Parallel Processing and Data Management

UNICOM Applied Information Technology

Each book in the series is based upon papers given at a seminar organized by UNICOM Seminars Ltd. The reports cover subjects at the forefront of information technology, and the contributors are all authorities in the subject on which they are invited to write, either as researchers or as practitioners.

1 **Fourth-Generation Systems**
Their scope, application and methods of evaluation
Edited by Simon Holloway

2 **Evaluating Supercomputers**
Strategies for exploiting, evaluating and benchmarking
Edited by A. van der Steen

3 **Failsafe Control Systems**
Applications and emergency management
Edited by Kevin Warwick and Ming T. Tham

4 **Computer Vision and Image Processing**
Edited by Anthony Barrett

5 **The Distributed Development Environment**
The art of using CASE
Edited by Simon Holloway

6 **Software Quality and Reliability**
Tools and methods
Edited by Darrel Ince

7 **Open Systems for Europe**
Edited by Tony Elliman and Colston Sanger

8 **Hypermedia/Hypertext**
And Object-oriented Databases
Edited by Heather Brown

9 **Software for Parallel Computers**
Edited by R. H. Perrott

10 **Object-oriented Programming Systems**
Tools and applications
Edited by J. J. Florentin

11 **Object-oriented Design**
Edited by Peter Robinson

12 **Software Reuse and Reverse Engineering in Practice**
Edited by P. A. V. Hall

13 **Parallel Processing and Data Management**
Edited by P. Valduriez

14 **Creating a Business-based IT strategy**
Edited by A. Brown

Parallel Processing and Data Management

UNICOM

APPLIED INFORMATION TECHNOLOGY 13

Edited by **P. Valduriez**
Director of Research, INRIA, France

CHAPMAN & HALL
London · New York · Tokyo · Melbourne · Madras

Published by Chapman & Hall, 2–6 Boundary Row, London SE1 8HN

Chapman & Hall, 2–6 Boundary Row, London SE1 8HN, UK

Blackie Academic & Professional, Wester Cleddens Road, Bishopbriggs, Glasgow G64 2NZ, UK

Van Nostrand Reinhold Inc., 115 5th Avenue, New York NY10003, USA

Chapman & Hall Japan, Thomson Publishing Japan, Hirakawacho Nemoto Building, 6F, 1–7–11 Hirakawa-cho, Chiyoda-ku, Tokyo 102, Japan

Chapman & Hall Australia, Thomas Nelson Australia, 102 Dodds Street, South Melbourne, Victoria 3205, Australia

Chapman & Hall India, R. Seshadri, 32 Second Main Road, CIT East, Madras 600 035, India

First edition 1992

Printed in Great Britain by T J Press (Padstow) Ltd, Cornwall

ISBN 0 412 42800 8   0 442 31580 5 (USA)

A catalogue record for this book is available from the British Library

Library of Congress Cataloging-in-Publication data available

CONTENTS

CONTRIBUTORS

D. R. Audley and A. E. Terrano
Financial Strategies Group
Prudential-Bache Securities
Prudential-Bache Building
New York
NY 10292
USA

P. Bryant
Stratus Computer Ltd
Central House
Lampton Rd
Hounslow
Middlesex
UK

C. Chachaty, P. Borla-Salamet and B. Bergsten
BULL Corporate Research Center
Avenue Jean Jaurès
78340 Les Clayes Sous Bois
France

J. P. Cheiney and Y. N. Huang
Ecole Nationale Supérieure des Telecommunications
46 Rue Barrault
74634 France

A. Davison
The Parlog Group
Dept of Computing
Imperial College
180 Queen's Gate
London
UK

D. DeGroot, E. Meyer and D. Wells
Computer Science Centre
Texas Instruments
Mailstation 238
Dallas
Texas
USA

T. C. Fogarty, J. G. Gammack, S. A. Battle and R. G. Miles
The Transputer Centre
Bristol Polytechnic
Coldharbour Lane
Bristol
UK

M. Freeston
European Computer-Industry Research Centre
Arabellastrasse 17
D-8000 Munich 81
Germany

O. Gruber
INRIA-Rocquencourt
B.P. 105
78153 Le Chesnay Cedex
France

G. F. J. Handley
Cray Research (UK) Ltd
Bracknell
Berkshire
UK

G. Haworth
ICL
Kings House
33 Kings Rd
Reading
Berkshire
UK

S. Jakobek
Meiko Ltd
650 Aztec West
Bristol
UK

R. G. Johnson, N. J. Martin, T. Wu and X. Zhao
Dept of Computer Science
Birbeck College
University of London
London
UK

J. Kerridge
Dept of Computer Science
University of Sheffield
Portobello Centre
Sheffield
UK

S. Lavington
Dept of Computer Science
University of Essex
Wivenhoe Park
Colchester
Essex
UK

P. A. Lee
Centre for Multiprocessors
Computing Laboratory
University of Newcastle upon Tyne
Claremont Rd
Newcastle upon Tyne
UK

J. C. Manley
Hewlett-Packard Laboratories
Filton Rd
Stoke Gifford
Bristol
UK

C. de Maindreville
INRIA-Rocquencourt
B.P. 105
78153 Le Chesnay Cedex
France

D. Moody
Intel Scientific Computers
Pipers Way
Swindon
Wiltshire
UK

M. Paci
European Computer-Industry Research Centre GmbH
Arabellastrasse 17
D-8000 Munich 81
Germany

J. Page
Teradata UK Ltd
Alwyn House
31 Windsor St
Chertsey
Surrey
UK

V. F. Rich
Encore Computer (UK) Ltd
Marlborough House
Mole Business Park
Leatherhead
Surrey
UK

J. Spiers
Oracle Corporation UK Ltd
Oracle Centre
The Ring
Bracknell
Berkshire
UK

K. Steer
Consultant to Strand Software
Technologies Inc.

P. Valduriez
INRIA-Rocquencourt
B.P. 105
78153 Le Chesnay Cedex
France

K-F. Wong
European Computer-Industry
Research Centre GmbH
Arabellastrasse 17
D-8000 Munich 81
Germany

Part One

Practical experiences with parallel database

1 Information flow in an enterprise

S. Jakobek
Meiko

True information flow in an enterprise – making both applications and data available wherever they are needed in a timely fashion – can only be achieved when we are able to distribute the information processing load across the enterprise.

The major issues involved in accomplishing this are: the problems of balancing the transaction processing and decision support load across a machine or a network of machines such that neither impacts the performance of the other; and the problems of streamlining networking and communications so that this load-balancing exercise is transparent to the user.

This presentation will consider these issues in more detail and propose solutions based upon our experience of similar problems encountered when designing and developing the technology for the new distributed memory parallel computers.

The distributed memory 'message passing' model, where hundreds and even thousands of processing nodes are loosely coupled to form one or more machines, owes its very existence to the fact that the inter-processor communications issues have been addressed, making it possible to distribute and balance processing load across many 'machines', and to ensure that data is delivered to these applications in a timely and effective manner.

We will describe how these parallel processing techniques can be applied in the context of Information Technology solutions and how the ORACLE user can now take advantage of them.

Research into changing business practices and new organizational trends has shown that the enterprises most likely to succeed in the 90s are the ones which have a fluid management structure and flexible procedures. If these companies are to fulfill their potential then this more adaptive style of working must also be reflected in their IT systems. We believe that the IT solutions of the 90s will be based upon an entirely new type of machine architecture.

Computer architects generally agree that the use of the classical Von Neuman approach to designing a uni-processor is now well understood, and they are capable of exploiting today's component technology to its limits. The way to improve computer performance with given technology and to improve the performance of computers beyond the limits of available technology involves the introduction of new architectures.

Specialized approaches have been used before, such as vector processing and pipelining, to create machines which are particularly good at scientific calculations. However, these are not general-purpose machines, being mainly deployed for numerically intensive problem solving.

The most hopeful means of achieving a scalable, yet general-purpose computing resource, is to use multiple processing elements within single machines. One approach is to link a number of processing elements all simultaneously executing an identical program but on different parts of the data. This is the SIMD (Single Instruction and Multiple Data) approach. This yields a very special purpose machine although in the IT context SIMD machines have only been successfully deployed in specialist applications such as text searching.

The alternative is to use multiple processing elements executing fragments of a program independently of each other. This is the MIMD approach (Multiple Instruction and Multiple Data). With the MIMD approach there is a further immediate choice available and this is between multiple processing elements sharing access to a single memory system, versus multiple processing elements each of which has its own dedicated memory system.

Superficially the shared memory system appears to be the more attractive. It is obviously simpler to imagine applications where individual processing elements get on with part of a task, but with reference to common data. The disadvantage of this approach is that each individual processor has to access the common data. The effect is that scalability of such a machine is limited by the speed of the memory access mechanism, and the speed of the memory itself. The memory system is therefore a shared resource and the architecture does not address the issue of scaling the size of the resource proportionally as the number of processing elements increases.

Consider the analogy of a busy office, where the tasks involve each worker in frequently accessing a single filing cabinet for filing and for reference to documents. As the office workload increases and as more workers are employed, it is clear that at some point the demands upon the filing system will cause workers to queue at the filing cabinet. There is clearly a finite level of work that this office can support, and this illustrates the limitations of the shared memory approach to computer architecture.

The alternative approach is the distributed memory machine, in which each processor has its own memory system and enjoys unimpeded access to that memory. This has the obvious benefit of allowing the performance of both the aggregate machine and the memory system to be proportional to the number of processing elements employed.

The disadvantage inherent in this system is that, in order to address a single problem, processing elements need to co-operate in passing information between each other. The problem presented to the computer architect in designing a distributed memory MIMD machine is to discover a communications medium that can increase its performance in proportion to the number of processing elements employed, while still allowing the processing elements to co-operate.

There exists a good analogy to this approach in the way in which organizations work, where an organization can grow in its capacity to deal with problems by employing more people, each of whom is capable of thinking and remembering and dealing with problems individually but who co-operate by communicating with one another. This is clearly acceptable within the context of a meeting room or a one-on-one meeting, but is also supported in larger communities by the telephone. The telephone is a good example of a communications resource which can be scaled in size and capacity in response to increasing demands from a growing working community. The essence of a distributed memory MIMD machine is therefore one in which there are many processing elements, each with their own memory, an inter-processor communications resource which allows those processing elements to co-operate on single problems by sending messages to one another, and where this communications resource is scalable, just like the telephone system.

With this model of computer architecture, there is no limit to the size of machine that can be produced. More and more processing elements can be added to deliver more and more computing power. As the size of the 'telephone network' increases, so more and more internal co-operation resource is also added. The only drawback with this kind of architecture is that of finding problems which are large enough to exploit such machines. I think that we will be able to demonstrate that the ORACLE user community presents the kind of problems which will justify the use of this new breed of machine.

For an Information Technology system to support the operation of an enterprise, there are three key issues which must be addressed.

- The IT solution must be capable of addressing the workload of the enterprise as characterized by the need to enter information, enquire on that information and provide management information in the form of consolidations and reports.

- The IT solution must be able to accommodate growth.
- The IT solution must be flexible so that new functions can be integrated, and changes accommodated in both user and structural requirements.

With a conventional computer system, i.e. a uni-processor environment, the machine is generally sized to support the workload. In reality, however, the machine is often undersized and does not support the workload! This situation arises because it is difficult to predict system loading given the dynamic nature of machine usage, making it hard to deliver an adequate service to users.

When employing a conventional computer system, a number of trade-offs need to be made. A compromise is made between the number of users that the system can support and the response which each user can expect. This is necessary to achieve a balance between the operating system burden imposed by users and the application burden which each of those users presents. *Ad hoc* query and reporting activities also create an unpredictable loading on the system. Usage of these functions is often restricted through system management procedures so that the load does not adversely impinge on any on-line users. Such trade-offs must be made in order that the workload across the enterprise can be supported.

The attraction of a multi-processor computer is that various parts of the total workload can be partitioned and allocated to one or more dedicated processing elements. The number of processing elements dedicated to a particular class of work or function can be determined dynamically, and this maintains a balanced and predictable service to the user community.

If we explore the nature of an Information Technology system workload, it can be characterized by a number of discrete classes of work: support of the operating system itself, which we regard as a significant computational load; secondly, support of the database which can be regarded as a server for the applications load; the applications themselves; and lastly, the processing associated with communications.

The operating system exists to clothe the underlying machine and present a conventional view of the machine to users. The database can be regarded as a service which is consuming processing resource and I/O capability and is used by applications which interact in a variety of different ways with the users. Some applications are transaction-based and provide an on-line operation for users, others are query-based and are used typically for management information enquiries, analyses, etc. The computational load presented by the communications protocol software is significant, but of vital importance if the machine in question is to co-operate with other machines in the enterprise.

ORACLE presents two major classes of workload: one is the applications and the other is the ORACLE kernel. Applications consume quantities of CPU resource per user and correspondingly occupy finite quantities of memory per user. Reports can consume even more memory and variable amounts of computing power depending on the nature of the reporting demanded. This application load controls the amount of work that the database kernel must do. So, the amount of computing resource required by the kernel is proportional to the application load at any point in time.

In an established Information Technology-using community, the number of people using an application can be predicted with each user having relatively predictable patterns. It is not the case that total workload is constant because it probably varies throughout the working day. However, it would be reasonable to say that total workload is repeatable in the short-term and growing in the long-term.

Many companies produce reports as an 'off-line' activity at the end of the working day because of the predictably heavy demands they place on the entire system. Reporting should be regarded as a first-class citizen in terms of workload and on a par with all the other applications which are being run. It need not be relegated to the times of day when its impact will be least disastrous, as is often the case. If this important management information could actually be obtained on-line, then it would provide a real-time picture, enabling better decision-making and potentially providing an important competitive advantage.

The kernel load is directly related to the total application load, so it follows that the number of users the system can support is a function of the capacity of the kernel. If we wish to support more users on the system, we must increase the capacity of the kernel. ORACLE is structured in such a way that one can have multiple copies of the kernel operating on behalf of groups of users. This allows scalable numbers of users to be supported. This is another area where Meiko's specific parallel processing insights have been brought to bear on the implementation of ORACLE.

We took as our goal the design of an architecture which will cater for the variety of demands made by an Information Technology workload, allowing us to deploy varying numbers of processing elements to different classes of work, and achieving a computer which is a balanced resource in all circumstances.

This is not as straightforward as it first seems. In reality, the workload and the mix of classes of work varies during the working day. Techniques such as multi-processor load balancing are used to share out the demands over 'pools' of processing elements. The constraint that we can employ to advantage is that we can restrict each class of work to its processing element pool, guaranteeing that there will be no incursion of one class of work into the resource that has been allocated for another. For example, we can ensure the Management Information System (MIS) reporting does not impinge on the responsiveness for interactive performance and we can deploy an appropriate pool of processing elements to support the expected number of users. We can also ensure that communications activities, e.g. electronic mail, which cause considerable consumption of computer power, each have dedicated resource. Thus, we can ensure that no activity will impinge on the responsiveness of any other user service.

To illustrate how this might work, load balancing with a pool of processing elements works just like a typing pool, where an organization has a pool of available typing resource into which hand-written documents are submitted. Typists pick up the next available piece of work and produce a document and give it back. Obviously the capacity of the typing pool is proportional to the number of typists and there is no particular relationship between the specific typists and the documents they are typing. Load balancing occurs when one typist with an empty in-tray takes work from the in-tray of a colleague.

In the multi-processor machine, the workload can be described as questions which are being asked. Each question requires some processing to be performed in order to produce an answer. Each of the processors which is available for answering questions simply takes the next question from the workload, performs the computation in order to calculate the answer, and gives back that answer. The model works effectively when the time it takes to ask a question is relatively short compared with the time it takes to compute the answer, because the cost of communicating the question is small when compared with the cost of actually answering the questions. This is where multi-processor computers succeed when networks and clusters fail.

Imagine a computer composed of processing elements like 'Lego' bricks with some elements which are specialized in nature, such as disk controllers and communications interfaces. A service machine is built by combining appropriate numbers of processing elements destined to perform specific classes of work, assisted by specialist intelligent I/O controller elements where necessary.

Within the Meiko architecture, which we call the Computing Surface, each processing element has the power of a conventional departmental computer. Computing Surface systems containing hundreds of such elements have been delivered. New processing elements can be added, one at a time. This means that capacity for transaction processing, for example, can be added in small, cost-effective increments. Therefore, when transaction capacity falls short by 10% the enterprise can simply add 10% more power.

This approach of incrementally boosting the power of an existing computer within the enterprise is actually quite different from adding a new computer to the enterprise. The intimacy of co-operation between the processing elements within a multi-processor computer is much greater than the intimacy of co-operation between disassociated computers across an enterprise. This directly addresses the need for enabling greater information flow within the enterprise while reducing the barriers to information flow within the IT resource. Departments become closer in terms of shared information.

Is the multi-processor architecture a sledgehammer to crack a nut? Clearly Meiko believe not. ORACLE's popularity is vested mainly in its flexibility to support a company's relational database solution. This encompasses the functionality of its tools which allow applications to be expressed rapidly, built rapidly and easily changed. However, ORACLE is not always renowned for its performance. The irony is that the benefits of ORACLE can create a performance problem. This may only become apparent as the installation grows, with an increasing number of users taking advantage of these benefits. The consequence is a premature overload.

There is good reason for using a scalable computer architecture as the delivery platform. It provides the ability to increase incrementally the available computing resource, able to serve the constantly growing demand for an ORACLE service. It is common sense. If a multi-processor computer is a sledgehammer, it is the right tool for the job.

Returning to the typing pool analogy, it becomes even stronger when individuals within the pool develop special skills. For example, a typist might become familiar with a particular individual's handwriting, and so will perform more efficiently on those documents than might another member of the pool.

The parallel to this is the use of optimizing techniques such as caching to remember most recently used data. Caching is used in the software architecture of ORACLE with great benefit. However, whilst caching improves the performance of the ORACLE kernel to the user, it also adds a level of complexity for people such as ourselves who are tasked with its implementation over multiple processing elements.

Cache consistency for ORACLE is a particularly difficult feature to implement on a multi-processor machine and is one which will differentiate the various implementations of multi-processor ORACLE, especially with respect to their scalability. Our solution to cache consistency, which, in ORACLE terms, is referred to as the 'Lock Manager Problem', is regarded as a Meiko proprietary area. It will not be surprising to find that transputers are used in a unique way here.

The danger with technologists championing their own technology is that they often get carried away with that technology and with its perceived benefits. Can this new technology be integrated into an enterprise? Meiko has devoted considerable attention to the issue of managing the transition from conventional to multi-processor computer solutions within an existing IT environment. Users need to be able to exploit the benefits of new technology without interrupting service, causing culture shock or requiring new skills. The technology can now be regarded as irrelevant except for the benefits it brings to bear.

ORACLE is an accepted standard, available under many proprietary operating systems, so Meiko has built hardware and software interfaces to existing proprietary machinery such as the DEC VAX. This means that the Computing Surface is employed, if you like, as an ORACLE turbo-charger connected to an existing conventional computer. The ORACLE workload is offloaded onto the Computing Surface, whilst leaving intact the user interface, the operational practices of users and their existing installation. This provides the means of transparently taking the first step from the existing environment to that of employing a massively parallel solution for database demands.

There is now a movement towards client/server styles of working, with workstations or personal computers networked within the working environment. The concept of the workgroup is emerging as a sympathetic model, where numbers of personal computers are connected to servers which provide the information resource for the workgroup. The cynical view is that the workgroup model is most sympathetic to the limited performance servers that it introduces – it does little to assist information flow between workgroups and is sticking plaster to address the information isolation caused by PCs in the first place. The Computing Surface can be regarded as a server for the workgroup, or an intimately connected server for the department.

Moreover, the case for the PCs is likely to be an historic one, and new users are probably better supported by sophisticated terminals such as X terminals, providing WYSIWYG (what you see is what you get) functionality, where documents appear to be like paper on your desk, unlike the conventional character terminal. The Computing Surface can now be viewed as a massive integrated Information Technology resource, whether used as a centralized computer or as a multiple distributed computer.

Information flow is not communication between computers. It is the exchange and sharing of information between individuals in an enterprise. Communication between computers is slow in comparison to the rate of information flow necessary between co-operating individuals. This is why databases are relevant; they consolidate the information needed by their user community.

The accepted approach to ensure adequate information flow within an enterprise is to perform an information needs analysis which reflects current business goals. These business goals determine the priorities within the IT strategy and a design and implementation then follows. It is often attractive to pursue a distributed computing policy, with the assumed dual benefits of achieving a scalable computing resource and relative autonomy within the enterprise.

This approach reflects the information needs for business goals and provides a set of dedicated information flows, or islands of information to meet those goals. However, business goals change. The excellent characteristics of small companies which large companies would like to emulate are those of versatility, flexibility and responsiveness in the changing marketplace.

The assumed benefit of autonomy implied by such a divisional computer strategy now inhibits change. Changing information flow needs can require the redefinition of information boundaries between islands of information. Maybe information boundaries can be moved, at a cost, but the computers in place cannot be redefined quite so easily. The result is a danger of organizational intertia.

An 'information needs' analysis is clearly not a once-and-for-all exercise; it is an on-going requirement of the enterprise. Your enterprise must be wary of a rigid IT solution; it can only be a short-term solution.

Information flow within an enterprise is therefore a dynamic requirement; it must be capable of reflecting changing business goals and subsequent information needs. The ORACLE relational database is chosen because of its ability to adapt to changing information needs. ORACLE should also be supported by a scalable technology resource which can be deployed and redeployed to reflect the instantaneous but changing divisional needs across the enterprise.

Meiko was founded in 1985 to exploit the opportunities just opening for parallel processing systems, which would supplant conventional computers over the next decade or so. Since its founding, Meiko has grown to become a clear leader in the field. Until recently, Meiko has addressed the high-end supercomputer market. The company is now driving its technology into the broader market for Information Technology systems.

2 Computational finance using the Intel iPSC family of concurrent supercomputers

D. Moody
European Manager, Intel Scientific Computers

2.1 THE iPSC/860 CONCURRENT SUPERCOMPUTER

2.1.1 Hardware

The Intel iPSC/860 is the third and latest member of the iPSC family of concurrent supercomputers. The system is upward compatible with its predecessors and incorporates the latest RISC microprocessors from Intel, the i860TM.

The iPSC/860 uses up to 128 i860 processors and offers peak performance levels of 10 GFLOPS (32 bit) and 7.6 GFLOPS (64 bit). It is a distributed memory MIMD system, each processor having 8 or 16 MBytes of private memory. The processors communicate with each other through the Direct-Connect TM communication system. which supports the exchange of data between any of the processors. Direct-Connect imposes negligible penalties on long-distance communication, nor do intermediate processors experience any interruption from messages which pass through towards another destination. The bandwidth of the Direct-Connect network is scalable, the aggregate message passing capacity of a 128 node system being over 700 MBytes/s. The major effect of Direct-Connect is to remove the need for the programmer to consider topology when mapping an application to the system. The system should be viewed as a pool of processors, each of which may be called up to do any job with no concern from the programmer about configuration or message routeing algorithms.

The flexibility of this architecture is one of the most important features. Code may be written which takes advantage of n processors, where n is the whole or a subset of the processor pool. When the number of processors available to a particular application changes, either through the addition of extra hardware or the need to allocate processors for other uses, the code will run unmodified on the new set[3].

Figure 2.1 shows an iPSC/860 node processor.

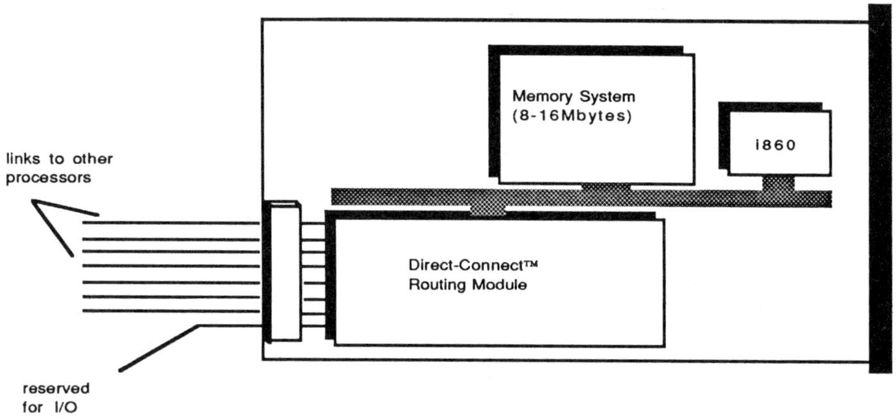

Figure 2.1 Compute Node with associated vector processor.

2.1.2 The development environment

The biggest criticism of concurrent computers is that although they have tremendous price performance characteristics, they are difficult to program. However, it is our experience that new programs may be written as quickly as normally expected for sequential systems once a developer has become familiar with the iPSC/860.

The standard languages included in the iPSC/860 Concurrent Work Bench are Fortran and C. Node 0 in the iPSC/860 is connected to an 80386 based super-microcomputer known as the System Resource Manager (SRM). The SRM is a standard computer system based on Unix V.3, providing all development services and access to the iPSC/860 itself. Hence, both the development environment and the languages of the iPSC/860 will be familiar to most potential users. The facilities to send data (synchronously or asynchronously) between nodes or between SRM and nodes are provided in the form of system subroutines which can be called from the high level language. Other functions within this library allow a software module to determine how many nodes are in the system and on which node it is runing. Processes may broadcast to all nodes, perform global arithmetic operations such as add, min, max etc., and directly perform I/O operations via the SRM.

Having developed a program (or programs) which will run in parallel it is necessary to have good debugging facilities. Concurrent WorkBench TM includes DECONTM, a source level symbolic debugger for concurrent programs. Breakpoints may be entered at statement level or on event (such as variable write, read or value reached) and variables may be examined and modified. Where this debugger differs from the traditional variety is the users have control over the context to which each command applies, i.e. all nodes, a specific node, a range of nodes, all processes, the SRM program etc. Also, all message queues are open to inspection through DECON – messages which have arrived but not been consumed, and messages which are expected which have not arrived. This allows the correction of problems caused by erroneous message passing.

A further feature of Concurrent WorkBench is the remote hosting facility, currently supported for Sun and Vax workstations (and others through the User Group Library). A library is provided for the workstations which allow programs to communicate directly with iPSC/860 nodes using the same subroutine calls as the nodes themselves use. This communication takes place over a TCP/IP Ethernet connection between the workstation and the SRM, so it is significantly slower than iPSC/860 message passing. However, the importance of this facility is that all human interface code may remain on a traditional workstation, while calculations are performed at supercomputer speed on the iPSC/860 – truly interactice supercomputing.

The remote hosting facility is also of major advantage when porting some existing scientific codes to the iPSC/860. Often large proportions of these codes are involved with graphics, data entry, preprocessing and other tasks which are not computationally intensive. These modules may remain on the workstation while the critical piece of the code is parallelized and ported to the iPSC/860, the linkage between the two systems provided by the remote hosting facility. An advantage of this approach is that the end-user of a particular package sees only a traditional workstation interface, and has no need to be concerned with the parallel computer system somewhere on the network.

The iPSC/860 should not be considered as a single-user system. Indeed applications or developers may request a specific number of nodes to be allocated to them, leaving the remainder for other users. This technique of allocating sole use of a subset of the processors is known as space-sharing. Since this allocation and deallocation is fully dynamic, the iPSC/860 together with the remote hosting facility becomes an extremely flexible computational server on a network of workstations.

2.1.3 Concurrent input-output system (CIO)

CIO is based on multiple I/O processors, known as I/O nodes, each dedicated to handling their own I/O devices. Up to 127 of these I/O nodes may be connected to the compute nodes of the iPSC/860 on a one-to-one basis using the Direct-Connect link reserved for I/O shown in Fig. 2.1. A diagram of the I/O node is provided in Fig. 2.2. Clearly, it is very similar to a compute node, but it has only one Direct-Connect link since it communicates with only one compute node. I/O nodes incorporate an SCSI controller and a minimum of 4 MBytes of memory. Optionally a Bus Adaptor may be connected in the next slot to allow the I/O nodes control of one or more VME devices.

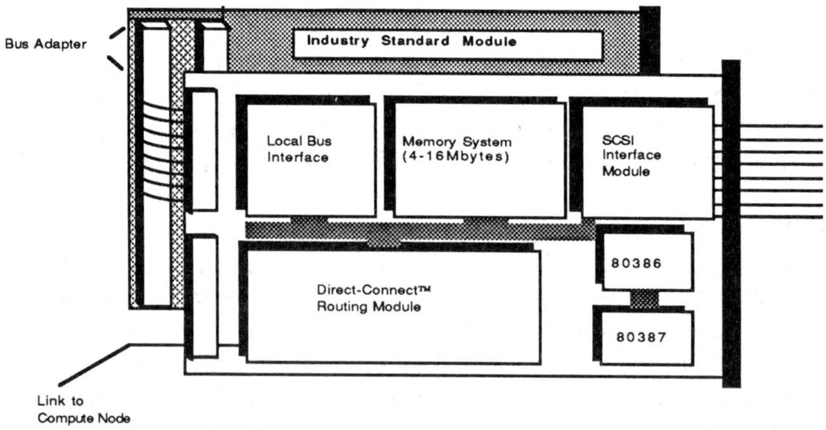

Figure 2.2 I/O Node with Multibus II or VME adapter plus SCSI interface.

Although an I/O node is physically connected to a single compute node the Direct-Connect network allows all compute nodes to communicate with each I/O node. A diagram of an iPSC/860 system with eight compute nodes, four I/O nodes and 8 GBytes of disk storage is given in Fig. 2.3.

The use of separate I/O nodes removes the need for compute nodes to manage I/O devices. In turn this ensures that applications can remain well balanced on the compute nodes since they will not be interrupted by other nodes requesting I/O support.

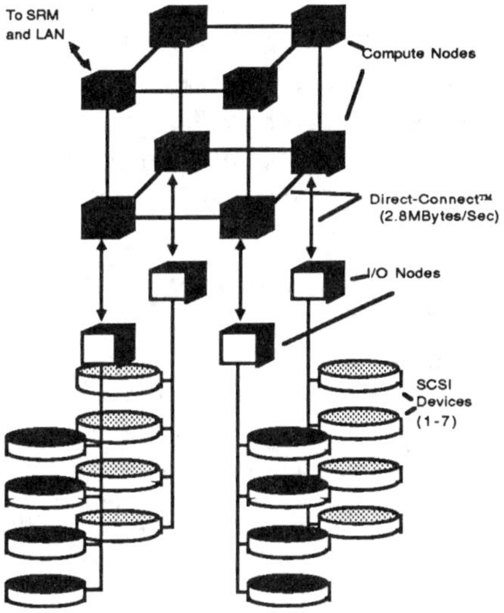

Figure 2.3 Schematic of an iPSC/860 system with 8 compute nodes, 4 I/O nodes and 8 GBytes of disk storage.

2.1.4 Concurrent file system (CFS)

CFS is the software which manages all disks connected to the iPSC/860 CIO system, its most important attribute being the ability to make the parallel nature of the I/O system transparent to the application and the user[4]. Unlike the programming of the computationally intensive portion of an application where parallelism is generally expressed explicitly, CFS can handle parallelism implicitly.

The problem of multiple disks on separate computing entities has been investigated in the past with a distributed computing model incorporating distributed file systems. NFS from Sun Microsystems is an example of such a file system. The major problem of this approach when applied to concurrent supercomputers is that any one file is constrained to reside on a single disk. This would clearly cause a bottleneck at the I/O node if data is required concurrently by several compute nodes co-operating in a single application. However, NFS and CFS complement each other extremely well and the integration of NFS into CFS will allow workstation users access to the capacity and performance of the CIO system.

Another alternative for combining many disks is disk-stripping. This method does not fit the concurrent supercomputer architecture well as it is best suited to providing high transfer rates over a single fast channel, rather than over several medium speed channels.

CFS manages all disks connected to the system as a single logical entity (up to 889 500 MBytes disk drives may be connected through 127 I/O nodes). The system allocates blocks to a file from all of the disks, a technique known as declustering[5]. The result is that the data required by multiple compute nodes, whether from a single file or multiple files, is likely to be on separate disks and can be transferred simultaneously. The user can create one file as large as the total disk capacity of the system, or hundreds of files across many disks without needing to know the physical location of any file, block or directory.

CFS works with file blocks of 4 KBytes in size. Each disk in the CIO system has a volume number so each file block is uniquely identified by a block number comprising the volume number and the logical block number on that volume. As a write operation is under way the file blocks are automatically distributed over all I/O nodes and disks by CFS. I/O nodes are usually able to receive blocks into a cache memory area of at least 2 MBytes in size, effectively removing delays caused by disk latency. This caching of data is completely transparent to the user.

Multiple compute nodes attempting to access parts of a single file will typically be receiving the data from multiple I/O nodes concurrently, these concurrent channels supporting an aggregate transfer rate of over a hundred megabytes per second (in proportion to the number of I/O nodes on the system). The application may restrict allocation to a specified set of disks if this form of tuning is beneficial.

CFS supports the same studio standard I/O library calls as the Unix operating system. Any application on any set of iPSC/860 nodes can create and access files through Unix style hierarchical directories. All iPSC/860 languages support the use of CFS. Users of these languages already performing file access through the iPSC/860 System Resource Manager will find their programs to be completely compatible with the new file system, with no changes required to exploit concurrency. A set of asynchronous read and write calls are provided to allow the overlap of I/O requests and computation within an application.

2.2 FINANCIAL SUPERCOMPUTING

Global competition, 24-hour trading and high market volatility are among the factors that have made decision-making very difficult in today's high stakes financial services industry. Powerful decision-making tools that provide timely insight on market movements and security valuations are becoming vital and this is where supercomputers are beginning to play a crucial role.

Supercomputing makes financial computations, which previously were too large to consider, practical and long-running batch operations interactive. Calculations and analysis which may consume hours of time on a traditional mainframe can now be completed while a client is still on the telephone. Clearly, institutions using such equipment may close business a day before their competitors are able to provide a quotation!

Traditional supercomputers have been extraordinarily expensive to own and operate. Physical constraints alone – including the need for several tons of equipment for cooling – have rendered such machines impractical for everyday commercial use. The arrival of parallel supercomputers has changed this completely. Machies such as the iPSC/860 represent a low-cost, high return investment and they are already in use at select financial institutions. Two examples of these applications are outlined below; others include asset pricing, econometrics, foreign exchange, portfolio evaluation, portfolio optimization and risk analysis.

2.2.1 Mortgage-backed securities

Computing the value of a mortgage-backed security is complicated by the uncertainty of the cash flows. Mortgage prepayments which can occur at any time are a major source of uncertainty. Additionally, adjustable rate mortgages have interest cash flows which depend on the special structure of these mortgages: the indexing of interest rate changes, special periodic and life-time interest rate caps and unique prepayment rules.

The usual method of dealing with the complexity of mortgage-backed securities is through the use of Monte-Carlo techniques. Computer-generated random numbers are used as the input to a model which generates interest rate movements through time. Then a prepayment model, specific to the security, is used to calculate interest and principle cash flows which are discounted to the present.

Several hundred of these cash flows models are needed for the computation, the final step being the averaging across such scenarios.

The Monte-Carlo method is notoriously computer-intensive, but well suited to the iPSC/860. The performance of the system in this application is given in Fig. 2.4 for system of approximately equivalent price.

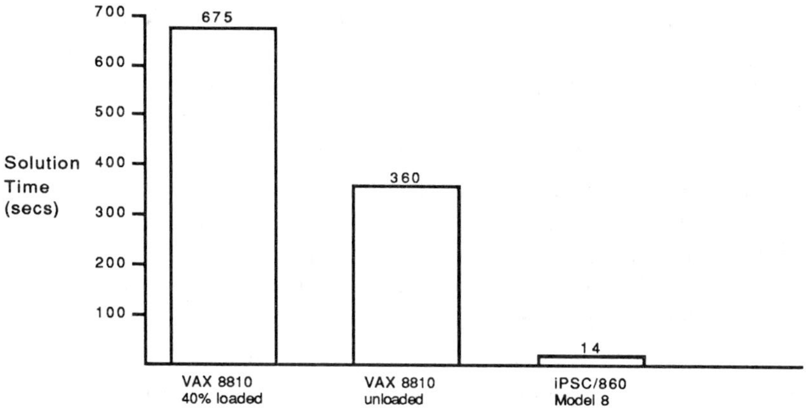

Figure 2.4 End-to-end response time as measured from a trader workstation in the valuation of adjustable rate mortgages.

2.2.2 Mortgage-backed financing

One of the critical steps in analysing mortgage-backed securities is to compute cash flows generated by the underlying mortgages. The mortgages, which are grouped into pools, will differ from pool to pool based on characteristics such as the number of remaining payments and the rate of interest. Typically, standard equations of finance are applied to each pool to compute the cash flows, interest payments and remaining principal. By summing these quantities for each pool, global quantities become available for further analysis. Sophisticated analysis, such as the MBS example above, may require generation of the cash flows for each pool under several hundred interest rate scenarios. Each security may consider of up to 1000 pools making the computational task extremely large. Mortgage pools may be distributed among the individual processors in the iPSC/860 supercomputer achieving excellent levels of parallelism. Since a significant number of parameters are associated with each of the mortgage pools and used during the calculation, efficiency requires adequate disk storage and I/O capacity. The iPSC/860 Concurrent I/O system described earlier fits this requirement admirably.

2.3 CONCLUSION

Parallel supercomputers have demonstrated their effectiveness in the field of computational finance amongst early adapters such as Prudential–Bache Securities[2]. The high returns which reward detailed and accurate financial modelling activity in the banking, securities and insurance industries will make the parallel supercomputer an essential competitive weapon for financial institutions in the 1990s.

REFERENCES

Penczer, P. (1989) Supercomputers: Era dawns on Wall Street. *Wall Street Computer Review.*

Supercomputer goes on-line at Pru-Bache (*Bondweek X,* **7**, 26 February, 1990).

Parallel Programming Primer (Intel Corporation).

Pierce, P. (1989) A Concurrent File System for a Highly Parallel Mass Storage Subsystem. *Proceedings of The Fourth Conference on Hypercube Concurrent Computers and Applications.*

Reddy, ALN. and Banerjee, P. (1989) Evaluation of Multiple Disk I/O Systems. Submitted to ICPP.

3 Parallel processing in the securities industry interactive supercomputing

D. R. Audley and A. E. Terrano
Prudential-Bache Securities

The crucial element in absorbing parallel processing into commercial applications is the ability to integrate it into existing computing systems. This is far more than plug compatibility: it is the ability of parallel processing to readily accept existing compute intensive applications, to accommodate the skills of application programmers; and in general to give computer scientist-free service. There is no doubt that the new generations of multiprocessors offer tremendous performance. But can this performance be delivered?

3.1 BACKGROUND – THE COMMERCIAL APPLICATION

Prudential-Bache Securities is a broad spectrum securities broker-dealer and investment bank, one of the largest securities firms in the world. The firm makes markets in securities on a world-wide basis, 24-hours a day. Its investment banking clients span the globe from Hong Kong Telecommunications Ltd. to Scandinavian Air System, from Dr Pepper/Seven-Up Companies to Elders IXL Ltd. It has a retail sales force of more than 5800 Financial Advisors in 320 offices in 20 countries, providing investment services to more than 1.8 million accounts. It is a member of The Prudential family, one of the largest non-bank financial institutions in the world, with consolidated assets of $164 billion.

Prudential-Bache is a big, widely deployed enterprise. It has a global communications and computer network. Its market activities demand that it keep track of tens of thousands of securities and their current prices, not only information about securities, but also about the portfolios of all its clients. All this information needs to be at the instant command of its sales and trading professionals. Opportunities in the securities markets last only as long as the time it takes for the first person to take advantage of it. This is a keenly competitive business. It is driven by speed of action and insight,

insight that comes from the quantitative analysis of the market. Competition has placed a premium on speed of computation and getting to the market first.

3.2 COMPUTATIONAL INTENSITY IN THE SECURITIES BUSINESS

There are many aspects of the securities business that have been strongly influenced by the advances in computation and communications. However, whole new activities have emerged from computational finance. Probably the most notorious are program trading and index arbitrage. But even more dramatic is the explosion of derivative mortgage- and asset-backed securities. In the case of Prudential-Bache, this has represented a major growth business.

Since their inception in 1983, Collateralized Mortgage-backed Obligations (CMOs) have grown from $16 billion in US issuance in 1985 to an aggregate amount outstanding of over $250 billion today. To give some insight into the potential mortgage securitization market, there are nearly $3 trillion of outstanding mortgage debt. Mortgages, especially as they are bundled into the nearly $1 billion in pass-through securities, are the raw material of the re-engineered mortgage-backed CMO. Beyond CMOs, the concept of collateralization is rapidly expanding into other areas and includes automobile debt, credit card receivables, even loans on recreational vehicles and pleasure boats. Almost as lucrative as the original issue business, is the process of maintaining an orderly secondary market. This is the business of supporting the exchange of these securities; by increasing their liquidity, their value is enhanced.

The computer is the factory of CMOs and asset-backed securities. It is only through analysis and computation that the arbitrage between the collateral and the tranches of the CMO can be designed with minimal risk. Historically, investors participated in the mortgage-lending market through pass-through securities. These securities, backed by individual mortgage loans, return monthly interest and principal that is passed through to security holders. Because homeowners have purchased a right to prepay part or all of their mortgage at any time, the exact timing and amounts of the cash flows may be uncertain. A CMO reduces this uncertainty by assembling a number of mortgage pools and creating serially maturing bonds, with varying senior claims, collateralized by the mortgage pools. As these securities obey the normal risk – return relationship, the riskier collateral can be purchased more cheaply than the choice, risk-controlled CMO bonds.

This is an ideal example of computer-aided engineering tightly integrated with production. The CMO issuance process follows from interactively analysing available collateral and structuring the CMO using models of homeowner prepayment behaviour and current market conditions (e.g. the term structure of interest rates). As blocks of collateral are offered in the market, the analysis and structuring must be performed in time to capture the offering, if profitable, to make a counter-bid, or to reject as unsuitable if a partial structure has been formed. Speed is an essential element of this process.

There are numerous other applications that are computationally intense, relative to the market-driven decision time-frame, which can benefit from parallel processing. This includes trading complex securities, portfolio structuring and management, active hedging and arbitrage.

In the financial industry today, parallel processing is thought of as a class of supercomputer – strictly number crunching. Serious thought is not now given to the possibility of massive data servers. In the securities business, this technology could certainly be revolutionary. As the availability of the early generation of parallel processors have opened the way to their use in computational finance, the availability of their massively parallel data capability will be critical to the expansion of the database dimension of parallel applications.

Prudential-Bache is a major business enterprise. Debt securitization is a big market with tremendous profit potential. We take parallel computing very seriously and consider it to be a key to our competitiveness. This did not come without a great deal of caution. Investment bankers can be very risk-averse. This is especially true with their aversion to computer technology. On the other hand, when there are profits to be made cost-effectiveness rules the day. How did the investment professionals at Prudential-Bache come to love parallel processing and how is it put to use?

3.3 THE FINANCIAL STRATEGIES COMPUTING COMPLEX

The Financial Strategies Group (FSG) computing complex at Prudential-Bache evolved from a cluster of Digital Equipment Corp (DEC) VAX/VMS minicomputers. The cluster started with a single VAX 8650 system, in April 1986. This computer supported custom analytics in a stand-alone mode through terminals located around the trading floor. It was also the home for the applications development staff. The programming language of choice was C. The Oracle database system was used to support a data base of several hundred securities with a daily load of prices. In addition, the VAX hosted the structuring of CMOs.

By the end of 1986, a second VAX (8700) arrived. Within a year a third machine (a VAX 8800 with 2 CPUs) was clustered with the first two. By this time there were well over 200 users on the system during the trading day. When CMO deals were to be done, higher priority was given to these users to support the time critical transaction. The rest of the users suffered accordingly. When this was not enough, outside computer resources were leased.

For one particularly intricate transaction in early 1988, Cray XMP 4/16 time was leased. The collateral was analysed on 3 CPUs and took approximately 100 minutes per run. The estimate of VAX time that would have been required to do this transaction was 16,000 minutes on a single 8800 CPU.

In an effort to balance to daily need of secondary market users, the development staff, and deal support, it was believed that this last need could be best served by workstations. This was done in 1988 with the addition of several Suns. Ultimately, transaction support was improved without detriment to the VAX (Sales and Trading) clients. However, as the secondary market in CMOs grew, there was a growing need to run CPU intensive applications similar to CMO new-issue analytics. Even though algorithmic approaches to accelerating the analysis were implemented, it was clear that something dramatic was needed.

By 1989 the FSG complex included 4 clustered VAXs (a 4 CPU VAX 6440 had been added) on a LAN with the Suns. The VAXs host a database of tens of thousands of securities, prices and the portfolios of the firm's institutional clients in addition to serving the computational needs of the secondary markets. These machines also host much of the application development work. In addition, there is a gateway to the firm's IBM 3090 600VF. This gateway supports data transfer from inventory and accounting systems as well as overnight batch jobs. The IBMs are too heavily used during the trading day to support interactive use. In this environment we undertook a search for what was perceived to be a need for supercomputer capability.

3.4 PARALLEL PROCESSING COMES TO WALL STREET

The search for a suitable platform for computationally intensive applications covered most of the usual sources as well as some unusual sources. The criteria for selection was three-fold. The computer had to:

1. have outstanding performance;
2. be friendly to application development programmers; and
3. provide interactive support for multiple users.

A set of three applications were identified for purposes of evaluating the criteria

- Adjustable Rate Mortgage (ARM) pricing model. This model is used to price ARM product. Competing vendors were invited to port at their effort for purpose of evaluating the first criteria. This application is characterized by its Monte Carlo nature.
- Arbitrage-Free Pricing System (APS). This system is used in many forms to price/value US Government securities, corporate debt, fixed-income options, futures and futures options. This port was to be done by FSG with vendor support, if needed. This was to be one vehicle to evaluate criteria 2 and 3. This application is characterized by the numerical solution of partial differential equations (PDEs).
- Mortgage Pass-Through Option Adjusted Spread (OAS) Model. This model was to be ported entirely by FSG programmers, without vendor support. It was to serve as the final test for evaluating criteria 2. This application is also characterized by Monte Carlo analysis.

Most of the following account relates to our experience with the Intel iPSC/2 32-node hypercube (as it is the system which was ultimately purchased and has now been upgraded to an iPSC/860). (Performance with the i860s is not reported here. This will be addressed in the presentation at the conference.)

3.5 PERFORMANCE

As expected, the cube performed very well on Monte Carlo applications, these being of the type often described as 'embarrassingly concurrent'. In comparison to the VAX, performance improvements of 15:1 were demonstrated in the trading environment in a production mode. The application was run on a 16-node sub-cube (i386 processors) and took about 25 seconds to run.

Similar performance was noted with other applications ported. While performance looks pretty good, it's not spectacular. It is expected that the i860 nodes will give an improvement of at least another factor of 5.

It is not surprising that the machine performed well. Fast computers can run code fast. What was surprising was that the technology was not as immature as originally feared. Programmers with no experience with parallel computers could make their code run fast.

3.6 USER FRIENDLINESS

User friendliness addresses the adaptability of a group of 35 applications programmers to the new world of concurrent programming. The experience here is good.

Within the first day that the 'cube was 'out of the box', code that had been running on a Sun was ported to a single node. With the modification of about 40 lines, the application was running in a concurrent form, on 16-nodes, within a week. The performance speed-up over the VAX was observed to be about 10:1.

The particular application that was ported was a CMO residual tax analysis model. This application has 120 000 source lines of code (SLOC). It is notable that this application was not one that was scheduled as an application to be part of the evaluation. Rather, an application programmer was curious about this thing called concurrent computing and thought he'd learn about it by porting a familiar financial model.

This experience turned out to be atypical, however. First, the issues of code portability had not been adequately addressed in FSG. While we had C-language applications running on the VAXs and the Suns, few had been cross-ported. Despite the fact that we thought this would be easy, it was not. The tax model compiled readily on the 'cube, having taken advantage of the previous port from the VAX to the Sun. The VAXs supported the ANSI standard, the Suns did not, and while the 386s were ostensibly able to deal with either, they didn't quite. The first release of the i860 compiler is only now available. Is this a parallel computing issue? No, but it's an issue for the commercial application of any computer. (I might add that a third-party public-domain compiler that could target the VAX, Sun and 'cube was useful in establishing portability.)

3.7 INTERACTIVE SUPERCOMPUTING

The most important aspect of integrating the 'cube into our application system was its ability to support interactive supercomputing. This is the functionality of bringing supercomputing power to bear on processes within an application where/when it will do the most good. This needs to be transparently accomplished in the context of the multi-user environment of financial professionals, not sophisticated computer users. These users do not care where an application runs, only that it quickly gets them their result.

There are as many 300 users logged-in to the VAX from (dumb) terminals. Most 'transactions' are simple. For example, fetching a security and its price from the database and doing a price-to-yield or yield-to-price calculation. Hardly the stuff of supercomputers. As few as 10% of these transactions, however, account for 90% of CPU usage. It is the functionality of providing horsepower to these processes, as available and when needed, that the iPSC/2 had to support.

The real-time, interactive functionality for the cube is provided through a compute server. In addition to handling any incoming requests for computation, the server also manages the resources on the cube. Since the node operating system does not support virtual memory or demand paging, an application must be preloaded in order to provide the real-time response which we require. The server, through its scheduler functionality, keeps track of current deployment and usage of resources. It employs a statically optimized load-balancing procedure for each of the several applications that are hosted.

When a request comes in, the server determines what application is being requested and whether it is available at this time or will be within a predetermined maximum latency interval. If the resource is not available, the request is refused. If the request is accepted, the request is assigned to a process and either executed or queued as appropriate.

The programmer's interface supports two paradigms: distributed function calls or co-operating processes. The simplest one to implement is the distributed function call. An existing, computationally expensive function can be executed from the VAX transparently on the cube: when the function is called, a channel is opened to the compute server, the appropriate application is requested, the arguments are transferred over the network to the cube where the computation is performed, and the results are returned to the process on the VAX, which has been simply waiting until the remote computation is completed. If the request is refused by the compute server, the computation is automatically performed on the VAX. Adding the remote call requires only trivial modifications to the existing VAX program.

The co-operating processes paradigm consists of fully parallel execution by both the VAX and the cube. In this instance, the application programmer must explicitly control the flow of data between the two processors, however each processor may continue executing until it cannot proceed without results from the other. In essence, the VAX CPU and the nodes on the cube function as co-equal members of a single, heterogeneous parallel computer.

This architecture has been extended to provide remote database support from the VAX for both the cube and the Sun: a database server accepts all remote requests for information, calls ORACLE directly and returns the desired data. For this purpose, the remote function call paradigm described above is sufficient.

3.8 SUMMARY

Is parallel processing mature enough for commercial application? Interactive parallel supercomputing is now routinely supporting the delivery of quantitative analytics at Prudential-Bache Securities. In sum, however, the experience has been trying. Parallel processors often come out of the box as stand-alone single-user machines. The 'cube was no exception. Commercial applications, on the other hand, demand all of the usual marketing hype – multi-users, networking, shared data, etc. We had to integrate the 'cube into this world. Surprisingly, though, it was not hard. Our development programmers, most of whom have never experienced parallel processing, have found it no worse than bringing in any other new computer. The real payoff is now that our software, including the development process, has assimilated the new technology, a tremendously cost-effective dimension for growth is now available.

Part Two

Parallel database servers

4 High performance database for client/server systems

J. Page
Teradata UK Ltd

4.1 INTRODUCTION

The concept of the relational model is that objects of importance to a business can be represented in tables which are both simple to understand and unambiguous in content. With such tables questions such as "who is buying which product" or "which product is the most popular for a particular class of customer" can be answered through the use of the standard Structured Query Language (SQL), with no knowledge of the physical format of the data. A perfect relational model should be able to serve all applications, from simple order-entry transactions through to the most complex marketing analysis.

The relational model is now available through relational database management systems (RDBMS) on all computing environments from personal computers through to the largest mainframe systems. However their benefit is perhaps best seen when the relational facility is applied to very large volumes of data, perhaps those typically found in large retail organizations. For marketing staff, the full detail of all transactions occurring over several years may be required to be able to analyse in depth the buying patterns of the customers. In this case the tables grow to extremely large sizes, and tables holding hundreds of millions of rows are not uncommon.

The challenge set to all computer and RDBMS manufacturers who wish to supply solutions to such problems, is to build a system which can handle these large volumes of data for both pre-defined and *ad-hoc* queries. At the same time we must consider that if the system is to fulfil the promise of being a single corporate data store, the system must be capable of maintaining that data through the use of on-line transaction processing (OLTP). The combination of high *ad-hoc* capabilities with high OLTP performance cannot be achieved by conventional computing architectures, and this paper seeks to illustrate a parallel-architected database machine, that has proved time and time again, that the goals above can be solved in a commercially viable way.

4.2 THE TERADATA DBC/1012 DATABASE MACHINE

It is obvious that any system which might meet the challenges outlined above would have to provide high computing power and high I/O performance. To be effective, this would have to be provided considerably more cost-effectively than conventional mainframe power.

The name Teradata arises from the original design objective of the system which was to be able to manage effectively up to 1 terabyte (1000 gigabytes or 10^{12} bytes) of data, but of course this on its own is not enough – any system created to handle relational databases must also be freely accessible to applications and users. The two main components of such access are the languages used and the physical mechanisms available to retrieve data.

To attain this requirement Teradata uses the industry standard SQL language as the only method of access to the DBC database system. As we shall show later, this enables the provision of interfaces to the major 3rd, 4th and 5th generation system development environments and gives portability between the DBC and other relational systems.

The objective of a relational database as a corporate data store, shared between multiple applications, should also permit sharing between different operating environments. The goal of the Teradata design is to permit access to the database equally from any user environment, regardless of the mainframe, mini or micro system which is being used.

4.3 MICROPROCESSOR DOWNSIZING

The table in Fig. 4.1 shows the relative growth rates of mainframe and microprocessor power during the 1980s. The faster growth rate of the microprocessors arises because of the increasing complexity of these devices (wordlength, instruction set etc), whereas the mainframes are limited to fixed architectures. Microprocessors leverage technology by gaining both speed and complexity benefits as technology shrinks in size.

DOWNSIZE → UPSIZE
TRANSISTORS COMPUTERS

	Mainframe Model	MIPS	Microprocessor Model	MIPS	Ratio
1982-1984	3080	9	8086	0.3	30:1
1985-1988	3090	15	80286	1.0	15:1
1988-1990	3090J	20	80386	2.5-3.5	7:1
1990+	Summit	40-50?	80486	8-10?	4:1

Figure 4.1 Computer downsizing.

The challenge, therefore, is to be able to devise an architecture which can harness the power of these new devices for special applications, such as relational databases.

It has long been recognized that for any given state of processor technology, limited by the size of electronic components and the speed of mechanical ones such as disks, the route to high power systems comes from replication. The nature of this replication governs the nature of the applications which such a system can process efficiently.

Computer systems making use of replication are generally categorized according to the instruction/data stream classification, as shown below:

Single Instruction Single Data stream
The classic Von Neumann computer, with a simple processor operating on one instruction at a time (e.g. IBM 7090)

Multiple Instruction Single Data stream (MISD)
Pipelined single processor systems, with separate parts of several instructions being processed in parallel for a single program (e.g. IBM 3083, ICL 3900)

Single Instruction Multiple Data stream (SIMD)
Multiple processors operating synchronously on a single application, with each processor handling a set of data (e.g. ICL DAP, Goodyear MPP)

Multiple Instruction Multiple Data Stream (MIMD)
Multiple processors operating independently on individual sets of data (e.g. Denelcor HEP, Cray X-MP)

Conventional multiprocessing systems such as the IBM 3090/400, with 4 CPUs operating independently, may be considered as MIMD systems, but the convention used above assumes that the complete power of the system can be harnessed to a single program (multiprocessing) rather than to aid multiple job streams (multiprogramming). Until recently, no commercial computer was available which successfully used MIMD techniques to provide very high power for single applications. All the SIMD and MIMD systems described above originate from the scientific world, with no equivalent systems for the general commercial workload.

With the advent of relational databases, which give the possibility of rapid development of flexible management information systems, the need for commercial computer power has risen rapidly. For typical marketing applications, where millions of customer records need to be joined to millions of order records, the power of a single conventional CPU using software-based RDBMSs such as Ingres, Oracle or DB2, is inadequate. The challenge, therefore, is to develop a parallel architecture specifically to handle this relational processing. As with scientific systems, the interconnection of the processors is of prime importance.

Relational processes are a combination of operations on single tables (project, select, restrict) and operations combining tables (join, union, intersect, minus). Since the relational model is completely flexible, any network of processors must be capable of supporting movement of relational rows between all processors in the system, because to join rows, demands that they be on the same processor. The Teradata DBC/1012 system employs a high-speed network called the Y-Net to perform such distribution.

The enormous sizes of relational databases also dictate that the system must combine both solid state and disk technology, with parallelism to provide high CPU power and high bandwidth to the disks, so we get a picture of a sophisticated computer utilizing parallel processing mechanisms to give access to enormous amounts of relationally held data.

4.4 DBC/1012 CHARACTERISTICS

The Teradata DBC/1012 was originally designed to meet the needs of Citibank in New York. Citibank required a system capable of holding up to 1 terabyte (10^{12}) bytes of data, accessed through many host systems, to act as a single data store for all customer information.

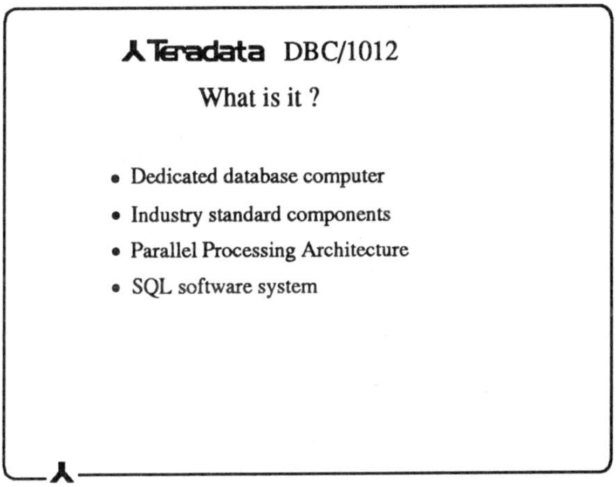

Figure 4.2 What is the DBC/1012?

A fundamental characteristic of the DBC/1012, as we have seen, is that is utilizes standard microprocessor technology in a system designed purely for relational database processing. Its design ensures that it is never constrained by any particular architecture or hardware limitations but we should remember that this specialized design ensures that it can in no way be considered a general purpose computer.

In fact the DBC/1012 does not function in a 'stand-alone' mode, but requires at least one general purpose system to connect to and house its user population. This is called the 'host' system, and the job of the DBC is to off-load from this system, all the work associated with relational databases. This will range from parsing the SQL to formatting the final results. The connectivity and the degree to which the host-offload approach is successful are shown in this paper.

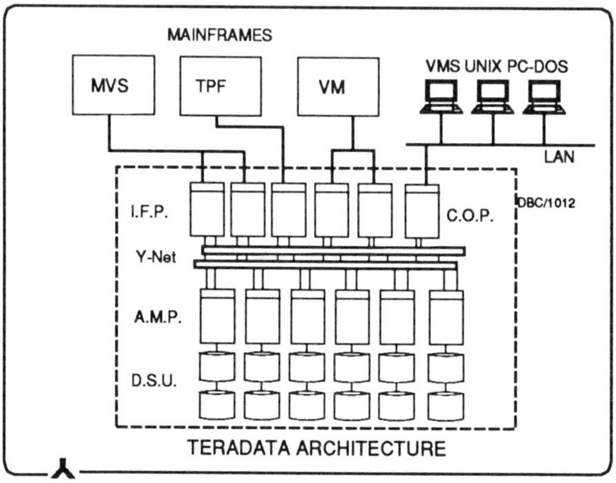

Figure 4.3 The DBC/1012 architecture.

Fig. 4.3 shows the basic components of the DBC/1012. The system consists of three types of processors, all using the same basic technology. The three types of processor are:

Access Module Processor (AMP)
The AMP is the database engine of the DBC, and manages database rows held on its associated disk storage units (DSUs). The AMP handles all aspects of database access, searching, updating etc.

Interface Processor (IFP)
The IFP has the role of managing the flow of requests and results between the DBC and an IBM, Bull or Unisys Block Multiplexor Channel. The IFP accepts SQL requests from the host system, chooses the appropriate sequence of actions, passes the actions to the AMPs to be processed, then returns the results to the host.

Communications Processor (COP)
The COP has essentially the same function as the IFP, but instead of handling a Block Multiplexor Channel, attaches directly to an Ethernet, and through this network to PCs, various Unix minicomputers and workstations, and the DEC VAX system operating under VMS.

4.5 HOW DOES THE DBC/1012 WORK?

As described above, one of the prime objective of a parallel system is to be able to deliver the complete power of the system to a single 'query'. For this to be possible using a relational operation, the tables participating in the query must be available to all the processors in the system. On the DBC each table is hash-distributed to all AMPs, so that each AMP receives an even portion of the rows. This enables a query that requires all rows to be accessed, such as a full table scan, to be processed in parallel by all the AMPs. As shown below, the power of the DBC is thus directly proportional to the number of AMPs in the system.

One of the initial design objectives of the DBC was that it should be a single corporate data store, capable of being accessed through many different host systems. Fig. 4.3 shows a configuration attached to three IBM hosts, under VM, TPF and MVS, and a network of PCs and minicomputers. As illustrated, this connectivity is made possible by the IFP and COP processors.

As well as providing physical connections, the IFP and COP systems also handle any conversions required between the DBC and the hosts, such as ASCII to EBCDIC, IEEE to IBM floating point, and byte conversions to the Bull system. All operations performed inside the DBC are identical, regardless of the host from which the request originated.

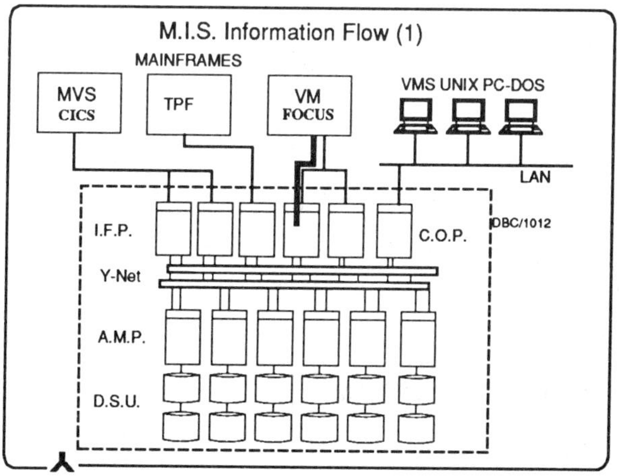

Figure 4.4 Origination of an MIS request.

The simplest way to explain the operation of the DBC/1012 is to follow the route of a query (transaction) from the user attached to an application on one of the host systems. Fig. 4.4 shows a Management Information System query being generated by the user of a FOCUS system running under VM.

FOCUS will automatically generate the required SQL to formulate the query using the definitions stored within its own data dictionary, in the same way as it would for DB2 or SQL/DS. In the Teradata case, the SQL is passed to the DBC/1012 via the host connection (channel). The SQL, still in its textual form, is received by the IFP.

The IFP handles the initial stage of SQL operation, by parsing the SQL statement to validate that it is a legal statement and that the user has the access rights to perform the requested action. Assuming a valid statement, the IFP then chooses the optimal access path to process the request.

The IFP does not, itself, hold any of the relational data, and at this stage must hand the steps of the request to the AMPs for the actual database operations.

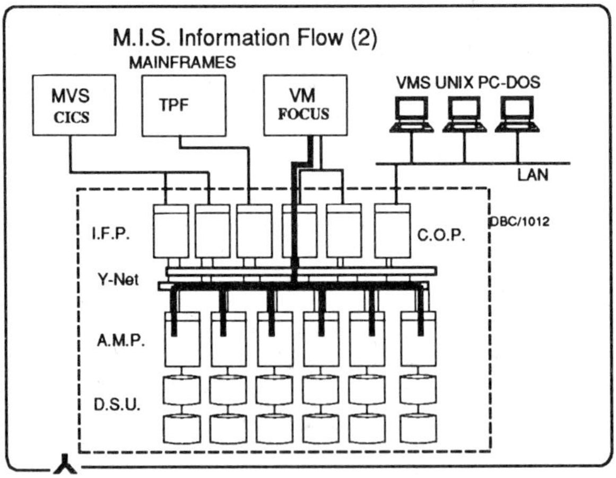

Figure 4.5 Executing data retrieval.

The architectural feature which enables the DBC/1012 to combine the power of multiple processors in answering a single SQL query, is the method of distributing data across all the processors. If we wish to make all the AMPs contribute to the processing of a request, they must all share part of the data.

In fact the data for each relational table in the system is spread equally across all processors and disks, through the use of a special algorithm. For example, on a 10 processor system, each AMP will hold 10% of each and every table. Because the data is evenly spread, each processor can contribute equally to handling the request, as shown in Fig. 4.5.

The IFP hands each stage (step) of the request to all the AMPs, which can then work independently on their own portions of the data. If movement of data is required for complex relational join operations, this is carried out automatically through the Y-Net.

When every AMP has finished its task, which may include selection, joining, sorting and formatting of the data, the IFP manages the transmission of the result set back to the host system. Special logic within the Y-Net ensures that partial result sets, which may have been sorted on the individual AMPs, are correctly merged on their way back to the host.

The complete process, from host to IFP to AMP and back via the IFP to the host, is designed to meet the original criterion of host offload, since the DBC/1012 has removed from the host all aspects of relational database handling, from parsing through to final result presentation.

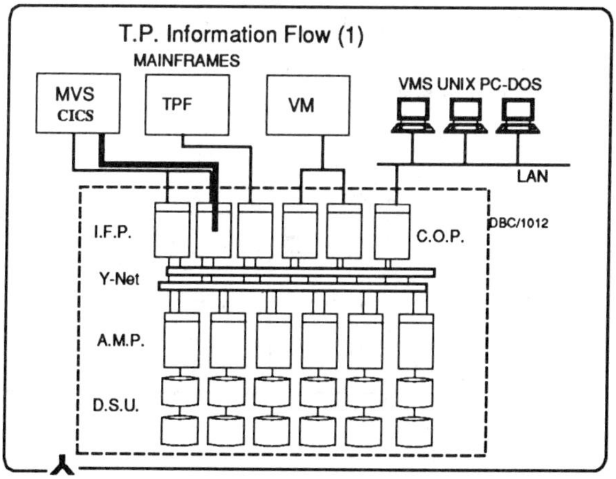

Figure 4.6 The TP request.

The case described above, where the parallel processing capability is brought to bear on a large MIS query, can be distinguished from the case of simple transactions such as found in high-volume On-Line Transaction Processing systems. Here, access is typically required to single rows (records), accessed by keys (indexes). In this case the requirement is to handle many simple transactions simultaneously, rather than large complex transactions.

The DBC/1012 architecture is designed to handle multiple simple transactions through the same distribution technique and multiprocessing system as used for the complex transactions.

Fig. 4.6 shows a transaction arising from a high volume MVS/CICS system, where the original application may well be a COBOL program with embedded SQL. As before, the transaction is passed, untranslated, to the IFP. During the analysis of the request, the IFP will have determined that the request is for an indexed retrieval, and generates the appropriate single AMP step.

This step, as before, is sent to the Y-Net, but this time is routed, through the distribution algorithm, directly to the AMP that contains the target row. All other AMPs are unaffected by the transaction.

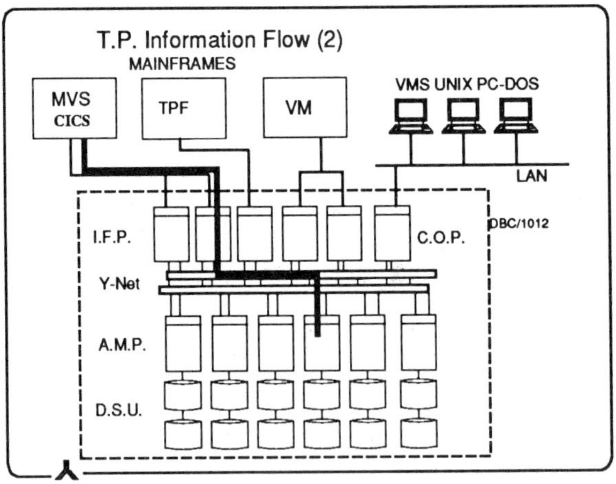

Figure 4.7 Retrieving a single row.

The target AMP is usually able to retrieve the row in a single disk access, or even directly from its data cache memory. The result row, or rows, are formatted and sent back to the IFP and then to the calling application.

Since each processor in the system is a complete, independent computer system, each is capable of full multiprogramming of tasks, and thus the system is able to handle many transactions simultaneously. In this way the DBC/1012 can be configured to give any required level of transactions per second. However, performance is not the only issue.

On a conventional Database system, each database or table resides on a specific set of disks, often with different tables on different disks. In the case of a disk failure, only a portion of the database will become inactive. For the DBC, where each table is contained partially on each AMP, and hence on at least one of the DSUs on each AMP, failure of a single AMP or DSU would render the table unavailable for operations which require full table scanning.

The DBC software system holds the solution to providing high data availability in the DBC/1012. Each row, as described above, is allocated to an AMP through a hashing algorithm. If the user selects the Fallback option, at the level of a database or individual table, the Y-Net uses a second hashing map to direct each row to a second, fallback, AMP, thus providing complete data replication. For update operations both rows will be updated simultaneously. For select operations, the primary copy of the row will be used. If the primary AMP is unavailable, all operations will automatically use the fallback copy of the row. Facilities are provided to bring the primary table up to date when the failed AMP is re-introduced into the system.

As well as the Fallback option for data, every other component in the system is duplicated. Typically a system will have several IFPs attached to a host computer and/or several COPs attached to LANs. The Y-Net itself is duplicated, with a single Y-Net having sufficient bandwidth to handle the complete workload of the system.

4.6 DBC/1012 software

The DBC/1012 is thus a completely self-contained database management system, handling all aspects of the relational model including SQL queries, database creation, maintenance and security as well as physical management of the system. Since the DBC may be accessed by many external host systems, all the database management must be internal to the DBC itself. The Teradata system also provides facilities on the various host systems to permit access to the database.

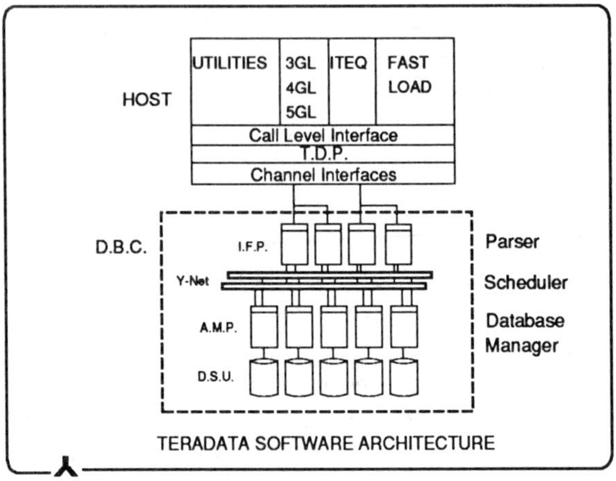

Figure 4.8 DBC/1012 software.

Fig. 4.8 shows the structure and location of the main components of the DBC software system, together with their physical locations.

DBC/1012

Teradata Operating System (TOS)
SQL parser, optimizer, dispatcher

Host (IBM)

Teradata Director Program (TDP) *
Call Level Interface software *
Various SQL pre-processors *
CICS and IMS interfaces
Bulk loading and archiving facilities
Interactive Teradata Enquiry system (ITEQ) *
Batch Teradata Enquiry system (BTEQ) *

Products indicated with * are also available on LAN-connected PC, Unix and VAX/VMS systems. Other collaborative arrangements are being discussed with third-party suppliers to provide interfaces to the SQL-based DBC system as illustrated below.

The basic functioning of the DBC relies on the fact that the traffic across the channel or LAN interface is SQL to the DBC and result rows back to the host. Other products such as Intellect and NOMAD, that generate SQL from their own enquiry languages, can thus also communicates with the DBC/1012 and use it as a database server. Such products can post-process the result set returned from the DBC/1012 to provide functionality such as cross-casting, and graphics which are not available from pure SQL. In this way the DBC takes maximum advantage of the development of existing 4GL systems, and the 4GL vendors can make efficient use of the enormous power available from the DBC with the minimum of development effort.

Fig. 4.9 lists various products that can currently communicate directly with the DBC/1012. Some of these use the Teradata CLI to achieve such communication, whilst others require a gateway to make the DBC/1012 mimic the proprietary database distributed with the specific product. Not included in this list is a growing range of Windows applications and tools using DDE communication protocols.

Teradata DBC/1012
Co-ordinated Products

- RAMIS
- NOMAD
- INGRES
- FOCUS
- PC/SQL
- INTELLECT
- AION
- METAPHOR

via API/TS
- QMF
- AS
- SAS
- SYSTEM W

Fig.4.9 DBC/1012 Coordinated Products.

4.7 GETTING SQL TO THE DBC/1012

The software architecture shown previously implies that any application using the DBC/1012 requires a combination of host processing and DBC/1012 processing. The balance between these two determines the extent to which the DBC/1012 can fulfil its promise of providing host offload.

As a test of this principle, a series of benchmark runs were performed for a UK banking customer. The customer had a standard series of complex FOCUS management information reports running on an Amdahl mainframe. The reports were taking excessive amounts of CPU time and were giving rise to long run times.

The reports were run as supplied, against the FOCUS database running on the mainframe, and the results were noted as a reference point. For the second series of tests, the database was converted into relational form and loaded onto the DBC/1012. The reports were run again, with only minor changes to use the FOCUS/DBC/1012 combination.

Teradata/Focus
Host Offload

	FOCUS HOST Elapsed	FOCUS HOST CPU	FOCUS/DBC Elapsed	FOCUS/DBC CPU
1	6 hours	390 secs	14 mins	2 secs
2	4 hours	280 secs	22 mins	3 secs
3	2 hours	150 secs	9 mins	9 secs
4	4.5 mins	9 secs	3 mins	3 secs

Figure 4.10 Processing offload.

The table in Fig. 4.10 gives the before-and-after performance figures in terms of run times and the amount of CPU work performed by the host. To some extent the run times are artificial, since the DBC/1012 times could be reduced by a considerable factor, either by changing to the newer Model 3 system, or by increasing the number of processors. The important factor is the amount by which the host CPU has been reduced, since this limits the ultimate speed improvement to be gained through off-loading the database work.

The first query shows that for a large report, of the 390 CPU seconds originally taken by FOCUS on the mainframe, 388 seconds were in the database part of the work, which is off-loaded to the DBC/1012, and in fact, the queries show that the more complex they are (many joins, agregations and sorts), the more effective the host offload and the greater percentage reduction in elapsed time.

4.8 DBC/1012 PERFORMANCE

Fig. 4.11 shows some statistics gathered when a DBC/1012 was working as a fast TP system with a mainframe transaction driver. The figures were taken in 1988, following the announcement by IBM of DB2 V2, with increased performance on a 3090-600E with ESA. The IBM system, with a CPU loading of more than 85%, achieved 438 simple enquiries per second for the 'credit check' benchmark.

The same tests were run on a 43x143x143 Model 2 DBC/1012 (43 IFPs, 143 AMPs and 143 DSUs), attached to an Amdahl mainframe. The system exceeded 1100 TPS, with the AMPs only 25% busy. A second test, with an MIS workload in the background, achieved over 1000 TPS. A sort process, which had taken 2 hours on an empty 3090-300, ran in under 12 minutes as a background task.

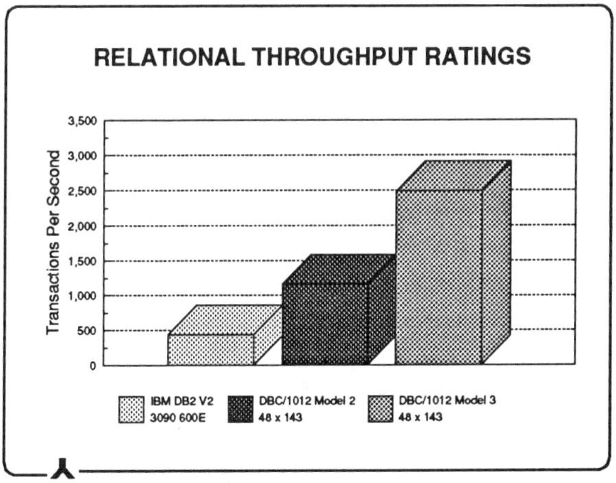

Figure 4.11 Transaction throughput.

Later that year, Teradata announced the Model 3 system, with performance 2.5 times faster for the TP workload. It was estimated that over 2500 TPS could have been achieved with such a DBC, and already a Model 4 is being developed with a further threefold performance increase.

4.9 LEVERAGING CURRENT TECHNOLOGY

One of the objectives of the DBC/1012 architecture was to be able to achieve high growth rates through the use of microprocessor technology. Fig. 4.12 shows the growth of the CPU power of a single processor as technology has moved through the Intel series of products, towards the 80486 processors. By the early 1990s, the power of the basic processor will have grown by a factor of more than 30 since its introduction in 1985.

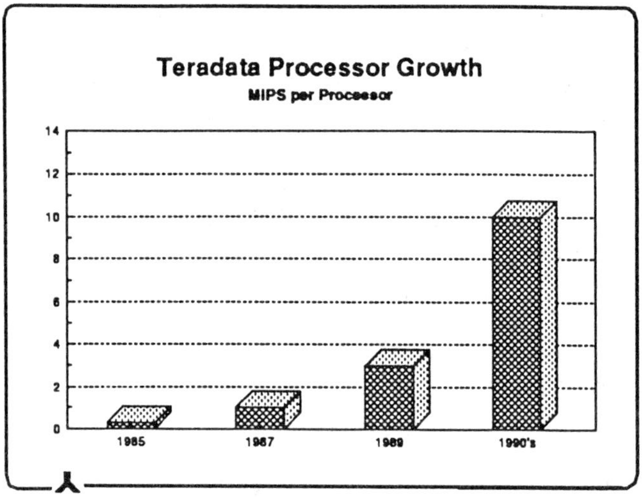

Figure 4.12 DBC/1012 processor growth.

Disk technology has also made rapid advances over the years, and these have been incorporated by Teradata. The original DBC/1012 systems used Eagle technology, with up to 4 500 MB drives in a single cabinet. The current product uses up to 16 1.2 GB drives in the same physical cabinet, giving a tenfold increase in usable storage, and a twelvefold increase in throughput.

Further advances in small disk drives, possibly with the incorporation of array technology, will be used as the product line evolves.

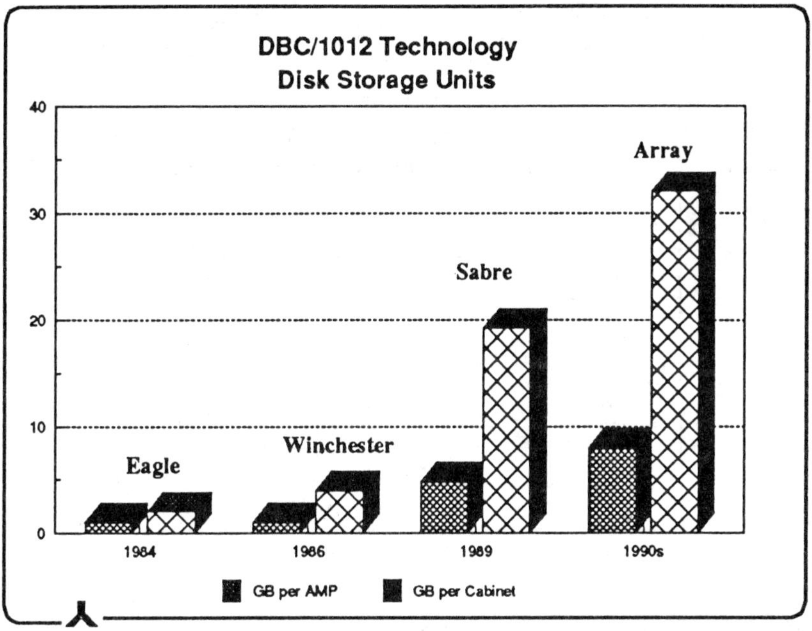

Figure 4.13 DBC/1012 disk growth.

Whilst the absolute growth rates of the product are impressive, it is useful to compare actual and theoretical maximum sizes with Mainframe systems.

Fig. 4.14 illustrates this comparison. In each grouping, the bar on the left represents the largest available mainframe from IBM at any point in time. The central bar represents the power of the largest installed Teradata DBC/1012 system, which in 1987 was the 260 processor Model 2 system installed at K-Mart in the USA. The right-hand bar represents the largest possible DBC/1012, with 1024 processors. Today, the largest installed systems approach 1,000 MIPS, with a maximum configuration of 3,000 MIPS. With the advent of 80486 and other technologies, systems in excess of 3,000 MIPS will be seen in the early 1990s.

As can be seen, the absolute rate of growth of the DBC/1012 is in excess of the mainframe system, and the system limits remain in excess of the largest user requirements, thus enabling the user to have a single data store, without fragmentation caused by technology limitations.

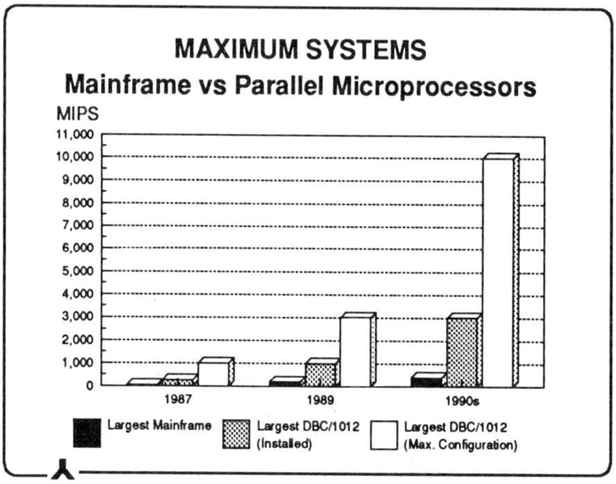

Figure 4.14 Maximum system sizes.

4.10 CONCLUSION

To summarize, the DBC/1012 had many design objectives to be met in its initial conception This paper has sought to explain how these objectives have been met.

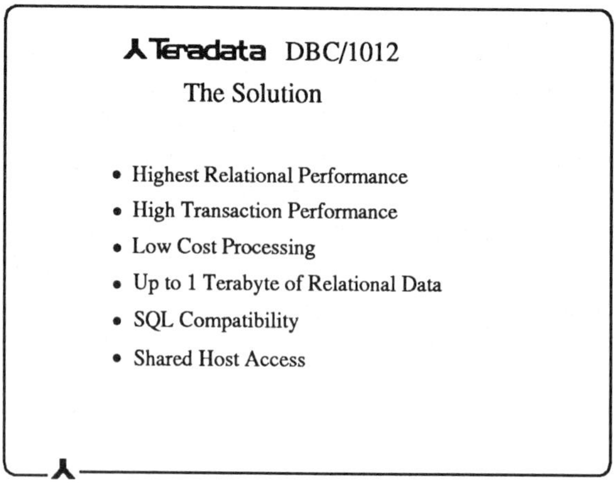

Figure 4.15 The Teradata solution.

To recap, these objectives were:

Highest relational performance
The use of multiple processors working in parallel to handle each relational process.

High transaction performance
The multiprocessing capabilities of the system to permit many simple transactions to be handled concurrently within the system.

Low cost processing
The use of microprocessor technology with much lower cost/performance than mainframes for special database work.

Up to 1 Terabyte of Relational Data
This has been exceeded with up to 1024 processors holding a maximum of 4 gigabytes of disk storage gives up to 4 terabytes of data.

SQL compatibility
The only interface to the DBC/1012 is through SQL, giving access to the major 4th generation productivity tools.

Shared host access
The DBC/1012 may be attached to multiple, different mainframe, minicomputer and workstations to provide a shared database resource.

5 Mapping a 4th generation DBMS to a range of parallel machines

J. Spiers
Oracle Corporation UK Ltd

5.1 INTRODUCTION

The role of a database management system (DBMS) is to provide data sharing – between different users, different applications and, increasingly, different locations.

The value of a coherent and consistent, shared information resource is now widely recognized and exploited. This leads to ever-growing demands for database performance to support more users of the resource. At the same time, there are ever-growing demands for enhanced database functionality – moving more 'intelligence' into the DBMS to simplify applications system development and end-user access.

The rise of the PC and of workstation technologies have increasingly brought into clear perspective the distinction betwen the personal needs of an individual 'user' and the shared aspects of an integrated multi-user system. In response, the role of client-server computing is to provide end-users with an independent and appropriate environment on which to work, with the server providing the essential access to shared data of traditional multi-user systems.

Increasingly, therefore, we see a growing focus on server-based systems, particularly database servers. The database server concept allows us to examine the issues of database management stripped to their bare essentials – a dedicated machine managing concurrent access, both read and write, to a shared database on behalf of a large number of users.

5.2 THE NEED FOR PARALLEL PROCESSING

Database management systems are, by commercial standards, heavy consumers of processing and I/O resources. But even more important, a DBMS is almost inevitably subject to growing workloads as the functionality and number of users increases. Indeed the benefits of using a DBMS can frequently create a performance problem as more users seek to take advantage of these benefits. Whilst relational databases are superior to older technologies in terms of productivity and ease of use, this must be bought at a cost in terms of processing power; this is illustrated by the following relative measures of performance (measured in TP1 transactions per second) in an IBM mainframe environment.

DB2	200 tps	(relational DBMS)
ORACLE	265 tps	(relational DBMS)
IMS Fast Path	600 tps	(non-relational DBMS)
TPF	1000 tps	(non-DBMS TP Facility)

Moreover, the higher performance levels can only be achieved at great expense; lower costs per tps can only be achieved by smaller systems delivering lower performance.

	TP1 tps	Cost	Cost/tps
IBM 3090 600S	265	$15m	$57k
DEC VAX 6360	66	$1.5m	$23k
Sequent Symmetry	124	$1m	$8k
PC 386	10	$10k	$1k

The traditional large scale computers are optimized to support a large number of concurrent local users; this is reflected not only by the hardware and by the accompanying systems software, but also in the pricing. Yet in the case of a dedicated database server, there will be no local user population at all.

The use of a database server configuration based on multiple parallel processors can offer a number of key benefits:

(a) Price/Performance: machines can be constructed from multiple, low-cost standard components leading to a lower system cost than a corresponding traditional uniprocessor. In database terms, this leads to a lower cost per transaction.

(b) Scalability: a system based on multiple standard components can offer modular growth through the addition of further components. Ideally this growth should translate directly into database throughput, allowing a database server of any required throughput to be constructed.

(c) Availability: a system with a failed processor can continue to be viable after a failure. Even when not specifically built to provide full fault-tolerance, systems based on parallel processing can generally be restarted either automatically or manually after a failure, and resume operation in the reduced configuration. As databases are more widely exploited, there are clear needs to provide high levels of reliability and availability, extending for many applications to non-stop 24-hour operation.

(d) Response: a parallel processing system can suffer less degradation in response times as the number of concurrent activities increases due to reduced context switching and dynamic scheduling across the processor pool. In a typical database application, the workload mix will typically vary throughout the day; in a parallel processing environment, techniques such as multi-processor load-balancing can be used to share out the work across the available processors. At the same time, however, we can restrict each class of work to particular elements, hence guaranteeing required levels of service to particular activities.

(e) Optimization: the flexibility and modularity of the hardware configuration means it can be optimized for its specific purpose; in turn, this may be further enhanced by optimized systems software. It is therefore possible to build systems which are specifically optimized for DBMS workloads.

(f) Centralization: a centralized system based on parallel processing allows the database resource to be more easily managed and controlled compared with a system based on multiple distributed processors. In addition, problems arising from the relatively low speeds and limited reliability of today's networks and of today's distributed database technology are avoided.

5.3 DATABASE MANAGEMENT IS A PARALLEL PROBLEM

It is important to recognize that the workload of a database server is inherently parallel – the total workload is made up of a large number of relatively small independent activities, originating from a large number of independent users. This is in total contrast with traditional applications of supercomputers and parallel processors, which are often concerned with small numbers of compute-intensive operations in areas such as image processing or text searching. The inherent parallelism of a DBMS workload provides an easy opportunity for exploiting parallel platforms, provided that the DBMS architecture is able to retain and exploit this inherent parallelism.

However, the nature of a DBMS is that it manages a shared information resource, which means that inevitably some of the independent parallel requests will require access to the same information and resources. Minimizing the impact of these points of serialization is essential to maximize concurrency and hence the scope for parallel processing.

Retaining and exploiting to the maximum, the inherently parallel nature of the workload is key to the exploitation of parallel hardware by a DBMS, since it directly impacts the total system throughput that can be achieved.

Beyond this inherent parallelism can be applied the traditional techniques of parallelization to identify and exploit opportunities for parallel processing within individual database operations. Such parallelism may be achieved through two broad strategies:

(a) function partitioning: to structure critical processes in such a way that separate functional sections can execute in parallel. This can be achieved either automatically by intelligent compilers, or explicitly by the developer, supported by specialized software tools such as parallel programming libraries and languages.

(b) data partitioning; to provide multiple instances of limiting processes, each working against an independent partition of the underlying data set.

A DBMS provides significant scope for both forms of partitioning. This is particularly true for relational systems which are non-procedural in their approach; complex database operations, for example involving nested sub-queries, are handled directly within the DBMS creating opportunities for function partitioning. In addition, the relational approach is set-oriented – a single request may require reference to and/or retrieval of an arbitrarily large set of data, providing opportunities for data partitioning.

Note however that, although the techniques of partitioning of atomic database requests can improve the response to an individual request, they will typically not affect the throughput of the systems as a whole. Only where the number of available processors is high in relation to the number of concurrently active database operations will it be necessary to parallelize individual operations to exploit all available processing power. However, such parallelization may be desirable in order to offer accelerated processing to high priority or long running database requests.

The architectural issues to be addressed by a DBMS running on a parallel platform may therefore be summarized as follows:

(a) retaining and exploiting the inherently parallel nature of the workload;

(b) minimizing the impact of the inevitable points of necessary serialization

(c) identifying and exploiting opportunities for parallel execution of sub-functions;

(d) identifying and exploiting opportunities for parallel execution through data partitioning.

5.4 ORACLE'S VERSION 6 ARCHITECTURE AND SHARED MEMORY PLATFORMS

The architecture of ORACLE version 6, the current release, is illustrated in Fig 5.1. This architecture was specifically designed to address the growing requirement to support large scale transaction-oriented workloads. The major focuses are therefore performance, concurrency, high availability, plus the ability to fully exploit shared memory parallel processing systems. ORACLE's shared memory symmetrical multiprocessing parallel platforms include the IBM 3090, Digital's VAX 6000 and 88x0 series, Convex, Pyramid and Sequent Symmetry.

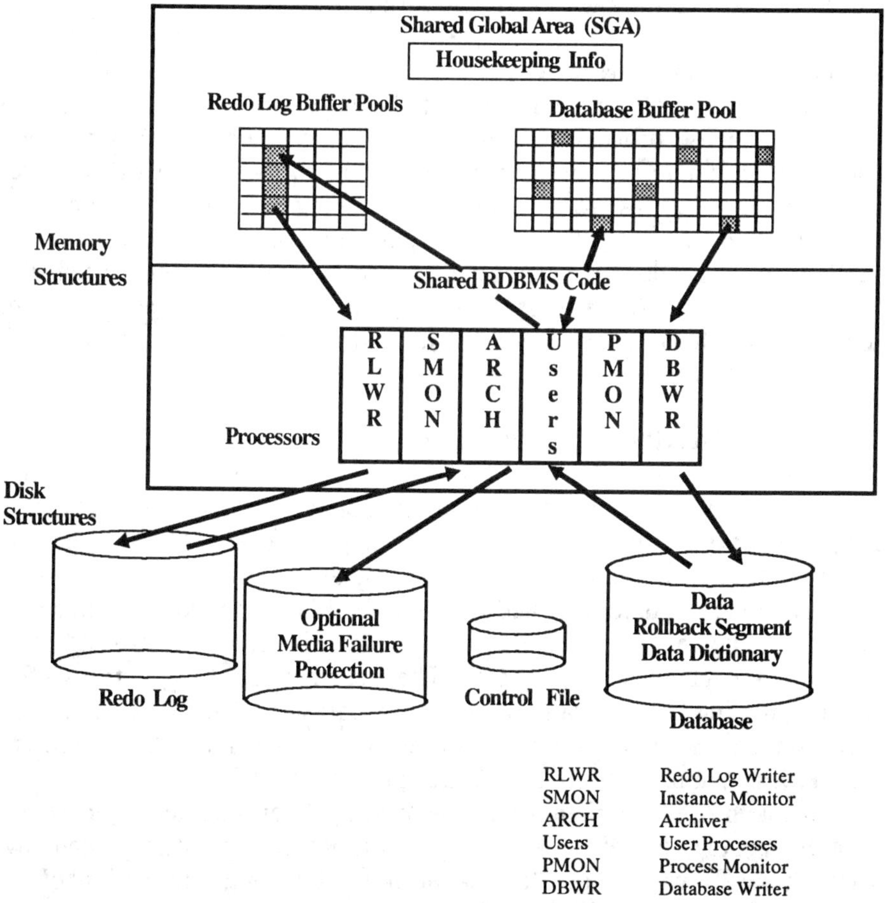

Figure 5.1 ORACLE V6 architecture.

5.4.1 System global area

The ORACLE version 6 architecture is based around a globally shared memory area accessible to all database processes; this area is known as the System Global Area (SGA).

The SGA is used for buffering disk I/O, to provide a database cache, to maintain details of database locks and to hold queues on shared system resources.

5.4.2 Parallel processes

The database processing workload is divided amongst a number of processes – the database server processes themselves, of which there is one for each concurrent database connection, and a small number of background processes undertaking the necessarily serial work.

The database server processes

For each concurrent connection to the database, there is a corresponding backend database process; all database processes execute the same code. The backend database process performs the majority of the work involved in processing a database request, including reading data from disk into cache memory where required. This 'process per user' approach fully exploits the parallelism in the incoming workload, with the operating system responsible for scheduling these processes across the available processors. The necessary serialization on physical disc read operations is imposed at the operating system level.

Transaction integrity and the Redo Log

Database update operations need to ensure transaction integrity, such that a set of related updates (a transaction) is applied in full to the database on disk, or (in the event of some error) not applied at all. Only in this way can the integrity of database structures be guaranteed.

As database updates are made, these are initially applied in the database cache. At the same time, a Redo Log record is created consisting of an image of the changed data bytes. The act of committing a transaction involves writing the relevant Redo Log records to disk. The Redo Log itself consists of one or more serial files, and for each such file there is a continuously running Redo Log Writer process (RLWR).

Although the underlying database has not been updated on disk, the system is protected against any failure by the Redo Log entries which have been physically written out to disk prior to signalling completion of the Commit. In the event of failure, the Redo Log contains a record of updates which need to be applied to the database proper to roll it forward to a consistent and up-to-date state.

This 'fast commit' technique is designed to reduce the work to be performed at the commit point to the absolute minimum sufficient amount. The work of physically updating the database on disk, which may involve many I/Os as disk blocks and index entries are reorganized, is deferred such that it can proceed in parallel with other activity.

This technique reduces the volume of disk I/O at the point of a Commit to a single serial write; indeed, the system also takes advantage of writing the Redo Log records for more than one transaction in a single I/O where possible, a technique known as group commit.

Deferred update

Database updates, which have to date only been applied within the database cache and protected by the Redo Log, need eventually to be physically applied to disk, either to free up space in the cache or to create a synchronization point for housekeeping purposes.

The actual database update operations are performed by a separate task known as the database writer which runs continuously in the background, and which of course can run in parallel with the processing of database requests. In appropriate circumstances, multiple database writer tasks can be used to allow write operations to separate portions of the database to proceed in parallel.

A reduction in total disk write activity is also achieved by virtue of the fact that, where a database record has been changed several times in the buffer cache, then intermediate updates are never physically applied to the database, only recorded in the Redo Log.

Benefits

The effect of this architecture is to exploit to the full the parallelism inherent in the incoming workload. At the same time, the amount of work performed at the Commit point, which is of necessity serial in nature, is reduced to a bare minimum. This not only maximizes the response time to the user but also minimizes the delay to other processes waiting to Commit. By deferring the task of physically updating the database, this work can be executed in parallel with other database activity, by a batch process able to exploit processing capacity not required by higher priority activities.

5.4.3 Concurrency

The ORACLE architecture also maximizes concurrency by minimizing the impact of database locks.

Data which is to be updated is locked at the most granular level; only the actual records which are subject to change are locked and there is no requirement to escalate locks to the block, table or file level. The ability to lock at the row level arises as a direct consequence of the deferred update mechanism. In a traditional architecture, the commit process involves physically updating the database on disk, which typically means reorganizing data at the disk block level, affecting other records held within that block and possibly beyond.

The ORACLE architecture also provides a read-consistent view of data without reducing the concurrency level. ORACLE does not take read locks, but retains before-image information as data is changed. Transactions reading from the database are guaranteed a consistent snapshot view of the data as it was at the commencement of the query, irrespective of the number of changes that may take place during the query. This feature is refered to as row-level multi-versioning.

5.4.4 Other features

The ORACLE version 6 architecture also provides for on-line back-up and recovery. Security backups can be taken whilst the system remains on-line, running in parallel with normal processing. Similarly, in the event of a partial failure, the affected area of the database can be restored in parallel with the continued processing of database activity against the unaffected areas.

A common bottleneck in transaction-based systems is the process of generating unique transaction sequence numbers – order number, invoice number and so on. Conventionally, this requires a database access and update operation. ORACLE provides a memory-based sequence number generation capability to minimize this common point of serialization.

5.4.5 Performance and scalability

The effectiveness of the ORACLE version 6 architecture is confirmed by the performance, and more particularly the scalability, achieved on shared memory parallel platforms. As an example, the performance figures achieved on Digital's VAX 63x0 platforms, measured in TP1 transactions per second, are as follows.

VAX 6000 Model 310	(1 processor)	13.5	tps
VAX 6000 Model 320	(2 processors)	26.5	tps
VAX 6000 Model 340	(4 processors)	44	tps
VAX 6000 Model 360	(6 processors)	66	tps

5.5 ORACLE FOR MASSIVELY PARALLEL SYSTEMS

The ORACLE version 6 architecture described above is dependent on the ability of all processors to access the same memory, the SGA; in hardware terms, the processors are required to share a common memory bus. Ultimately, the performance of the system will be limited by a shared memory bottleneck.

In contrast, traditional loosely coupled hardware architectures, such as the Digital VAX cluster or Tandem systems, are not based around shared memory; each processor has its own local memory and communicates with other processors by passing messages over a common interconnect – a bus or even a LAN. However this arrangement ultimately leads to an interconnect bottleneck, limited by the fixed bandwidth of the interconnect.

Massively parallel systems eliminate the shared memory bottleneck by employing a distributed memory structure in which each processing node consists of a processor and local memory. The interconnect bottleneck is removed by virtue of an interconnect scheme which not only provides high-speed connections, but which also incrementally scales the total interconnect bandwidth as the number of processors increases.

ORACLE for Massively Parallel Systems is designed to deliver a broad range of cost-effective performance, up to very high transaction rates of 1000 TP1 transactions per second and beyond, on today's emerging massively parallel platforms. These include the the Meiko Computing Surface, the Parsys Supernode 1000 Series, and the NCUBE 2 Scalar Supercomputer. Although implementation details vary between these platforms, the architectural principles are common.

This architecture is illustrated in Fig. 5.2. In effect, each processor carrying out database work maintains a buffer cache in its local memory to store the data blocks required by the transactions it executes. Again, background processes executing at each node are responsible for writing Redo Log records to disk at the point of commit, and removing data blocks from the cache by physically applying database updates to disk.

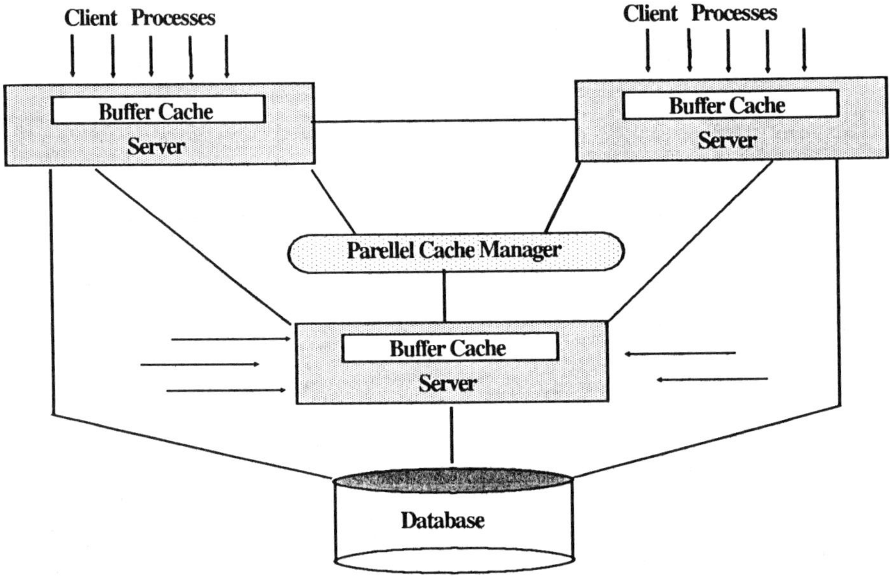

Figure 5.2 Parallel cache management.

When the Parallel Server requires a data block that is not already in local memory, it uses the facilities of the parallel cache manager to determine whether the block is in the memory buffer cache of another node. If it is, the block is physically moved across the interconnect to the node that needs it; otherwise, the block is obtained from disk storage in the conventional way.

5.5.1 Concurrency control

A unique feature of ORACLE is its support for unrestricted row level locking; this provides the finest granularity of concurrency control, minimizing contention between transactions, and maximizing the extent to which transactions can be executed in parallel with one another.

The higher the throughput becomes, the more important it is to minimize bottlenecks since the probability of multiple users accessing the same disk block is a direct function of the number of concurrent users. This issue is most critical for index blocks, since not only are index entries accessed most frequently, their small typical size means that a single page may contain perhaps several hundred index records.

Even in the massively parallel environment, full unrestricted row level locking is supported. When a data block is transferred from processor to processor, information on any row level locks held on the data is also passed. Thus multiple transactions executing on different processors can modify different rows in the same data block without ever waiting for each other to release a lock.

Multi-version concurrency control to provide read consistent images is also particularly important in massively parallel environments with their high workload of concurrent read and update transactions. As in the standard version 6 implementation, when a transaction updates a row in a table, a copy of the previous contents of that row can be generated to provide a read consistent image. Moreover, if a data block is transferred to another node, the local copy is retained to allow query operations to proceed without waiting for the block to be transferred back. Furthermore, additional queries on the same data block may be performed at the same time by other servers once they acquire a copy of that data block in their local memory. Thus multiple operations on the same logical row of data can be processed in parallel without interfering with one another and whilst keeping the number of data blocks transferred between processors to a minimum.

The standard ORACLE version 6 fast commit, group commit and deferred write features minimize disk I/O. In a large massively parallel configuration, with aggregate memory measured perhaps in gigabytes, large databases may indeed be effectively cached entirely in memory; in such cases, only the highly efficient logging information needs to be physically written to disk. Even where the available cache memory is less than the total database size, the most active data is likely to remain permanently in memory.

Massively parallel platforms also require support from new database administration facilities. Each node effectively runs a complete 'instance' of the ORACLE DBMS; in a configuration with perhaps hundreds of nodes it would be inconvenient, to say the least, to require a database administrator to manually start-up, shut down and monitor these instances individually. As a result, new database administration tools are being built to assist in the parallel management of multiple parallel database instances.

5.6 APPLICATIONS OF MASSIVELY PARALLEL DATABASE PLATFORMS

The implementation of ORACLE on massively parallel platforms opens up the possibility of a variety of configurations addressing a wide range of requirements.

The first style of configuration is a complete fully-functional platform for database applications. Here both the applications and the DBMS itself run together on a single massively parallel machine. Such a platform can provide a cost-effective and more flexible alternative to conventional mini or mainframe systems.

Secondly, the massively parallel platform could be configured as a dedicated network database server. Applications would reside on other computers, perhaps workstations, accessing the database by passing database requests over a network. Such an approach offers distributed client-server computing, combining the front-end of today's workstations with a flexible back-end server optimized for database performance.

Thirdly, a massively parallel system can be configured as a closely-coupled database back-end, connected via a local high-speed connection (e.g. 'channel attached') to a conventional computer running the applications. Such systems could be configured as database add-in cards or add-on cabinets to conventional machines from the very small to the very small, extending the performance and capabilities of an existing hardware or software investment.

5.7 DEDICATED DATABASE MACHINES

The possibility of dedicated database servers and add-ons suggests the possibility of constructing purpose-built machines, based on parallel processing, specifically optimized for, and dedicated to, DBMS processing. Two such machines are briefly descibed below.

5.7.1 The charles river data systems relational accelerator

The Relational Accelerator is an example of a custom device, specifically sold as an ORACLE accelerator for Digital VAX computers. The accelerator uses up to 4 processors, plus special-purpose disk subsystem, operating system and interconnect to the VAX system.

Because the Relational Accelerator is not a general-purpose computer, its design objectives are optimized solely to the needs of a DBMS. The scheduler is of particular importance because of the high number of processes generated by concurrent DBMS activity, and the tendency of Unix to thrash under large number of processes due to its scheduling mechanism. The Relational Executive provides a fast context switch (of approximately 300 microseconds), based partly on the knowledge that floating point registers can generally be ignored since DBMS operations rarely use floating point. Similarly, a specialized memory allocation scheme is used since conventional virtual memory mechanisms are hardly relevant to systems dedicated to running multiple copies of identical processes.

DBMSs use disk resources intensively because of the random nature of data accesses in many applications. Given that disk drive manufacturers cannot significantly improve on today's access speeds, the only ways to achieve better disk performance are through the use of alternative storage devices (e.g. RAM disks), or through parallelism – multiple controllers, multiple drives and efficient buffer and space management.

The Relational Accelerator optimizes disk I/O for DBMS purposes by spreading the database across spindles using an interleaving technique; this effectively randomizes and parallelizes accesses amongst the available drives. A separate drive, supported by a battery-backed cache, is dedicated to logging so that these accesses, which are essentially sequential, will generally find the head already correctly positioned.

The multiple processors of the Relational Accelerator all have shared access to a global memory area which holds the SGA. In addition, however, each processor has a 32 Kb high speed cache which means that most references to global memory can in fact be satisfied by the local cache; this minimizes contention on the shared memory bus. The cache remains fully transparent to software through a coherency mechanism which monitors traffic on the bus and purges cache entries which another device has updated; this requires a write through cache mechanism whereby all updates pass all write cycles immediately out on the bus to global memory. The Relational Accelerator is restricted to a practical limit of 4 processors by the bandwidth of the memory bus.

In addition, each processor is equipped with 16 Mb of local RAM. As well as being accessible locally, this can also be accessed from the system bus by both other processors and from DMA devices.

All memory, both global memory and the local memory associated with each processor is mapped onto a single uniform address space, such that any CPU needing access to any piece of the shared kernel state can directly address it. Moreover all changes become immediately visible to all cpus. The key function of the Relational Executive is to ensure that objects are allocated to the right RAM, global for system-wide data and local for per CPU objects

No automatic load balancing mechanism is provided. Instead, incoming connect requests are assigned to the most lightly loaded of the CPUs, ensuring rough balance at peak loading.

The Relational Accelerator may be viewed as a specialized data storage server that is further specialized for ORACLE RDBMS execution, through parallelism in its disks, CPU and operating system.

5.7.2 The REAL database servercharger

The ServerCharger is another configuration built and optimized specifically for the purpose of running the ORACLE DBMS. It consists of a minimum of 4 loosely coupled processors dedicated to specific tasks:

between 1 and 4 RDBMS processors running the ORACLE DBMS processes under a dedicated special-purpose operating system

network I/O processor

disk I/O processor

DBA Processor running standard Unix and dedicated to the front-end workload of the database administrator

The ServerCharger is configured and sold as a dedicated ORACLE database server, receiving requests from conventional applications machines over a network or bus.

5.8 FURTHER DEVELOPMENTS AND APPLICATIONS

As described in this paper, ORACLE's work to date has been concerned primarily with efficiently mapping the inherent parallel workload of a database environment onto both shared memory and non-shared memory parallel systems. This allows multiple database operations to be executed in parallel on different processors.

At the same time, the emergence of specialized hardware architectures optimized for, and dedicated to, running standard ORACLE DBMS software is already visible. Unlike the dedicated database machines of the past which ran dedicated DBMS software, these can provide easy migration of an existing database workload from conventional systems, and also retain the option of portability and freedom of hardware choice into the future; ORACLE today supports over 100 different environments.

Future developments of the ORACLE architecture will address the requirement to allow multiple processors to share the workload of a single transaction, using techniques of data partitioning, for example for large sort operations, and function partitioning, for example through the decomposition of complex queries into parallel subqueries. In addition, work is in hand to optimize the ORACLE implementation on various parallel platforms through exploiting the specific software environment and development tools provided to support the hardware.

With the availability of parallel systems offering potentially unlimited amounts of processing power, centralized computing can regain its position as a cost-effective alternative to distributed computing. The degree of decentralization can be selected based upon considerations other than the price of hardware. Centralized information systems can avoid the performance and manageability problems inherent in the use of networked configurations, and allow managers to more easily retain desired levels of control, security and reliability.

Part Three

New architectures for parallel database systems

6 Developing concurrent databases using distributed objects

K. Steer
Consultant to Strand Software Technologies Inc.

6.1 INTRODUCTION

As the cost of computer hardware and networking decreases, there is a trend towards computer networks. This, coupled with cheaper secondary storage has allowed much larger database systems to be developed.

Quite often large databases are stored on mainframe computers which are concurrently accessed via the network. As more users are added to the system, the response time degrades. To improve response time, a faster mainframe can be installed which is costly and may only reduce the response time by a factor of two or three. However it does not remove the user I/O bottleneck.

An alternative option would be to distribute the database over a number of processors and enable user interaction via dedicated I/O channels directly connected to the processor. The access time of a single request will be of the same order, but on multi-user systems, these accesses are made concurrently giving a much faster response time, provided the distribution of the database matches the view of the users.

Thus, there is a large potential market for multi-processor databases both in existing DP markets requiring faster transaction throughput, and also new areas, for example data fusion, where are large volume of real-time data is being fused together in some coherent form. The problem is how to rapidly develop these systems and try alternative versions without interrupting existing operations?

Database systems can be roughly divided into two levels of abstraction i) the physical database which handles the file and disk access, and ii) the logical database that reflects the users' conceptual view. Concurrency can be applied to both levels, but it is desirable to make this transparent to the conceptual view of the user. Therefore it is necessary for a concurrent system to translate a user's request into a distributed transaction and provide an appropriate interface to support these transactions. This interface must be flexible and reconfigurable allowing both parallel and remote network access, depending where the physical resources are located.

6.2 AIMS OF THIS PAPER

We aim to show how a concurrent language, can be used to model objects of a database system allowing the developer to generate an arbitrary network. By providing a high level view of the physical distribution, different networks can be generated and tested to run across parallel processor architectures.

Although concurrency can be exploited in various ways, i) multi-user access, ii) distribution across multiple processors and iii) replicated databases, the paper discusses the second form of concurrency showing how a database is decomposed into a set of smaller ones without affecting the conceptual schema and views onto it.

An example is developed showing how Strand models database architectures as concurrent objects communicating via message streams. These objects are linked together and distributed over the available physical resources. The example is simple and most emphasis is on how Strand overcomes implementation problems.

The last section discusses future directions of STRAND88 and concurrent database design, for example, to redistribute dynamically the physical database structure if a processor fails or differing views require a more efficient distribution.

Throughout this paper 'STRAND88' and 'Strand' are interchanged; but Strand is the specification of a parallel processing language whereas STRAND88 is an implementation of Strand by AI Limited. The term 'processor' is used to mean part of the parallel machine that includes its own working memory and file system, rather than just the physical processor itself.

6.3 WHY ARE CONCURRENT DATABASE MORE PREVALENT?

Matching the physical distribution to the users' view can be a problem, often only found by experimentation. Therefore a database system is required that allows the database administrator to try different distributions easily, but hide these changes from the end user.

There has been much work on distributed databases, showing how response times can be improved for specific requirements. Often by providing a distribution layer on top of existing database systems. Unfortunately, the user has to know where the data is physically located to access it. On the other hand, concurrent databases provide a global view onto the system, hiding the physical distribution from the user.

An alternative method, would be to take a single database system and split it over a number of physical processors. It has been shown that for the equivalent processing power there can be a 5:1 hardware cost benefit using multiple processors systems instead of single mainframe systems. As with all potential benefits there are trade-offs to consider including investment in existing code, cost in developing parallel code, reliability of new system, choice of parallel machine, future trends, and how to code parallel systems.

Unfortunately one never gets anything free; various problems occur when developing concurrent databases, which include:

matching	- distribution to user's view
testing	- alternate views, need to redefine distribution
access rights	- who can read and write simultaneously
independence	- between abstract levels
reliability	- across networks
security	- of data transfer
integration	- of existing databases
global schema	- semantic conflict, disagreement of values

Having developed an application, how can you redistribute the physical database without changing the conceptual schema (e.g. to fine tune the system)? We consider here one possible solution using STRAND88, a concurrent dataflow language, that allows a parallel algorithm to be defined independently of the machine architecture.

With STRAND88, existing sequential code (for example C) can be incorporated into an application via the foreign language interface. These features allow existing database code, e.g. Informix, ORACLE to be incorporated to handle database access on each processor with STRAND88 providing the communication 'glue' between them. As STRAND88 is portable, changing the parallel hardware only requires the foreign language interface to be relinked with database code for that machine.

6.4 EXAMPLE - A BOOKING DATABASE

To illustrate concepts and problems, we consider a simple example of a booking database. Bookings are made for travel (air, sea), accommodation and sightseeing throughout the world. The database is accessed regularly by the agents and accountants. There are unacceptable response times on a single processor system. A system is required to provide a faster response time that can be upgraded with minimal effort.

Various questions need to be considered:

- Improved response time?
- Comparison of different distributions?

- Scalability, adding extra processors?
- Flexibility, convert existing distribution to another one?
- Failure recovery, transaction processing?
- Reusability, incorporate existing code?

Analysis shows possible methods of distributing the bookings by:

type	- air, land, accommodation etc.
location	- UK, Europe, US, rest of world
department	- group booking agents together
client	- group clients
date	- dynamically add monthly databases
generic	- based on a set of key attributes
views	- split into views

Often bookings are made for flights, trips and accommodation making location a better distribution. Whereas air bookings may include UK and foreign flights making the type distribution better. The problem with the third option is that the accountants would have to know who made the booking in order to access the record. The generic solution of distributing the entity set based on the value of a key attribute provides a simple method of trying different distributions. However, a global conceptual schema is still necessary to provide consistent access to these subset entities.

As this paper is primarily concerned with exploring how to distribute data for a single entity type, the example is simplified to the single entity set **booking** in Fig. 6.1 and used to illustrate different methods of splitting a single database into subsets of related entities. The booking tuple (or record) defined is

```
booking(Client, Type, Loc, Date, Cost, B_no, Agent)
```

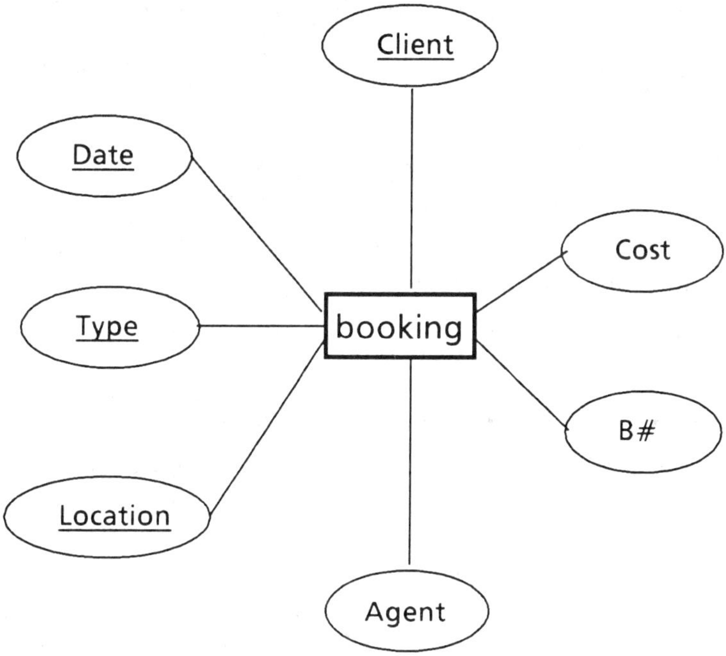

Figure 6.1 Simplifed entity relationship diagram for booking.

6.5 COMPONENTS OF A CONCURRENT DATABASE SYSTEM

Having defined the problem, components of a typical database system are listed along with extra ones defined to handle physical distribution.

Query language – provides a language to access databases (e.g.SQL) either directly or via a host application to add control and expressive power.

Conceptual schema – provides a consistent interface to the distributed system. Definition and mapping written in a Data Definition Language (DDL), describing the conceptual level by providing a data model of entities and relationships.

Views – provide user groups with views onto the conceptual schema. Abstraction or a subscheme of the DDL, e.g. "Retrieve from booking all flights booked by Whale on July 15".

Transaction processing – encapsulate database accesses into transaction requests.

Distribution layer – handles physical distribution of the database system.

Physical layer – handles files, indices and storage structures, (often written in C).

Well defined interfaces – provide independence between levels.

Data definition compiler – compiles data definitions.

Distributed system compiler – provide a method of reconfiguring the distribution of an entity set.

Dynamic distribution – run-time copying of old distribution set to a new set.

Concurrent access rights – either in file manager or distribution layer.

Security – ensure data security and correct access across parallel hardware.

Error recovery – maintain a history of transactions.

Backup – provide methods of backing up parts of the database system.

An extra level of abstraction in the database system is required. Fig. 6.2 shows a standard view of a database system, whereas Fig. 6.3, shows how it is modified to handle distribution over physical processors.

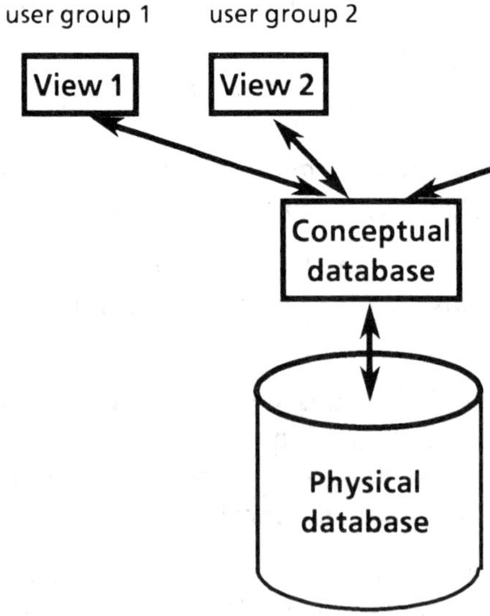

Figure 6.2 Levels of abstraction in a database system.

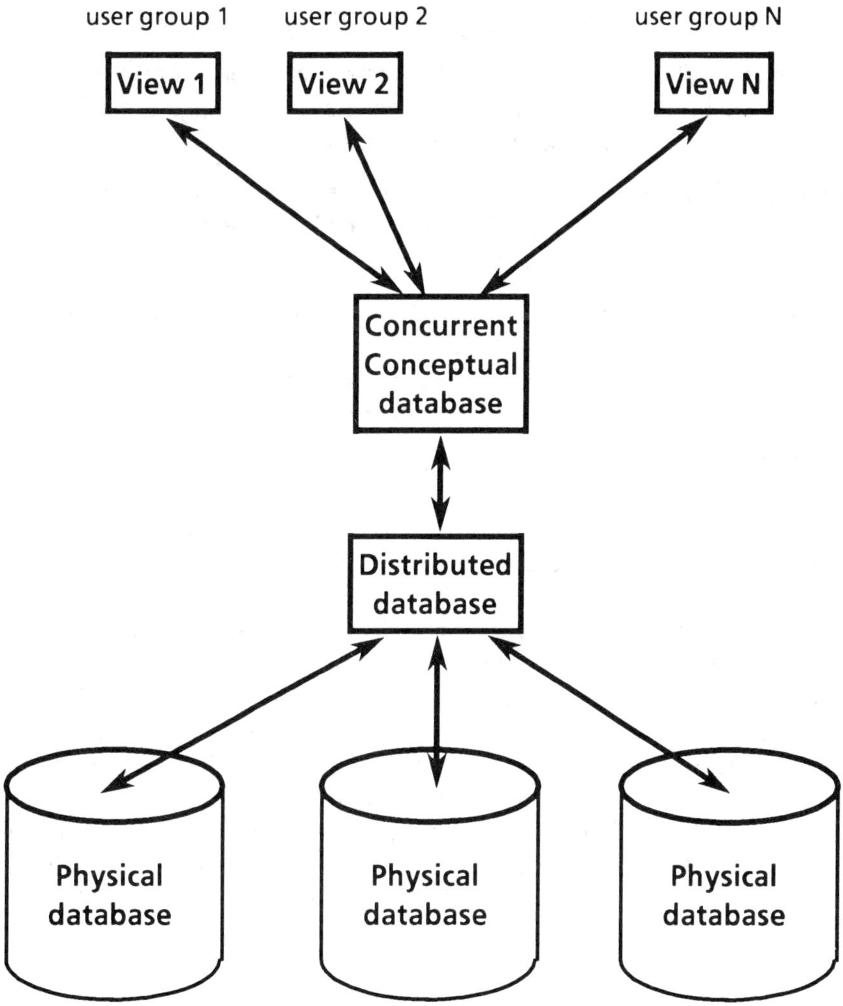

Figure 6.3 Levels of abstraction in a concurrent database system.

6.6 INTRODUCTION TO STRAND

A detailed knowledge of Strand is not assumed in this paper, and because of this assumption only top-level code is shown in the examples later. This section discusses the concepts and techniques of Strand. To implement and test concurrent databases efficiently requires a scalable and portable parallel programming language. Various alternatives were considered, including Actors, Linda, Parallel C, but Strand was selected for the following reasons:

Parallel semantics – STRAND88 is one of the few commercial languages that has architecture independent fine-grained parallel semantics.

Uniformity – the implementation is portable and relatively insensitive to the underlying architectures, because the language expresses inter- and intra-resource parallelism uniformly.

Efficiency – the implementation is scalable allowing it to utilize highly parallel machines and allows C code to be linked and run for lower level optimization.

Clarity and conciseness – Strand is a declarative language, making the source code easier to read. In addition, use of explicit synchronization in transaction processing makes it easier to rigorously argue about correctness.

Strand is a modular programming language for parallel processing that includes data flow, synchronization and process to processor assignment. STRAND88 is a version of Strand developed by AI Limited; currently running on Suns, Intel iPSC/2, Sequent Symmetry, Symmult, and Transputer boards.

A Strand program can be conceptually viewed as a pool of light-weight concurrent processes distributed across a number of physical resources (processors). Processes communicate with each other via a shared variable mechanism, which uses the same mechanism for inter- and intra-processor communication. This means that processes can easily be redistributed without altering the correctness of the program.

The actions of a process are defined by a procedure, that is composed of a number of clauses. Procedures are grouped together in module files. Each module has a number of public procedures that can be called external to that module; the rest are private. A clause has the form:

```
r(t1,...,tn) :- <guard conditions> | <body relations>.
```

This clause is part of a procedure with name r and parity n (specified as r/n), for example transaction (Operation, Key, Result) is defined transaction/3. The '|' delimits the guard conditions and body relations, t1 .. tn are argument terms. The <guard conditions> and <body relations> are conjunctions of relation calls, with the <guard conditions> | being optional.

When a call db:transaction (fetch, Key, Result), is evaluated, the module db is loaded and every clause of the procedure transaction/3 is searched for a candidate clause. A candidate clause is one where the head pattern matches and all guard conditions succeed. For example, a procedure transaction could be defined to handle 'fetch' and 'delete' operations:

```
transaction(Operation, Key, Result) :-
        Operation == "fetch" |
                db_fetch(Key, Result).
transaction(Operation, Key, Result) :-
        Operation == "delete" |
                db_delete(Key, Result).
transaction(Operation, Key, Result) :-
        otherwise |
                Result := error.
```

Arguments starting with uppercase letters are variables, lower case are strings. The declarative reading of transaction is

```
if the Operation is "fetch"
        then call the db_fetch/2 primitive
if the Operation is "delete"
        then call the db_delete/2 primitive
otherwise assign the Result to "error"
```

Communication occurs by one process assigning a variable that other processes are waiting on, for example Result := error. Messages are sent via communication streams and can be of any format e.g. strings, numbers, lists, tuples or user defined. For example the tuple defined as:

```
sql (select(cost),
     from(booking),
     where(date, "15 july", client, "Whale"))
```

could be used to make a SQL request:

```
SELECT      cost
FROM        booking
WHERE       date = "15 july" AND client = "Whale"
```

An object-based style of programming can be developed directly in Strand, by setting up a network of perpetual processes communicating with each other through message streams. Each perpetual process does a specific job, waiting for new messages on their input streams, processing them and passing on new messages before processing new input messages.

A simple database system can be composed of two concurrent objects, a query_language processor, receiving query requests from users and a database object which processes the transaction requests. These processes communicate with each other via the Query stream. A configuration procedure, system can be defined to create the processes:

```
system :-
        query_language(Query),
        database(Query).
```

In Strand, each physical resource is identified by an integer which allows run-time allocation of processors using the @ N operator:

```
distributed_system :-
        query_language(Query),
        database(Query) @ 3.
```

The call db:distributed_system starts a query_language process locally and a database process running on resource 3. Processes still communicate across physical processors via the shared variable Query. Run-time allocation of processes has the additional advantages of being able to dynamically reconfigure the system in event of resource failure, not discussed in this paper.

As there is no need to set up specific inter-processor communication channels, code can be developed and tested on a sequential machine and then transferred to a parallel machine where the database application runs. A major benefit of portable code is that there is no need to interrupt the existing application to test ideas because the concurrent version is being developed and tested on different hardware.

6.7 DATABASE IMPLEMENTATION

The interaction of database components is shown in Fig. 6.4, which is appropriate for a single processor. However, for a concurrent implementation, an extra component is required to distribute the requests to the specific processor.

Adding a distribution manager to the system produces the architecture shown in Fig. 6.5. It may seem more natural to place the distribution above the database manager, which is a valid alternative but more suited to distributed databases. By placing the distribution layer below the database manager, the global view is maintained until there is a need to physically distribute the requests. The distribution manager receives requests from the database manager, locates the correct file manager from the distribution description tables and routes the message. Selection is made from one or more key attributes, either via lookup tables or hashing functions.

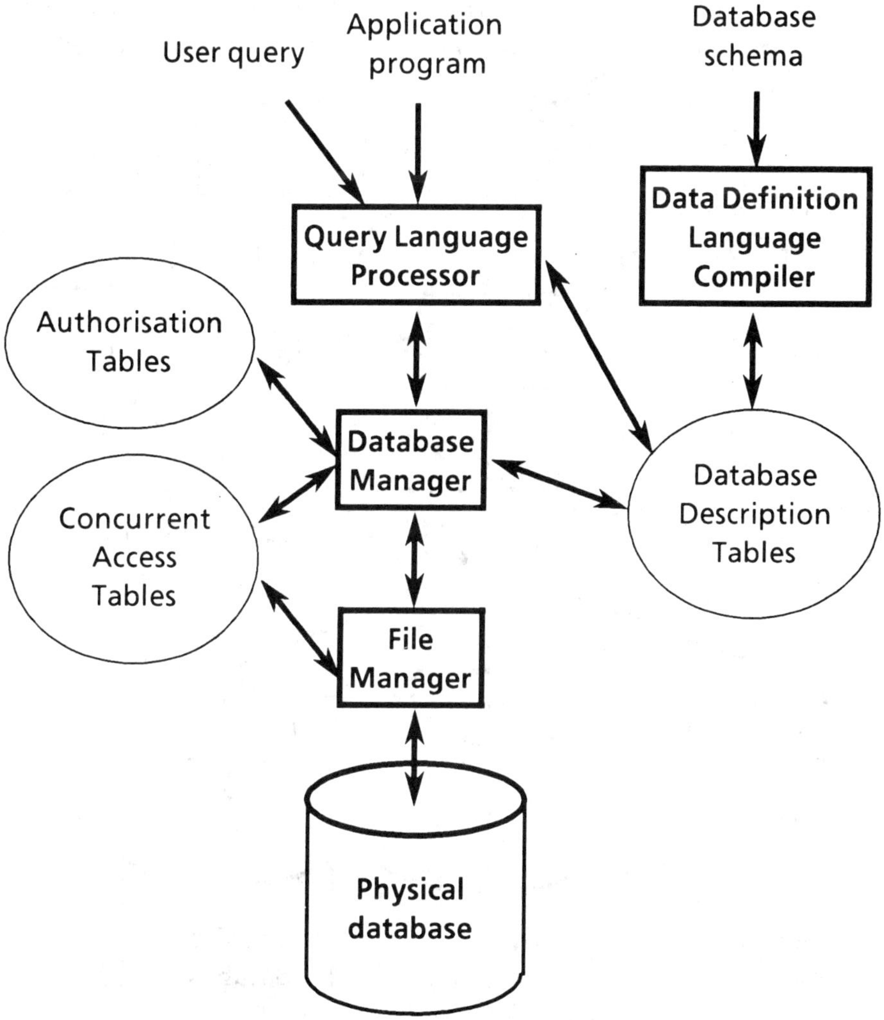

Figure 6.4 Components of a standard database system.

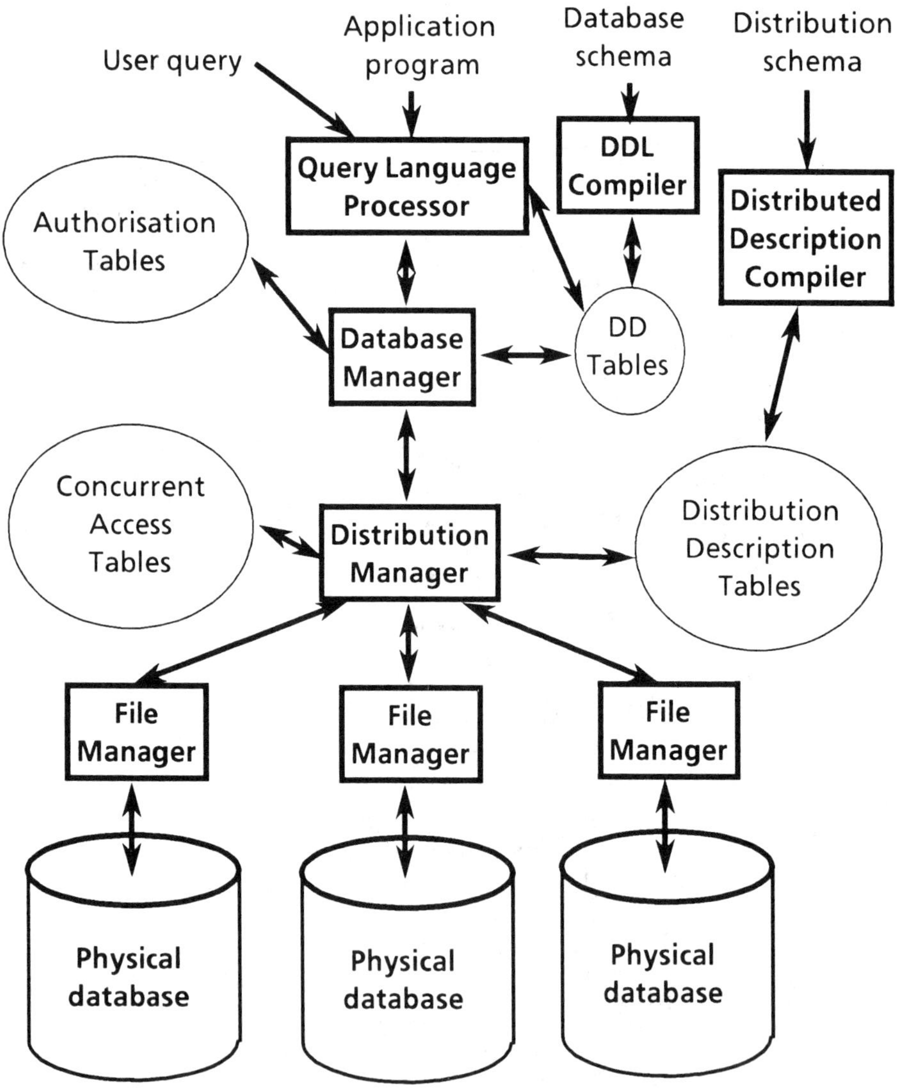

Figure 6.5 Components of a concurrent database system.

6.8 DATA DESCRIPTION LANGUAGE

We begin by specifying a limited Data Description Language that the query language processor understands for example requests to find, insert, delete and modify records based on key attributes. The syntax is based on a subset of SQL (formerly known as SEQUEL developed by IBM), for example

```
SELECT <attribute1>, ... , <attributeN>
        FROM <relation>
        WHERE<key1> fn1 <value1> AND ...
                                AND <keyN>fnN <valueN>;

INSERT INTO <relation>
        VALUES (<attribute1>, ... , <attributeN>);
```

6.9 DEVELOPING DISTRIBUTED DATABASE COMPONENTS

A high level view of the database system architecture is required which allows a programmer to easily reconfigure the design, for example if more physical resources are added to improve performance. Strand provides this using an object-based style of programming, discussed previously. Each component in the system is developed as a separate object communicating through specific channels. Objects run concurrently and only respond to message of correct format.

The simplified architecture in Fig. 6.6, shows a distribution over four physical processors (identified as 1, 2, 3 and 4 respectively) with the rest of the system running locally. A procedure can be defined to represent this:

```
system(User_query, Dist_scheme) :-
        qlp(User_query, Db_request),
        db_manager(Db_request, Distribute),
        distribution(Distribute, DB1, DB2, DB3, DB4),
        file_manager(DB1) @ 1,
        file_manager(DB2) @ 2,
        file_manager(DB3) @ 3,
        file_manager(DB4) @ 4,
        dist_compiler(Dist_scheme).
```

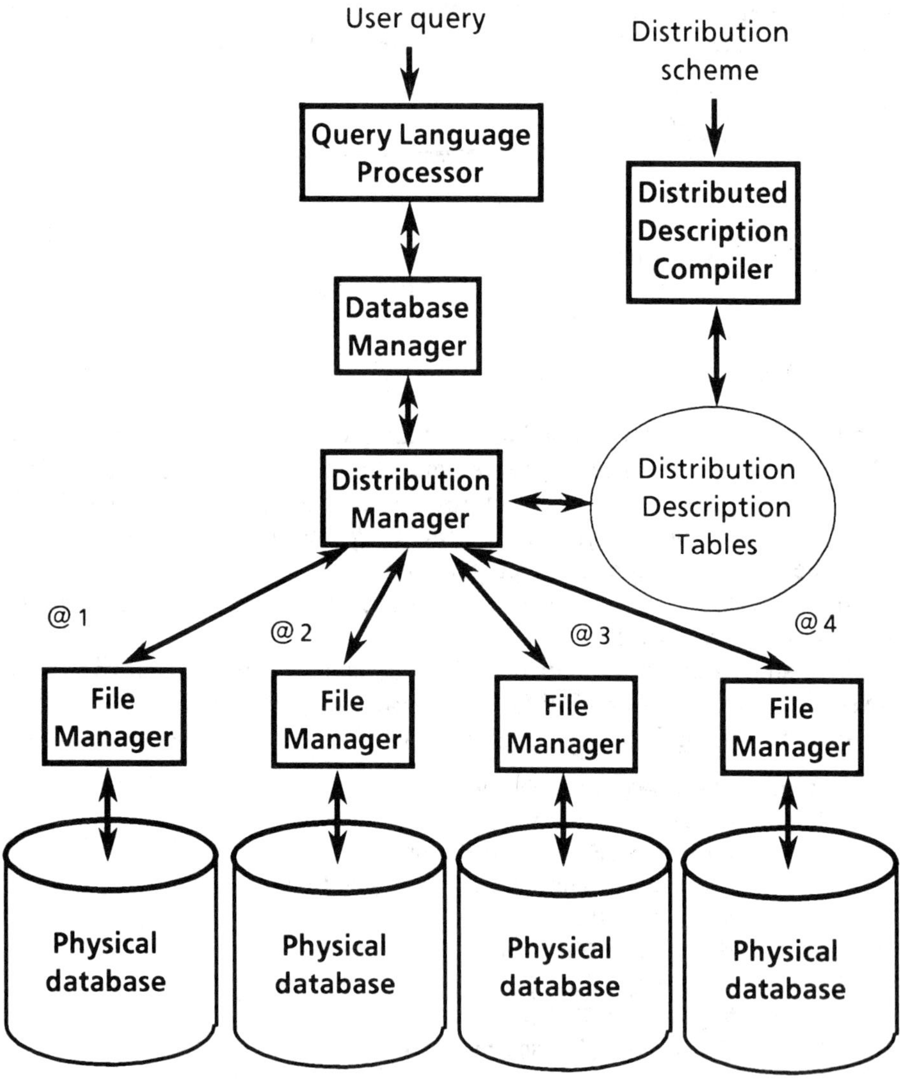

Figure 6.6 Simplified concurrent database system.

The query language processor parses the request and generates a specific tuple message per query, for example:

```
select(User_id, Attributes, Relation, Key, Result)
insert(User_id, Relation, Key, Entity, Result)
create(User_id, Relation, Key, Specification, Result)
```

where each message encapsulates a transaction request. The variable Result is used to signal the completion of a transaction, return required data or signal an error if the transaction fails.

The database manager db_manager/2 checks if the user has correct access rights to that relation and if valid routes the message onto the distribution manager. Each object has its own error recovery and signals a transaction failure by assigning the Result to some form of error message.

The distribution manager distribution/5 perpetually

- receives a message request from the database manager;
- identifies the relation name and key attributes for the DDT;
- looks up the processor and file id in the DDT;
- distributes the message to the specified processor;

if the key is insufficient to identify a specific file manager, the message is broadcast and the returned results combined as a difference list.

The file manager could be written entirely in Strand, but this is probably less efficient than one written in C. However, STRAND88 provides a foreign language interface which allows foreign code to be defined as user kernels and linked into the environment.

A set of database primitives is required to manipulate the physical level which are linked as user kernels into Strand. These user kernels specify the interface between the file manager and the physical level and may be considered as Abstract Data Types. Provided their use is fully specified, they can be redefined in another language and after relinking the file manager will still provide the same functionality. For example:

```
db_create(Relation, File, Specification, Stat)
db_retrieve(File, Key, Result)
..
db_modify(File, Key, Attributes, Stat)
```

The file manager receives requests from the distributor and uses these kernels to locally access the required file.

6.10 DISTRIBUTED SYSTEM COMPILER

The distribution manager uses the distribution data tables to select the desired processor and file. This section discusses the distributed system compiler that enables a database administrator to redefine the distribution data tables for a given relation.

A distribution may be specified explicitly, or as a hashing function or by specifying a single default file. An explicit specification has the form:

```
CREATE DISTRIBUTION
        FOR             booking
        ON              type
        USING       air:1:airbooking,
                        sea:2:seabooking,
                        land:3:landbooking,
                        accommodation:4:accbooking,
                        tour:5:tourbooking
        OTHERWISE   1:booking;
```

This creates a distribution description table for the relation booking based on the key type to identify the location of records. The physical location is specified by processor_id and file_id. The OTHERWISE provides a default processor and file for values not matching any of the above.

6.11 HOST APPLICATION FOR TRAVEL AGENCY EXAMPLE

So far we have shown how a concurrent database can be implemented in Strand, but not how multiple users interact with it. A host application is required that can receive requests from an arbitrary number of agents and accountants, both with a different view, as shown in Fig. 6.7.

The host application again uses reusable objects for agents and accountants that interact with terminals. The merge object takes a list of streams as its input argument generating a single output stream of all requests. The agent_view and accountant_view are defined to provide differing views onto conceptual schema. The host configuration then becomes:

```
application :-
        db:system(Query, Dist_scheme),
        db_administrator(Q_dba, Dist_scheme),
        merge([Q_agents, Q_accnts, Q_dba], Query),
        merge([A1, A2, ..  , AN], Q_ag),
        agent_view(Q_ag, Q_agents),
        agent(A1), agent(A2), .., agent(AN),
        merge([Ac1, Ac2, ..  , AcM], Q_acc),
        acc_view(Q_acc, Q_accnts),
        acc(Ac1), acc(Ac2), .., acc(AcM).
```

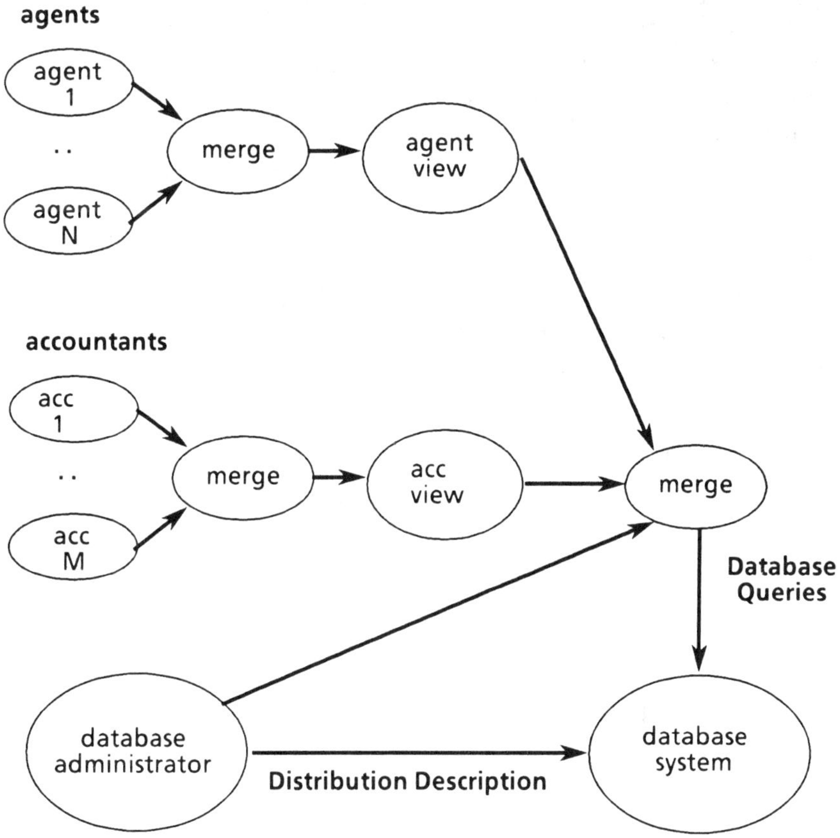

Figure 6.7 Host application for travel agency.

Note: the existing database code has not been altered. The merger processes allow an arbitrary number of agents and accountants to be added to the system, plus because Strand allows new process to be dynamically created at run-time, it is possible to add and delete users as required.

Unfortunately, this configuration still poses a potential bottleneck because there is only one query language processor available. The discussion section shows how to overcome this bottleneck as more processors become available.

6.12 DISCUSSION AND FUTURE DIRECTIONS

Components of a database system have been developed that allow the programmer to reconfigure an application by distributing the network of objects across the available processors. Strand provides a transparent intra-processor communication mechanism to utilize available resources. By grouping functionality together as a pool of processes on the same resource minimizes communication overheads.

There is no 'best' way to distribute a system as this depends on who is using it at the time. With this kind of system, a high level specification of a concurrent database is provided which encourages the developer to compare alternative versions.

The database administrator defines both the relation and its distribution via the database and distribution language. To the user, the conceptual view of the database remains the same.

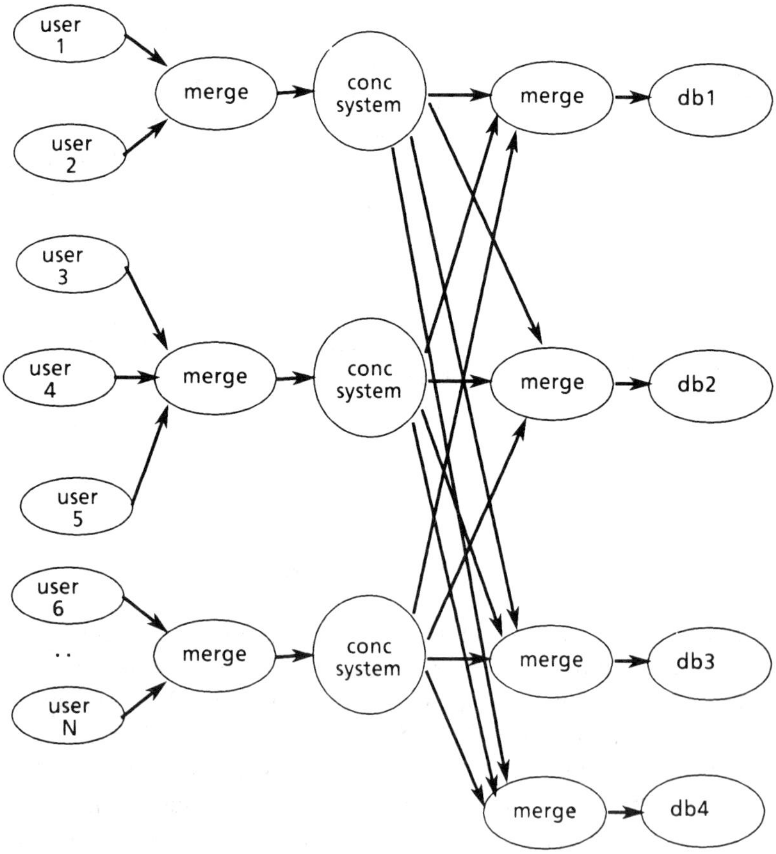

Figure 6.8 Replicated database system.

Objects and message streams provide well-defined interfaces between each level of abstraction in the database system. The use of the Strand otherwise guard allows error detection and correction to be defined. Transaction requests are encapsulated in partial data messages, allowing the receiving object to decide if the transaction is valid or not and signalling the suspended sending object.

The foreign language interface allows existing code to be incorporated into the Strand environment, providing a method for distributing an existing application across a number of processors. Most commercial database systems provide some form of C interface to their applications, for example Informix provide a utility called ESQL/C (embedded SQL for C), that allows SQL commands to be embedded into C code. A pre-compiler converts this to C which can then be linked into the Strand environment.

Distributing the booking relation over a number of processors, allows response times to be measured. A profiling package is included in Strand which graphically displays the utilization of processors during a run-time session. Different distributions can then be tested by creating new distributions. There is a need to transfer the old distribution to the new one, which can be achieved by a suitable backup and recovery mechanism. Given a single backup file, a new distribution can be configured from this, in a similar way to recovering an old version of the relation.

Unfortunately, there is still a bottleneck caused by the single query language processor (QLP), which sequentially processes user requests. Given more resources, the QLP, database manager and distribution manager could be replicated to provide concurrent access, as shown in Fig. 6.8. The object conc_system incorporates the QLP, database manager and distribution manager:

```
conc_system(Query, DB1, DB2, DB3, DB4) :-
        qlp(User_query, Db_request),
        db_manager(Db_request, Distribute),
        distribution(Distribute, DB1,DB2,DB3,DB4).
```

Future work is required to map the relational data model into Strand, possibly via tuple relational calculus. Previous work has been done on representing data flow diagrams in Strand; it should be possible to map entity-relationship diagrams into an object model. This would allow the user to draw the E-R diagram and automatically generate the desired database system. For distribution, an extra relation part_of could be added relating an entity set to a group of subsets.

Other related research topics that are being investigated by SST are data fusion and free text retrieval. We are investigating whether the declarative languages combined with pattern matching are useful mechanisms for making searching for free text easier over multiple processor architectures. This work is still in a very early phase.

In summary, this paper has attempted to stimulate ideas on how existing database systems can utilize parallel processing. Strand provides an entry into this market, by allowing various ideas to be tried before committing to specific hardware.

6.12 ACKNOWLEDGEMENTS

The author wishes to thank AI Limited for their help in writing this paper, especially David Catton for his comments and criticisms, plus Dr. M. Gittins and the research group who developed STRAND88.

REFERENCES

Boral, H. and DeWitt, D. (1982) Applying Data Flow Techniques to Data Base Machines. *IEEE Computer.*

Dinn, A., Foster, I. and Taylor, S. *Strand: a Practical Programming Tool.* Strand Software Technologies.

Informix-ESQL Embedded SQL and Tools for C, User Manual, 1989.

Integration of Expert Systems and Databases. CCTA 1988.

Litwin, W. and Abdellatif, A. (1986) Multidatabase Interoperability. *IEEE Computer.*

Reches, E., Gudes, E. and Shapiro, E. (1988) Parallel Access to a Distributed Database and its Implementation in Flat Concurrent Prolog. *The Weizmann Institute Technical Report CS88-11.*

Roussopoulos, H. and Kang, H. (1986) Principles and Techniques in the Design of ADMS. *IEEE Computer.*

Schneider, D. and DeWitt, D. (1989) A Performance Evaluation of Four Parallel Join Algorithms in a Shared-Nothing Multiprocessor Environment. *Proceedings of the 1989 SIGMOD Conference, Portland, OR.*

Snodgrass, R. (1986) Temporal Databases. *IEEE Computer.*

Steer, K. (1989) Developing and Maintaining Concurrent Databases. *UKCMG89 conference.*

Steer, K. (1989) *Objects as distributed perpetual processes*. Strand Software Technologies.

STRAND88 Buckingham User Manual. Strand Software Technologies. 1990.

Ullman, J. *Principles of Database and Knowledge-base Systems*. Computer Science Press. 1988.

Weiderhold, G. (1986) Views, Objects, and Databases. *IEEE Computer.*

Weinreb, D., Feinberg, N., Gerson, D. and Lamb, C. (1987) *An Object-Oriented System to Support an Integrated Programming Environment*. Symbolics, Inc..

7 The development of advanced databases exploiting parallel transputers

R. G. Johnson, N. J. Martin, T. Wu, X. Zhao
Department of Computer Science, Birkbeck College, University of London

7.1 INTRODUCTION

The limitations of the conventional von Neumann computer architecture for data processing have long been recognized. Current solutions to the problem of supporting the expanding information processing needs of users include client–server architectures, distributed databases and multi-processor machines. All of these embody the key principle of allocating more than a single processor to a data processing task – parallelism.

Whilst research into specialized hardware database machines to support large-scale parallelism has been carried on over a number of years, the commercial impact of such database machines has been limited. However, the recent availability of parallel machines with very high processing capabilities using off-the-shelf hardware has now opened up the possibility of the much wider use of parallel computers. In particular, the development of the Inmos transputer has resulted in the commercial availability of machines such as the Meiko Computing Surface and the Parsys Supernode which provide high performance parallel processing using large numbers of processors.

Parallel computing is a key developing technology of the 1990s. Many computer manufacturers and software product companies are actively pursuing research and development in the area. In May 1990 the UK Government announced a three-year 40 million Parallel Computing Programme to encourage the commercial application of parallel computing, in the belief that the area will be commercially very important by the mid 1990s.

This paper presents the key technical issues in the development of databases exploiting large-scale parallelism. The authors are developing a high-speed database management system based on transputers – the

ADEPT system (Advanced Databases Exploiting Parallel Transputers). A prototype implementation is already working. The architecture of ADEPT and technical implementation issues are described.

7.2 PARALLEL COMPUTING ARCHITECTURES

A common classification of computer architectures, due to Flynn [1], is on the basis of the number of instruction and data streams supported:

- Single instruction stream and single data stream (SISD)
- Multiple instruction stream and single data stream (MISD)
- Single instruction stream and multiple data stream (SIMD)
- Multiple instruction stream and multiple data stream (MIMD)

A conventional uni-processor computer is a SISD machine. ICL's CAFS associative disc architecture is an example of a MISD machine – the hardware supports multiple search conditions to be evaluated in parallel against a single data stream. AMT's distributed array processor is an example of a SIMD machine – a single instruction stream is executed with reference to the parallel data stream elements of an array. However, with the recent development of general purpose machines based on the Inmos transputer, much interest now centres on the MIMD machines which are now a reality.

The term 'transputer' refers to a family of VLSI devices, both general-purpose processors and special-purpose devices. The currently available general-purpose 32-bit processor is a single chip containing processor, RAM and four communication links. The communication links enable direct connections between transputers, permitting multiple transputer systems of various network topologies such as rings, trees, arrays and so on to be built by connecting the links. The point-to-point links between transputers means that the communication between processors is not limited by the potential bottleneck of an external bus. Link interfaces independently manage communications on links enabling communication to be taking place on all links of a tran- sputer simultaneously whilst a process is executing. Transputers with more than four links are already technically feasible. At present transputers function at speeds up to 10 MIPS, with a data transfer rate on each link of up to 20 megabits per second.

7.3 PARALLEL DATABASES ON TRANSPUTERS

Both commercial and academic groups are pursuing research and development of database management systems (DBMSs) based on transputers. The authors are developing the ADEPT system described in the following section [2]. Complementary research on formal modelling of parallel database processing is also being carried out at Birkbeck College [3]. A group at Sheffield University has developed a transputer-based DBMS architecture, with particular emphasis on the support of a database application generation system, P-DB4GL [4,5]. Meiko have announced a product, The Relational DataCache, which provides a back-end ORACLE relational DBMS machine attachable to Digital VAX computers.

In designing a MIMD transputer-based DBMS, a number of different ways exist in which parallelism may be exploited. Consider a relational DBMS supporting SQL. A conventional SISD DBMS may construct a parse tree representation of an SQL query, with particular nodes in the parse tree representing primitive tasks such as relational algebra selections, projections and joins.

From a parallel database viewpoint:

- Each primitive database task may be allocated to a distinct transputer processing in parallel with other transputers. In the simplest case each parse tree node representing a task is allocated to a separate transputer. Tasks corresponding to nodes at a particular level in the parse tree may be carried out in parallel. Parallelism may also be exploited through pipelining if the data produced by parse tree child node tasks may be processed as input by a parent node task whilst the child tasks continue to process data.
- Multiple transputers may be allocated to each primitive database task. Rather than having a primitive database task allocated to a single transputer, a group of transputers may be used. For example, a relational selection on a particular table may be allocated to a group of transputers. The data in the table may be horizontally partitioned to give each transputer a distinct set of data to operate on.

Given these fundamental ways in which parallel processing may be exploited, there still remain many detailed technical issues to be addressed in a MIMD transputer architecture, as is now considered.

7.3.1. Processor specialization

A transputer-based system may be designed so that a particular transputer performs a particular primitive database task, or each transputer may have the ability to perform a number of tasks. For example, transputers may be programmed just to perform join operations or the full range of relational algebra operations. Specialization enables smaller processes on each transputer, thus enabling more memory for data buffering. However, transputers which can only perform a specialized task will lie idle when that task is not required, thus limiting overall throughput of the system.

7.3.2 Task synchronization

With the distribution of processing, the problem of synchronisation of tasks processing in parallel arises. In some cases task start-up may be on a pipeline basis. If, for example, an SQL query is decomposed into a relational algebra join of the results of two relational algebra selection operations, then the join may begin as soon as result rows from the selections start to be produced. In other cases a task may only start-up when a related task has completed. For example, a relational algebra selection selecting rows with values NOT IN the result of a nested query, may only be computed when the full result of the nested query has been generated. It must be possible to recognize any ordering constraints between tasks, and to control the orderly commencement and termination of those tasks.

7.3.3 Multi-user support

Databases must enable the sharing of information among concurrent database users. The problems introduced by concurrent users may be seen as adding a further complexity to the task synchronization requirement noted above. In addition, general concurrency control and related data recovery facilities will be required. Techniques developed in distributed database technology – such as two-phase commit – may be applicable.

7.3.4 Data distribution

The need for designing the distribution of processing – how tasks are allocated to processors – has already been noted. Particular distribution strategies may themselves result in a requirement for the same data to be sent to more than one transputer for processing. For example, some join algorithms would require rows in one table being joined to be sent to a number of processors, each of which might be receiving matching rows from the second table. Hence, a dynamic replication of data might be needed. In any case, as in distributed database technology, a decision must be made whether to replicate not only database data but also data dictionary and data directory data.

7.3.5 Task algorithms

The point just raised about the dynamic replication of data that might result from a particular choice of join algorithm may be generalized. The choice of task algorithms will fundamentally affect the processing and data distribution characteristics of a design. In particular, algorithms which minimize the need for the movement of data between transputers would seem to be preferable. However, if algorithms result in particular transputers being overworked whilst others lie unused the movement of data may be preferable.

7.3.6 Message protocols

The architecture of a transputer means that for best performance one large message is preferable to a number of small messages, since each message initiation requires some processor overhead. However, large messages require large buffers with a resultant reduction of memory for task processes. In addition to the need to balance memory requirements, it must also be borne in mind that with tasks interacting in a pipeline mode, the holding of results for transmission to the next task in the pipeline until a large message can be filled results in a cumulative delay down the pipeline.

7.3.7 Network topology

A further topic related to message protocols is the choice of network topology. One effect of the point-to-point communication between transputers is that messages passed from one transputer to another may need to be passed through a number of intermediate transputers. This routeing requires the existence of routeing processes on each transputer. Hence, the cost of sending a message to a nearby transputer is less than that of sending it to a far one. This fact will influence the network topology chosen for a DBMS architecture. Also, the modular nature of transputers and the resultant ease with which processors may be added to an existing system mean that the architecture network topology should be smoothly scalable as transputers are added to the system.

The Meiko Computing Surface enables the links between transputers to be dynamically switched electronically. This opens up the possibility of dynamically changing the network topology to support the particular database tasks processing at a particular time. Whilst this potentially gives rise to novel optimization techniques, the complexity of managing different simultaneous switchings needed for concurrent tasks is a problem.

7.3.8 Summary

The design issues in developing a transputer-based database management system are such that each has an effect on some other aspect of the design. Hence, the processing distribution strategy, data distribution strategy and task algorithms are all intimately connected and are themselves dependent on the network topology and message protocol. This presents an opportunity for many optimization possibilities. The challenge is to achieve a design balancing these issues to enable the great processing power available in parallel systems to be fully utilized in the data management tasks. A particular approach is now described.

7.4 THE ADEPT ARCHITECTURE

The ADEPT project is developing a high speed relational DBMS based on a set of transputers. The target application area is the management of data, such as temporal and spatial, which incorporates intervals. This involves a number of computationally intensive processes. Extension are being developed to SQL to support the manipulation of intervals, and are described in [6,7]. The DBMS described in this paper is designed to run this extended version of SQL.

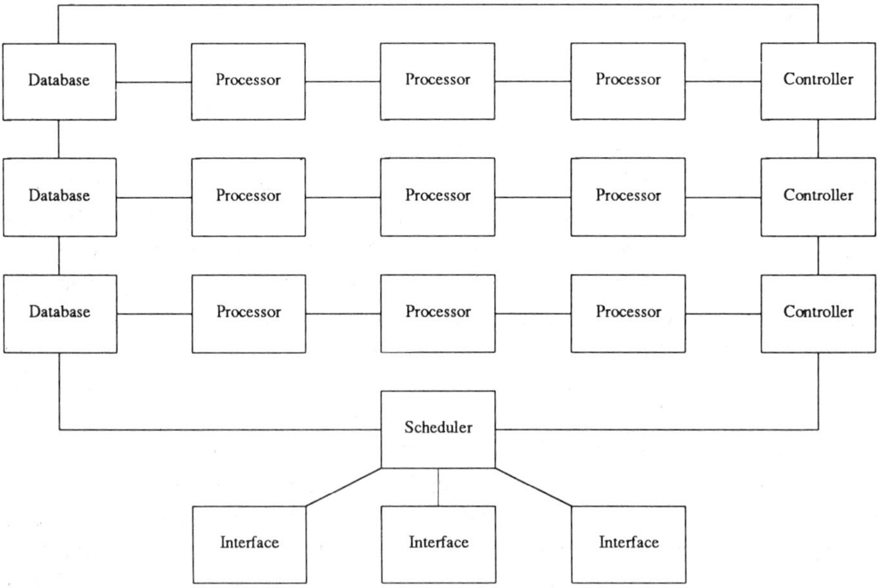

Figure 7.1 Architecture.

Fig. 7.1 shows the design, which is currently under construction. Each box in the design represents a transputer. The system has been deliberately designed with a modular and hierarchical structure. Specifically, the design can be thought of as being a series of nodes forming a distributed database system. Each node is formed by a linked set of transputers, including one, designated the Database, managing the local database, another designated the Controller controlling and monitoring the work being carried out at the node, by those manipulating the data, designated the Processors.

The allocation of work to each of the nodes is controlled by the Scheduler. The Scheduler receives transactions from Interfaces. An Interface provides user access to the database, and presents the results of each transaction to the user. Alternative interfaces could be readily provided if desired. The nodes are connected together in a ring, which passes through each Controller and Database, as well as the Scheduler.

Throughout the design, the emphasis has been on having the maximum number of opportunities to exploit the parallelism in the architecture, and to reconfigure the components. In particular, the numbers of nodes within the system and processors within a node are defined by a simple parameter file.

In terms of the design issues presented in the last section, the architecture has been designed to support high-speed database processing through both of the main ways in which parallel processing may be achieved. First, the Scheduler allocates distinct tasks to distinct nodes with pipelining arising where possible between tasks. Second, the Controller of a node may allocate multiple Processor transputers to each task. Processor specialization is taking place at one level – the distinct interface, scheduling, controlling, database and processor activities are handled by specialized transputers. However, each Processor transputer may perform any of the low-level relational algebra tasks to ensure that Processors do not lie idle because a particular relational algebra task is rarely required. The network topology supports a smooth expansion as transputers are added to the system, and particular tasks are carried out on Processor nodes with short distances between transputers. The fact that the architecture builds on existing distributed database technology is particularly important in developing solutions to the support of concurrency control and recovery mechanisms for multi-user systems.

There now follows a more detailed discussion of the major components.

7.5 INTERFACE

Users access the system, in the initial version, via an SQL interface. The interface parses the SQL and converts it to a sequence of 'tasks' in an internal language which is similar in expressive power to relational algebra. The interface determines for each task whether any constraints exist on the sequence of execution of the tasks. These can arise from the need to complete an earlier task prior to carrying out a task such as sorting the tuples in a relation. Otherwise, all tasks are assumed to be executable in parallel. Inherent in this assumption, is the ability of the system for one task to start before the relation it uses as input has been completely generated by a previous task. This achieves a form of pipelining through the architecture, which reduces bottlenecks that would result from sequential processing.

In order to provide uniformity in the physical stored data a lexical token converter is used on all alphanumeric fields. This function is carried out in the Interface. It replaces all alphanumeric fields with fixed size numeric tokens, thus converting all variable length fields to a fixed size.

The interface also labels each task with an internal identifier which identifies the task, SQL query and interface at which the task originated.

7.6 SCHEDULER

The Scheduler receives tasks from the interfaces. These are added to the list of other tasks being carried out. The scheduler can resequence tasks, subject to the constraints identified by the interfaces and rules intended to ensure consistent processing of data when updates are being carried out.

The scheduler allocates tasks to nodes depending on the location of relations to be processed and the existing workload of each node. The size of a task is estimated by reference to the size of the relation and the operation specified. This gives a rough measure of the workload. The decision on which node to employ is based on the node at which the relation is currently stored and the node to which the result is sent. Nodes are able to operate only on local data, although the resulting relation can be sent to any other node. However, the scheduler can move data to any node prior to being processed.

These options provide the scheduler with the ability to carry out a static optimization of the task sequence and location. Overall, the intention is to ensure that maximum use is made of all nodes while avoiding excessive movement of data between nodes.

Initially, relations will not be partitioned or replicated. However, horizontal partitioning is supported within the design and it is expected to be employed as a scheduling technique at an early stage. Replication raises many more serious problems, particularly relating to update and a very thorough analysis of the costs and benefits would be needed prior to its incorporation into the system.

7.7 NODES

Each node operates autonomously within the system. The Controller receives tasks from the scheduler and allocates processors to that task. The database supplies the data to be processed to the transputers allocated to the task. As transputers finish their processing they report their availability for further work to the controller. The operation of the three components of the node are now described in more detail.

7.7.1 Controller

The controller receives tasks from the scheduler. It maintains a list of what task, if any, each processor within the node is processing. The tasks waiting to be executed are divided between the processors available. Initially equal numbers of processors are applied to each task, although it would be possible to use the estimate of the size of the task obtained by the scheduler to weight the number of processors allocated.

Having made the allocation, the processors selected are sent the task to be carried out. Simultaneously, this list of processors and the relations they require are sent to the database.

At the end of the task, each processor reports to the controller that it is available to execute further tasks.

One major class of constraint on sending tasks to a node is that of the completion of the creation of a relation. Since this may involve the transfer of the relation in portions between processors, special checks have had to be built in to ensure that all portions of the relation have reached their destination. This is achieved by each processor informing the controller at the end of a task the number of pages output during that task. When all processors have notified the controller that they have completed their part of the task, the controller sends the size of the new relation to the database receiving the relation. Comparison of the size as advised by the controller with that of the portion received at the destination enables the destination to determine when the whole relation has arrived. Messages containing data are 1K in length providing a balance between processor overhead and cumulative delay in pipelines through buffering results.

7.7.2 Database

The database manages the relations held at the node. The relation is held in 1K pages which are chained together. When a task reaches the controller it advises the database which relation, or relations, are needed by which processors. The database then begins to transfer pages of data along the channels to those processors.

This process continues until all the pages from the relevant relation have been processed. A special termination page is then transmitted causing each processor to close down its processing of the current task.

In the system under construction the databases hold all data in memory. However, they operate as though acting as a cache memory for a disc drive attached to the transputer. It is intended to install such discs as soon as possible in the development.

7.7.3. Processor

The allocated processors receive from the controller the task to be carried out. The database at the node has been advised simultaneously of the relation, or relations in the case of a join operation, to be sent to the processors. The database begins sending pages to the processors. Each page is marked with the processor to which it is being sent. In this way pages of data are distributed to all the transputers allocated to the task. Pages containing the results from the processors are transmitted to the destination node designated by the scheduler and specified in the task as received by the controller from the scheduler.

A special termination page is transmitted by the database at the end of the relation causing each processor to close down its current processing and to advise the controller of the number of pages of data output for the resulting relation and that the processor is available for a new task.

7.8 IMPLEMENTATION

The ADEPT design is being implemented by the authors using a Meiko Computing Surface with OPS (Occam Programming System). The software is being written in Occam 2 and C. A prototype became operational in October 1990.

Work on the prototype implementation has been concentrated on implementing the fundamental processes of the distribution of tasks and data to transputers, and the collection of results, following the ADEPT architecture of Section 7.4. The prototype enables a user to enter a SQL query. The query is converted into a schedule of tasks, each task being allocated to a group of Processors on a particular node. Messages specifying tasks are sent to the allocated Processors as well as Database transputers holding relevant data, with that data then being sent to the Processors. Tasks may result in intermediate relations being formed. As a block of rows in the result relation is computed, it is returned to the originating Interface transputer for display.

The optimization strategies inherent in the scheduling of tasks are the subject of ongoing research. In the prototype implementation, tasks are allocated to nodes on a round robin basis. Algorithms for carrying out the primitive tasks such as relational algebra joins are also the subject of study and evaluation. Hash-based join algorithms [8] are one way of reducing the message traffic between Database and Processor transputers. Pending the outcome of this study, a straightforward algorithm is implemented in the prototype whereby each Processor allocated to a join task receives a distinct set of rows arising from the horizontal partitioning of one of the relations, and all rows from the second relation for processing using a nested loop approach.

The prototype implementation consists of about 7900 lines of code of which about 65% is Occam 2 and the remainder C. Occam 2 has been chosen as the major development language in view of its clean support for parallel processes at the language level - Occam 2 has been designed around concurrent constructs rather than having such constructs added on to an existing sequential language. Occam 2 code runs exclusively on the Scheduler, Controller and Processor transputers. However, C is used on the Interface and Database transputers. Occam 2 does not support recursion or dynamic memory allocation. The SQL parsing process is inherently recursive and hence C has been used in implementing the interface on the Interface transputers. Dynamic memory allocation is used in managing database, data dictionary and data directory structures. Hence C has also been used for implementing those management routines.

The prototype implementation has been tested with relations in excess of 1K rows with encouraging performance on all queries including joins. Benchmarking of results as a basis for testing different optimization strategies and task execution algorithms is now under way.

7.9 CONCLUSIONS

This paper has discussed the design decisions in the development of transputer-based database management systems and presented the major features of the design of a transputer-based database management system – ADEPT. The main design objectives were:

1. Multi-user DB system, running a version of SQL extended to support intervals.
2. Modularity of design to provide simple enhancement of the system.
3. Structural simplicity of design to provide for ease of study and analysis.

As the design has progressed it is apparent that this architecture provides many opportunities for exploring alternative strategies at a series of levels. These vary from low level developments in the processing techniques employed within a processor to the creation of a new interface based on other types of query language such as object or functional based languages.

The authors, therefore, believe that the design when fully implemented will provide not only for the processing of data incorporating intervals but also a highly flexible platform for a wide variety of other possible developments.

7.10 ACKNOWLEDGMENTS

The Meiko Computing Surface used by this project is funded by the Esprit Basic Research Actions programme. X Zhao is supported by an SERC Research Grant. T Wu is supported by the British Council.

REFERENCES

Flynn, M. J. (1972 : Some Computer Organizations and Their Effectiveness. *IEEE Transactions on Computers* **C-21**(9) pp948–960.

Johnson, R.G., Martin, N. J., Wu, T., and Zhao, X.(1990) : A Transputer Architecture for Database Management. *Proc. of Commercial Applications of Parallel Processing,* Unicom Seminars, London.

Leung, C. H. C., Ghogomu, H. T., and Mannock, K. L. (1990) : High Performance Relational Database Systems on Transputers. *Proc. of Transputer Applications '90.*

Kerridge, J. M. (1987) : DRAT – A Proposal for a Dynamically Reconfigurable Array of Transputers to Support Database Applications. *Proc. 7th Occam User Group Meeting,* Grenoble, France, 1416, pp29–45.

Gray, J. P. and Poole, F. (1990) : A Transputer Based Implementation of a Parallel Database System. *Proc 8th British National Conference on Databases,* A. Brown and P. Hitchcock (eds.), Pitman, pp32–63.

Lorentzos, N. A. and Johnson, R. G. (1988) : Extending Relational Algebra to Manipulate Temporal Data. *Information Systems* **13**(3), pp289–296.

Lorentzos, N. A. and Kollias, V. J. (1989) : The Handling of Depth and Time Intervals in Soil Information Systems. *Computers and Geosciences,* **15**(3), pp395–401.

DeWitt, D. J. and Gerber, R. (1985) : Multiprocessor Hash-based Join Algorithms. *Proc. 11th Very Large Data Bases Conference,* A. Pirotte and Y. Vassiliou (eds.), pp151–164.

8 Transputer topologies for data management

J. Kerridge
Department of Computer Science, The University of Sheffield

8.1 INTRODUCTION

The history of commercial data processing is littered with projects that initially fulfilled their design requirements but which subsequently had to be discarded because the system was incapable of expanding to meet changing needs. There are two main reasons why this arises. First, demands are made upon the system that were not originally specified and what was an initially successful implementation becomes overloaded. Secondly, the organization expands its operation and thus requires larger data processing resource which the designed system is incapable of providing.

It is therefore a requirement of any system design that from the outset the major components of the system architecture can be individually increased in size to deal with changing organization requirements. These major components can be categorized as: data storage, processing and the user interface. Each of these components should be able to change independently of the others to reflect organizational needs. A typical scenario that occurs is that one user is provided with new capability for a specific and well-defined purpose. The co-workers then see this additional capability and request that they are given access to it. This immediately makes demands upon processing requirements and the usual situation is an overload on the machine until the next upgrade cycle.

Most large organizations are in a situation where they are in a regular upgrade cycle of between 12 to 24 months. During the first part of the cycle, just after an upgrade, there is usually spare capacity. During the middle part of the cycle requirements and capability are in balance, In the final part of the cycle there is insufficient capacity. The major cost of most upgrades is the purchase of higher performance disc systems as this is the perceived bottle-neck. For some organizations this can form 50% of their capital expenditure.

For many organizations the era of the relational database has not yet arrived simply because the data volumes associated with their operation are so large that current relational database technology could not support their requirements. However, locked away in their existing computer system is much vital management information which cannot be extracted because the computer system is solely satisfying the mission critical computing of that organization and there is no spare capacity to undertake management information type processing. There are countless examples of warehouse control systems that only produce a stocking schedule by the end of the week for which the schedule was required, rather than the beginning of the week.

If organizations are going to unlock this information from their data stores then mechanisms are required that will allow the use of relational database technology and which will allow the components of a computer system to be individually scaled at low cost. The problem for larger organizations is that an upgrade to a computer system can usually be measured in millions of pounds. What is required is expansion of the parts that are showing signs of stress at a specific well-defined cost. There is therefore a need to design an architecture that has this capability of localized scalability. With current technology this can be achieved by the use of parallel processing techniques.

8.2 THE TRANSPUTER AND ITS APPLICABILITY TO DATA PROCESSING

The transputer is a Very Large Scale Integration (VLSI) device comprising, processor, memory and communications on the same piece of silicon. Because the transputer was designed to implement the Communicating Sequential Process [1,2] paradigm, it contains explicit provision to support parallel operation. As such it is the only currently available microprocessor that had, as one of its design goals, scalable parallel operation. To achieve parallelism the transputer employs synchronized point-to-point communication rather than a shared resource such as memory or a single communications bus. Thus each time a transputer is added to a design not only does the processing capability of the complete system increase but also the total communications bandwidth. If a shared resource is used then there will come a point when the bandwidth of the shared resource is saturated and the addition of further processors has no appreciable benefit.

The integration of memory and communications onto the same piece of silicon as the processor also enable an increase in functionality due to the closeness of the components. The transputer has been organized so that processing and communications can be overlapped. This is achieved by making the communications links Direct Memory Access (DMA) devices. The internal memory can be augmented by external memory as required by an application.

The transputer is not just one processor but a family of processors each with the same basic architecture. The basic architecture is shown in Fig. 8.1.

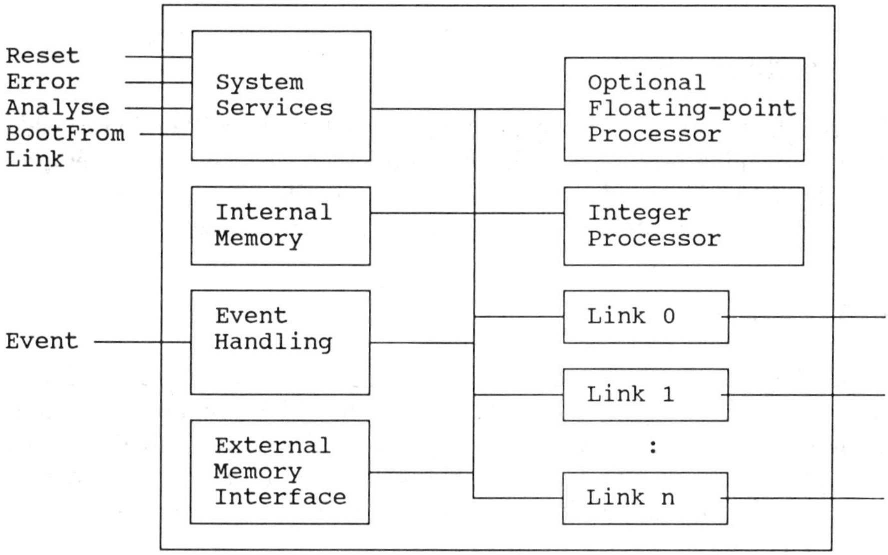

Fig. 8.1 Generic transputer architecture.

8.2.1 System services

Systems services provides the basic housekeeping signals for the transputer. Reset sets the transputer to a pre-defined state. Error indicates when an illegal state has occurred within the transputer. Analyse can be asserted after an error has occurred so that the state of the transputer can be examined. BootFromLink is a signal that indicates that the program to be loaded into the transputer will be downloaded through one of the links. If this signal is not asserted then the program to be loaded in the transputer will be saved in some form of read-only memory. In a large system it would be invidious to have read-only memory located with each transputer. Thus all that is required is a single root transputer which can access the program to be loaded into each transputer which it then communicates to all the connected transputers.

The transputer also contains a clock mechanism which enables processes to determine a time value relative to the transputer upon which it is executing. The time is implemented as a free running counter which any process can access by means of a communication. Any number of timers can be declared. The granularity of a timer is either 1 microsecond or 64 microseconds. A process accesses a timer by means of the same communication primitive that is used for inter-process communication. A timer is always ready to communicate so that a process accessing a timer channel never has to wait.

8.2.2 Integer processor

All transputers contain an integer processor that is either 32 or 16 bits wide, thereby defining both 16 and 32 bit transputers. The integer processor is capable of 10 million instructions per second (MIPS). This performance will be increased to 15 MIPS when faster parts become available.

8.2.3 Internal memory

Depending on the particular variant the memory could either be 2 or 4 Kbytes in size. Due to the nature of the internal transputer instructions memory is used very efficiently to express an algorithm. This means that for a large class of embedded control systems the internal memory may be sufficient to store all the instructions and data. Future transputers may have larger amounts of on-chip memory.

8.2.4 External memory interface

Most systems will require some external memory and an interface is provided that enables external memory to be easily interfaced. For 16-bit transputers the total memory that can addressed is 64 Kbytes and for 32-bit transputers 4 Gbytes. The external memory interface has been designed so that it can be configured to enable different memory types to be placed at different places in the memory map. This reduces the number of chips that are required to implement the hardware of a system.

Peripherals and devices are memory mapped into the external memory interface. Such devices are accessed using the same communication primitives that are used to communicate between processes. The only difference is that a device is always ready to communicate and thus a process never has to wait to communicate with a device.

8.2.5 Link engines

A transputer can have either 2 or 4 links each of which is capable of communicating in both directions at the same time. That is, each link engine comprises two DMA devices, one for input, the other for output. However, each link has to be connected to a single link connection on another transputer because the reverse direction is used to acknowledge messages. Data is transferred at either 10 or 20 Mbits per second (0.8 or 1.6 Mbytes per second). Data is communicated using a serial connection. It does not matter whether the communication is directed to internal or external memory.

8.2.6 Event handling

A transputer will accept a signal from a peripheral device to indicate that the device has completed an operation. This is equivalent to an interrupt on a traditional processor design. The event handler achieves the same effect but in a manner that is consistent with the communication mechanism rather than something that causes the processor to halt what it is doing and deal with the interrupt and then return to where it was before the interrupt occurred. The event signal is effectively an output communication from a hardware process which is then input to a process executing on the transputer. A process can be made to wait until an event occurs when it completes the communication by inputting the event message.

8.2.7 Optional floating point processor

Some versions of the transputer (T8s) have a 64-bit floating point processor that can operate in parallel with the integer processor. Thus floating point operation can be overlapped with address calculation. The floating point processor is capable of 1.5 million floating point operations per second (MFLOPS).

8.2.8 Process scheduling

The transputer has a process scheduler implemented in the microcode. This avoids the necessity for a real-time executive or operating system. The process scheduler provides a two-level priority scheme. It is relatively easy to construct a system that implements multi-level priority if that is required. High priority processes execute until they attempt a communication for which the other process is not yet ready. They are also descheduled when they delay themselves until a particular time has occurred. In addition, low priority processes can also be descheduled when they obey a conditional jump instruction, at which point any waiting high priority process will be scheduled. It takes less than one microsecond to switch from one process to another.

In general, communication-bound processes execute at high priority and compute-bound processes execute at low priority. This means that a system can be constructed in which data is received by a high priority process, which does not require processor intervention as communication is controlled by a link engine. Meanwhile, the processor can be processing, at low priority, the previous data set that was transferred to the processor. In a similar manner, results of the processing can be output by another high priority process. It is therefore easy to design a double-buffered system which overlaps processing with input and output communication.

8.2.9 Communication control

It does not matter whether a communication is between processes on the same transputer or between processes running on different transputers. The semantics are identical. The process which attempts to communicate first is made to wait until the second process is ready to communicate. The communication then takes place and the first process is added to the list of processes ready to execute. The second process just continues processing without waiting.

8.2.10 Applicability to data processing

It has to be appreciated that the transputer was designed for embedded control systems and not as a generally applicable microprocessor for use in workstations. It may therefore seem surprising to consider its use in a database environment. In fact most systems that run a database management system run only that system because it consumes so much resource. The operating system is just an overhead that allows the database management system to operate within a file system provided by the computer manufacturer. We can actually view a database management system as a collection of embedded systems that communicate results amongst themselves in order to achieve a desired end result.

The data storage subsystem is an embedded controller that accesses the disc to obtain records which are then passed to another subsystem which then processes the records which are then passed to another subsytem which generates the user view. The file system which most computer manufacturers make available is geared towards traditional file structures such as indexed and random access. A database system does not require these organizations, some form of B-tree mechanism would be far more appropriate. Thus many database systems map a B-tree mechanism onto the operating system supplied file organizations. It may be better to build specific processes that implement data storage access mechanisms that are appropriate to database requirements rather than use outmoded file organizations. The transputer architecture lends itself to this approach very easily.

Consider the case of processing records from two different tables to form a joined view. The processor that undertakes this operation is essentially an embedded system that accepts inputs from two different sources and then undertakes the necessary processing the result of which is then output.

It can be seen therefore that we are constructing a pipeline of operations which starts with the selection of data from the data storage subsystems. These data streams are then passed to a relational processing engine which passes the resultant view to the user process. An immediate advantage becomes apparent at this point because the data storage subsystem has processing capability of its own. Data that is retrieved from the disc can be filtered so that only those records that satisfy the required selection predicate are passed to the relational processing engine for subsequent processing. It is well known that the hit rate for a general 'what if' type query is very low. With this architecture we can reduce the amount of data that is sent for relational processing to that which is known to satisfy part of the query predicate.

Consider the following relations:

Employee(E#, name, address, age, sex, ...)
Salary(E#, amount, tax-code, ...)

and the query to find all male employees that have a salary less than 10000. The equivalent SQL query could be formulated as :

```
SELECT E#, name
FROM Employee, Salary
WHERE (sex = "M") AND                    -- predicate 1
      (amount < 10000) AND                      -- predicate 2
      (Employee.E# = Salary.E#)          -- predicate 3
```

We will assume that the Employee and Salary tables are held on different data storage subsystems. We can therefore process each table at the same time. Predicate 1 applies only to the Employee table and can thus be evaluated by that data storage subsystem. Predicate 2 similarly applies only to the Salary table and can be evaluated by the corresponding data storage subsystem. Only predicate 3 applies to both of the tables and thus has to be evaluated by the processor undertaking the relational operation. However the relational processor only receives data that satisfies predicates 1 and 2 and thus these predicates do not have to be re-evaluated when the data arrives at the relational processor. Thus the data storage subsystems act as filters only passing data that is known to satisfy part of the relational query. Depending on the organization of the tables the relational processing may be more or less complicated. If the data is held in sorted order of E# then a simple merge process is required. Conversely if the data is held unsorted then a Cartesian product processor is required. Yet a third mechanism could occur where one of the tables is sorted and the other is unsorted and it would be more efficient to sort the unsorted output. This can be simply achieved by incorporating a sort engine into the data stream between the unsorted data storage subsystem and the relational processor. These scenarios are summarized in Fig. 8.2, where DS is a data storage subsystem. Fig. 8.2a shows the case where the tables are sorted, Fig. 8.2b the case where neither of the tables are sorted and Fig. 8.2c the case where one of the tables is sorted. Consideration of these examples leads to the conclusion that what is required is a communication mechanism that enables a data storage subsystem to be connected to any relational processing engine, and that the relational processing engines can be allocated on an 'as needed' basis as required by particular user queries. It should also be observed that a data storage subsystem could support more than one query provided it had several filter engines associated with it. The nature of the transputer is that it requires a static allocation of processes to transputers. This leads to the conclusion that the system installer can set the limit of the number filter engines in each data storage subsystem above which subsequent requests will be rejected until resource is available. If this is a continuing occurrence then the amount of processing resource allocated to a particular filter can be incremented or the table itself split over more than one data storage subsystem. The effect of these choices will be considered in the next section which were first described for a database machine called DRAT[3].

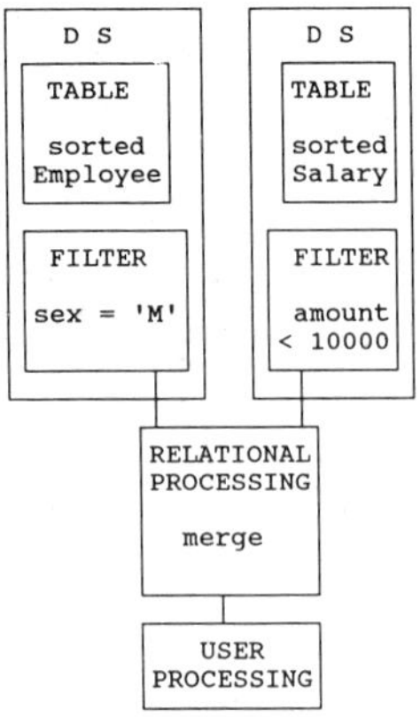

Figure 8.2a

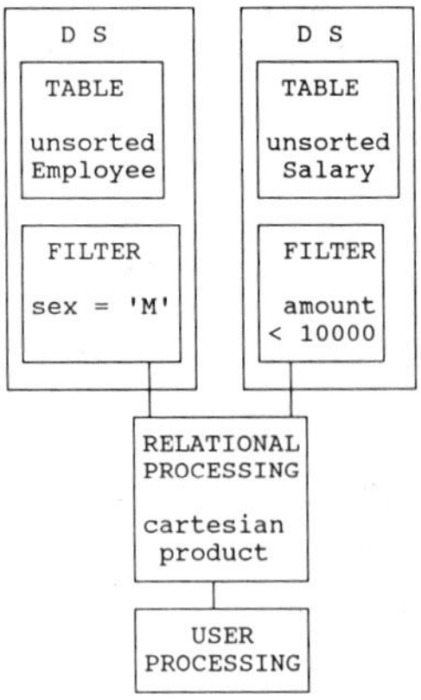

Figure 8.2b

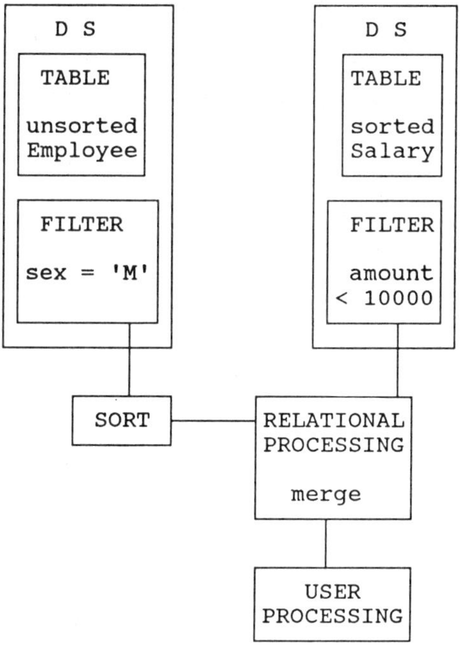

Figure 8.2c

8.3 PROCESSOR INTERCONNECTION

The main requirement of the processor interconnection mechanism is to enable any data storage subsystem to be connected to any relational processing engine, which can then be connected to the processor undertaking the user processing. The communication mechanism should allow each of these three components to be expanded or contracted independently. A further requirement is that the communication mechanism itself must be scalable so that its bandwidth can be modified to deal with changing interconnection requirements. For the duration of a user query the relational processing engine is connected to a single user processing engine and thus this connection can be made more specific. This cannot be done so easily with the connection between the data storage subsystems and the relational processing engines because a single data storage subsystem could be supporting several user queries in parallel and therefore it needs to be able to send its data streams to several relational processing engines. A basic architecture is shown in Fig. 8.3, where DS is a data storage subsystem, R is a relational processing engine, U a user processor and Q is the query decomposition and optimization processor which analyses each query and through access to an active data dictionary D determines where the components of a query should be sent. It also allocates processing resources for the query. The communication network is implemented using a completely separate set of processors C.

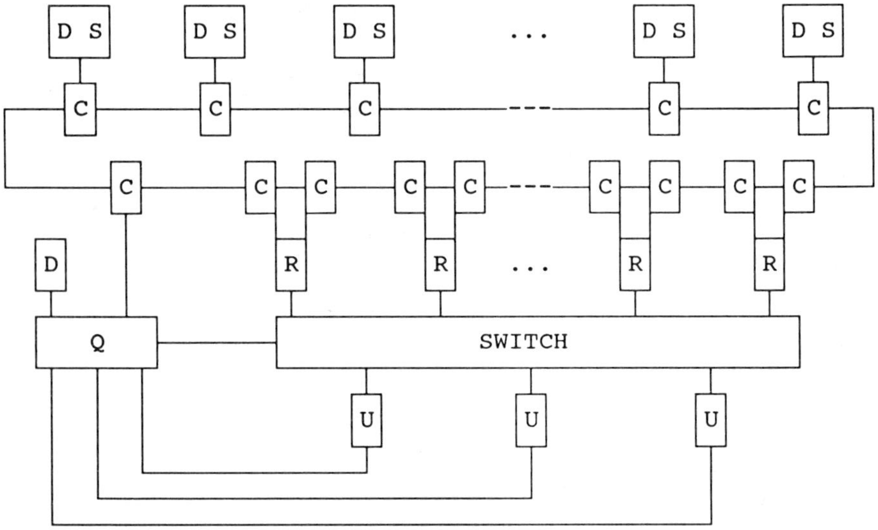

Figure 8.3 Basic architecture of a query processing system.

The switch is capable of connecting any processor R to any of the user processors U. This is achieved by sending control signals from the processor Q. Once a query has been decomposed by Q the processing requirements can be determined. The data dictionary, as well as knowing the structure of the database itself, will know the current resource utilziation within the database machine. Assuming resource is available the processor Q can send control information to the DS processors that specify the filter to be applied and to which R processor the data stream should be sent. The processor Q can also send messages to the R processor that has been selected, indicating the operation to be undertaken and any necessary predicate. This message is sent via one of the C processors connected to the R processor.

The format of data messages is very simple in that it contains the destination and source of a message together with the data string. A C processor receives such a message, determines whether the message is for it and if so passes the message to the associated processor, otherwise the message is passed on to the next C processor in the network. Thus the communication network does not have to be informed of the specific requirements of a particular query. The communication path that is chosen is determined by the relative positions of the source and destination nodes within the network and the path that requires the least number of hops is chosen. Due to the nature of query processing, the number of hops taken to pass the data will not be crucial in the overall timing associated with query processing because in general there will be a stream of records passed from a DS processor to an R processor. Thus a pipeline will be set up between the DS and R processors and thus the overhead will be the pipeline fill time. A much more crucial factor will be the amount of traffic on the network which requires the use of the same communication links. The communication architecture shown in Fig. 8.3 is however scalable because there is one spare link on each of the C processors. Therefore we can place another complete C ring inside the existing one thereby doubling the bandwidth of the communication network. This mechanism can be repeated until the required bandwidth is achieved. Performance monitoring tools will be required to determine the state of the network to ascertain whether there is a lack of bandwidth. The detail of the communication mechanism is described elsewhere[4] but it should be noted that a communication processor can be implemented using a 16-bit transputer with 32K bytes of memory at an approximate cost of 40 in volume.

A further refinement is possible which takes due account of the nature of the relational join process undertaken using a Cartesian product. In this case, one of the tables has to be compared with all the rows of the other table. Thus one table is processed once, whilst the other table is accessed many times. For this latter table much traffic would be generated over the network. A better solution could be achieved if there were a direct connection between the DS processor and the R processor. This can be achieved by use of another switch that allows dynamic connection between the DS and R processors via any intermediate C processors using the last remaining link on the innermost C processor.

Finally, the communication architecture described does afford the capability of dealing with failure of C processors when there is more than one ring of C processors. It should however be noted that the failure rate of links is the same as the failure rate of an internal computer system bus. The more likely occurrence is the failure of a complete transputer which would remove all its links as well. The communication process can easily be modified to deal with this type of failure.

8.4 FURTHER REFINEMENTS

So far we have considered the situation where a single table has been stored on one data storage subsystem. It is not worthwhile considering the case where more than one table is stored on the same data storage subsystem because this reduces parallelism. We should however consider the case where a table is partitioned onto more than one data storage subsystem because this does enable further parallelization within the query, provided there is sufficient processing resource available.

Consider the join of two tables A and B in which A is partitioned over three data storage subsystems and B two such systems. After simple analysis, shown in Fig. 8.4, it becomes apparent that there are four interesting cases depending upon the processing resources that are available.

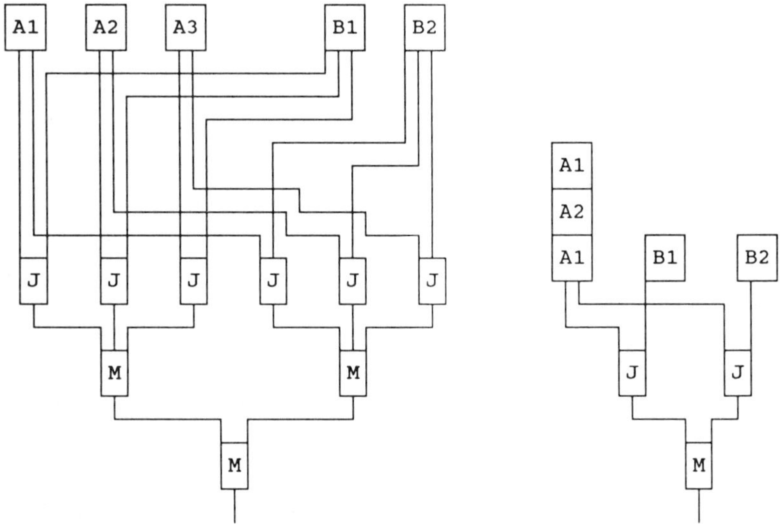

Figure 8.4 Extractable parallelism with partitioned tables.

The time taken in each of these cases is summarized in the following table:

Resources	Time
9	J + M + M
4	2 * (J + M)
3	3 * (J + M)
1	6 * J

where J is the time to undertake a Join and M is the time taken to Merge the results of a previous operation.

In the case when 9 transputers are available all the joins can be carried out at the same time, which uses 6 transputers. Two transputers are used to merge the outputs from the join processors and a final transputer is used to merge the outputs of the merge processors. In the case where 4 transputers are available the operations have to be sequenced. The first sequence undertakes the join of the partitions of A with the first partition of B, which uses 3 transputers and the fourth is used to merge the outputs. The process is repeated for the second partition of B. If 3 transputers are available then the partitions of B are joined to the partitions of A in sequence. Finally, if only 1 transputer is available then the partitions of each table have to be joined in sequence and this does not require any merge operations.

Finally, query optimizations can be undertaken with partitioned tables if the data dictionary knows the predicate upon which the partitioning has been undertaken. If a query contains a selection predicate based upon the partitioning predicate then it may be possible to restrict query processing to those data storage subsystems that are known to satisfy the predicate. It is becoming necessary to develop a language that allows a Database Administrator to specify precisely the placement of tables onto data storage and the way in which they are partitioned. Such a language was developed for network model databases, called the Data Storage Description Language[5]. Work has been undertaken by the BCS Database Administration Working Group to develop such a language for SQL based systems[6].

8.5 CONCLUSIONS

This paper has briefly considered the role of parallel processing in database applications and the use of the transputer in particular. It has demonstrated for query processing how it may be possible to provide an architecture which has high performance. A further advantage of the architecture is that the individual components can be scaled at a low well-defined cost. In order to take full advantage of the architecture it may be necessary to throw away some of the aspects of traditional system such as the operating system and file management system. This may not be as dramatic as it first appears because current operating systems are a hindrance to efficient database performance on traditional machines.

REFERENCES

1. Hoare, C. A. R. (1987) *Communicating Sequential Processes,* CACM.
2. Hoare, C. A. R. (1987) *Communicating Sequential Processes*, Prentice-Hall International.
3. Kerridge, J. M. (1988) DRAT - A Dynamically Reconfigurable Array of Transputers for database applications, in *Parallel Programming of Transputer Based Machines*, Muntean T. (ed), IOS, Amsterdam.
4. Kerridge, J. M. (1990) *A Scalable Communication Network For Highly Parallel Data Management Applications,* paper submitted to the Occam User Group meeting to be held in York.
5. BCS/DBAWG, 'Data Storage Description Language', Appendix to the *CODASYL Database Language Journal of Development*, Canadian Federal Government, 1981.
6. BCS/DBAWG, *Relational Data Storage Description Language*, Standing Paper, available from The Secretary of DBAWG, BCS, London.

9 The Cray Research architecture for high performance applications and data management

G. F. J. Handley
Cray Research (UK) Ltd

9.1 INTRODUCTION

Cray Research is well known for its support of numerically intense computing (NIC) in the scientific and engineering communities. Today I want to present to you the architecture that we have built up in support of NIC; this architecture embraces high performance and parallel applications support, large scale data management and also includes many other features necessary to spread Supercomputing throughout an organization.

Our approach is to offer the best performance available with all the familiarity of general purpose computing. This combination has great advantages in enabling organizations to move their computing strategies along evolutionary lines. In particular it minimizes the need for retraining as processing needs grow.

9.2 COMMERCIAL PARALLEL PROCESSING

A multiprocessor architecture is the first step in offering parallel processing. Cray's architecture offers parallelism at the instruction level through the vector registers and functional units, at the loop level through micro-tasking, at the subroutine or function level through multi-tasking, and at the process/job-step level through the independent scheduling of individual processors. Above and beyond compute side parallelism, we also use parallelism to increase the throughput of I/O operations.

Besides a multiprocessor architecture, what is necessary to meet production information processing needs is a commercial-strength operating system. I define the functionality of a commercial-strength OS to include:

- Parallel processing. Let the application developers exploit the machine.
- Networking - to provide access to the whole organization.
- Data management - disk, tapes and DBMS. Enough storage at the right price and good access.
- Security - to protect an organization's information.
- Standards.
- Accounting, system administration.
- Job (batch) and resource control.
- Real time features.
- Checkpoint/restart - recoverability from unavoidable failure.
- User interfaces - to build accessible applications.
- Rich functionality - make it easy to do things.
- Ease of use and familiarity.

Clearly standard UNIX does not yet meet this requirement. Cray Research's UNICOS does.

9.3 BALANCED ARCHITECTURE

Supercomputers requires a balanced architecture; processing power must be matched by sufficient memory and memory access speed, by data storage capacity and access speed. In addition there must be sophisticated system functionality and ease and speed of access throughout the network.

9.4 HIGH PERFORMANCE AND PARALLEL PROCESSING

Cray Research provides between 1 and 8 processors now and up to 16 in the future. This provides headroom for organizations to grow and allows them to dedicate processor power to mission critical tasks.

The Cray Research architecture supports a 'coarse grain' form of parallel processing with relatively few very large and fast processors with an integrated vector facility. We choose this architecture over large or massively parallel architectures since in the real world there are many problems which necessarily include single threaded portions of code, as there are also many existing applications which, although they are potentially parallel, will not or cannot be converted to a parallel implementation. In both these cases parallelism offers no help.

Best performance improvement comes from use of vector registers by an application. Typically vectorization will speed up a piece of code by a factor of 10. Vectorization achieves performance improvement by chaining together operations such that the result from one operation is immediately used as an input operand to a parallel operation.

Where one processor is not enough for an application, UNICOS provides multi-tasking to allow applications to use more than one processor to increase throughput or decrease response times. Multi-tasking is hardware supported by the provision of shared registers and semaphores. There are three software components of multi-tasking:

> Macro-tasking – multiple processes within a task. Use for long running jobs due to set up overhead. Implemented using a set of library routines to start tasks and to synchronize their activities.
>
> Micro-tasking – operates at the function/subroutine/loop level; low set up overhead; implemented using compiler directives. Functions regardless of the number of processors available. Uses shared semaphores and hardware registers.
>
> Auto-tasking – second generation micro-tasking; done by the compiler so that the user does not have to alter the program. Auto-tasking is the second generation development of micro-tasking.

9.5 NETWORK SUPERCOMPUTING

Support an environment in which all machines interoperate in a way that is transparent to the user. Where other vendor systems cannot operate in this environment provide as effective a means of interoperation as is possible to those systems.

Permit an organization to locate functions where they are most cost effective to the whole organisation, but still permit departments enough autonomy to be able to adapt to meet their goals.

The Network Supercomputing pieces are necessarily standards oriented since the hardware environment is heterogeneous.

9.6 STANDARDS

We follow and adopt standards wherever appropriate, but where performance suffers we will develop proprietary solutions as well.

Standard operating system:

> **UNICOS**
>
> **A.T. & T. System V and Berkeley 4.3**
>
> **POSIX conformant in 1991**

Standard connection media:

- **Ethernet (10 Mb/s)**
- **FDDI (100 Mb/s)**
- **NSC HYPERchannel (10 – 100 Mb/s)**
- **HPPI (800 Mb/s)**

Standard 'transport' protocols

- **TCP/IP**
- **ISO OSI**

Standard applications protocols

- **SQL**
- **X-Windows**
- **NFS**
- **NQS/RQS (Batch)**
- **File transfer (FTP and FTAM) and managed file transfer**
- **Distributed applications (RPC/XDR, sockets etc.)**
- **Telnet, VT**

Network management

- **SNMP**

9.7 LARGE SCALE DATA MANAGEMENT

Provide the means to give an organization access to its mission critical data on-line. Avoid the overheads and inefficiencies of artificially splitting the business over multiple mainframes.

Where all the data does not fit provide sophisticated tape management and archiving systems.

Cray Research supports:

Up to 500 GB on a YMP-2E

Tape robots such as the STK4400 directly connected provide enormous off-line storage capability.

Data Migration Facility provides transparent management of an over-full file store.

Quota management for keeping users in check.

Data management applications also require rich system functionality to support their development; these include:

Contiguous allocation of files on disk.

Striping of files over many spindle.

Secondary storage device (SSD) for simultaneously cacheing of data, in-memory file systems, and extended memory for applications.

Executing multiple I/O requests with one system call.

Guaranteed write to disk.

Raw and asynchronous I/O.

9.8 DATABASES

RDBMS is a significant example of a data management application. We support the relational database management systems that users want. This implies more than one vendor's product being available. Right now Informix, Ingres and /rdb are available; Oracle is porting to the Cray.

Ingres release 5 is available now and release 6 by 1991 for X-MP and Y-MP.

Informix is available for Cray-2 and being ported to the X/Y-MP range.

Oracle server expected mid 1991.

Looking at the features discussed above we can see that these are indeed the features which most of the RDBMS vendors are using in their latest products. The best RDBMS will provide:

High performance server on the Cray utilizing multiple processors.

Networked connections from front ends to the Cray using standard protocols. These can be used either to locate the front end tools on a user's machine and the server on the Cray or to locate the numerically intensive piece on the Cray using the front end tools to access the data wherever it is in the network.

Gateway connections to other databases wherever they are in the network.

We do not have hardware shared memory, but using macro-tasking we can form a group of processes that share memory and can use multiple processors to perform their task.

9.9 SECURITY

UNICOS provides multi-level security to access of objects on the machine and to network connections. UNICOS MLS is based on DoD evaluation criteria for trusted computer systems; we are implementing to B2 level with some B3 functionality. The clearance we apply for will depend on various criteria, such as time the process takes and customer requirements.

It includes:

Secure compartments, levels and permissions.

Discretionary access control.

Mandatory access control.

Trusted facility management capability.

Security log.

Access control extends to cover networking (socket) connections.

Part Four

Concurrency and fault-tolerance in parallel systems

10 Concurrency within the Mach operating system and its use in DB server applications

V. F. Rich
Encore Computer, London, England

10.1 INTRODUCTION

Computer purchases in the late 1980s have confirmed the trend away from proprietary hardware/software and towards open systems based on Industry Standard Computer architectures. End users and owners of computer systems are eager to relinquish dependence on any one computer vendor and to increase their purchasing power by stimulating healthy competition amongst computer vendors. The Unix operating system has acted as a powerful catalyst in this process by providing levels of portability of both programs and programmers hitherto unknown in the computer industry.

Unix supports seamless networking of heterogeneous computer systems into one virtual computer system tailored to the users needs. Specific computing components in the network can be optimized according to function, for example one component can be a database engine serving other components with the results of database enquiries, and this engine need not support any facilities beyond those required for database serving.

With the demise of proprietary architecture computers, computer vendors have chosen to standardize on Central Processing Units (CPUs) designed and produced by a small number of semiconductor manufacturers (typically Motorola, Intel and National Semiconductor). These 'merchant microprocessors' exhibit excellent price/performance ratios due in part to the Large Scale Integration (LSI) techniques applied and in part to the amortization of the development costs over a large number of production units. Typical price/performance ratios are three to four times better than a conventional proprietary superminicomputer and up to ten times better than a mainframe class computer.

In order to further enhance program portability, the concept of the Applications Binary Interface (ABI) has been developed. This involves the standardization of the lowest level interface between an applications program and the underlying operating system. The executable image of a particular applications program can then be moved from one make of computer to another providing that they both use the same CPU and adhere to a common ABI. Several industry groups have been formed to promote ABI products for specific classes of CPUs, one of the most prominent groups being the 88open consortium which is encouraging the production of ABI compatible products for computers based upon the Motorola 88000 family of Reduced Instruction Set Computers (RISC). The 88open ABI is known as the Binary Compatibility Standard (BCS) and a wide range of products including database systems either have been (or are in the process of being) ported to the 88open BCS. Such products are informally known as being 'shrink wrapped', a name that implies the software supermarket/target system independent approach to software procurement.

An individual merchant microprocessor is unlikely to be able to offer the raw computing power required to support very high performance database serving and so systems must be constructed from multiple processors. Many different interconnection strategies exist ranging from a tightly coupled system where all processors can directly access all of memory, to a loosely coupled system where individual computers communicate with each other through a Local Area Network (LAN).

Loosely coupled systems suffer from the replication of program code and data on each node, communications latency on the network and acute difficulty in maintaining the global locks required to maintain the integrity of the database management system. The tightly coupled approach offers elegance and simplicity in interprocessor communication but provides substantial challenges for the designers of the computer hardware and operating system software in order to prevent performance degredation as the number of processors increase. The most advanced tightly coupled configuration is known as the Symmetrical Multiprocessor. Any processor can execute any part of the applications program and any part of the operating system as well as access any disc or other peripheral device. Despite the engineering difficulties, the symmetrical multiprocessor is poised to become the dominant computer architecture of the mid and late 1990s.

10.2 ISSUES OF CONCURRENCY

An advanced Symmetrical Multi-Processor (SMP) employs a very high speed backplane bus to interconnect the basic system components of CPUs, memory boards and peripheral device controller boards. A prominent example of this class of machine is the Encore Multimax which supports up to twenty CPUs together with 160 megabytes of memory and 70 gigabytes of disc storage. As all main memory accesses are via the backplane bus, steps must be taken to ensure that this component does not cause performance degredation as additional CPUs are added. This is accomplished on the Multimax by the incorporation of a two-level cache memory subsystem on each CPU board, the purpose of which is to hold the most recently accessed program statements and data for instant reuse, thereby minimizing references to the main memory.

The Operating System is commonly the major bottleneck in an SMP system. The original implementations of Unix were on small single-user computers which were only capable of executing one applications program at a time. As computer power and users needs increased, Unix evolved into a time-sharing system, where each program was sequenced to give the illusion of concurrent execution. The design of the Unix Kernel (the core part of the operating system) was simplified by inhibiting the switching from program to program whilst any one program was executing the kernel. This avoided problems of re-entrancy but reduced the responsiveness of the system to external events such as peripheral device interrupts.

The non re-entrant kernel is even more of a problem in a multiprocessor system. In such a system, if one applications program calls the Unix Kernel to initiate a disc operation then any other CPUs that attempt to call the Unix Kernel will be blocked (i.e. suspended) until the kernel completes its currently assigned activity. This could be disasterous in a large scale database application where substantial amounts of input/output are being performed and therefore each database server program would spend much of its time waiting to access the kernel.

At Encore, work has proceeded on two separate fronts to resolve this problem. The first approach has been to enhance the Unix Kernel to make it multi-threaded and truly concurrent. Applications programs executing on different CPUs may, at the same moment in time, call the Unix Kernel for service. The system is fully symmetric as any CPU can execute any applications program and any part of the Unix Kernel. Within the Kernel, data structures and critical code sections are protected from attempted concurrent access by the use of locking flags (or semaphores). These will hold off a second or subsequent CPU for a few microseconds if exclusive access to a data structure or code section is required by a CPU. Practical trials have shown that the SMP coupled with a multi-threaded implementation is a very effective combination offering an almost linear increase in database performance as CPUs are added to the system.

One issue with Unix is the granularity of the unit of concurrency. On Unix, each applications program is compiled into machine code and becomes a single Unix process. Unix assigns CPUs on a per process basis and allows processes to dynamically replicate themselves as well as activating other processes. The number of processes currently scheduled for execution should be substantially larger than the number of CPUs in order to ensure that each CPU can be kept busy at all times.

Unfortunately, large numbers of processes can lead to a loss of efficiency due to the time required to create and start a process as well as the time taken to switch between processes.

10.3 THE MACH OPERATING SYSTEM

The Mach operating system, developed at Carnegie–Mellon University, targets a broard range of computer architectures including uniprocessor, multiprocessor and distributed systems. Mach is a compact and efficient kernel upon which is layered a 4.3BSD Unix interface.

The development of Mach was funded in part by the US Defence Advanced Research Projects Agency (DARPA) and the initial port of Mach to the Encore Multimax is part of a 1000 MIPS general-purpose version of the Multimax that is also being sponsored in part by DARPA.

The Encore implementation of Mach has been recently adopted by the Open Software Foundation (OSF) as the nucleus of the first OSF operating system, OSF/1. In addition, the Encore Multimax has been selected as the OSF multiprocessor reference architecture.

In addition to providing 4.3BSD Unix compatibility, Mach offers a number of new facilities. The most important of these facilities is the support for multiprocessors through the separation of the process abstraction into tasks and threads.

A task is an execution environment in which threads may run and is the basic unit of resource allocation. A Mach task includes a paged virtual address space and protected access to system resources such as processors, files, etc. A thread is the basic unit of CPU utilization and is equivalent to an independent program counter operating within a task. The Unix notion of a process is, in Mach, represented by a task with a single thread of control. Any Mach task may at any moment in time contain multiple threads each executing a specific function within the task. Threads can be deemed lightweight in nature as the number of CPU instructions required to create a new thread is approximately an order less than the number of instructions required by Unix to 'fork' a new process.

With a traditional Unix-based multiprocessor system, multiple Unix processes were required in order to exploit the available parallelism as the operating system could not schedule two or more CPUs to co-execute the same process at the same moment in time. Database server applications can be constructed from multiple Unix processes communicating via shared memory, but the use of Mach tasks and threads offers the database server designer improved management of concurrency and higher levels of operating system efficiency.

The Encore implementation of Mach contains inherently parallelized Mach code and serial code from 4.3BSD Unix. The original 4.3BSD kernel was designed for uniprocessor operation with kernel data structures being protected by disabling interrupts at appropriate times. This code has been substantially rewritten and major parts of the 4.3BSD code (e.g. interrupt handlers and the file system) have been parallelized. This work, which is continuing, has involved the addition of twelve new threads to operating system components and 35 new Kernel internal locks.

10.4 SUMMARY

Symmetrical multiprocessors based on merchant microprocessors offer substantial technical and economic advantages over proprietary monolithic solutions. Unfortunately, standard Unix is not an ideal fit due to the cumbersome nature of the process model.

The Mach operating system has been designed from scratch for multiprocessor operation and offers a far more effective method of utilizing multiprocessors. As the usage of Mach increases through its incorporation in OSF/1, each of the major database vendors will implement servers that utilize Mach tasks and threads thereby further increasing the performance of their products.

11 Multiprocessor system for performance and fault tolerance

P. A. Lee
University of Newcastle upon Tyne

11.1 SHARED MEMORY MULTIPROCESSORS

In general, shared memory multiprocessors consist of a number of CPUs connected to a shared address space in which memory modules and I/O devices reside. Table 11.1 outlines some of the overall characteristics of a selection of present-day and future commercial shared memory multiprocessor systems, covering both parallel systems designed for performance, and systems designed for fault tolerance. It seems clear even from the small selection of systems outlined in Table 11.1 that the shared memory multiprocessor architecture is set to become the standard architecture of the 90s, covering the whole spectrum of computing systems from the high price, top-end supercomputers down to the low price workstation.

From the multiprocessor systems currently available, five main developments of the architecture can be seen:

1. Shared memory implementation, with a (usually small) number of proprietary CPUs (most mainframe/supercomputer manufacturers)
2. Shared memory implementation, using a modest number of standard microprocessors for processing power (e.g. Encore Multimax, Sequent Symmetry)
3. As 2., but with additional specialized floating point processors (e.g. Alliant FX/80)
4. As 2., but with additional redundancy to provide fault tolerant behaviour (e.g. Sequoia, Stratus)
5. Shared memory semantics, but with a distributed memory implementation and a (large) number of standard microprocessors (e.g. BBN Butterfly)

Of these threads of development, those based on the use of standard microprocessors are particularly interesting for two main reasons: firstly, because of the price/performance characteristics of such systems; and secondly, because of the staggering increases in MIPS/MFLOPS (Millions of Instructions Per Second/Millions of FLoating point Operations Per Second) rating of recent microprocessors, and hence of the systems in which they are embedded.

Table 11.1 Shared memory multiprocessor systems.

System	Number of Processors	Processor Types	Performance
WORKSTATIONS			
Stardent	1 - 4	MIPS R3000/10	32-128 MIPS 192 MFLOPS
Human Devices Inc Chorus	4 - 16	RISC	5-80 MIPS 2-32 MFLOPS
Solbourne Series 5 600/800	1 - 4	Cypress SPARC	22-65 MIPS
MAINFRAMES			
BBN Butterfly TC2000	8 - 504	Motorola M88000	10 GFLOPS 9,576 MIPS
Alliant FX/2800	8 - 28	Intel i860	340 MFLOPS 1.12 GFLOPS
Encore Multimax 520	2 - 20	NS32532	170 MIPS
Sequent Symmetry	2 - 30	Intel 386	6-90 MIPS
Digital VAX 9000	1 - 4	custom	100 MIPS
SUPERCOMPUTERS			
IBM 3090/380J	1 - 3	custom	50-70 MIPS
NEC SX-3/11/44	1,2,4	2.9 ns cycle, custom	1.37- 22 GFLOPS
Fujitsu VP2000 /VP2600/20	1,2	4 ns cycle, custom	2 - 4 GFLOPS
Cray-3	16	2ns, custom	1 - 16 GFLOPS
FAULT TOLERANT			
Stratus/XA600 IBM System/88 (1989)	6	M68010	Fault tolerance
Sequoia (1988)	64	M68020	Fault Tolerance

Considering price/performance, it is rather difficult to give precise comparisons between systems due to the different characteristics and emphases in each. However, as a general guide one can observe almost an order of magnitude difference in the 'price per MIP/MFLOP' of microprocessor-based shared memory multiprocessors when compared with traditional mainframe systems. Typically, around 1988 a traditional mainframe system (i.e. a fault intolerant uniprocessor) with its proprietary CPU architecture covering one or more circuit boards had a list price of the order £40-60K per MIP; microprocessor-based multiprocessor systems typically cost approximately £4-6K per MIP. The paper by Bell [Bell 85] examines some of the reasons for this discrepancy and concludes that multiprocessors "are an order of magnitude cheaper to use for traditional computing than mainframes".

11.2 MULTIPROCESSORS FOR PERFORMANCE

First let us consider the application of shared memory multiprocessors in the quest for enhanced computing power, and in particular, concentrate on the systems which adopt microprocessor chips for their processing power, rather than the more specialized (and expensive!) systems based on proprietary CPUs. In fact, it is of interest to note that, apart from the more specialized market places such as for the supercomputers, manufacturers are moving away from having their own proprietary CPU architecture and adopting the 'commodity' CPUs provided by the chip manufacturers. For example, Alliant rely on proprietary hardware for floating point operations in their current FX/80 systems, but have announced adoption of the Intel i860 micro for their next generation system. Note also that even the proprietary CPU supercomputer manufacturers have adopted shared memory multiprocessor architectures for higher system performance, albeit with small levels of parallelism.

The main reason for interest in microprocessor-based shared memory multiprocessors is, as mentioned above, the explosive advance of the MIPS ratings of the microprocessor chips. Table 11.2 shows some of the manufacturer's figures for what might be termed the first generation 32-bit microprocessors, together with those of current and emerging microprocessor generations. The computing power promised from these chips is quite astonishing. Also noteworthy is the fact that the current and emerging microprocessors have very respectable MFLOPS ratings (e.g. 16-60 MFLOPS for the i860) as compared with the first generation systems where floating point performance was rarely considered important (or even necessary!).

Table 11.2 Microprocessor characteristics.

Manufacturer	Chip	Year	Type	Clock	Performance
FIRST GENERATION					
National Semiconductor	32032	1984	CISC	10 MHz	0.75 MIPS
Motorola	68020	1985	CISC	15-25 MHz	1.5-4.5 MIPS
Intel	386	1985	CISC	13-25 MHz	1.2-5.7 MIPS
National Semiconductor	32332	1986	CISC	15 Mz	2 MIPS
MIPS	R2000	1987	RISC	16.7 MHz	15 MIPS
CURRENT AND EMERGING					
National Semiconductor	32532	1988	CISC	30 Mz	8.5 MIPS
Motorola	88000	1988	RISC	20-33 MHz	17-28 MIPS
Intel	i486	1989	CISC	25-33	15-20 MIPS
MIPS	R6000	1989	RISC	??	55 MIPS
Motorola	68040	1989	CISC	25 MHz	20 MIPS
Intel	i860	1990	RISC	33-40 MHz	60 MIPS
H-P and Hitachi	Bi-CMOS PA	1991	RISC	??	100 MIPS

The improvements in speed come from three main sources. Firstly, the chip designers are getting better at making the chips run at higher clock speeds, either though improvements on earlier designs of chips in the same family, or by adopting new architectures such as those based on RISC. Secondly, the advances in VLSI technology result in smaller, and hence faster, components. Thirdly, VLSI advances also permit more functionality to be placed on a chip. Thus, while features like caches, instruction pipelining, multiple function units and virtual memory were originally only to be found in mainframe computers, modern microprocessor chips also incorporate such features – one of the reasons for the dramatic rate of improvement in their speed over their predecessors. The projected continued improvements in VLSI technology suggest that future chips will continue the upward trend in speed.

The advantage of these developments to the manufacturer of multiprocessor systems (and hence to their customers) is twofold: firstly, they can easily incorporate these new chips into their systems and hence 'ride' the technology curve, and when the new chips are software compatible with the previous, moving the software base is straightforward. The second advantage is that the manufacturers can continue to offer multiprocessor systems with ever-increasing processing power, and hence their customers have the promise of a long-life system with an upgrade path that can incorporate significant expansion, both through an increase in the number of CPUs in a system as well as adoption of new technology CPUs.

For example, Encore has so far developed three generations of processor board for the Multimax using the NS32000 processor family, approximately one every two years. In one 6-month spell we experienced all 3 generations in our Multimax systems. The latest generation boards gave an order of magnitude speed improvement over the first generation boards, without any software changes.

It is important to note that shared memory multiprocessors are very much an evolutionary and general-purpose architecture for parallel processing, as compared with the revolutionary and specialized aspects of more highly parallel distributed memory machines such as hypercubes or the AMT DAP. They are evolutionary in that they are an evolution of the traditional von Neumann model of computation, albeit extended with shared memory and making use of the technological advances which have made CPUs no longer the expensive part of the system. They are general purpose in that they can run 'normal' sequential programs as well as parallel applications, and have no specialized constraints because of the interconnection scheme. Most shared memory multiprocessors are also general-purpose in that they can support multiple simultaneous users by supporting a normal Unix-based time-sharing operating system. The features of virtual memory and protection mechanisms in the microprocessor are necessary for such support; hence transputers, which have no protection features, cannot be safely used in such systems.

A common organization for microprocessor-based shared memory multiprocessors is shown in Fig. 11.1. The architecture is tightly coupled, with global memory equally accessible to all processors over a global high-speed bus. The architecture is symmetric in that all CPUs are equal, and can receive interrupts, run the operating system (see below), run user programs, etc. (in contrast to earlier asymmetric multiprocessor systems based on the master/slave principle).

11.3 MULTIPROCESSORS FOR FAULT TOLERANCE

Unreliability in a system is caused by faults, which generate errors which can subsequently cause a system to fail. Faults are the cause; errors are the effect. A system is said to be fault tolerant if it contains redundant hardware and software components such that the occurrence of component failures does not cause the system itself to fail to provide its specified service.

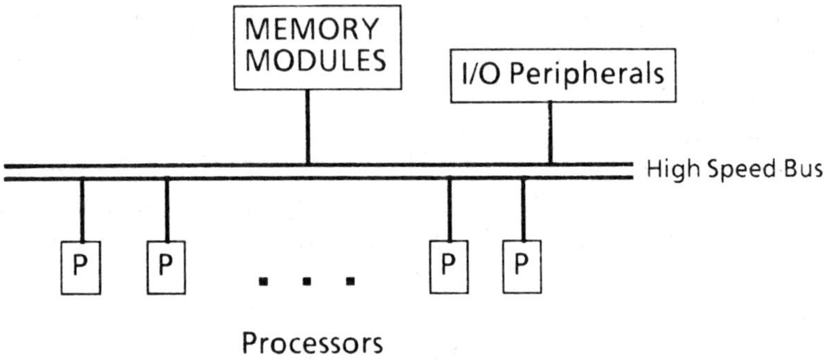

Figure 11.1 Shared memory multiprocessor architecture.

That a significant number of computer users have a requirement for high reliability and hence for fault tolerance, has been demonstrated by the commercial success of the Tandem company, with its Tandem/16 and Tandem/32 systems (which are not shared memory multiprocessor architectures). More recently formed companies such as Stratus and Sequoia are trying to emulate Tandem's success, although are adopting tightly-coupled shared memory multiprocessor architectures as compared to Tandem's loosely-coupled, distributed memory system.

Fault tolerance can be implemented in a system in several ways, and some of the approaches adopted by Sequoia and Status are discussed below. However, the principles of fault tolerance are system-independent and relatively straightforward [Lee 90]. A fault tolerant system must:

1. Detect errors and deal with these errors (error detection and error recovery)
2. Deal with the fault which caused those errors (fault location and system repair).

The primary concern of present-day fault tolerant systems is to prevent failure of hardware components from causing system failures. Three main potential components failures are normally considered:

(i) processors
(ii) memory
(iii) disks

All fault tolerant systems depend on redundancy in some fashion. Multiprocessor systems which contain multiple copies of the above components form a natural basis for a fault tolerant system.

All multiprocessor systems contain some fault tolerant measures such as SEC/DED on memory, and coding checks on disk operations. Some manufacturers, such as Encore and Sequent, currently provide no further fault tolerance. Their emphasis is on price/performance, and in consequence they do not wish to add the expense of the additional mechanisms to be discussed below. However, if a fault does occur in one of the replicated components, and can be located by diagnostic programs, then that component can be deconfigured and a reduced-configuration system brought back into operation. This is an option rarely available with more conventional uniprocessor systems.

As mentioned earlier, manufacturers like Stratus [Taylor 89, Harrison 87] and Sequoia [Bernstein 88] have designed additional redundant hardware into their systems to improve their reliability through increased fault tolerance. Indeed, their primary aim is to try to ensure that any hardware faults which do occur are masked from, and not apparent to, any user-level programs running at the time the hardware component failure occurred. They aim to provide the abstraction of a highly reliable hardware interface, through the incorporation of redundant hardware with additional assistance from the operating system. The following sections outline the main strategies they adopt.

11.3.1 Processor failures

Processors, consisting essentially of irregular logic, can only be sensibly checked by replicating the CPUs and comparing the answers they generate. This is the basic strategy adopted by Stratus and Sequoia – a processor board actually consists of 2 CPUs operating in lockstep with a comparison check between them. (Thus the processor numbers in Table 11.1 refer to processor boards – the actual number of microprocessors in the system is two times the number given.) If a discrepancy is detected by the check, one of the CPUs may be faulty, and that processor board can be excluded from further participation in the system's activity until it has been replaced (or deemed to have been suffering from a transient fault).

Since the job that was being executed when the fault occurred is held in the shared memory, it is straightforward for another processor to pick up that job and continue its execution. However, some of the state of that job is bound to be local to the faulty processor and hence not available following the failure of that processor. For example, state such as the CPU registers and the program counter, and data contained in local caches, may be lost and must be replaced if correct execution of the job is to ensue. Stratus and Sequoia achieve this in different ways.

In the Stratus system, a program is actually executed by 2 processor boards in lockstep (each board contains 2 CPUs), i.e. by 4 CPUs in all. If one processor board fails, execution can be continued by the other, without interruption, and an additional processor board can be employed by the operating system to replace the faulty one to maintain the four-way execution.

In the Sequoia system, the strategy for recovering from a failed processor board is based on maintaining a recovery point in shared memory for each job. A recovery point is a point in the execution of a program at which the state of that program can be recovered and restored and hence execution restarted from that point. If a processor fails, the job can thus be picked up and restarted by another processor from a recovery point. To maintain the consistency of recovery points, memory updates generated by a processor after a recovery point has been established are cached locally to the processor and not permitted to update the shared memory. When this cache is full (or at other suitable intervals), a new recovery point for the program is generated by carefully flushing the cache (together with the processor state) back to memory, and the job can then continue execution. Care has to be taken when establishing this new recovery point that a fault during the flushing operation can also be recovered from (basically, by not discarding the old recovery state until it has been established that the new state has been safely recorded).

Thus both Stratus and Sequoia achieve the same effect (masking of processor failures which is transparent to the executing application), but with different trade-offs in the redundancy they use. The Stratus system uses more hardware than Sequoia (4 CPUs instead of 2), but recovery from a failed processor is very fast. The Sequoia approach incurs the overhead of recovery point establishment, and restart after recovery necessarily involves some reprocessing, but requires less hardware in the system and is presumably a less-costly system to purchase.

11.3.2 Memory failures

As mentioned earlier, all multiprocessor systems known to the author utilize coding checks on memory to enable single-bit errors to be detected and corrected and all double-bit (and some higher order) errors to be detected

(SEC/DED). The Stratus system can also duplicates memory components in a manner similar to that used for its processing elements – each memory card contains two controllers checking each other, and two memory cards can be used together so that a failure of one results in the backup providing/storing the data.

In the Sequoia system, two memory cards can be paired together under the control of the operating system, with write operations going to each card so that a failure of one card (indicated by the coding checks discussed earlier) can be recovered from by using the second card of the pair. In both systems, this pairing is controlled by the operating system and so can be enabled or disabled as desired. For instance, in the Sequoia system, read-only pages of memory (e.g. code pages) are not paired since a backup copy exists on disk and that copy can be used for recovery in the event of a memory failure.

11.3.3 Disk failures

In all of the fault tolerant multiprocessor systems under consideration here, databases are of particular importance since these systems are primarily intended for transaction-based applications. Thus the integrity of the retained data is of paramount importance. Disks are the main stable storage available (i.e. they retain state even in the presence of power failures) but are perhaps the most unreliable part of the hardware. Thus Sequoia and Status (and Tandem) put significant emphasis on trying to ensure that single-disk failures do not cause loss of important data or system failure. Mirrored disks (i.e. each logical disk actually consists of two physical disks which contain identical data) are the main redundancy strategy used.

In the Stratus system, the disk controller is duplicated and cross-checked. When mirrored disks are employed, each disk + controller is duplicated by a second disk + controller, and writes occur to both mirrored drives. However, the mirrored drives do not work in lockstep like the other components in the Stratus system. Also, an error detecting code is stored with each disk record so that media failures can be detected.

In the Sequoia system, mirrored disks can also be used. However, the Sequoia disks are dual-ported, so that a controller failure does not necessarily make the disk it was controlling unavailable.

11.4 CONCLUSIONS

Summarizing, there are five main facts that will, we believe, cause microprocessor-based shared memory multiprocessors to become one of the dominant computer architectures in the very near future:

(i) they offer attractive price/performance characteristics, essentially bringing the cost advantages of microprocessors to mainframe-like machines for the first time, both for users interested in performance (parallel processing) and for those interested in fault tolerance;

(ii) they represent an evolutionary rather than a revolutionary step to the use of parallelism, with the prospect of achieving very significant speed increases on individual applications;

(iii) they are particularly suitable for time-sharing and 'conventional' processing, as well as for parallel processing;

(iv) they are easy and inexpensive to upgrade and expand;

(v) the microprocessors on which they are based are becoming ever-more powerful.

It is clear that shared memory multiprocessors based on the global bus organization will never be able to achieve the high levels of parallelism that the Butterfly or other distributed memory systems will be able to offer. The global bus is bound to limit the power of the system, and cannot provide the increases in interconnection bandwidth that are obtained when multistage networks are used to implement a system.

However, bus-based shared memory multiprocessors approaching 200 MIPS are commercially available, and 1000 MIPS looks attainable – indeed, Encore has a research contract from DARPA to build a 1000 MIP shared memory multiprocessor, providing several hundred CPUs. The system will actually consist of several Multimaxes linked together with high-speed links and sophisticated and large caches to continue to provide the abstraction of shared memory to the programmer without bottlenecks in the overall system's performance.With such developments together with the advances in microprocessor technology, the overall hardware picture for high performance future shared memory multiprocessor systems looks very bright.

The replicated components in a multiprocessor also make it a natural basis for fault tolerance. Again the microprocessor revolution has had a significant effect on the strategies adopted. Checking a CPU's operation through replication has always been potentially feasible, but limited by the cost and engineering difficulties of this approach when the CPU covers many circuit boards. However, with cheap microprocessor chips, a replication check is quite feasible and cost-effective.

The long-term future of parallel processing systems seems secure. It seems unlikely that any one parallel processing architecture will completely dominate the field – each has advantages and disadvantages, and can in general be regarded as providing complementary features. For a complete picture of the possibilities of parallel processing it is important to understand the characteristics of each architecture, since many combinations are possible. For instance, a highly parallel supercomputer might in the future consist of many nodes interconnected in a hypercube, where each node is itself a shared memory multiprocessor augmented with fine-grain parallelism support! As a general-purpose parallel processor (if there is such a thing), however, the shared memory multiprocessors have many attractions.

11.5 Acknowledgements

This work has been supported by a grant from the DTI. Thanks are due to Michael Stoker for preparing the tables of system and microprocessor characteristics.

REFERENCES

Bell, C. G. (1985) Multis: A New Computer Class of Multiprocessor Computers, *Science 228,* 462–467.

Bernstein, P. A. (1988) Sequoia: A Fault-Tolerant Tightly Coupled Multiprocessor for Transaction Processing, *IEEE Computer* **21**(2), 37–45.

Harrison, E. S. and Schmitt, E. J. (1987) The Structure of System/88, A Fault-Tolerant Computer, *IBM Systems Journal* **26**(3), 293–318.

Lee, P. A. and Anderson, T. (1990) *Fault Tolerance, Principles and Practice,* Springer-Verlag.

Taylor, D. and Wilson, G. (1989) Stratus, *Dependability of Resilient Computers,* (ed. T. Anderson), BSP Professional Books, Oxford 222–236.

12 Parallel processing, fault tolerance and open systems

P. Bryant
European Product Marketing Manager, Stratus Computer Ltd

12.1 INTRODUCTION

This session was initially titled just 'Fault Tolerance and Open Systems' – as the theme of the conference is 'Parallel Processing' this was assumed. Indeed one of the interesting, fortunate and somewhat hidden side effects of producing fault tolerant systems is the use of parallel processing techniques in the accomplishment of fault tolerance.

Fault tolerant systems 'came of age' in the 1980s and will continue to play an increasingly important role in the 1990s. This 'coming' of age coincided with the emergence of 'on-line transaction processing' as an increasing trend. The techniques used in producing modular OLTP systems (requester/server or client/server) architectures are a natural fit for the commercial use of parallel processing systems. These factors have come together and will dominate the terminal and transaction based systems of the 1990s.

The name of the game is 'CONTINUOUS AVAILABILITY', fault tolerance being a means to achieving this. You cannot have a 'Premium Guaranteed' service without fault tolerance. A distinction must be drawn between CONTINUOUS AVAILABILITY and HIGH AVAILABILITY. In some applications HIGH AVAILABILITY is all that is required and a 'lesser' solution, where seconds or even minutes of down time are acceptable, is appropriate. This paper will discuss these differences; but will primarily focus on fault tolerance.

Open systems are naturally what users want – it is a buyers market; however in many cases the expected gains in terms of portability and flexibility must be offset by the product not 'delivering the goods' – that is the open products may not perform the actual task required in as effective a way as a proprietary purpose-designed solution.

In many ways the desire to couple fault tolerant equipment with open systems provides a doubly complex task for the computer manufacturer – the added degree of complexity being greatly influenced by the actual means chosen to achieve fault tolerance.

This paper discusses the whole scenario of parallel processing, fault tolerance, comparative fault tolerant solutions and how these map into an open systems environment.

12.2 PARALLEL PROCESSING

We will first discuss parallel processing and what we choose to mean by it. How many processors are there in your processor? Clearly in today's computers there are many processors operating in parallel. In many ways what one considers a uniprocessor mainframe there are many ancillary processors.

In Stratus largest computer for example, if fully configured for communications there are 192 main processors, and more than 1900 ancillary processors. This configuration delivers 48 truly parallel streams of user work and can be networked to other similar systems. The 192 processors delivering 48 parallel streams is due to the way Stratus implements fault tolerance. This will be discussed later in the section on comparative fault tolerance. The ancillary processors operate at the I/O controller level and also at the peripheral level, i.e. offloading much of the character level interrupt handling from the main processors.

Another view of parallel processing is seen in the way that a Mainframe, FEP, Workstation architecture is implemented with different parts of the functionality being handled at different levels. This is not the aspect of parallel processing that immediately springs to mind, neither is it the one we will be primarily concentrating on – but it is hard to to draw the definitive line in terms of 'client/server' processing either where the client/server could both exist in a tightly coupled symmetrical multi-processor architecture; or could be spread in some way within the 'Mainframe or FEP or Workstation' domain. Indeed many users are seeking a seamless heterogeneous architecture in which their modules can run in parallel in any component of the system and even be moved or load balanced dynamically.

In considering different parallel scenario they range from those discussed above through WANs, LANs, multiprocessors with dedicated tasks, multiprocessors with dedicated memory to tightly coupled symmetrical multiprocessors with shared memory.

Parallelism is emerging from the numeric and scientific market-place, where array and transputer-type technology demand special 'micro' techniques, into the commercial 'macro' market-place where the actual processing 'chunks' are relatively small and unable to 'parallelize' to any great extent; other resources other than 'mill' processing are the constraints.

The ability to parallelize at a micro level is to some extent handled by today's commercial microprocessors and their pipelining techniques. At a higher level as long as the object(s) of work can be split into discrete tasks then as long as there are no conflicts for resources these tasks can be mapped into parallel processors. This is analogous to running 6 streams in six uniprocessor batch machines side by side. In the transaction environment the client/server architecture neatly packages the work into units that are independent and can be fed to parallel processors. In some architectures a chosen processor will then process the whole package of work; in others (of which Stratus is an example) the package of work will be handled on whichever processor or processors happen to be best available at the time instructions need to be executed.

On the terminal side the client (or requester) is generally handling the context for many 'independent' terminals – so there is generally no conflict for processing resource at the although there may be conflict for the bandwidth of a multidrop or multiplexed communications line. At the server end however, which is commonly used for database handling there is usually conflict for resources and the ability to parallelize is often limited by the granularity of locks within either the database system, the TP system or the operating systems itself. This should really only be a constraint when databases are updated; in read-only mode the locks are not the problem – in this case the disks themselves are the limiting factor.

The characteristics of a TP system are many terminals, performing a lot of different tasks on a 'shared' database. Almost by definition the thing that you want to share is the factor that will inhibit the ability to parallel process. In the quest for openness the ways in which the commercial database products e.g. Oracle, Ingres, Informix and Sybase develop and refine their distribution and locking technologies will limit the ability to increase the levels of parallelism.

12.3 FAULT TOLERANCE = CONTINUOUS AVAILABILITY

How much do you need continuous availability?

How much does it hurt if your application is down?

I say application is down rather than computer is down advisedly, the computer may well be 'up' performing a recovery; but to the users the service is down!

It's all a matter of degree. The more it hurts if the computer is down the more continuous availability is required – and the level of 'fault tolerance' purchased reflects the pain felt, i.e. whether the business can afford to be off the air for sub-seconds, seconds, minutes or hours. Today's business are increasing becoming 'mission critical' – that is the computer's availability is vital to the running of the business. In many cases backup systems are impractical – in a recent failure in an Italian supermarket when the computer failed the customers were told they could take the goods away 'for free' – it was easier than causing a riot and attempting to get goods back on shelves. There have been many similar occasions in the UK but not always with such a 'generous pragmatic approach'.

Remember fault tolerance is a means to continuous availability. What then is fault tolerance? Hardware fault tolerance, pioneered by Stratus, defines it as "Fault tolerance is the ability to stand the failure of any component in the system without any interruption or degradation of the user service". As all items in a Stratus system are paired this extends to tolerating the failure of 'one of everything' within the system (i.e. 50% of boards could be missing) and the user would never notice the difference.

A more general and slightly more relaxed definition of fault tolerance is "Fault tolerance is the ability to stand the failure of any component in the system without any interruption of the user service". The subtlety is the exclusion of the word 'degradation'. In many solutions where duplicated/redundant hardware is put to good use doing other work; then when something fails there are less engines to handle the workload and the performance suffers. This is clearly dependent on the percentage utilization of the equipment and the ratio of the failed equipment to the total equipment available – if one processor out of six fails it is not so dramatic as one processor out of two fails. In this definition the 'no interruption' is also subject to interpretation – no interruption may mean 'less than a second' interruption. If it is many seconds interruption we move out of the domain of Continuous Availability into High Availability.

Let's explore what these definitions mean a little further. In the first and tighter definition what happens in the event of a failure? As said before there is no interruption or degradation of service. There is no switchover time – because the tasks are already being performed in multiple places already. Note this is not parallel processing in the sense that the user would see – this is parallel processing to achieve fault tolerance. Some systems, like Stratus, superimpose 'user parallel processing' on top of the 'fault tolerance parallel processing'. There will be no loss of data or loss of transactions in event of a failure.

In the software fault tolerant schemes, if a failure happens there is a possible degradation of the system, dependent on the percentage of the hardware that is down. There will usually be some switchover time as the software 'regroups' to run on the remaining hardware. Again in fault tolerant systems there should be no loss of data or transactions. The performance will depend on the configuration available. Software fault tolerance has the advantage of maximizing the use of the available hardware (i.e. no exact duplication of tasks) at the expense of switch over time and reduced service in the event of a failure. To guarantee service levels it may be required to over-configure the systems, which negates some of this advantage. Also, as we will see when discussing open systems, the relative simplicity of the software in the 'hardware fault tolerant scenario' makes for a far more easily portable environment.

Why Continuous availability? What can go wrong? Firstly, hardware failures, this is what we have primarily talked about so far, and they are something that can be avoided. Coupled with the hardware failure is the diagnostic mechanism, who notices the failure, how is the part replaced, what happens with transient failures etc. Hardware failures, software failures, power outages and operator error are all major hazards for Continuous Availability. Software failures will happen. In application code these are generally contained by the operating system and it is up to the application to have some form of recovery – generally the TP side of the operating system will cope with database integrity/consistency after an application (or other) failure. Whether in the hardware or software fault tolerant scenario the manufacturers do/should employ the highest Quality Standards in the production of the operating system itself. Although software fault tolerance claims slightly reduced odds in the event of an operating system crashing the user service in practice any failure or 'almost failure' is suspect and what matters more is the protection of data, the automatic recovery or dump/recovery and the minimizing of any downtime.

Operator errors are a major factor in downtime. There have been cases of operators powering off the systems when they thought they were powering off a magnetic tape. Clearly steps can be taken to eliminate simple mechanical problems like this. Clear instruction, education and security protection levels all play an important part in the containing of operator errors. Perhaps one of the major factors is also the simplicity of the machine itself. There is a catch here in that because fault tolerant systems are so reliable operators get very little practice in using the system. If you only walk up to the machine once a year in the event of a failure one is naturally ' a little rusty'. Again, simplicity and tools like on-line help play an important part.

Power failures are an important source of downtime. Generally the continuous availability is compromised more by the recovery time than the downtime. This recovery time is a major factor in all down situations – not just power failures. It is especially noticeable with power failures as 95% of power failures last less than 5 seconds – which might result in a downtime of several hours. Clearly UPS systems can be used as protection external to the machine, but this may not protect terminals or let the computer know that terminals need to be refreshed after a failure. Most fault tolerant systems have some sort of battery backup for memory protection. Stratus has taken this a step further with automatic hardware provision for the whole system to 'ride through' power failures of less than 5 seconds. This process is invisible to the user and thus handles 95% of power failures with no recovery software being brought into play at all.

Service, preventative and curative maintenance are generally activities that require all or part of the system to be taken down. In the Continuous Availability scenario the ideal is that there is no preventative maintenance that compromises the system in any way and that failed parts should be replaceable on line. This includes the obvious items like CPU boards, memory boards etc., and the less obvious items like power supplies and fans. It's very sad to have to switch your computer off to replace a £5 fan unit! The various vendors meet these challenges with different levels of success. Another aspect of the service is the ability for the service 'engineer' (whoever he/she is) to get things wrong and replace a working component – thus taking the system down. Again, as with the operator interface simplicity, clarity and where possible mechanical checks should be use to minimize this danger.

As an extension to 'on-line service' , on-line upgradability is also an important factor. In this parallel processing world of modular hardware and software it should be possible to add hardware modules on-line without powering down the system. This includes all sorts of upgrades; CPU, memory, disk to chains, new disk chains etc. And having added the new hardware, or changed the usage of a communications line, it is vital the the system has 'on-line configurability'. The should be able to pick up, change and drop devices dynamically, without resorting to a sysgen and an off-line boot of controller devices.

Indeed the 'scalability' of the system is a most important – in many cases users are unable to accurately size workloads and the ability to start with a small system and 'grow it' can be of vital importance. Thus ability to grow within the architecture, without getting into a dead and capping situation, and growth within a totally and 'cloning' software environment, means the user can increase his computer power by just adding hardware without cutting any extra code! Shortly we will be comparing the currently available fault architectures and seeing how they handle some of problems. Generally on the hardware side they to a greater or lesser extent have duplicated CPUs, controllers disk drives – in some cases the degree of fault tolerance is selectable.

12.4 COMPARATIVE FAULT TOLERANCE

The architectures we will look at include various standby mechanisms, Tandem's software fault tolerance, Stratus' hardware fault tolerance, Tandems new IS2 machine, DEC's ft3000 machine and the HP/Sequoia box.

Cold Stand By : prior to 1970 when fault tolerance first became commercially available some form of resilience was achieved by standby mechanisms – in some way the duplication of parts of the hardware to allow switchover in the event of a failure. Cold standby falls far short of our definitions of fault tolerance but is a useful reminder of 'what went before' and a worrying reminder of what still happens today. The switching on and running up of a backup computer is a slow way to restore a service in the event of a failure, and the costs of the original machine, plus the cost of the backup will generally be a lot greater than an off-the-shelf fault tolerant machine. Companies who are not 'mission critical', that is who are not using the computer at the heart of their business may well be slipping into a non-competitive situation.

Many systems today run in hot standby mode, where the spare equipment is already fired up and running and can take over the workload with only a small delay. Many airline ticketing systems use this and have multiple mainframes. These solutions grew before fault tolerance became commercially available and whilst they produce what is required, it is at enormous cost. In these cases the users are generally locked into the situation due to the immense investment in existing software.

Fault tolerance came of age in the beginning of the 1970s when Tandem produced its non-stop systems. Here was a system that had multiple processors (up to 16), parallel processing and the ability to cope with single points of failure. The processors are linked by a very fast bus. The processors run true parallel streams. To achieve fault tolerance each process (or program) running has a shadow process running in another processor. These shadows receive checkpoints from the active process periodically and are ready to take over in the event of the active process disappearing; either due to a software or hardware error. If it is a software error the chances are the shadow will fail as well! This shadow process concept applies to parts of the operating system itself as well as user applications. So although the processors are generally running different jobs a percentage of the processing power is used in running the shadow process and there is a software performance and complexity overhead in maintaining the software fault tolerance, checkpoints, restarts etc. There is a small delay when the shadow process takes over; and in the event of a hardware failure the system is now running on less hardware resource. This means if one processor fails in a two-processor system and they were previously both 75% utilized; then the remaining processor has to achieve 150% of its potential to provide the same service to the users. This it clearly can't to do so in the user's eyes it slows down. If this degradation is unacceptable it may lead to 'over configuration' to compensate. Clearly the larger the number of processors the smaller the proportional effect when one fails. Disks are also mirrored with multiple paths through multiple controllers, so one disk and one controller can fail and the system is still running.

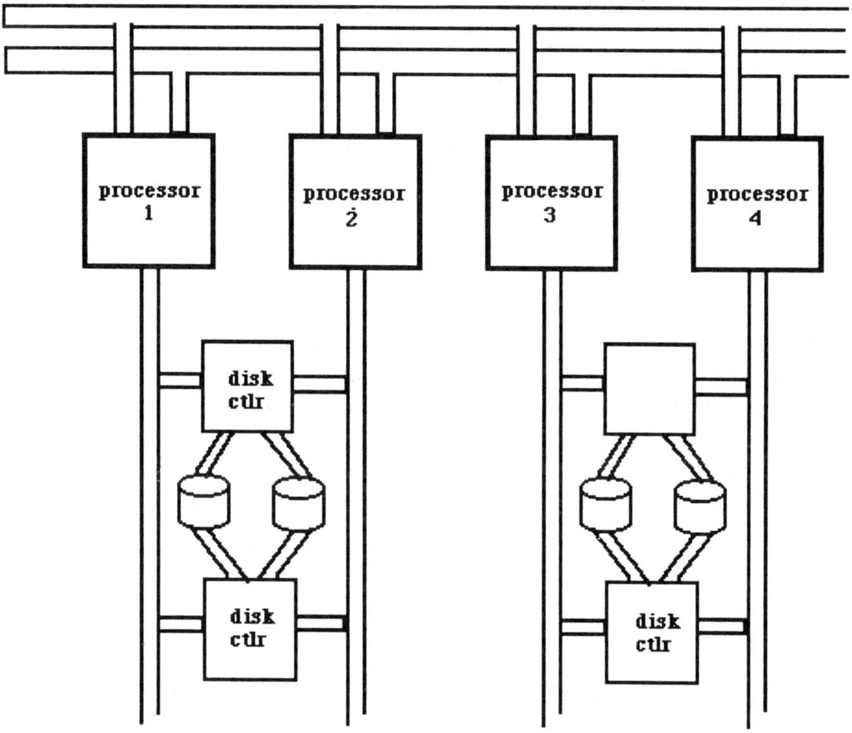

Figure 12.1 Tandem guardian architecture.

(The Guardian operating system is message and process based, in contrast with Stratus's call based system.)

The original non-stop systems have evolved through nonstop2, VLX and currently available in the Cyclone range of 'Mainframe Style' processor. Cyclone systems come with four processors and have multiple IO buses.

In the 1980s, with the evolution of powerful off-the-shelf processors (e.g. the 68000) Stratus approached the problems from a radically difference direction. Rather than achieve fault tolerance by software mechanisms Stratus decided to solve the problem in the hardware. The problem was solved by in effect making each user visible parallel processor from a matrix of four processors. These four processors solved the fault tolerance problem. As far as the user and software is concerned there is just one processor which is 'always there'. This leads to simple software design and other important advantages. The way this 'quad modular redundancy' technology works is as follows:

We will consider a processor, but the some logic applies to all the controller boards in the system. Take a processor board; at each clock tick the work is done twice and compared by a hardware comparator (all on the same tick – the checking steals no cycles from the processors). If the results of the comparison is good the data is then output to the bus. Actually there are two of these boards. Each of the boards carries out the same task on each clock tick. If one of the boards has a failure, detected by the comparator it then shuts itself off from the bus and goes into diagnostic mode. Meanwhile the remaining board fully supports the user workload, the performance of the system hasn't changed, and the user doesn't notice a thing. If the diagnostics detect a permanent failure the computer automatically telephones the service centre and a replacement is dispatched (the user exchanges the component him/herself). If it is an intermittent failure the board may put itself on-line again. However thresholds can be set that a chosen rate of intermittent failures is unacceptable – it this is exceeded the phone call is made and the board is replaced.

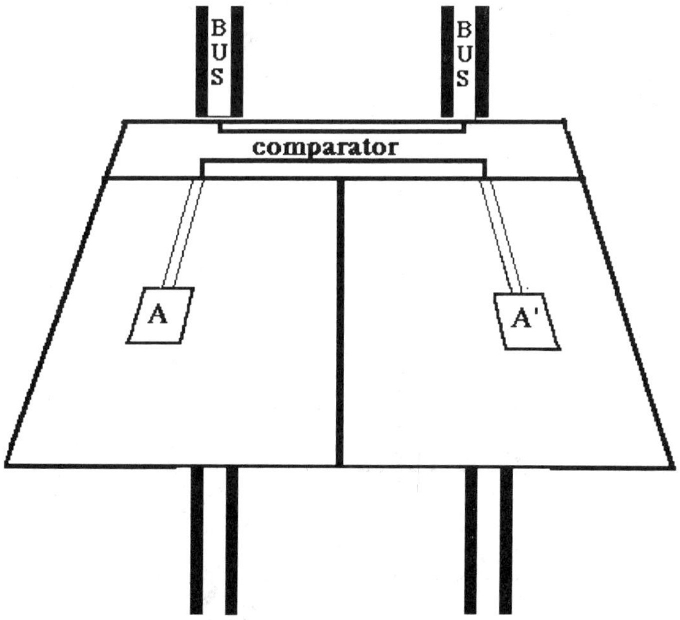

Figure 12.2 Stratus processor board.

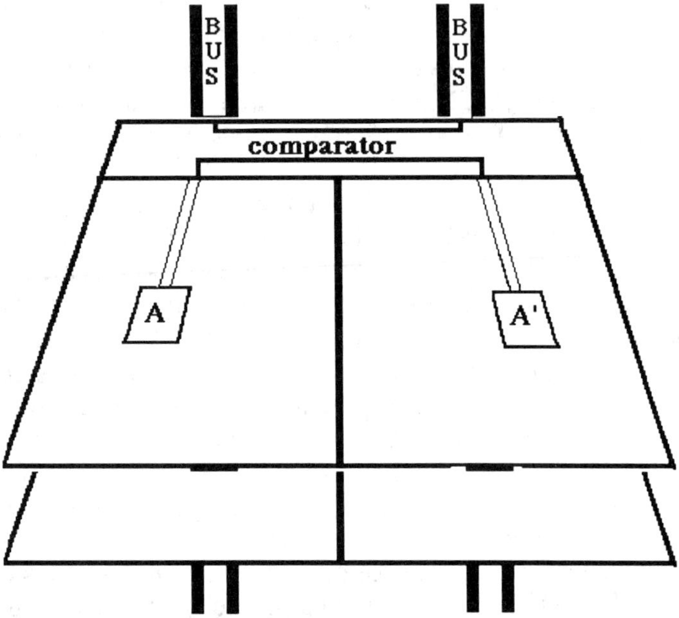

Figure 12.3 Stratus processor boards.

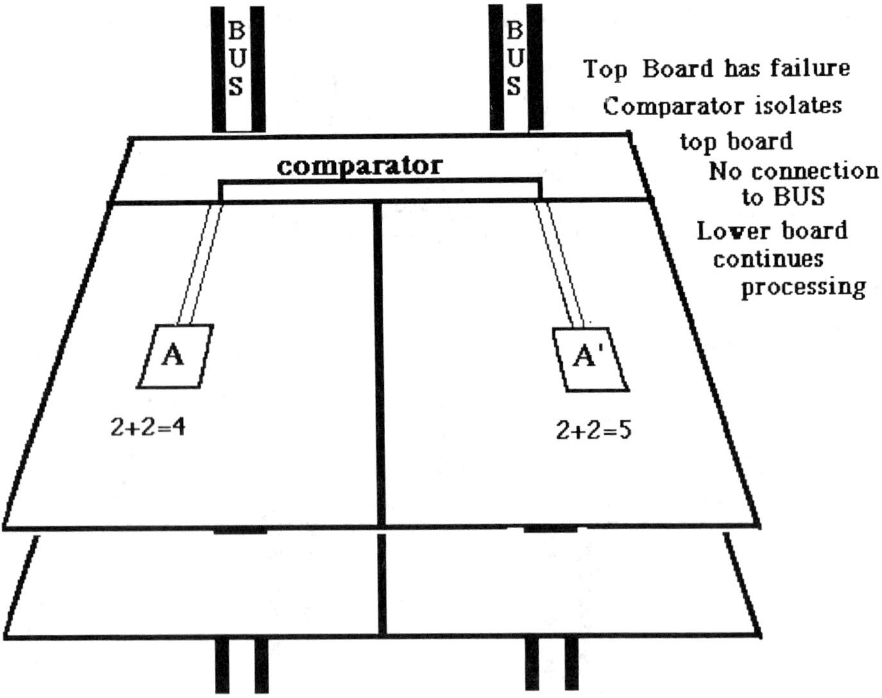

Figure 12.4 Stratus processor boards.

What we have been considering so far is how four actual processors are couple to provide one 'guaranteed available user processor'. In fact there can be up to six guaranteed available user processors closely coupled symmetrical multi-processors in a Stratus module – all sharing the same memory. Each time a task is ready for execution it is executed on the 'most readily available' of the parallel processors. There is no dedication of processing power. This approach provides great flexibility and modularity and a self tuning/self balancing system. Indeed processors can be added on-line and will automatically pick up their share of the work.

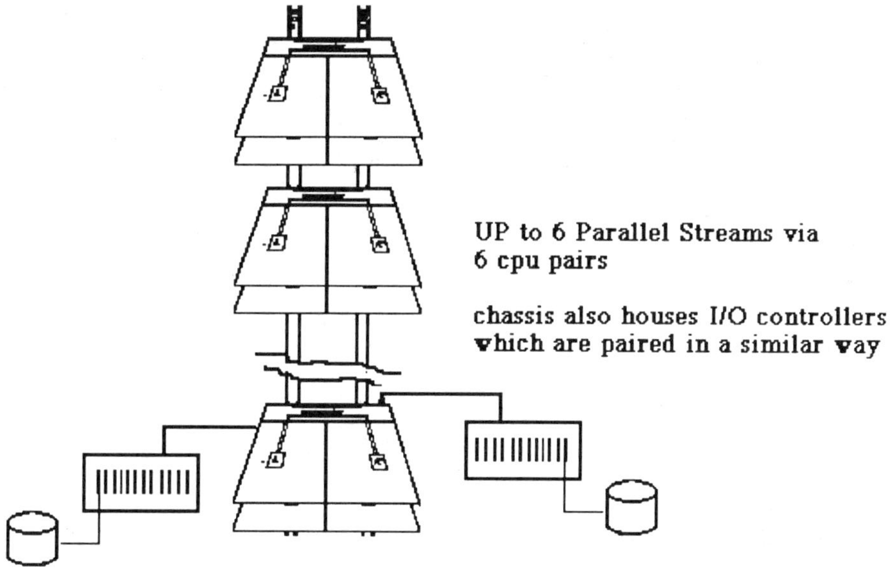

Figure 12.5 Stratus processor boards.

Disks are mirrored and also can be replaced and added on-line.

Note that because the fault tolerance is solved in the hardware any software can be run on the system and it is automatically fault tolerant. Stratus recently announced Unix products run on the whole range of hardware, the same hardware, as its VOS and PICK products. Also this technology also paves the way for easy migration to the upcoming i860 RISC architecture.

Tandem has recently announced its Integrity S2 architecture running Unix. This is a completely separate range from the Guardian systems and is implemented in hardware by Triple Modular Redundancy. In this case the work is executed 3 times and a voting system is used to check the results. In the event of failure two of the three processors should agree and the voting system 'votes out' the offending processor which is then replaced. The processors have local memory as well as global memory and the processors are synchronized in a more relaxed way than the 'clock tick' of Stratus. The synchronization occurs when global memory is accessed, on interrupt or every 1000 instructions. There is no parallel processing as far as the user is concerned and the machines processing power cannot be increased.

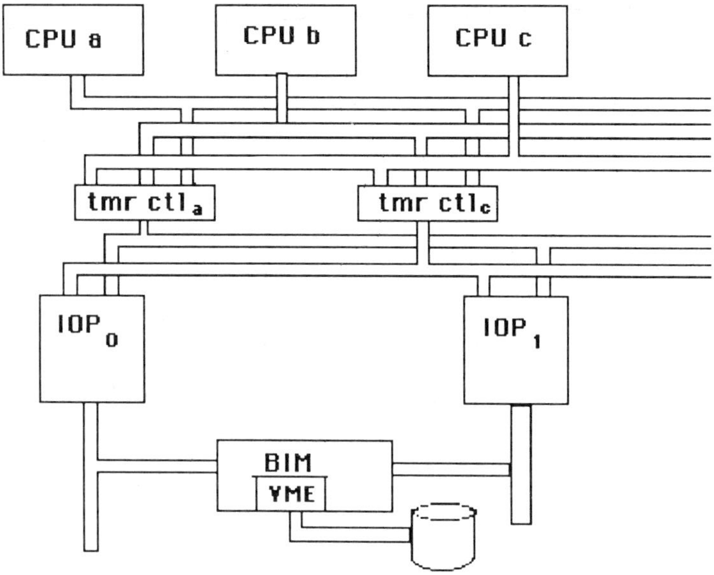

Figure 12.6 Tandem IS2.

Unlike Tandem's earlier Guardian systems which were based on proprietary chips the IS2 system uses a powerful MIPS RISC chip.

The system mirrors disk and has the advantage of being able to connect to industry standard VME cards.

Although having high availability systems with its VAX clustering approach, DEC recently entered the Fault Tolerant Area with its VAX 3000ft 310 product. This is a VMS-only system aimed at the Continuous availability TP market-place. The fault tolerance is achieved by duplicating the hardware into two zones. The zones are two separate cabinets and a zone can take a failure leaving the other zone providing the service to the user. A failure however will take out a zone so two failures of different items, one in each zone, could take out the whole system. This contrasts to Tandem Guardian and Stratus systems where many failures can be tolerated as long as 'both items of a pair' do not fail. The zones are driven by a master clock (in one of the zones) and if a failure occurs the system in effect provides an almost instant hot backup situation.

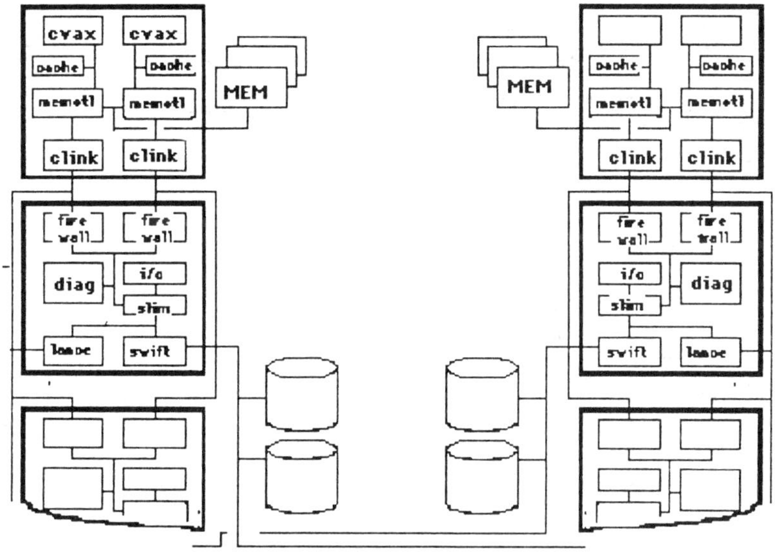

Figure 12.7 DEC VAX 3000ft.

Mirror disks are catered for, as are duplex memory and IO controller.

The system is a single processor as far as the user is concerned – there is no user parallel processing.

Sequoia systems have been available from Sequoia, from ITL and are now marketed by HP. Like Stratus, Sequoia's systems are 68000 based and use tightly coupled processors. The philosophical difference is while Stratus puts in enough 'spare' hardware to make sure the user is never compromised Sequoia thinks that as hardware seldom fails it is better to make use of all the hardware in a productive way; with a resynchronizing delay and a reduced service in the event of a failure. A failed component isolates itself, and the operating system reconfigures and continues the work from a checkpoint. A hardware checkpoint mechanism is used on cache memory to facilitate this with minimal delay. The architecture supports duplicate disk and IO controllers and mirror disks. A multibus adaptor is available.

Sequent have produced their SYMMETRY systems which use a tightly coupled SMP architecture – currently 80386 based and shortly to be 80486 based. This is a high availability solution which uses mirrored disks and automatic software recover. Software is V.3 Unix-based. The systems available are quoted at between 8 and 120 MIPS for the S81 maximum configuration. The systems feature dynamic balancing across the multiprocessors.

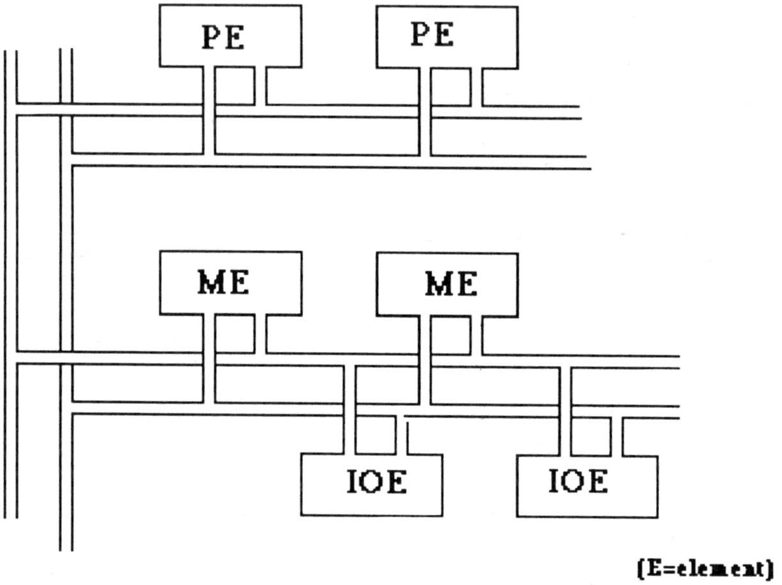

Figure 12.8 Sequoia architecture.

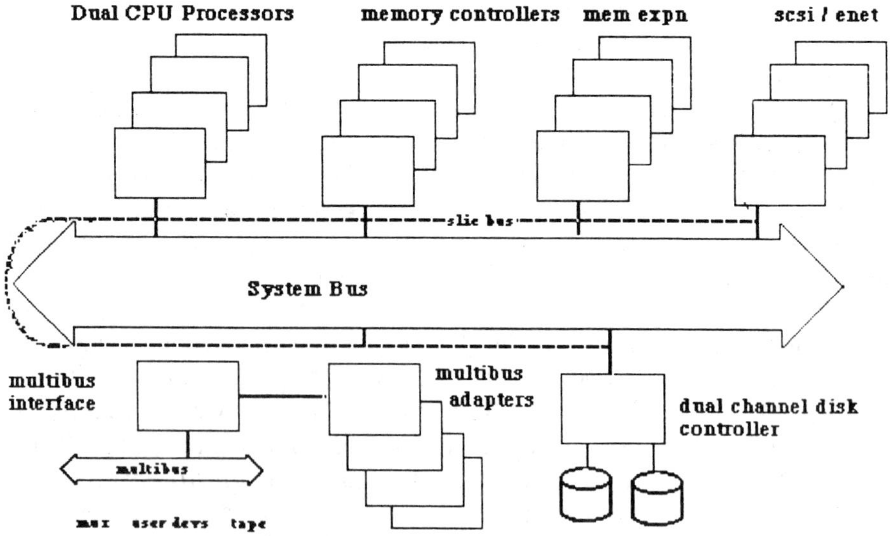

Figure 12.9 Sequent 'symmetry' architecture.

12.5 OPEN SYSTEMS

Openness, fault tolerance and parallelism are all intertwined; we have touched on openness previously but now we shall look at degrees of openness.

The hardware itself can be open, that is, the processor components that are used can be either proprietary or 'off the shelf'. It used to be the case that proprietary always meant faster and better. With some of the latest generation of chips this is not necessarily the case. The advantages of 'off the shelf' hardware include the ability to multi source components, the ability to cross licence manufacturing easily and the benefits of a common platform, both in interfacing technology and in base software. For example, there will be 'off the shelf compilers' for a public technology – which decreases the time to bring product to market; particularly in the Unix world. In the fault tolerant market-place it is only the Tandem Guardian range and DEC 3000ft which use proprietary chips. The remainder use CISC 68020/30, 80366/486 and RISC i860/MIPs technology. Currently RISC technology seems to be demonstrating the required performance growth profile; although there are schools of thought that CISC will have a comeback when the clock cycle situation is improved.

As well as benefiting from standard core hardware manufactures are also extending out into open bus technologies, for example Tandem with VMEbus with the IS2 and Sequoia with multibus.

On the software side the 'one standard' of Unix seems to be the way forward (or what should be one standard!). Clearly the user base wants standard software so hardware can become a commodity product. This is not so immediately in the manufacturers' interest, other than if that's where the market is, then that is where the manufacturer must be. A wider net in terms of standards is given by POSIX. Some manufacturers, e.g. DEC support a POSIX interface in their proprietary operating systems. Although this is a 'half way' stage and in many ways is a 'best compromise' as it gives the richness of a proprietary system with portability, in general it is felt that what users want is 'real Unix' and the task over the next few years is to develop Unix to have the 'richness of features'.

One problem with Unix is that manufactures have to conform to one release (say V3.2) and then another a year later (say V4) – this means that any software modifications and enhancements have to be reapplied to the kernel. This can be particularly onerous in the case of fault tolerant manufacturers as by the nature of their products they have to add features over and above the standard Unix kernel. In this respect Stratus is in a good position as nearly all of the fault tolerance is solved by hardware therefore does not need to be carried forward to the new release as software fixes.

Even with Stratus, the fixes to handle mirror disks and the service network do have to be carried forward. Other manufactures are not so fortunate as Stratus and may well have many-fold the work to reapply the fixes to each new kernel release. As Unix is not a resilient operating system these manufacturers are all, to greater or lesser extents trying to solve the reliability problems of Unix itself, as well as adding the fault tolerant features. Ways in which Unix must be improved include better handling of resources, elimination of panics, improved file systems, TP systems and security features. As these problems have to be resolved it points to the scenario that when Unix becomes established there will be great inertia that will slow moves to new releases. It is not clear that the 'reliability' lessons learnt and applied by the computer manufacturers will actually be standard and delivered to them in the next Unix kernel (not clear is a euphemism!). However the kernel will have to develop with more TP and reliability features to enable it to provide as good a solution in the TP market-place as today's proprietary systems.

The message may be 'if you want reliable TP systems today – proprietary is best', 'if you want Unix today - Unix' is best; but users beware, Unix may give you a handle on the manufacturers but it may not give you what you want!

On the communications side, standards are becoming clearly defined and manufactures have to have a complete repertoire in order to play in the market. OSI and SNA will remain the two overall umbrellas, with LAN technology X400/X500 and EDI playing an increasingly important place.

The other important area of standards is that of presentation; here the industry is split between the PC-based presentation manager standards and the emerging GUI and Xwindows standards. These are increasingly being demanded of manufacturers; the latter particularly in the Unix environment.

As well as the 'designed' open standards there are *de facto* standards emerging, where software runs on multiple platforms; in forms systems such as JYACC, UNIFACE and the forms front-ends to database products.

In both the communications and presentation standards areas these standards are demanded in both the Unix and non-Unix environments. This is appropriate as these are 'intercommunication' and 'look-feel' standards across varying platforms. Even if an open operating system is not chosen, systems must be able to communicate and provide a common interface. This is particularly relevant in distributed architectures where client/servers may exist in a variety of places and common database engines (e.g. ORACLE/Sybase) provide library and graphics standards across multiple platforms.

With the database and forms 4GL products providing the user environment, it may be that the operation system question is of no relevance and Unix only comes of age as a tool for software house developers – perhaps Unix will be leap-frogged? Surely not? But there are some signs of this already, for example with 4GL techniques being taught to users on one type of hardware, irrespective of the actual hardware the users will be eventually working on!

12.6 CONCLUSION

What comes first? Fault tolerance leads to modular architectures and client/server processing. Modular architectures lead to parallel processing. Parallel processing is bottle-necked due to locking at the shared resource level. This is in a sense parallel processing top-down rather than bottom-up – perhaps that is what commercial parallel processing is.

Open standards in terms of operating systems provide the openness and portability that application developers require. Today they may well not provide the features that the end users require or demand from fault tolerant continuous processing systems.

Parallel processing, fault tolerance and OLTP have come together as the 'heart of on-line systems' and by the mid 1990s Unix may well be there too.

Part Five

Parallel knowledge base systems

13 kbProlog: a language for knowledge management

J. C. Manley
Hewlett-Packard Laboratories, Bristol

Knowledge Base Management Systems will increasingly become a major component of commercial information processing platforms. kbProlog is a logic-programming-based language designed to support software architectures for knowledge management. The prototype Knowledge Base Management System KBMS1, which comprises an interpreter for kbProlog tightly coupled to persistent store, is described. The existence of theories in kbProlog is seen as central to the use of parallel hardware for supporting the efficient processing of large-scale knowledge bases. We argue that the most fruitful application of such hardware initially will be to the clause selection process.

13.1 INTRODUCTION

An important development in commercial information processing will be the emergence of Knowledge Base Management Systems (KBMSs) [Brodie 86; Schmidt 89; Ullman 88,89] as a major platform component. KBMSs will be adopted because of the need to handle and share much richer forms of information than are currently allowed by Database Management Systems (DBMSs). Commercial information processing will begin to change from the building of application programs accessing databases to the construction of knowledge bases. We believe that the correct basis for such a KBMS is Logic Programming and will describe a prototype system, KBMS1, being built at Hewlett-Packard's European Research Centre.

The transition to knowledge base technology will involve a radical change in the way that information processing is carried out; most of the information that is currently hidden away in immutable and unsharable application code will become part of the knowledge base. Application development will become the construction of knowledge bases which, in DBMS terms, contain both the data and the application programs.

Companies and market-places are becoming increasingly dynamic; the only way in which the information processing needs of an enterprise will be met is through users having control over their data. An appropriate platform for supporting this new regime is Knowledge Base Management Systems. Such a platform creates the possibility of end users maintaining most aspects of the applications and data for which they are responsible, leaving the Management Information Services to carry out major projects instead of being swamped by minor change requests to existing applications.

Given that the adoption of KBMSs is likely, it is then right to ask what impact parallel processing will have. We will discuss the most fruitful areas for parallel support when dealing with logic-programming-based KBMSs, and in particular KBMS1.

13.2 KNOWLEDGE BASE MANAGEMENT SYSTEMS

The aim of a KBMS is to enable investment in large knowledge bases that are extensible and maintainable over long periods of time, in much the same way as databases have enabled long-term investment in data. The most serious failing of, say, a relational database is its representational ability. Its data is in the form of ground structureless facts arranged as tables. Any other information which is not of this form has to be incorporated into application programs. If a more powerful language is made available for storing and manipulating this information then it becomes declarative, dynamic and sharable in the same way that the relational database data is. As a result the application programs become more compact and more easily maintained because all the knowledge is now declaratively expressed and not partly embedded in application code.

What is the difference between data and knowledge? We will take it as axiomatic that data comprises ground facts, and that knowledge comprises arbitrary facts and rules. Knowledge is declaratively-expressed factual and procedural information; a delegation procedure for expense authorization is as much knowledge as a table of employee names and tax codes. Because the knowledge is declaratively expressed, it is reasonable to assert that representation is equivalent to implementation; once the knowledge has been expressed it can become active through the application of an interpreter for the relevant language.

An evolutionary or a revolutionary approach can be taken for the construction of a KBMS [Mylopoulos 86]. The evolutionary approach uses an existing DBMS as the starting point and tries to add those capabilities required in a KBMS, principally rule-processing. This is a short-term solution and is consequently of limited interest. Large knowledge bases will have rules as a major component, and these will be rules requiring, in some cases, very intensive inference. It is not sufficient to treat the rule handling as a 'bolt-on'; it has to be at the very core of the KBMS. Thus attempts to couple a rule engine to a DBMS will provide a system capable of supporting minor applications, but it will not provide a path to the support of large-scale knowledge bases. Alternatively the evolutionary approach could take a knowledge-engineering environment or a logic-programming system and add the capabilities missing there, principally persistence, transaction management and multi-user access control. The drawback here is that the representation language is that of the rule-processing system chosen. If this is, for example, Prolog then the KBMS inherits the well-known shortcomings of Prolog, as well as the lack of a knowledge-structuring mechanism.

The revolutionary approach starts from a knowledge-representation framework and builds a KBMS and a methodology around it. This is, of course, very much a long-term approach, but if the language is correctly chosen it will provide the principal information-processing platform for the next generation of application requirements. This is the approach taken with KBMS1, the prototype KBMS discussed in the next section.

A KBMS is a very powerful system. It subsumes the functionality of databases and their embedding languages, but it also subsumes expert systems, knowledge-engineering environments and logic-programming systems. The base language of the KBMS must be looked on as an assembly language. Higher-level modelling languages can be built on top of this base language. These modelling languages will reflect models that the end users have of their information and will allow its manipulation and display in a natural and intuitive manner. Applications can then be coded in terms of these models, which gives rise to the notion of model-oriented programming [Harrison 90], a major new paradigm supported by KBMSs.

13.3 KBMS1

KBMS1 [Black and Manley 87; Manley 89] is a prototype Knowledge Base Management System designed to allow the representation, storage, retrieval and update of large amounts of declaratively-expressed knowledge. The development of KBMS1 has been driven by a number of beliefs.

- Logic Programming is the proper foundation for a KBMS.
- A structuring mechanism for the knowledge is a fundamental requirement.
- A tight-coupling between the interpreter and secondary storage is essential.

The principal Logic Programming language is Prolog. Prolog systems are, in general, designed for relatively small applications where the 'database' can be populated at the start of a session either from a saved image or from files. The notion of a persistent database that reflects updates as they occur is not part of traditional Prolog systems.

In Prolog, information is expressed as clauses (facts and rules). Clauses which share the same primary functor and arity are grouped into procedures. A higher-level of structuring is sometimes afforded through the use of modules. Modules are side-effectable partitions of the database which often have ill-defined semantics and so are of limited practical use. The construction of a logic-programming-based KBMS revolves around the scaling in size of a Prolog-like database. This scaling introduces some new requirements, in particular the need for a fundamental structuring mechanism in the 'database'.

A major difference between Prolog and kbProlog (the language of KBMS1) is the abolition of Prolog's global database and the introduction of a new first-class object, the theory [Bowen 85]. In KBMS1, a knowledge base is exhaustively partitioned into theories – a theory is a collection of kbProlog clauses. A theory is also a true kbProlog term and as a result updating is non side-effecting: updating a theory results in the formation of a new theory (term) which differs from its parent theory by the update. The parent theory is not destroyed by the updating operation. This leads to a very powerful in-built theory-versioning facility which allows a completely general tree-based evolution of a theory. Other consequences of theories as terms are that all updates are backtrackable, and that metaprogramming is facilitated through the treatment of fragments of knowledge as individual objects. We believe that kbProlog, a Prolog-like language in which theories are introduced as a first-class object, is a proper foundation for the development of a KBMS.

KBMS1 comprises a novel interpreter for kbProlog tightly coupled to a storage manager. The interpreter has support for theories and their operations built into its core. The apparent need for theory copying during updating is obviated through the maximal sharing of common substructure. The present version of the storage manager is based on DBCore, which is the record manager of Hewlett-Packard's relational database product Allbase [Brown 86]. The tight-coupling enables the interpreter to access and update the disk-resident knowledge base in an efficient manner without the need to proceed via a wholly inappropriate query language as is the case with loosely-coupled Prolog/expert systems and databases. The primary-memory structures of KBMS1, in particular their sharing, are reproduced on disk leading to an efficient transfer of data between the storage manager and the interpreter and a space-efficient representation of theory versions.

KBMS1 provides the ability to build and experiment with software architectures for the management of knowledge through the features of kbProlog (theories, versioning, metaprogramming) and through persistence.

One such architecture we have designed has a set of knowledge base management primitives built from kbProlog's theory-handling primitives. This higher level of abstraction for handling theories allows the assignment of names to theories and the association with named metatheories. A system theory represents the relationship between a (object) theory, its name, and the names of its interpreter theory, assimilator theory and attribute theory. An interpreter theory handles querying in its associated object theories – it might be required for inference control when the default, built-in interpreter's strategy would be too inefficient and so, for example, lemma generation, goal reordering or a more global view of the search space is needed. An assimilator theory handles updating in its associated object theories – if an object theory has a specialized assimilator theory, then that controls all updating, usually through the enforcement of local and global integrity constraints. Attribute theories allow the abstraction of object-theory-specific metadata from interpreter and assimilator theories thereby enabling their re-use on more than one object theory. The five-place relation represented in a system theory may be many-to-many-to-many-to-many-to-many. For instance, a given theory name may be associated with more than one actual object theory. The implied choice here may be exploited either through backtracking, or through a decision made on the basis of metadata in, say, the system theory's attribute theory.

System theories, interpreter theories, assimilator theories and attribute theories are themselves first-class theories, and so they in turn have names and associated metatheories. This apparent infinite regress is usually quickly terminated by the built-in metatheories: the underlying kbProlog interpreter; an assimilator that adds or deletes clauses exactly as instructed; and an empty attribute theory.

Since theories are terms, a system theory contains all theories it names. In other words, a system theory is a knowledge base. A system theory evolves as a series of versioned knowledge bases as the theories it contains evolve. A system theory version enables the dereferencing of a theory name to the appropriate version of an object theory, this gives a powerful mechanism for handling the complexity generated by full theory versioning.

In a large knowledge base, theories will be of many different complexions: some will be like conventional relational database tables with very large numbers of ground structureless facts; others will be small collections of rules which entail long complex inference; the majority will be collections of varying numbers of facts and rules. KBMS1 provides the ability to realize particular theories in foreign subsystems, thereby enabling an appropriate treatment of theories based on their characteristics. As an example, there might be theories which are best treated in a relational database because their contents are very large procedures composed entirely of ground structureless facts, and that all operations performed on these theories are set-based. Another reason for having theories realized in foreign systems is that it may not always be possible to transfer their contents to a knowledge base as the foreign system has to remain 'live' because of existing applications. We will see that this realization in foreign systems also offers the opportunity to exploit parallel support for particular theories.

Other features of KBMS1 include the ability to embed queries in foreign programming languages (this has been used for integration into a distributed object management facility), the ability to implement kbProlog procedures in languages other than kbProlog, a form of transaction management, an integration with the X11 Motif widgets (this allows declarative specification and maintenance of user interfaces from KBMS1), a global side-effectable theory, and the specialized treatment of 'database-like' theories within the standard storage manager.

KBMS1 is a prototype system, and as such does not yet support multi-user access to shared knowledge bases. However the system is of sufficient maturity to allow the development of large-scale applications and one such is described in the Section 13.5.

13.4 KBMS1 AND PARALLELISM

Given that KBMSs will be important component of the next-generation platform for commercial information processing, and that a logic-programming foundation is the correct basis for such a system, what will be the impact of parallel processing support? The greater power and flexibility of KBMSs must have implications for their performance characteristics, especially when dealing with tasks already handled by DBMSs. This performance loss must somehow be regained, but also the much richer forms of access and manipulation of information that KBMSs will encourage must receive adequate support.

KBMS1 may be viewed as a logic-programming system that enables the treatment of very large numbers of kbProlog clauses. This view forces a change of emphasis from a language to a repository, and this in turn creates a similar change of emphasis when looking for the most fruitful areas for parallel hardware support.

KBMS1 processing of any kind (storage, retrieval/inference, update) is a succession of steps of inference. The approach to incorporating parallelism into standard logic-programming is to search for methods of executing steps of inference in parallel. This is, in our opinion, not the right place to start looking for parallelization in a KBMS.

Each step of inference may be regarded as a sequence of four operations:

1. Goal selection - choose a goal from the set of outstanding goals on which to attempt satisfaction next;
2. Clause selection - find a suitable clause from the database/knowledge base of clauses with which to attempt satisfaction of the chosen goal;
3. Unification - unify the chosen goal with the head of the chosen clause;
4. Goal combination - combine the goals in the body of the chosen clause with the set of outstanding goals.

Fig. 13.1 demonstrates, the major difference between the language and the repository is that the set of potential candidate clauses for each chosen goal can be very large, perhaps in excess of clauses. Logic-programming systems generally have quite crude mechanisms for locating candidate clauses in procedures since a linear search, or a partially-assisted linear search (using an impoverished first-argument indexing) is usually adequate – procedures containing a single clause are quite common, more than ten clauses are quite rare unless they are 'data'.

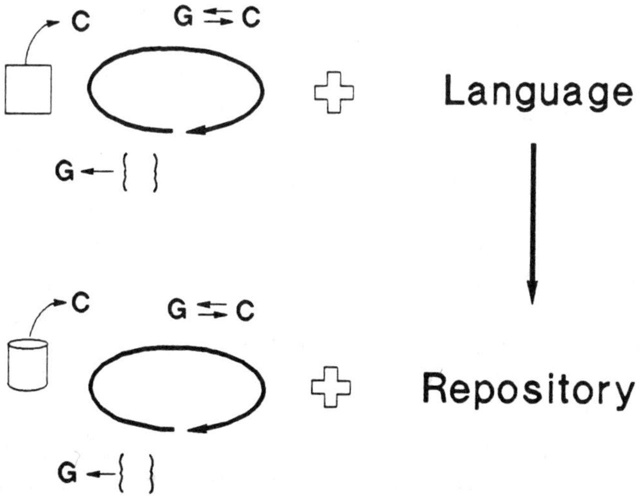

Figure 13.1 The four stages in a step of inference for the language and the repository.

In the repository the rate-limiting step is most likely to be clause selection. It is here that the largest return in performance will be given by the use of parallel hardware. A major difference between the way in which clauses are located in a KBMS and the way in which tuples are located in a DBMS is that the clause selection does not necessarily return guaranteed candidates. In a DBMS a template is constructed which essentially contains logical variables. This template is then matched against the database under the control of a predicate tree, which embodies the selection criteria, and any indexes built on the relevant table. All tuples found are true candidates.

In inference engines the clause selection is usually not an accurate filter. One reason for this is that the test for candidancy is much more complex and is only confirmed through full unification of the template (the current goal) and the head of the clause chosen. In a DBMS, the pattern matching is one-way since only the template can contain logical variables, and in general neither the template nor the tuple contain structured arguments. In the KBMS case the matching is two-way since both the goal and clause head may contain logical variables and both may also have structured arguments. The structured arguments may be partially ground in that logical variables can appear at any level within their structuring.

If the clause selection were to perform perfect filtering a full unifiability test would be required, and this is potentially an expensive operation to perform at this stage of the inference procedure, unless very much more sophisticated indexing is available to help locate candidates more reliably before the unifiability test is applied. The structured nature of the clause arguments clearly poses problems for efficient indexing. Because the filtering is not perfect candidate clauses can be rejected at the unification stage, and this causes the clause selection process to be reinvoked in the same step of inference – this cycling is repeated until a true candidate is found, it is not the same as backtracking.

The task of clause selection is thus: given a goal, to locate a single candidate clause as reliably as possible, but with no absolute guarantee that the clause found will unify with that goal. However the process must not fail to find any of the true candidates. It is an advantage to try to determine whether any further candidates exist within the relevant procedure since this gives a pointer as to whether or not the current goal will be satisfied deterministically.

A complicating feature is that clause ordering within a procedure is significant. In other words, candidate clauses must be found in order. This adds a further burden on any indexing scheme employed. However, with large procedures it is likely that operations are set-based since they are usually modelling the type of knowledge found in traditional database tables

– clause ordering is then not so important and this removes the apparent sequentiality in the processing.

The role of parallelism in supporting inference over large bodies of knowledge now becomes clearer. A candidate clause has to be found in a large procedure. That procedure may be of homogeneous data: a large number of ground structureless facts as found in database tables. But it may also be inhomogeneous: a large number of interleaved facts and rules with logical variables and arguments of arbitrary complexity in their heads. The clause found might be as part of a series of related retrievals, as with set-based operations, or it might be a single act of location where clause ordering within the relevant procedure is of primary importance. Indexes, or more generally partial indexes, may be available to help constrain the search, but the presence of logical variables and arguments of arbitrary complexity might make the index of limited use. For every clause a unifiability test, or a partial unifiability test, has to be applied to determine the clause's candidature.

Parallelism offers the opportunity to de-emphasize the reliance on indexing or even dispense with it entirely, particularly in the case of large procedures. The expensive unifiability test can be applied to candidate clauses in parallel which offers the opportunity to consider a full unifiability test in each case, instead of truncating it through the number of arguments and the number of levels of structuring considered. The full unifiability test will ensure perfect filtering by the clause selection process and will thus remove the internal cycling in a step of inference described earlier.

KBMS1 offers some attractive features when considering the role of parallel hardware. The most important of these is the existence of theories. For this purpose theories may be thought of as black-box encapsulations of knowledge with well-defined and simple querying and updating interfaces. As discussed earlier, a large knowledge base will be composed of theories of many different complexions. Because of this, it is possible to implement different theories in technologies that are well-suited to their characteristics. Most theories will be realized in the built-in persistent store of KBMS1, but it is possible to have chosen theories held in specialized hardware stores, or other subsystems, and for them to appear as part of a single knowledge base.

The requirements on specialized persistent stores for theories containing large procedures are severe. In addition to requiring search engines that are able to perform configurable unifiability tests on structured, non-ground terms and able to handle clause ordering, the store must support theory versioning in an efficient and space-effective manner.

We are currently investigating with the University of Essex the potential for using their Intelligent File Store (IFS) [Lavington 88] for the storage, retrieval and update of large complex theories. It appears that the IFS is capable of responding to demands of handling KBMS1 versioned theories, and as a result this integration will provide clear evidence of the potential of KBMSs and specialized hardware support in large-scale commercial information processing.

If we move up one level and consider the complete satisfaction of goals instead of individual steps of inference, then further opportunities for the use of parallel hardware become apparent. In KBMS1 the satisfaction of a top-level goal may be seen as the satisfaction of a series of sub-goals in particular theories. The satisfaction of a goal within a theory can be regarded as an atomic operation – the theory which requested that satisfaction is not interested in how that satisfaction was obtained, only that the underlying inference performed is sound. As a result set-based operations, transitive closures, unions (joins) and other similar operations can be 'pushed down' into the specialized support.

Finally, in future it may well become beneficial to consider parallel processing of the inference procedure itself, perhaps through the introduction of parallel-processing-related devices into kbProlog. There is no barrier to this, but we believe the major gains initially will come from the parallel support of particular theories, not from parallelization of the language.

There are many potential applications of Knowledge Base Management Systems technology to the commercial processing world, some of these will pose challenging requirements on the performance of their applications. Specialized hardware support will be justified as the benefits of KBMS technology over existing technologies for the building of next-generation applications are clear.

13.5 APPLICATION AREAS

The use of KBMS1 and similar KBMSs will gradually embrace the whole spectrum of commercial information processing. Initially, however, applications will have a number of distinguishing features that will necessitate the use of such a technology: the need to regard a much larger fragment of the knowledge inherent in a set of applications as sharable, inspectable, modifiable; the ability to provide flexible *ad hoc* access to data; the ability to integrate diverse knowledge sources and provide an abstraction that gives the appearance of a single body of knowledge; the rapid and compact development of applications.

GAP [Harrison 90] is a prototype application developed using KBMS1 as the sole implementation technology. It is a project expense monitoring and planning system that gives *ad hoc* access to sets of "expense forms".

The user interface enables end-users to query and maintain their own expense forms, and other data, through the use of user-centred models which allow the building up of a dialogue between the user and his information system in pursuit of the user's end goal. This end goal might well be fuzzy or ill-defined to begin with – he thinks he has spotted an anomaly and wants to investigate it further, for example. The building up of a dialogue means that he can home in on the query, or more usually the set of queries, he wants answered.

GAP was developed in just over five man-months, including the experiments with how interaction with the user-centred models should be conducted and how dialogues with the system could be built up. The final knowledge base consists of about 70 theories holding all the data, the models, the construction and maintenance of the user interface, communication with GAP systems operated by other project managers, a knowledge-based spreadsheet, and the general 'program-like' knowledge needed to provide a complete application. These theories contain about 1900 kbProlog clauses, expressed over about 11000 lines. System analysts estimate that to emulate GAP in Pascal would require about 50000 lines. An important outcome is that the performance of the final system is sufficient to remove any inclination to recode it in an imperative language.

GAP is an indication that large-scale KBMS commercial applications are viable, but more importantly they have huge advantages in the time taken to develop applications, the ease with which such systems are maintained (most of an application is declaratively expressed), and the ability to offer uniform and unified solutions to complex problems.

13.6 SUMMARY

Knowledge Base Management Systems are likely to become an important component of commercial information processing applications. Their ability to represent and manipulate larger fragments of the knowledge implicit in all applications, and their ability to make that knowledge declarative, dynamic and sharable will lead to end-user programming. The rapid development of compact and easily maintained applications will encourage a transition to this new technology.

kbProlog is a representation language designed to support KBMSs. KBMS1 is a prototype system which consists of an interpreter for kbProlog and a tight-coupling with persistent store. Novel software architectures for knowledge management can be built in KBMS1, and one such has been described.

A logic-programming-based KBMS has a number of implications for the use of parallel hardware. In particular, the emphasis changes from the support of a language to the support of a respository. The role of kbProlog's theories is central to use of such hardware.

13.7 ACKNOWLEDGEMENTS

KBMS1 is a system that has evolved through the contributions of several people. Damian Black, Alasdair Cox, Keith Harrison, Mark Syrett and Dave Wells have all been responsible for its design and implementation.

REFERENCES

Black, D. S. and Manley, J. C. (1987) A Logic-based Architecture for Knowledge Management, *Proc 10th Int Joint Conf on Artificial Intelligence,* Milano, p87.

Bowen, K. A. (1985) Meta-level Programming and Knowledge Representation, *New Generation Computing,* **3**, 359.

Brodie, M. L. and Mylopoulos J. (1986) *On Knowledge Base Management Systems*, Springer-Verlag.

Brown, A. S., Hirata, T. M., Koehler, A. M., Vishwanath, K., Ng, J., Pechulis, M .J., Sikes, M. A., Singleton, D. E. and Veasey, J. E. (1986) Data Base Management for H P Precision Architecture Computers , *Hewlett-Packard Journal,* **37** (12), 33.

Harrison, K. A. GAP: An Exercise in Model-Oriented Programming, *Proc 1990 Ann Conf UK Assoc for Logic Programming.*

Lavington, S. H. (1988) Technical Overview of the Intelligent File Store, *Knowledge-based Systems,* **1**(3), 166.

Manley J. C. (1989) kbProlog: A Language for Knowledge Management, *Proc SERC/IED Workshop on Handling Large Knowledge Bases Declaratively,* University of Essex.

Schmidt, J. W. and Thanos, C. (1989) *Foundations of Knowledge Base Management*, Springer-Verlag.

Ullman, J. D. (1988) *Principles of Database and Knowledge-Base Systems,* Volume 1, Computer Science Press.

Ullman, J. D. (1989) *Principles of Database and Knowledge-Base Systems,* Volume 2, Computer Science Press.

14 A parallel platform for a KBMS

M. Freeston
European Computer-Industry Research Centre, FRG

14.1 INTRODUCTION

The European Computer-Industry Research Centre is a joint research organization founded in 1984 on the initiative of three major European manufacturers: Bull, ICL and Siemens. Its activities are intended to enhance the future competitive ability of the European Information Technology industry and thus complement the work of national and international bodies.

The Centre is intended to be the breeding ground for those ideas, techniques and products which are essential for the future use of electronic information processing. The work of the Centre focuses on advanced information processing technology for the next generation of computers. There are approximately 60 researchers, currently drawn from 21 countries around the world, but predominantly from Germany, France and Britain. The activities of the centre are divided into four research groups: computer architecture, logic programming, human-computer interaction and knowledge bases. These groups reflect the original conception of the overall objective of the centre: to develop a complete decision support system – from user interface down to hardware – based on logic programming.

Although the ensuing studies have generated many promising new avenues of research, and initial ideas have naturally been modified greatly as progress has been made, the original conception remains as a cohering theme between the groups within the centre. Indeed it seems that we may be only now really beginning to reap the benefits of focusing our efforts on a central theme. The problems of developing and assembling all the elements of a new technology, from hardware to user interface, were daunting. But fortunately a policy was adopted of letting these elements develop naturally, rather than trying to force them into an artificial cohesion. Consequently, whatever has been lost in administrative convenience has undoubtedly been gained many times over in creativity. And now the overall conception is more clearly seen, the detail is better appreciated, and the disparate elements are coming together.

14.2 THE INITIAL CONCEPTION

At the beginning, there were fundamental uncertainties about the very nature of the hardware and software required for a decision support system. It was always appreciated that, however clever a system may be at making decisions, it cannot do so without unimpeded access to the facts on which any decision must be based. This led – as with the rest of the research community in this field – to the notion that the way forward lay in a connection or coupling between an 'expert system' and a database management system. The obvious attraction of this model was that both elements of the connection already existed: the DBMS had been refined for twenty years, and logic programming had been recognized as a powerful, though not yet fully developed, tool for building expert systems. Our efforts should therefore be concentrated on the expert system component: using an existing logic-programming language – Prolog – as the basis, we should build parallel processing hardware to make Prolog programs go faster, and see what kinds of reasoning could be supported by a (possibly modified) Prolog program connected to a DBMS.

But cracks in this conception began to appear. Prolog has been its own worst enemy in this, since Prolog programmers refer to their programs as databases. But Prolog programs are not, of course, databases, in the sense that any user of a database management system would recognize, for three obvious reasons: the components of the program are not persistent, not individually updatable, and cannot be shared concurrently between several users. On the other hand, whereas DBMSs contain only extensional data Prolog programs contain intensional data in the form of deduction rules. And yet the whole idea of many expert systems – and certainly any decision support system – depends on the dynamic acquisition and update of knowledge: deduction rules as well as facts. It may well be necessary also to obtain this knowledge from several concurrently contributing sources, and to check that the contributions are consistent.

It has often been argued that it doesn't matter if the intensional component of the knowledge lies only in the main-memory program, rather that in the supporting DBMS, on the basis of the space occupied: because the number of deduction rules will be far less than the number of facts, main-memory overflow is unlikely, especially since memory is getting so cheap that every thing, including the whole DBMS, will soon be the main-memory anyway. This argument completely misses the point. It is not a question of whether there will be enough main-memory for the rules.

It is a question of how to control both rules and facts by the same mechanisms within the environment of a DBMS. Whether and how a DBMS should be modified if it becomes main-memory resident is a quite separate issue. Why then are Prolog programs so insistently described as 'databases'? Because in Prolog there is no distinction between program and data: rules and facts are treated exactly alike.

14.3 TOWARDS A TRUE KNOWLEDGE BASE MANAGEMENT SYSTEM

Suddenly when we assemble these thoughts, we see before us the prospect of reaching the Holy Grail of Computer Science (well, one of them!): if we could somehow store and retrieve the rules in a DBMS exactly in the same way as the data, then we could execute a Prolog program which was entirely resident on permanent storage. If this were disk storage, then the program might run very slowly. But nevertheless we would have created a true persistent programming environment which would be entirely transparent to the programmer; the program would contain no additional code for transferring permanent data between the program and the database; and a program modified itself – either rules or data – would remain modified if halted and reloaded. The 'impedance mismatch' between database environment and host programming environment would disappear completely.

This would not be the first attempt to create a persistent programming environment. But it would be unique in a number of respects. It would be the first persistent logic-programming environment, and a true Knowledge Base Management System (KBMS). For purely declarative procedures at least, the granularity of persistence would be the individual Prolog clause (rule or fact), rather than the whole procedure or module. The notion of program transformation – either by itself or by another program – offers possibilities from dynamic query optimizers to advance CASE tools. In the latter case, there could be complete integration within the KBMS of data dictionary, source and object code control systems, the programs themselves, and integrity constraint checking.

But would it work? Surely such a program would run desperately slowly if it were stored entirely on disk? Here we note two points that are so obvious that they are often overlooked. First, every program that is stored on disk must be loaded into main memory before it can be run. Second, all database programs retrieve their (extentional) data from disk, and sometimes have to wait for it. Therefore any procedural module which is stored in the persistent store, but which never accesses it while executing, will run as fast as any other program in the main memory, provided that the module can be stored in compiled form in the KBMS. If, on the other hand, the execution of a clause in main memory prompts an access to an individual clause in the persistent store, there is no reason why it should take longer than any conventional database access, if equivalent access methods and indexes are provided. In fact, there are two good reasons why it could be much faster than a conventional.

In conventional DBMSs the overhead in transforming data between the external database representation (i.e. fixed-structure tuples) and the internal representation of the programming language can be considerable - so much so, that it can dominate the computation. The same is true for the assertion of new facts in Prolog. If however the clauses could be stored in relocatable compiled form in the KBMS, both overheads would be avoided.

A second, but in some cases even more significant reason, is that the ability to represent and transfer data in its intensional form can greatly reduce knowledge base accesses and associated disk traffic, relative to the equivalent, purely extensional representation. For example, it is easy to find circumstances where a single rule can replace tens or even hundreds of facts. This becomes potentially even more important when considering the overheads of inter-processor communication in parallel processor configurations.

14.4 THE MEGALOG SYSTEM

Of course, the simplicity of the conception belies the difficulties of its implementation. In practice it has proved necessary to begin again absolutely from scratch to realize such a system. But we have now succeeded. The **MegaLog** system is the result of five years' research and development within the Knowledge Bases Group at ECRC. MegaLog provides a persistent logic programming environment, and the basis for a true Knowledge Base Management System, along the lines described above. It is described as a platform for a KBMS, rather than a KBMS itself, because it provides a firm foundation with which to experiment in a new technology, but it leaves many choices open for systems built above it – even a choice of computational paradigm.

It is not our intention to give a detailed description of MegaLog here. We give only references [2, 3, 4, 5, 6, 7, 8, 9, 10, 11, 13, 14, 15]. We want to emphasize here its main features, in relation to the way in which its execution engine can be parallelized. The MegaLog system is based on an abstract machine which contains three major components:

1. An inference engine based on a derivative of the Warren Abstract Machine (WAM);
2. A relational engine built over a BANG file management system;
3. A main memory management subsystem providing full support for dynamic allocation of memory on demand, extensible and performing full garbage collection.

The host programming language extends a full implementation of Prolog with a set of relational operators. The provision of full garbage collection is believed to be unique among Prolog systems, despite the fact that it is an essential prerequisite for the support of a continuously operating DBMS. The familiar concept of the relation is extended to that of the 'deductive relation' which, in general, contains both facts and rules. A special indexing mechanism, based on the BANG file, is used to access facts and rules alike, taking into account uninstantiated as well as instantiated terms in the generation of index keys from the clause heads. The indexing mechanism thus acts as a pre-unification filter. Relocatable compiled code (WAM code) is associated with the heads of the stored rules.

If the operands of the relational operators are fully extensional relations, then the result of the operation will also be an extensional relation. MegaLog thus subsumes conventional relational systems – an important advantage by providing upwards compatibility with current database technology. But if the operands are fully or partly intensional predicates i.e. deductive relations, then the result of a relational operation may also be represented as a deductive relation. In particular, joins on deductive relations can be much smaller and hence much faster than on their fully extensional equivalents, since a single rule may replace a large number of equivalent facts. Such a transformation does not always result in a predicate which is easier to materialize, but the average overall effect of such a representation is to reduce computation and to reduce communication overhead.

It is important also to emphasize that, although Prolog has been chosen as the logic programming element in MegaLog, this is not an inevitable choice of the technology. The essential element is the computational paradigm based on clause head matching – i.e. unification. It is this which makes such a complete integration of programming language and database system possible.

14.5 PARALLELIZATION OF MEGALOG

Quite separate from this development, the computer architecture group at ECRC began the PEPSys project – an in-depth study and evaluation of new ways of parallelizing the execution of logic programs. The inherent OR and AND parallelism in declarative logic languages makes them particularly attractive prospects for parallel implementations. Essentially, the objective of the project was to decide upon an abstract machine supporting a computational model which was able to take advantage of a multi-processor architecture – and overcome the concomitant difficulties. The model had to be sufficiently flexible to allow different architectural configurations, and the logic language supported – Prolog – needed to be extended to include pragmas i.e. requirements or hints from the programmer about what parts of the program could be – or might profitably be – parallelized.

Since the computational paradigm is unification, the basic problem of parallelization is how to maintain all the variable bindings, to keep track of them, and to share them between parallel processes. Detailed descriptions of the solutions adopted are given in [16, 1, 12, 17, 18, 19]. But most importantly, at least from the point of view of the present discussion, the abstract machine chosen was an extension of the WAM. The PEPSys study therefore provides a strong basis for parallelizing the MegaLog system. MegaLog's emulator for the WAM is written in C, since portability across Unix systems has been regarded from the beginning of the project as of higher priority than performance (and the emulator can always be re-written in native code for a particular machine if there is a sufficient need). So it proved very easy to port MegaLog from its original SUN3 development environment to a (single processor) node of a SEQUENT multi-processor, used as a test-bed by a team within the Computer Architecture Group. The current objective of the team is now to apply the techniques developed in the PEPSys project to the full unification parallelization of the MegaLog architecture.

14.6 CONCLUSION

We have provided here only the briefest sketch of a major research effort. But the bibliography gives a fairly complete list of available papers relating directly to the development of MegaLog, and to the PEPSys project, and these references will lead the interested reader back through the relevant research literature in the field.

The successful integration of logic programming and database technology which MegaLog represents shows great promise for the future.

We believe that it provides a firm foundation for supporting deductive – and also object-oriented – database systems with a paradigm which is ideally suited to parallelization.

14.7 ACKNOWLEDGEMENTS

The work described in this paper represents the efforts of many people over the last six years. Although not exhaustive, the bibliography cites many of those who are or who have been actively involved, and gives an indication of the particular area of their own contributions. On this occasion it has been the task of the present author simply to recount their efforts, and record a little of their considerable achievements.

REFERENCES

1. Baron, U., Ing, B., Ratcliffe, M. and Robert, P. A. (1987) Distributed Architecture for the PEPSys Parallel Logic Programming System. In *Technical Report 25, ECRC.*
2. Bocca, J. (1986) On the Evaluation Strategy of EDUCE. In Zaniolo, C. (editor), *Proc. 1986 ACM-SIGMOD International Conf. on Management of Data.* ACM, Washington, DC, USA.
3. Bocca, J. (1986) EDUCE - A Marriage of Convenience: Prolog and a Relational DBMS. In Keller, R. (editor), *Proc. '86SLP Third IEEE Symposiumon Logic Programming.* IEEE, Salt Lake City, Utah, USA.
4. Bocca, J., Decker, H., Nicolas, J-M., Vieille, L. and Wallace, M. (1986) Some steps towards a DBMS. In Kugler, H-J. (editor), *Proc. 10th World Computer Congress.* IFIP, Dublin, Ireland.
5. Bocca, J. and Bailey, P. (1987) Logic Languages and Relational DBMSs - The point of convergence. In Atkinson, M., Buneman, P. and Morrison, M. (editor), *Proc. Appin II Workshop on Persistent Object Stores,* pages 346–362. Computing Sc. Department - Glasgow University, UK.
6. Bocca, J. and Pearson, P. (1987) On Prolog-DBMS Connections: A Step Forward from EDUCE. In P. Gray and R. Lucas (editor), *Proc. Workshop on Prolog and Data Bases.* Coventry, England.
7. Bocca, J., Dahmen, M., Freeston, M., Macartney, G. and Pearson, P. (1989) KB-PROLOG, A Prolog for Very Large Knowledge Bases. In *Proceedings of the Seventh British National Conference on Databases* (BNCOD-7). Edinburgh, UK.

8. Bocca, J. (1989) EDUCE* - A logic programming system for implementing KBMS's. In *Proceedings of the Seventh British National Conference on Databases* (BNCOD-7). Edinburgh, UK.

9. Bocca, J., Dahmen, M., Macartney, G. and Pearson, P. (1989) KB-Prolog User Manual. *Technical Report KB-31,* ECRC.

10. Bocca, J. (1990) Compilation of Logic Programs to Implement Very Large Knowledge Base Systems - A Case Study : Educe*. In *Proceedings of the Sixth International Conference on Data Engineering*. IEEE, Los Angeles, California, USA.

11. Bocca, J. and Freeston, M. (1990) Aspects of Knowledge Base Management System Research at ECRC. In *Proceedings of the UK IT 1990 Conference*. IEE, University of Southampton, UK.

12. Chassin, J., Westphal, H. and Peterson, D. (1987) The Implementation of PEPSys on a MX-500 Multiprocessor. In Internal Report. ECRC.

13. Freeston, M. (1987) The BANG File: A New Kind of Grid File. In Dayal, U. and Traiger, I. (editors), *Proc. 1987 ACM-SIGMODInternational Conf. on Management of Data*. ACM. San Francisco, USA.

14. Freeston, M. (1989) Advances in the design of the BANG file. In Litwin, W. and Scheck H.-J. (editors), *Third Int. Conf. on Foundations of Data Organisation and Algorithms*. Paris, France.

15. Freeston, M. (1989) A Well-Behaved File Structure for the Storage of Spatial Objects. In Buchman, A., Guenther, O., Smith, T.R., Wang, Y.-F. (editors), *Symposium on the Design and Implementation of Large Spatial Databases*. Santa Barbara, California, USA.

16. Hailperin, M. and Westphal, H. A. (1986) Computational Model for PEPSys. In *Technical Report CA-16*. ECRC.

17. Ratcliffe, M. and Syre, J.-C. (1987) The PEPSys Parallel Logic Programming Language. In *Proc. 10th IJCAI*. Milan, Italy.

18. Robert, P. (1987) An Emulator for the PEPSys Abstract Machine. In Internal Report PEPSys 17. ECRC.

19. Westphal, H., Robert, P., Chassin, J. and Syre, J.-C. (1987) The PEPSys Model: Combining Backtracking, AND- and OR-parallelism. In *Proc. 1987 Symposium on Logic Programming*. San Francisco, USA.

15 Intelligent decision support using on-line databases

T. C. Fogarty, J. G. Gammack, S. A. Battle and R. G. Miles
The Transputer Centre, Bristol Polytechnic, UK

15.1 INTRODUCTION

The research outlined in this paper is being undertaken as part of the IDIOMS project. First an overview of the IDIOMS project as a whole is given to put the ideas advanced in a practical context. Constraint networks are proposed as a flexible representation of knowledge that can be implemented on parallel computer systems. How constraint networks are related to data classification is described. The genetic algorithm is proposed as a suitable machine learning algorithm in this domain that can also be implemented on parallel computer systems. How the genetic algorithm can be used to generate constraint networks is outlined. Finally the relationship between constraint-based representations of knowledge and rule-based decision support systems is described.

15.2 OVERVIEW OF THE PROJECT AS A WHOLE

IDIOMS is a collaborative project involving The National Transputer Support Centre at Sheffield University, Artificial Intelligence Limited, The Transputer Centre at Bristol Polytechnic and The Trustee Savings Bank (Retail). IDIOMS stands for "Intelligent Decision making in On-line Management Systems". It is partially funded over a period of two years by the Department of Trade and Industry under the Information Engineering Advanced Technology Programme. Broadly the aims of this programme are to investigate the use of novel architecture concepts, to develop techniques and tools to implement these technologies and to exploit them in a cost effective manner.

Many organizations in industry and business build and use large volumes of data. The manipulation of this data is paramount in their operation and further, this data must be kept up to date. To increase profitability these organizations need to improve their systems and to extract management information from the data. Previously it has not been possible to run on-line transaction processing and management information systems at the same time due to insufficient processor resource. Using large parallel systems it now seems possible to achieve this goal.

The aims of the project are to research and demonstrate the following:

- an SQL database engine which will efficiently provide for both on-line transaction processing and the answering of database queries at low cost;
- a machine learning tool which is flexible and adaptive and which will demonstrate the use of machine learning in management decision support;
- a multi-user version of Strand88 and a parallel interface from Strand88 to SQL so as to act as an interface between the machine learning tool and the database engine;
- the application of the machine learning tool to three areas of Trustee Savings Bank (Retail) activity so as to build concept demonstrators that show the functionality of the system.

The National Transputer Support Centre at Sheffield Unversity is undertaking to research and develop the SQL database engine. Artificial Intelligence Limited is to build the multi-user version of Strand88 and to build a parallel interface to SQL. The research and building of the machine learning tool is being undertaken by The Transputer Centre at Bristol Polytechnic. The three concept demonstrators are being built by The Transputer Centre in conjunction with The Trustee Savings Bank (Retail).

15.3 CONSTRAINT NETWORKS FOR DATA CLASSIFICATION

All Artificial Intelligence systems require their data to be pre-classified in some way. Many require all relevant data be presented to them and they are sometimes even incapable of handling irrelevant data. From earlier work we believe that most of the knowledge of an expert is classification knowledge. There is a familiar feeling when solving problems that on finding the correct way of looking at a problem then the answer easily follows. One aspect of classification that we have therefore decided to investigate is the partitioning of variables into small sets of non-overlapping sub-classes of values. We do this within the context of trying to discover the relationships between a set of variables within a database containing sample data. Once a classification scheme has been learned, we build a probabilistic model of the database in terms of the conditional probabilities exisiting between the new sub-classes. The classification scheme should be optimal with respect to this model.

The conditional probabilities between the variables can be seen as constraints that allow us to infer the probability distribution of the sub-classes of one variable from another. They form a network over the variables that allows the inference process to be designed as a distributed system. Each node in the network maintains and distributes the probabilities for each sub-class of a single variable and updates them in accordance with information received from its neighbours. If the nodes are to communicate sensibly they must also share a common language; that is, they must share a common classification scheme. We will investigate the trade-offs between imposing a global classification scheme, and allowing nodes to employ local schemes that improve predictive accuracy.

15.4 OPTIMIZING CONSTRAINT NETWORKS WITH THE GENETIC ALGORITHM

The genetic algorithm can be used to learn rule-bases [Fogarty, 1989] but an approach which is more akin to human learning is to use the genetic algorithm to find a good neural network for a task. This is inherently a noisy process and therefore suitable for the genetic algorithm. The main problem here is defining high-level abstract parameters to specify the space of possible networks for a particular task.

Constraint networks to represent relationships between variables in a database can be specified by categorizations of the variables, the structure of the networks and the weighting of the links is then just a matter of database look-up. The value or cost of each of such networks will depend upon a number of factors.

Gammack, Battle and Stevens [1989] showed how expert knowledge of a domain can be represented in a constraint matrix which could then be implemented as a constraint network on a multi-processor system to give a flexible inferencing tool.

If the results of expert decisions reside in a database then, rather than asking the expert to provide the information necessary to build a constraint matrix, this can be generated from the raw data. If the database is very large, storing the results of the decisions of many experts, then the job of generating a constraint network is a monumental task. The genetic algorithm can be used for this purpose. What it searches for is a good categorization of each of the variables. This is done by generating categorizations for all of the variables which are used with the database to construct constraint networks. These are evaluated along a number of dimensions to give a cost for each network.

The genetic algorithm [Holland, 1975] usually takes as its raw material strings of binary digits. The space of possible solutions to the problem at hand is generally expressed as all possible bit strings of a given length. There must be a method for assigning to each possible solution a cost or value which is the sole measure of its worth, though this may vary.

The algorithm generally proceeds as follows: a number of strings of bits, depending upon the length of the string and computing facilities available, are randomly generated. These are evaluated and each is assigned a probability of being selected based on its relative value. New strings are then generated by selecting pairs of old ones and recombining them using the genetic operators of crossover and mutation. The resulting strings are then evaluated and replace old members of the population so that over a large number of evaluations the population of strings converges to a solution. Crossover copies parts of either of two strings to make up a new one while mutation randomly flips one of the bits in a string with a low probability.

The genetic algorithm proceeds at a graceful pace, that is why it is so tolerant to noise, but can be speeded up when implemented on parallel or distributed processing systems. This is especially important on large problems requiring long bit strings, and thus a large population, each member of which takes a long time to evaluate. Evaluations can proceed in parallel and the population can be distributed over a number of processors.

15.5 CONSTRAINT NETWORKS AND RULE-BASED SYSTEMS

We take the position that information relevant to answering multifarious questions is implicit in the database as relations between simple entities. However, the particular relationships relevant to answering a question are dynamically determined through construction of the search strategy. A facility to allow natural querying of the database through informed construction of rule-based search strategies will be provided. Information from the data itself will be suggested to the user to aid in production of specific search strategies, so that an expert knowledge of SQL or the like is not required.

The constraints implicit in the database can be represented as rules for the purpose of indicating trends, biases and patterns in the data, in a manner that may be understood naturally. For instance, if nobody is buying a particular product, or if there is a decline in a particular type of consumer, this pattern can be detected and conveyed as a quasi-English rule, giving a snapshot of the database with respect to a given concern.

This property of generating an up-to-date rule-base description of the information on the market, avoids two major problems. Firstly it avoids the obsolesence of any ‘snapshot’ rule-base built at a given time, and secondly it avoids the emergence of rules from empirical rather than theoretical grounds. Expert systems which derive from a session with a domain expert are based on the state of play at that time, and in any dynamic field are likely to become increasingly irrelevant. In addition, standard knowledge acquisition techniques force experts to express elements of what they know about a domain into rules, which are often unforgiving in the thresholds they set. Augmenting these with probabilistic information estimates is fraught with problems, since firstly, experts cannot reliably judge the numeric values, and secondly, slight errors propagate along inference chains often rendering a final value meaningless. Rules, whether fuzzy or not, suffer from the problem of essentially being a high-level summary of a number of empirical observations, and those empirical data are the underlying description of the real domain. If there are changes in the world, such as new products being introduced, the balance among those empirical observations will shift, and new rules summarizing the trend will be required. To be of use to a manager making strategic deci- sions, the support system must be sensitive to this aspect.

We contend that rules emerge as heuristic approximations of a trend in a set of data, and that the empirical data itself should be used to set the threshold for the rule. Producing a rule-based description by requiring the database to 'explain itself' in that form allows the user at any time to see patterns in the current database, in a way which is explicable in linguistic, rather than purely statistical terms. As a management decision aid, this may be expected to provide a much more direct insight into patterns in the data, with obvious implications for strategic decision making.

15.6 CONCLUSION

The paper has outlined a novel approach to building intelligent decision support systems on top of databases. This approach uses the genetic algorithm to construct a network of constraints reflecting relationships between variables in a database. Rule-based systems can be supported by the constraint network representation of relationships in the data and also allow the user to impose structure from above. The techniques of genetic algorithms and constraint propogation are robust but, computationally, very expensive. However, they are natural candidates for parallel implementations. In order to be used with on-line database systems they rely upon the speed-up offered by parallel machines.

REFERENCES

Fogarty, T. C., (1989) Learning New Rules and Adapting Old Ones with the Genetic Algorithm, in the proceedings of AIENG-89: Applications of Artificial Intelligence in Engineering, Cambridge, July 1989, published as *Artificial Intelligence in Manufacturing* edited by G. Rzevski, Springer-Verlag, pp 275–290.

Gammack, J. G., Battle, S. A. and Stephens, R. A., (1989) A knowledge acquisition and representation scheme for constraint based and parallel systems, *1989 IEEE Conference on Systems Man and Cybernetics,* Cambridge, Massachusetts, November, 1989.

Holland, J. H, (1975) *Adaptation in Natural and Artificial Systems.*

Part Six

Parallel data processing

16 Issues in parallelizing object oriented database systems

D. DeGroot, E. Meyer, D. Wells
Computer Science Centre, Texas Instruments

16.1 OODB INTERFACE AND FUNCTIONALITY

There is not a uniform definition of either the functionality or interface desired from an OODB [Joseph *et al.*, 1990]. This is a direct result of the fact the OODB technology has evolved from three distinct disciplines: object-oriented programming, databases and logic programming. The domain of object-oriented programming brings notions of encapsulation, object identity, inheritance, and strong typing. Databases bring persistence, transaction atomicity, controlled sharing, recoverability, and query capabilities. Logic programming brings semantic modelling constructs, memorization, and techniques for lazily evaluating requests. The ability to evolve type definitions and techniques for long and co-operative transactions seems to be an issue only in OODBs. Fig.16.1 illustrates the contributions of the various capabilities.

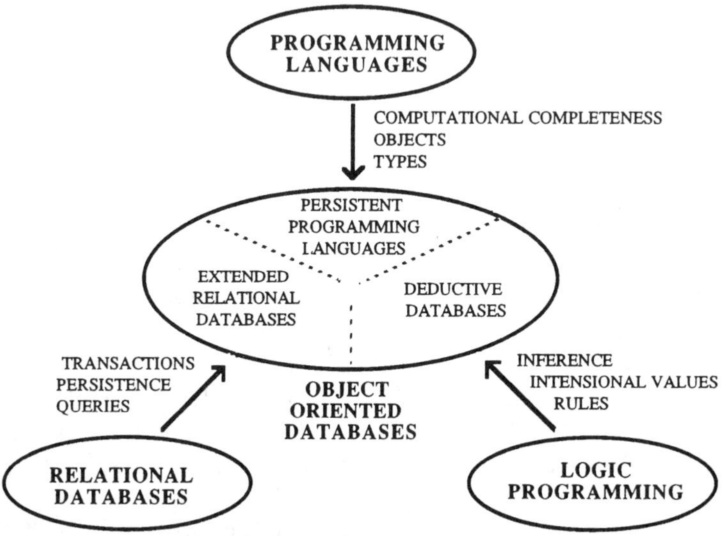

Figure 16.1 Three disciplines contribute to OODB technology.

Since OODBs are growing from three distinct ancestries, there is no standard definition of the required funtionality and interface. While there is agreement on what minimal properties any OODB must exhibit there is no agreement on how these capabilities will be achieved, how they will be presented to applications, or which should dominate. As such, existing OODB implementations tend to reflect the origins of their developers. OODBs arising from object-oriented programming tend to emphasize accessing the database by following embedded inter-object references, whereas relational database extentions consider accesses to be based on SQL-like queries, for example, with the queries themselves perhaps embedded within objects.

Programming language based OODBs generally allow an object's methods to be written in a computationally complete language; relational database languages do not, due to both their need to optimize query plans and to the current infeasibility of doing this in the presence of arbitrary (anything other than relational algebra) functions. Logic-based OODBs allow an application to specify that query results should be generated lazily (and to short-circuit a query if it does not need to see any more results), since logic programming expert systems often ask a query to determine if a constraint is met, not to determine all objects satisfying the query are needed. These two assumptions of how query results will be used result in radically different query plans and performance characteristics (each appropriate to the underlying assumptions). Programming language based OODBs are much more concerned about maintaining a seamless interface to a language than are RDB extentions, and generally do a better job of it. The list of differences between OODBs with different origins is of course much longer than this, but the above examples illustrate the basic problem – there are simply many ways in which what appears to be the same capability can actually be defined and presented.

Ultimately, OODBs will converge to providing functionality in the union of the currently implemented and proposed systems. Thus it is necessary to consider this entire set. However, we believe that there are some fundamental differences in emphasis between the three approaches that will lead to future OODBs being biased toward one paradigm or the other, at least in terms of performance.

There are a great many opportunities within an OODB for exploiting parallelism to improve performance, especially within deductive or computational OODBs, where both extensional and intensional objects are manipulated. In addition, there are many techniques such as improved access methods, caching, clustering, and prefetching that are applicable to both sequential and parallel environment. We define the following levels of an OODB application at which to consider performance improvements:

1. the OODB management system (the OODBMS);
2. the stored objects;
3. the query engine;
4. the application code.

16.2 PARALLELISM WITHIN THE OODB MANAGEMENT SYSTEM

The OODB management system (OODBMS)[1] consists of the modules that support and maintain database objects. The modules in the OODBMS are more likely to resemble 'hard core' systems code rather than application code; they are likely to exhibit a great many side effects; and they are likely to exhibit complex control flows. Consequently, their internal parallelization will likely prove difficult. However, the overall OODBMS can be parallelizable as a collection of loosely-coupled tasks corresponding to the individual modules.

It is at the OODBMS level that techniques from relational data bases are most applicable. These may be categorised in three general areas: storage techniques for value-based retrieval (SELECTION), special processors for activities such as locking and better backup and recovery techniques. Selection may be based on any attribute, and as such, indices are often maintained on non-key attributes. To avoid one disk access per tuple identified by the index, a list is often generated of tuples to be selected and this list is ordered to minimize I/O. A drawback to indexing is the non-trivial cost of maintaining them when tuples are added or updated. Also, if a selection predicate involves more than one attribute, either multiple indices must be used, or composite indices over combinations of attributes must be maintained. The latter is more efficient for selection, but since the number of such indices possible for an n-attribute relation is 2^n, choosing the right attribute combinations to index is non-trivial. Another approach to selection is the use of 'associates memory' [Nakano], in which it is possible to ask all memory locations whose contents meet some criteria to identify themselves. These locations can then be read. The advantage of this approach is that no indices need to be maintained. However, associates memory is expensive and in general volatile. A notion similar to associative memory has been to create associates disks, in which a processor able to determine which tuples meet a criteria is placed on the disk channel (e.g., CASSM and RAP [Lipovski, 1978, Ozkarahan and Sevcik, 1977]. In such schemes, indices are used to determine which tracks to scan, and then all

---

1 We also refer to the OODBMS as the persistent language for convenience

tuples on those tracks are examined by the channel processors. Multiple head disks with a processor per track allow an entire cylinder to be filtered in one revolution. Various levels of sophistication have been proposed for the channel processors, from simple comparisons up through regular expression recognizers. Special hardware for functions such as concurrency control did not have a high payback in relational databases, since these tasks were not bottlenecks. However, the issue may be worth revisiting in OODBs.

Certain components of OODBMS may prove to constitute significant bottlenecks. In this event, these components must be parallelized. However, to guarantee a given level of predictable performance on primitive tasks necessary to support time-constrained transactions, this parallelism will almost certainly be static rather than dynamic, and will probably be highly tuned and 'hand tweaked' to achieve every last bit of parallelism and performance. Unlike the other levels identified above, the OODBMS must necessarily be treated as a separate layer with respect to parallelism. Techniques such as dynamic load balancing, throttling of parallelism, and data table migration will prove both unnecessary and undesirable. Additionally the parallelization of a specific OODBMS module will (and should) prove independent of the ways in which other OODBMS modules are parallelized and from the ways parallelisms are exhibited in the OODB or application. Thus, we can consider parallelization of the OODBMS separately from the other levels in the overall OODB application.

16.3 OBJECT-LEVEL PARALLELISM IN AN OODB

The set of known objects may be resident in the long-term, persistent store, in application memory, or both. The objects are likely to be highly interconnected through pointers into large networks (graphs) of interrelated objects. Many objects will be extensional, that is, they will exist as 'real' entities in the object store – their size is known, their backing store location is known, and their attributes and components can be directly accessed by the code defining the methods that operate on the object. Other objects, however, will be intentional, or computational, objects; they must be first computed before they can be examined.

Objects, whether intentional or extensional, will contain both code and data. Some code will be encapsulated into the definitions of the methods which access the values, attributers, and component objects of an object. Other code will be collected into procedures which are responsible for computing an object, that is, for making it extensional. Both method code and intentional object code may contain both unrestricted host programming language expressions and unrestricted data manipulation language expressions, query engine expressions, and query procedure invocations. All of these constitute candidates for exploiting parallelism; the challenge is to find techniques for doing so that are applicable to all types of expressions and across expressions.

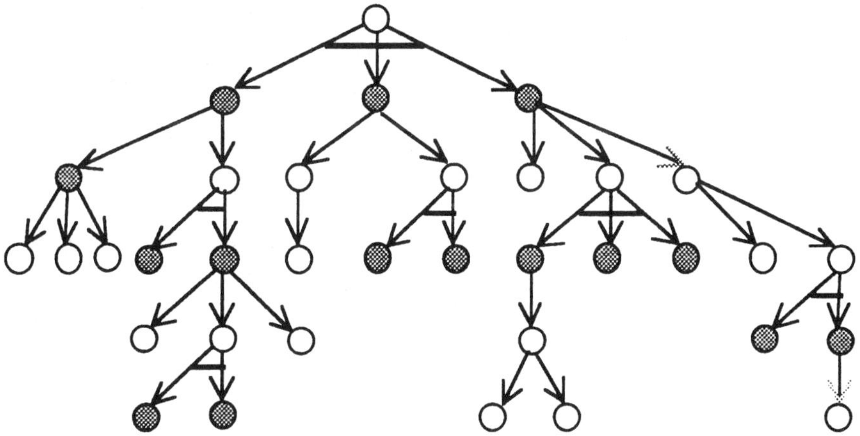

Figure 16.2 Method execution tree considered as layers of and-nodes and or-nodes

The execution of a method involves a combination of data manipulation statements and invocations or other methods. The data manipulation instructions are performed by the method itself; the submethods can be invoked as independent tasks that execute their own code, possibly in parallel, or they can execute sequentially on behalf of the parent method. In any event, we can view the execution tree of a method as a collection of and-nodes and or-nodes [Conery, 1988]. And-nodes are nodes which appear in a conjunctive expression within a method, as in Lisp's and, progn, and let forms, for example [Steele, 1984]. All expressions in such a form must complete execution for the form itself to complete; such forms are called conjunctive forms, and we speak of their subexpressions as being and-expressions. Or-nodes are nodes which appear in a disjunctive expression within a method, as in Lisp's or, cond, or if forms, for example [Steele, 1984]. Only one expression in such a form is required to complete execution for the form itself to complete; such forms are called disjunctive forms, and we speak of their subexpressions as being or-expressions. A method execution tree can be considered to consist of descending layers of both and-nodes and or-nodes, as in Fig. 16.2. The and/or execution tree is traversed during the execution of the method whether the method is evaluated sequentially or in parallel. However, these trees also nicely demonstrate opportunities for task-level parallelism within the evaluation of a query, as each node in the tree may potentially execute in parallel (barring data and I/O dependence, of course). In fact, a great deal of research has focused on the parallel evaluation of and/or task trees, especially in logic databases [see Overbeek and Lusk, 1989, for example]. Unfortunately, most of the research in that area has focused on only all-solution query models (defined below), that is, they have focused on only the data retrieval aspect of databases; the other aspects reasoning about, filtering, and manipulating data – have largely been ignored.

Possibilities exist for parallel expression evaluation, parallel recursion, parallel tasking, producer-consumer parallelism (including pipelining), and low-level data manipulation parallelism, among others. Significant compiler analysis will be required for the automatic parallelization of computations within an object, for the parallel combination of sets of objects, and the like. Interprocedural parallelism can be significantly increased in logic and deductive databases through techniques of synchronizing I/O and other major side-effects within parallel, recursive, deeply nested sets of procedures [DeGroot, 1987, Muthukumar, Chang and Chiang]. Because OODBs and OODBMSs are likely to exhibit large amounts of I/O and side-effects to shared system tables, this method will likely prove useful for parallelizing them.

Because multiple query parts and multiple methods may be in execution simultaneously, the parallel execution of one may interfere with the parallel execution of another. Thus it is necessary to consider throttling and dynamic load balancing in any overall system approach to effective parallelism.

16.4 PARALLELISM IN THE QUERY ENGINE

There are three aspects to improving the performance of the query engine:

1. Parallelizing the low-level set operations such as intersection, union etc.
2. Optimizing the query execution graph to minimize the work done.
3. Parallelizing the evaluation of the query graph.

16.4.1 Parallelization of low-level set operations

This has been examined extensively in the relational database world with many special-purpose architectures devised to perform relational algebra operations such as JOIN, PROJECT, etc. ([Kitsuregawa and Tanaka, 1988], for example). Algorithms to optimize joins in distributed environments such as 'semi-joins' are of limited utility since there is no clearly analogous operations in OODBs. However, many architectural features used for these purposes seem to be applicable to the parallelization of the set operators required by OODB queries.

16.4.2 Query optimization

Ullman [1988] attempts to reduce the overall effort required to evaluate a query by rearranging the evaluation tree for the query according to a set of algebraic equalities that specify legal transformations and to a set of heuristics describing which ones are likely to be useful in a given circumstance. Issues dictating which heuristics apply are relation sizes, presence of indices or relation ordering, expected size (selectivity) of a join between two relations, etc. The basic idea is to perform first those operations that are either easy or serve to reduce the sizes of intermediate data sets. Such techniques may be applicable in OODBs, however, as pointed out by Graefeand Maier [1988], the presence of arbitrary methods whose algebraic properties are unknown, and/or about whose performance little can be said, causes discontinuities in the graph, around which optimization is not possible.

16.4.3 Parallelizing the evaluation of the query graph

This is a very promising way to improve performance. Queries to an OODB can take many forms. When a query is made to an OODB, the method invoked is responsible for returning values or objects which satisfy the meaning of the invoked method. Clearly, input parameters passed to the method delineate the meanings possible, and thus the result of the method is a function of its input parameters. The method may be defined (programmed) so that it always produces 1) the entire set of values or objects that satisfy the meaning of the method, 2) any number of values or objects, but only one per invocation, and a different one on each invocation until there exist no further valid answers, or 3) only one object that satisfies the query, even if there are others, and even on successive invocations. These are known respectively as

1. all-solutions queries
2. many-solutions queries
3. single-solution queries.

Depending on the type of query made, different amounts and types of parallelism can be exploited.

All-solution queries return the set of possible answers to a query. Given that many answers may be produced, it is possible that parallelism may be used internally within the method to produce the set, such as creating one task to produce each object within the answer set. If the set produced is large, many tasks will be created, and significant parallelism will result. Clearly, however, it is necessary to ensure that the grain size of each created task is sufficient to ensure the absence of thrashing.

An all-solution query can return the answer set in two ways: 1) all at once, or 2) one object at a time, as they are produced. With all-at-once method, the consumer of the set must wait for the producer to produce the entire set before resuming computation. With the one-at-a-time method, the answer set is streamed from the producer to the consumer; as soon as one object is produced by the product, it is delivered to the consumer. While the consumer operates on that object, the producer can work on producing the next object in the answer set. In the all-at-once method, either the producer or the consumer is active; in the one-at-a-time method, both the producer and the consumer are active. We refer parallelism resulting from the one-at-a-time method as stream parallelism or producer–consumer parallelism; such parallelism occurs independently of parallelism internal to a task, and thus may be easily exploited.

A many-solutions query is interested in examining the set of answers to the query, but only one at a time and only until a satisfactory element of the set is found. Once a satisfactory answer is found, the remaining answers are no longer of interest, whether they have been returned or not. When one answer is returned from the producer to the consumer, the producer may eagerly compute the next answer. However, unlike all-solutions queries, the producer keeps the next answer until it is demanded by the consumer. The producer only works ahead a little bit, say from one to five precomputed answers; once that number of answers have been eagerly produced, the producer goes to sleep in order to prevent wasting system resources. If the producer resumes production and answers until its reserved set of answers is one again full. Many-solution queries are parallelized much as are stream-parallel, all-solution queries. They can be considered an optimization of all-solutions queries, and a more flexible version of single-solution queries.

A single-solution query is interested in any one answer to a query, even if more exist; further, it is not at all interested in determining whether the returned answer is more or less valuable than the other possible answers. Single-solution queries are typical of 'committed-choice' logic languages [Shapiro, 1989]. Interestingly, the single-solution query method is useful for both producing a single answer to a query and for checking whether a provided object (the input parameter) is in the set of possible answers that could have been produced by an all-solutions query to the same method. Thus single-solution query methods are useful for reasoning about objects and values; consequently, they are the hallmark of efficient deductive capabilities in OODBs. Notice that in single-solution queries, the producer and consumer do not execute in parallel.

16.5 THE APPLICATION CODE

The application code may itself be parallelizable in a variety of ways. Some of these ways will be consistent with the ways in which the OODB can be parallelized and some will not. In this effort, we are interested in the parallelization of the application code only to the extent that it interacts with the parallelization of the OODB itself.

Since a query or method invocation typically invokes other queries and methods, different forms of parallelism may be used at each succeeding level. Some combinations of parallelism will be inappropriate. For example, if the top level query requires a single solution, it does not make sense to eagerly generate all solutions at a lower level. To address this issue requires a means of passing down into the OODB from the parallel application an indication of the nature of the parallelism that is occurring at the application's level; only when this is know is the effective parallelization of the OODB possible.

16.6 IMPEDIMENTS TO PARALLELISM

Unfortunately, it is not always possible to exploit parallelism in a computation. First, the computation may be inherently sequential, in which case it simply cannot be decomposed into multiple parts capable of simultaneous execution. Such situations, though undesirable, are nevertheless understandable. Unfortunately, there is another situation in which parallelism may not be possible and that is not tolerable. This occurs when a parallel computation cannot be determined to be parallel. Numerous research efforts are aimed at eradicating this problem.

Several cases for lack of parallelism in a computation can be identified. The most well-known involve various forms of data-dependences in the code [Banerjee *et al.*, 1987]. Data-dependences all involve some form of race condition between read and write operations on shared data, such as read-write, write-read, and write-write. For example, if one program statement writes a value into a data object and another reads the new value, the two statements cannot execute in parallel, for then the read might actually precede the write, and an error will have occurred. Two statements performing I/O to a common I/O device constitute another cause for lack of parallelism and forced sequentiality. Frequently, data dependences introduced into a computation by a programmer can be removed by a parallelizing compiler, but not always. Parallelizing compilers, however, are usually capable of removing I/O dependences.

The causes for failing to identify an algorithms as being parallel generally result from an inability of the compiler or programmer to prove that a given computation does not possess any I/O or data dependences. When the absence of data dependences cannot be proven, their existence must be assumed, and the code being considered must be executed sequentially just in case it does not contain such dependences. Thus the ability to parallelize a computation depends on being able to prove the absence of data-dependences.

This is fairly easy for short sequences of simple expressions. However, if any expression within such a sequence calls some other subroutine of procedure, the problem becomes greatly complicated. If this called subroutine or procedure is very simple, if the data requirements of this procedure can be accurately determined, and if it can be determined that the data accessed by the statement sequence is not dependent on the data accessed by the called procedure, then the expressions in the statement sequence can be executed in parallel. But unfortunately, making these determinations is difficult for any but the simplest of called subroutines and procedures [Polychronopolous, 1988]. If the called procedure is complex, it is unlikely that even the most sophisticated parallelizing compiler will be able to prove the absence of data dependences between the statement sequence and the called procedure; the result is that the parallelism must be limited to executing the statements preceding the procedure call in parallel, executing the procedure call, and then finally executing the statements following the procedure call in parallel – a serialization point will occur at the procedure call, and the total parallelism will have been significantly reduced.

Notice that parallelizing the statement sequence requires examining the code of the called procedure. This requirement violates incremental compilation techniques. Further, it is infeasible in OODB applications for a compiler to examine the source code defining each possible object the application program may access, due to issues of time, cost, propriety, security, 'dusty decks', etc. Consequently, parallelism within the application code is likely to be serialized across call to the OODB; similarly, as described above, parallelism with the OODB may be serialized across calls to the OODBMS.

16.7 CONCLUSION

Though there are numerous opportunities for parallelism in Object Oriented Database systems and applications, great care has to be taken to ensure that the parallelism employed is properly managed to achieve optimal performance improvements. Excessive or poorly managed parallelism can easily result in speed-down rather than speed-up of database applications!

REFERENCES

Banerjee, J., et al., (1987) Data model issues for object-oriented applications, *ACM Transactions on Office Information Systems.*

Chang, S.-E. and Chiang, Y. P. Restricted And-Parallelism Execution Model with Side-Effects, *Procs. of the North American Conference on Logic Programming,* Vol. **1**, MIT Press, pp. 350–368.

Conery, J. S. (1988) The AND/OR *Process Model for Parallel Interpretation of Logic Programs,* Kluwer Academic Publishers, Boston, MA.

DeGrout, D. (1987) Restricted And-Parallelism and Side-Effects, *Procs. of the 4th Int'l Symp. on Logic Programming,* IEEE, pp. 80–89.

Graefe, G. and Maier, D. (1988) Query optimization in object-oriented database systems: A prospectus, in *The Proc. of the Second International Workshop on Object-Oriented Database Systems,* Heidelberg, West Germany: Springer-Verlag, pp. 359–363.

Joseph, J. Thatte, S. Thompson, C. and Wells, D. (1990) "Object-oriented databases:Design and implementation," to appear in Proc. of the IEEE, 1990.

Kitsuregawa M. and Tanaka, H. (Eds.), (1988) *Database Machines and Knowledge Base Machines,* Kluwer Academic Publishers, Mass, 1988.

Lipovsky, G.J. (1987) Architectural features of CASSM: A context addressed segment sequential memory, *SIGARCH Newsletter,* **6** (3).

Overbeek, R. and Lusk, E. (Eds.), (1989) *Procs. of the 1989 North American Conference on Logic Programming,* MIT Press.

Ozkarahan, E.A. and Sevcik, K.C. (1977) Analysis of architectural features for enhancing the performance of a database machine, *ACM Trans, on Database Systems.*

Constantine Polychronopolous, (1988) "Compiler optimizations for enhancing parallelism and their impact on architecture design," *IEEE Trans. on Computers,* pp. 991–1004.

Ehud Shapiro, (1989) The Family of Concurrent Logic Programming Languages, *ACM Surveys,* **21**(3); 412–510.

Steele, G. L. Jr., (1984) *Common Lisp: The Language,* Digital Press.

Ullmanm, J. D. (1988) *Database and Knowledge-Base Systems:Vol.1,* Computer Science Press, Rockville, Maryland.

17 Object oriented databases in Polka

A. Davison
The Parlog Group, Department of Computing, Imperial College

17.1 INTRODUCTION

A language called Polka has been developed [Dav 88a] which combines object oriented programming (OOP) techniques [StBo 86] with the concurrent Logic Programming (LP) language Parlog [ClGr 87]. This allows the creation of concurrently executing logical objects, which communicate via message passing. Polka objects exhibit two forms of concurrency: external and internal concurrency. External concurrency allows many objects to execute at once, while internal concurrency permits an object to process many messages simultaneously. One of the other key properties of Polka is that both objects and Parlog predicates can be utilized in a program.

Polka will be examined by showing how a simple database server can be encoded. This will illustrate both the object oriented features of Polka, and the concurrent LP features which are used for such things as rule-based search, access control, and message manipulation. Also, an augmented database server will be defined by inheriting most of its functionality from the original database server.

One problem with internal concurrency is that the processing order of messages can be indeterminate, which can have serious consequences on the resulting behaviour of the object. Rather than force the object to execute sequentially, the answer put forward here is to define constraints between messages. This is possible in part because of a novel form of communication in Polka called suspendible message passing. The constraints will be defined using a synchronisation object which will enable the synchronization and functionality issues involved in application design to be separated. An example of this approach will be based on the readers–writers problem as applied to databases.

17.2 AN OVERVIEW OF PARLOG

Parlog differs from Prolog in three important respects: concurrent evaluation, don't-care non-determinism and its (optional) use of mode declarations to specify communication constraints on shared variables.

A Parlog clause is a Horn clause optionally augmented with a commit operator, ':', which is used to separate the right-hand side of the clause into a conjunction of guard conditions and a conjunction of body conditions:

```
r(t1, . . ., tk) ← <guard conditions> : <body conditions>
```

where t1, . . ., tk are argument terms. A clause without any <guard conditions> does not need to include a commit operator ':' between the '←' and its <body conditions>. Both the <guard conditions> and the <body conditions> are conjunctions of predicate calls. There are two types of conjunction: the parallel ',' (C1 , C2) in which the conjuncts C1 and C2 are evaluated concurrently and the sequential '&' (C1 & C2) where C2 will only be evaluated when C1 has successfully terminated. The use of the parallel conjunction allows Parlog to display and- parallelism in the execution of its goals.

During the evaluation of a call r(t1',..., tk'), all of the clauses for the predicate 'r' can be searched in parallel for a candidate clause. The above clause is a candidate clause if the head r(t1,...,tk) matches the call r(t1',..., tk') and the guard succeeds. It is a non-candidate if the match or the guard fails. If all clauses are non-candidates the call fails, otherwise one of the candidate clauses is selected and the call is reduced to the substitution instance of the body of that clause. There is no backtracking on the choice of candidate clause since we 'don't care' which candidate clause is selected. In practice, the language implementation dictates that the first one (chronologically) to be found is chosen.

The absence of backtracking in Parlog is compensated for by guard tests which guarantee that the correct clause is chosen. This idea has been more formally stated in Gregory's sufficient guards law [Greg 87], which identifies the situations under which a Parlog computation returns a solution to a query, if a solution exists. It states that Parlog predicates should be written so that guards in each clause guarantee that if a clause is selected to reduce a goal then either:

- a solution to the call can be computed using this clause, or
- no solution can be found using any other clause

The search for a candidate clause can be controlled by using either the parallel clause search operator '.' or the sequential clause search operator ';' between clauses. For instance, if a predicate is defined by the clauses:

Clause1.
Clause2;
Clause3.

Then, Clause3 will not be tried for candidacy until both Clause1 and Clause2 have been found to be non-candidate clauses. The presence of the parallel search operator allows Parlog to display or- parallelism during the search for a candidate clause.

A Parlog predicate definition may have a mode declaration associated with it, which states whether each argument is input (?) or output (^). For example, the predicate 'merge' has the mode (?, ?, ^) to merge lists 'X' and 'Y' to create list 'Z' :

```
mode merge( ?, ?, ^ ) .
merge( [ El | X ], Y, [ El | Z ] ) ←
        merge( X, Y, Z ).
merge( X, [ El | Y ], [ El | Z ] ) ←
        merge( X, Y, Z ).
merge( [ ], Y, Y ).
merge( X, [ ], X ).
```

Syntax similar to that of Dec-10 Prolog [ClMe 81] is used for program examples throughout.

The first clause places an element from the 'X' list onto the 'Z' list, while the second does a similar task for an element from the 'Y' list. The parallel search operator between these two clauses means that a non-deterministic choice will be made between them if there is a 'merge' call with elements on both 'X' and 'Y'. The third clause allows 'Y' to become the remaining part of the 'Z' list by unification since the 'X' list has terminated. Similarly, 'X' becomes the rest of the 'Z' list when the 'Y' list is exhausted.

A query for 'merge' might be :

```
← merge( [ 1, 2, 3 | X ], [ a, b, c | Y ], Z )
```

which may produce the binding :

```
Z = [ 1, a, b, 2, 3, c | _ ]
```

The anonymous variable '_' at the end of the list indicates that the list is only partially instantiated because both the 'X' and 'Y' lists are not fully bound. This will mean that the evaluation of 'merge' will deadlock and then terminate after producing the 'Z' binding shown.

Non-variable terms that appear in input argument positions in the head of a clause can only be used for input matching. If an argument of the call is not sufficiently instantiated for an input match to succeed, the attempt to use the clause suspends until some other process further instantiates the input argument of the call. For example, the first clause for 'merge' has

[El | X] in its first input argument position. Until the call has a list or partial list structure of the form [El | X] in the first argument position the first clause is suspended. If all clauses for a call are suspended, the call suspends but a candidate clause can be selected even if there are other, suspended, clauses.

More details on Parlog can be found in [Conl 89].

17.3 POLKA

Polka is an object oriented language implemented on top of Parlog, which offers all the standard object oriented programming (OOP) features such as encapsulation, information hiding, message passing, inheritance, and self communication. In addition, all the underlying properties of Parlog are retained, which allow objects to execute concurrently, to contain predicates, and to use the logical variable and unification. One important feature is the representation of message streams by logical variables which means that they are first order entities in the language. This permits them to be passed between objects as messages, or manipulated inside predicates. Another useful technique, which is used in the 'augmentedDb' class given in section 17.3.2, is to select messages from the input stream in some order other than 'first come first served'.

17.3.1 A database server

In this example, an object oriented database server is represented as a Polka class which stores its database as a hidden state variable. An instance of the class is then equivalent to a new database with its own server.

The class called 'database' given below accepts two sorts of messages:

```
new(Key, Data, Done)
```

and

```
extract(Key, Data, Done)
```

A 'new' message causes its 'Data' value to be added to the database, and 'Key' is used as a means of identifying the data in future communication. After the data has been stored, the 'Done' variable is bound by the object and this is automatically communicated back to the message sender because of unification. In this way, 'Done' is treated like a simple form of reply mechanism. If the data addition is successful, 'Done' is bound to 'done', but if data with the same key is already present, then the new data is ignored and 'Done' is bound to the term:

```
already_present(Key)
```

An 'extract' message causes the database server to remove the data with the given key value from the database. If the operation is successful, the 'Data' variable is assigned the data, and 'Done' is bound to 'done'. However, if the key entry could not been found then 'Data' is left unbound, and 'Done' is assigned the term :

```
no_such_entry(Key)
```

The object will print an error statement if it is sent any other type of message.

The definition of 'database' is :

```
database % basic database class
invisible Store state     <= [] % internal database store
clauses
        new(Key, Data, Done)            <= present(Key, Store):
                                        Done = already_present(Key);
        new(Key, Data, Done)            =>Done = done,
                                        Store becomes [d(Key, Data) | Store].
        extract(Key, Data, Done)        =>extract_data(Key, Store, Data,#Store):
                                        Done = done ;
        extract(Key, Data, Done)        =>Done = no_such_entry(Key).
code
        mode present( ?, ? ) .          % find the key in the store
        present(Key, [ d(Key, Data ) | Store ]);
        present(Key, [ D | Store ])
                present(Key, Store).
        mode extract_data(?, ?, ^,).  %extract data with specified key
        extract_data(Key, [ d( Key, Data) | Store ], Data, Store);
        extract_data(Key, [ D | Store ], Data, [ D | Store1])
                extract_data(Key, Store, Data, Store1).
end.
```

A sentence following a % is a comment, and can be ignored. 'database' has one invisible state variable called 'Store', which means that it can not be directly manipulated by the user . The invisible declaration also states that 'Store' is given an initial value of [] when a 'database' instance is invoked.

The clauses section contains four clauses which illustrate the format of a Polka clause:

<message> ⇒ <actions >

Each clause can be separated from its neighbour by either the Parlog parallel search operator '.', or the sequential search operator ';'. The '.' and the ';' are used in the same way as in Parlog, and a newly arrived message is used to select a clause by unifying with the message pattern specified in the clause's <message> part. As in Parlog, if several clauses can handle a message, then one is chosen non-deterministically. In this class, there is only one message on the left-hand side of the '⇒', but several messages from several input streams can be specified.

The <actions> part of a clause can contain guards and use the Parlog parallel conjunction ',' or the sequential conjunction '&', to separate its actions. Actions can consist of either Parlog predicates or Polka operations.

The two clauses for a 'new' message are defined first. The first clause makes a guard call to 'present' which succeeds if data with the given 'Key' value is already in 'Store'. This leads to the message being ignored and 'Done' is bound to the 'already_present' term by using the unification operator '='. If 'present' fails, then the second clause is executed, which binds 'Done' to 'done' and updates the 'Store' value. 'becomes' is a Polka operation which has the effect of making the value on the right become the new value for 'Store' after the end of the clause. This means that if 'Store' was used again in the clause it would still have its old value. The implementation of 'becomes' is not a form of destructive assignment as it might appear, but is based on argument replacement, as explained in [Dav88a].

'Store' holds data as a list of the form:

```
d(<key>, <data>)
```

This permits Parlog predicates to be utilized to search through the list and manipulate it in various ways. This is helped by Parlog's unification, which subsumes simpler forms of pattern matching.

An alternative approach is to store data as objects rather than as terms, and this is possible in Polka. However, in this example the utility of term manipulation outweighs the benefits of an object oriented view of data.

The 'present' predicate is central to the functionality of the 'new' message clauses and is locally defined in the code section in the class. The succinctness of this definition shows that a predicate is the natural way to carry out a search of the database store, but such an approach is not possible in concurrent LP-based OOP languages such as Vulcan [Kahn 87], which only permit objects to be utilized at the language level. 'present' can also be viewed as a form of access control since its success causes the message to be ignored.

The third and fourth clauses deal with an 'extract' message. The third clause calls 'extract_data' which attempts to remove the data with the 'Key' value from the store, and returns the data in 'Data' and the new store in '#Store'. The '#' annotation is a Polka operation and is another way of specifying an update and, as with 'becomes', does not take effect until the end of the clause. The use of '#' can always be replaced by a slightly longer piece of code which uses 'becomes'. Thus:

```
extract(Key, Data, Done)        ⇒extract_data(Key, Store, Data, #Store):
                                Done  =  done;
```

is the same as:

```
extract(Key, Data, Done)        ⇒extract_data(Key, Store, Data, NewStore):
                                Done  =  done ,
                                Store  becomes  NewStore;
```

The fourth clause is called if the 'Key' value can not be found in the store, and so 'Done' is bound to the 'no_such_entry' term. In effect, it is acting as an alternative to the third clause since it is only tried when the guard of that clause fails.

In addition to the clauses given here, the Polka compiler also adds default clauses when necessary, and in this example it will add a termination clause and an error handling clause. The termination clause will terminate the object when the input stream is bound to [], and the error handling clauses will report an error when the object can not understand a message. The programmer can define his own termination and error handling clause, if he wishes. The definition of the class finishes with the **end** key word.

An instance of 'database' could be created like so:

```
←database(Ins),
Ins  =  [ new(1, a1, D1), new(2, a2, D2),
          extract(1, Data1, D3),
          extract(14, Data2, D4) ,
          hello  |  _ ]
```

The argument of 'database' is its input stream which has five messages put on it. These produce the bindings:

D1 = done	D2 = done
Data1 = a1	D3 = done
Data2 unbound	D4 = no_such_entry(14)

and the printed error message:

did not understand the 'hello' message sent to 'database'

Objects are invoked and communicated with in this way so that Polka and Parlog programs can be easily combined. The important assumption made in order to do this is that the input stream 'Ins' can be treated as a partially instantiated list. Inside an object, each of the elements of this list becomes a message, and the object will suspend when it reaches the variable at the end. Once the variable is bound to further list elements, the object will resume.

The execution of an object can actually be more complicated than the explanation above would indicate, since an object can have more than one input stream, and can execute independently of input. However, these extensions will not be considered here.

This example does not exhibit much internal concurrency because of the simple nature of the 'Store' data structure. To increase the concurrency, the database server could maintain a list of smaller 'Store' lists so that searches through the separate lists could be done in parallel.

External concurrency in Polka allows objects and predicates to execute simultaneously. An example of this is the combination of a 'merge' call (as defined in section 2) with 'database':

```
←merge(FirstUser, SecondUser, Ins) , database(Ins)
```

This permits two user to use the same database, and also illustrates the utility of mixing predicates and objects in a single language.

17.3.2 An augmented database server

One of the major benefits of OOP is the way that new classes can be quickly built and tested. This is partly due to the use of inheritance which enables one class to reuse and specialize the functionality of another class. Multiple inheritance is possible in Polka but the example given here will only require single inheritance to demonstrate how the basic database server can be extended.

The augmented database server, called 'augmentedDb', will be able to accept one new message in addition to the 'new' and 'extract' messages. Also, it will change the implementation of the 'new' message, but this alteration will be invisible to the user.

The new message is:

```
replace(Key, NewData, Done)
```

Its purpose is to replace the data with the specified key value by the new data in 'NewData'. When this has been achieved, 'Done' is bound to 'done', but if the database server did not find any data then the variable is bound to:

```
new_entry(Key)
```

The 'augmentedDb' class is :

```
augmentedDb              %   augmented database class
inherits database
clauses
    replace(Key, NewData, Done)   ⇒   super :: extract(Key, OldData, Ok),
                                      extracted(Ok, Key, NewData, Done).
    new( Key, Data, Done )        ⇒   remove_others(Key, Ins, #Ins),
                                      super :: new(Key, Data, Done).
code
    mode extracted( ?, ?, ?, ^).
```

```
                    % send a 'new' message after the old data has been removed
    extracted(done, Key, NewData, Done)←
            super :: new(Key, NewData, Done) .
    extracted( no_such_entry(Key ), Key, NewData, Done)
            super :: new(Key, NewData, Ok) ,
            data(Ok) &
            Done = new_entry(Key).
    mode remove_others(?, ?, ^).
                    % remove useless 'new' messages from the input stream
    remove_others(Key, Ins, Ins)
            var(Ins) : true;
    remove_others(Key, [ new(Key, D, Done) | Ins ], Ins1)
            Done = already_present(Key),
            remove_others(Key, Ins, Ins1);
    remove_others(Key, [ Msg | Ins ], [ Msg | Ins1 ])
            remove_others(Key, Ins, Ins1).
end.
```

The most important new feature shown here is on the second line:

```
inherits database
```

This enables 'augmentedDb' to accept all the messages dealt with by 'database'.

The first clause of the class handles a 'replace' message by sending an 'extract' message to the inherited object. This is done by using a super message which has the form :

```
super :: <message>
```

'super' is a Polka keyword which denotes the first object named on the inherits line. An alternative message, which would achieve the same thing, is:

```
database :: extract(Key, OldData, Ok)
```

This is called a named message and is more useful when multiple inheritance is utilized, and several objects are inherited.

In parallel with the super message, a call is made to 'extracted' which suspends until the 'Ok' variable from the 'extract' message is bound.

The first clause of 'extracted' deals with the case when the old data has been removed and the new data must be added. This is carried out by sending a super message from inside the predicate. Such operations are not allowed in ordinary Parlog predicates, but Polka has extended their functionality so that certain OOP operations are available. The 'Done' variable in the 'new' message is unified with the fourth argument of the head of 'extracted', and in turn the same argument of the call to 'extracted' is unified with the 'Done' variable in the 'replace' message. All of these unifications mean that the 'Done' variable in the 'replace' message is the same as the one in the 'new' message, and so will only be bound when the 'new' message has completed its processing. This can be thought of as a constraint between messages, which can only be expressed in such a concise form because of the presence of logical variables in Polka.

The second clause of the 'extracted' predicate deals with the situation when the 'extract' super message has not extracted an old piece of data. This has no effect on the sending of the 'new' message but means that its 'Ok' reply variable must be treated differently. 'data' is a built in primitive which suspends until its argument is bound, and when it is combined with the '&' 'Done' is only bound after 'Ok' is bound. As in the first clause of 'extracted', the binding of 'Done' causes a binding in the 'replace' message.

The 'extracted' predicate illustrates two points: the use of super messages, and the way that logical variables can act as constraints between messages.

One drawback with 'database' is that after a 'new' message has added some data to the store, any further 'new' messages associated with the same key are ignored only after a search of the store. This will be a time-consuming activity once the database has become large, which is why the action caused by a 'new' message is redefined in 'augmentedDb'. The new clause overcomes the problem by removing as many 'new' messages as it can from the input stream before they reach the object. This is only possible because message streams are represented as logical variables and so are first order entities in the language. This means that the input stream of 'augmentedDb' can be manipulated by the 'remove_others' predicate.

Normally, all the stream and state variables for a class are explicitly defined, but a class is allowed to forgo the definition of its input stream if only a single input stream is being used. In that case, its name is 'Ins' by default, and this is why 'remove_others' uses 'Ins' as its second argument. The third argument is '#Ins', which indicates that the value output will be the new input stream after the completion of the clause.

'remove_others' manipulates the input stream by treating it as a partially instantiated list, which can be seen in the first clause when the variable at the end of the list is detected by using a 'var' test. The second clause deals with the case when a 'new' message with the same key is found. The message is discarded but its 'Done' variable is correctly bound. The third clause handles the situation when a message is not relevant, and so is passed over.

'remove_others' is a time dependent predicate because it can only search through the messages which have arrived so far. It does not prevent further 'new' messages with the same key arriving later.

The most important point about 'remove_others' is that it demonstrates the way that predicates can manipulate message streams, which is useful in this case for improving the efficiency of the augmented database server.

The other job of the second clause of 'augmentedDb' is to forward the 'new' message to 'database', since the original definition for a 'new' message can be used to add the data to the store. This shows that although the original definition has been overridden by the new one, it can still be accessed.

A call to 'augmentedDb' might be:

```
←augmentedDb(Ins),
Ins  =  [ new(1, a1, D1), new(2, a2, D2),
          replace(1, a3, D3),
          extract(2, Data1, D4)  |  _ ]
```

The messages produce the bindings:

D1	=	done	D2	=	done
D3	=	done			
Data1	=	a2	D4	=	done

17.4 MESSAGE ORDERING

The order of a sequence of messages may change three times after they are sent to an object by some other object (or user). These ordering are called:

- the arrival order,
- the selection order,
- the completion order.

The arrival order is the order in which messages finally arrive at the input stream of an object. In Polka, this order can be varied by passing streams through processes or objects which can access their messages. A simple example of this is 'merge' which removes messages from two input streams and puts them onto a new output stream. It does not alter the relative ordering of the messages from the same input stream, but it could do so quite easily.

The 'remove_others' predicate in the 'augmentedDb' class illustrates the selection order of messages, which is the order in which messages are removed from the input stream, and start to be processed.

The completion order is the order in which the processing of messages is completed. In sequential languages with no internal concurrency, the completion order is always the same as the selection order, since only one message can be processed at a time, However, internal concurrency permits the processing for several messages to be carried out at once. This makes it quite likely that the completion order will be different from the selection order.

These orderings are important because of their effect on the meaning of messages sent to an object. For instance, most users of object oriented databases would think that sending a message to add data to a database, followed by a second message to remove that data would be perfectly safe in a single user environment. This is not the case if the ordering of these two messages can change.

Many languages avoid such problems by making sure that messages sent to an object always stay in the same order in relation to one another. This has a number of serious consequence, including the removal of all internal concurrency to ensure that the selection order for messages is the same as their completion order. This seems too drastic since it means that even harmless parallelism is ruled out.

The answer is not to force messages to follow some implicit ordering, but rather to explicitly state the required orderings between messages. In fact, this approach can be seen in action in all of the previous programs. For example, it is utilized in the first clause of the 'augmentedDb' class where the 'new' message sent from inside 'extracted' is dependent on the completion of the 'extract' message. Similarly, the completion of the 'replace' message is dependent on the completion of the 'new' message.

To aid this style of programming, one further Polka construct called a suspendible message will be introduced. The important attribute of this construct is that it is used in the object which is sending the messages, rather than in the recipient object. Its main purpose is to constrain the arrival order of messages at the recipient.

Output messages in Polka have the format:

```
<output stream>  ::  <message>
```

An output stream is a variable defined as an ostream at the start of the object. The construct can also include an on part like so:

```
<output stream>  on  <variable>  ::  <message>
```

In this form, the message is known as a suspendible message, and is guaranteed not to arrive at the object at the other end of the output stream until the variable in the on part becomes bound. This is demonstrated in the 'taxi' class below, which uses an output stream called 'ToScheduler'. This output stream will be linked at invocation time to a taxi scheduler, which will use it as its input stream.

```
taxi      ToScheduler  ostream
invisible  Status state
clauses
          pick_up_customer ⇒    ToScheduler:: picking_up(Ok),
                                ToScheduler on Ok:: set_status(busy).
          :
end.
```

The clause of 'taxi' states that when a customer is picked up, a 'picking_up' message is sent to the taxi scheduler. The behaviour of the scheduler is such that the 'Ok' variable in the message will not be bound until the message has been fully processed. In that case, the use of the suspendible form for the 'set_status' message enforces a dependency between the two messages, which guarantees that the taxi scheduler will not process the 'set_status' message until the 'picking_up' message has finished. It may be that the scheduler would process the 'picking_up' message before the 'set_status' anyway, but by using this technique, the correct processing order can be guaranteed without the programmer of 'taxi' needing to know or rely on the internal dependencies of the taxi scheduler.

17.5 SEPARATING SYNCHRONIZATION AND FUNCTIONALITY

The main drawback of the approach described above is that it increases the complexity of messages. At the very least, extra arguments must be included inside messages which will signal the completion of some important event. Extra code is also required if messages need to be constrained and it is likely that such constraints will be complex in many cases. There are no absolute answers to these problems but the technique proposed below does help to simplify the user interface to an application.

A user often wants to ensure that one message has been processed to completion before another is sent to the object. This can be thought of as a synchronization problem, which is separate from the functionality offered by the application. To mirror this, the user's synchronization constraints will be encoded inside an object called a synchronization object which acts as an interface to the application object. This approach means that the user can send messages to the synchronization object without constraints, and also not be aware of the separation of synchronization and functionality.

17.5.1 The readers–writers problem

To illustrate this coding technique, a new class will be defined which permits access to a simple database class called 'db' and also deals with the readers – writers synchronization problem [Cour 71]. In the database context, this problem specifies that many readers are allowed to access a database at once, but only one writer may change it at a time, and while a writer is manipulating the database, no readers are allowed. In addition, a scheduling property can be included which states that all readers and writers must eventually access the database.

We shall assume the presence of a 'db' class which can accept two sorts of message:

```
read(R, Ok)
```

and

```
write(W, Ok)
```

The 'R' variable in the 'read' message will contain a partially instantiated term which will be used to find a value in the 'db' object . When this value is unified with 'R', bindings will be returned to the sender and at the same time 'Ok' will be bound. The 'write' message causes the contents of 'W' to be added to the database in some fashion, and when this is done 'Ok' is bound.

The synchronization class for 'db' will be called 'db_sch' and will accept messages of the form :

```
read (R)
```

and

```
write(W)
```

One of 'db_sch' jobs will be to add 'Ok' arguments to the messages it receives, so relieving the user of that task. However, its main job will be to enforce the synchronization criteria for 'db'. The definition of 'db_sch' is:

```
db_sch                    % fair scheduling carried out on the database
invisible       ToDb ostream,
                Readers state <=[], Writer state  ok
initial    db(#ToDb) .
clauses
        read(R)         =>      ToDb on Writer ::  read(R, Ok),
                                flush(Readers, Readers1),
                                Readers becomes  [Ok | Readers1].
        write(W)        =>      all_done(Readers) &
                                ToDb on Writer ::  write(W, #Writer).
code
        mode all_done( ? ).   %  wait for all the 'read' 'Ok' vars to be bound
        all_done([]) .
        all_done([ Rd | Rds ])
                data(Rd) &
                all_done(Rds).
```

```
        mode flush(?, ^).
                % remove all the bound 'read' 'Ok' vars from the readers list
        flush([], []).
        flush([ Rd | Rds ], [ Rd | Rds1 ])
                var(Rd):
                flush(Rds, Rds1);
        flush([ Rd | Rds ], Rds1)
                flush(Rds, Rds1).
end.
```

The actions that 'db_sch' carries out can more clearly be understood by considering the dependencies for each 'read' and 'write' message. A 'read' must wait until the earlier 'write' has finished, while a 'write' must wait until the earlier 'write' and all the earlier 'read's have finished. In fact, a new 'write' will only depend on one or other of these, but we test for both to simplify matters. These dependencies are encoded as the state variables 'Readers' and 'Writer' : 'Readers' contains a list of 'Ok' variables for every 'read' sent to 'db', while 'Writer' contains the 'Ok' variable for the last 'write'.

The 'ToDb' output stream is a slight misnomer since it does not actually leave 'db_sch' but instead is linked to an invocation of 'db' which is created in 'db_sch's initial section. An initial section can contain an arbitrary conjunction of Parlog and Polka commands, which will all be carried out before the object accepts any messages. This means that the user can not access the database directly but must go through 'db_sch'.

When a 'read' message is processed in 'db_sch', it gains an 'Ok' variable and is sent to 'db' as a suspendible message, which will not arrive until 'Writer' becomes bound. In addition, the new 'Ok' variable is added to the 'Readers' list. The call to 'flush' is optional and is used to remove all bound variables from the 'Readers' list, which reduces its size.

The processing of a 'write' message starts by checking that all the readers have finished. This is done by calling 'all_done' and when this is finished, a suspendible 'write' message is sent to 'db'. The 'Writer' variable, which makes it suspendible, is the 'Ok' variable from the last 'write' message, so enforcing the ordering between 'write' messages. After the clause has finished, 'Writer' is updated so that it contains the 'Ok' variable for the 'write' message just transmitted.

A typical call to 'db_sch' might be:

```
←db_sch (Ins),
Ins  =  [ write(el(1, a )),  read(el(1, Val )),write(el(2, b)) |_]
```

which binds:

Val = a

This shows how the synchronization details can be hidden from the user.

A variation of the readers–writers problem, which gives priority to readers over writers, is investigated in [Dav 88b]. To represent such a priority in 'db_sch' would mean a slight change to the second clause and one new predicate in the code section. However, 'db' would not need to be changed, which shows the benefits of separating the synchronization and functionality issues.

Similarly, the writer priority version of the readers–writers problem requires small changes to the 'read' clause of 'db_sch'.

17.6 CONCLUSION

Polka differs quite radically from languages like Vulcan [Kahn 87], which also combine concurrent LP and OOP, since Polka allows the use of objects and predicates. The benefits of having both available were seen in the simple object oriented databases encoded in Polka. The OOP features encourage abstraction, encapsulation, reuse and a simple user interface, while the concurrent LP features were utilized for rule-based search, access control, and message stream manipulation.

Some of the problems related to the arrival, selection and completion orderings of messages were discussed, along with Polka constructs such as the suspendible message which helps to alleviate the problems. A programming technique which separates the synchronization requirements of an application from its functionality is also helpful, as was demonstrated by the solution to the readers–writers problem.

REFERENCES

Clark, K. L., and Gregory, S., (1986) PARLOG: Parallel Programming in Logic, *ACM Trans. on Programming Languages and Systems,* **8** (1), pp. 1–49.

Clocksin, W. F. and Mellish, C. S., (1981) *Programming in Prolog,* Springer-Verlag, New York.

Conlon, T., (1989) *Programming in PARLOG,* Addison Wesley.

Courtois, P. J., Heymans, F., and Parnas, D. L., (1971) Concurrent Control with 'Readers' and 'Writers', *CACM,* **14**, (10), pp. 667–668.

Davison, A., (1988a) *Polka : A Parlog Object Oriented Language*, Dept. of Computing, Imperial College, London.

Davison, A., (1988b) *Separating Synchronisation and Functionality in Polka*, Dept. of Computing, Imperial College, London.

Gregory, S., (1987) *Parallel logic programming in PARLOG,* Addison Wesley.

Kahn, K. M., Tribble, D., Miller, M. S., and Bobrow, D. G., (1987) "Vulcan : Logical Concurrent Objects", In *Concurrent Prolog,* ed. Shapiro, E.Y., MIT Press.

Stefik, M., Bobrow, D. G., (1986) "Object-Oriented Programming: Themes and Variations", *The AI Magazine,* pp. 40–62.

18 Parallel processing of AI structures

S. Lavington
Department of Computer Science, University of Essex

18.1 INTRODUCTION

Data-intensive applications involving symbolic (i.e. non-numeric) information offer much scope for parallelism. This is because they depend on generic operations such as search, intersection, transitive closure, etc. – all of which are based on the comparison of one data value with many other data values. The data values are themselves part of user-defined structures (or objects, or abstract data types). An analysis of 'smart' information systems which incorporate AI-related techniques reveals that the commonly-occurring data structures include sets, graphs, networks, tables and relations. Since graphs can be represented as relations, the super-type relation is useful as a unifying conceptual framework. In many relational operations, the order in which data comparisons is carried out is not significant. This fact can be used when planning parallel evaluations.

Although there is much natural parallelism in database and knowledge base applications, the cost-effective exploitation of this parallelism is not easy. This is because conventional (von Neumann) computers, and their software, operate at a level of data granularity far finer than that implied by the above set and graph manipulations. Put another way, the primitive types found in most programming languages are not rich enough to support adequately the abstract data types desired by applications programmers. An exception is SETL [Dewar 1983]. This has the desired relational primitives, analagous to the matrix primitives in APL, but is very inefficient because of the mis-match between SETL primitives and the computational facilities offered by conventional hardware.

The mismatch between the programmer's ideal and conventional hardware support is also seen in the memory-management domain – especially the management of persistent objects. Although memory management is not a main theme of this paper, we make reference to memory management requirements when presenting our analysis of the problems to be overcome before parallelism can more easily be exploited during the manipulation of AI structures.

A new architectural approach is required. We address the central issue of data granularity. Related practical problems, familiar to all database practitioners, are how to localize searching and how to avoid the unnecessary movement of data. We tackle these problems with particular reference to Artificial Intelligence because the structural complexity of many AI applications is not readily tamed by conventional software strategies. When the volume of stored knowledge becomes significant, as in large knowledge-bases or persistent object systems, the performance of conventional computers leaves much to be desired. A call for two orders of magnitude improvement in performance in run times for AI applications is not uncommon [Lavington 1988].

In Section 18.2 we introduce the architectural concept of active memory, as a means of improving the performance of conventional computing systems. Now that the object-oriented paradigm is being applied to databases, the requirements of persistent object management are included in an analysis of the active memory's advantages. More details are given in [Lavington 1990]. In Section 18.3 we state the desired functionality of an active memory from the users' viewpoint. This leads on to a discussion in Section 18.4 of low- level procedural interfaces and information representation. For these topics, we draw on our operational experience of an existing knowledge-base server. In Section 18.5 we outline the hardware implementation of an active memory from off-the-shelf components such as transputers, showing how SIMD-parallel techniques are used to provide both associative (i.e. content-addressable) memory and the desired structure manipulations – all in the one unit. The performance of this unit is described in Section 18.6, firstly in terms of the raw speed of generic operations such as search, insert and transitive closure. Finally, a case study is given which indicates a speed-up of up to three orders of magnitude when the SIMD parallel techniques are applied to a practical management information system.

18.2 THE CONCEPT OF ACTIVE MEMORY

The programming community readily accepts the idea of add-on hardware support for certain well-defined tasks such as graphics and floating-point calculations. Such special-purpose hardware is acceptable because the cost-effectiveness is clear and because the functional interface is easy to use. We now introduce a new add-on device which we call an active memory unit. We justify this novel concept via an analysis of the shortcomings of conventional memory systems.

Fig. 18.1a shows a conventional hierarchy of memory devices, M1 (faster, volatile) and M2 (slower, non volatile). For present purposes it is not necessary to know whether this hierarchy is connected to one CPU or to several CPUs. Accordingly, we show the memory hierarchy controlled by a single box labelled Locus of Computational Control (LCC). In Fig. 18.1a data processing can only proceed if the data to be processed is within the LCC's addressing range (here M1). Thus, persistent data structures are in general moved from M2 to M1, whereupon the LCC takes (reads) fine-grain elements of the data structure in order to operate upon them. There are three points to note about the conventional computing environment represented by Fig. 18.1a:

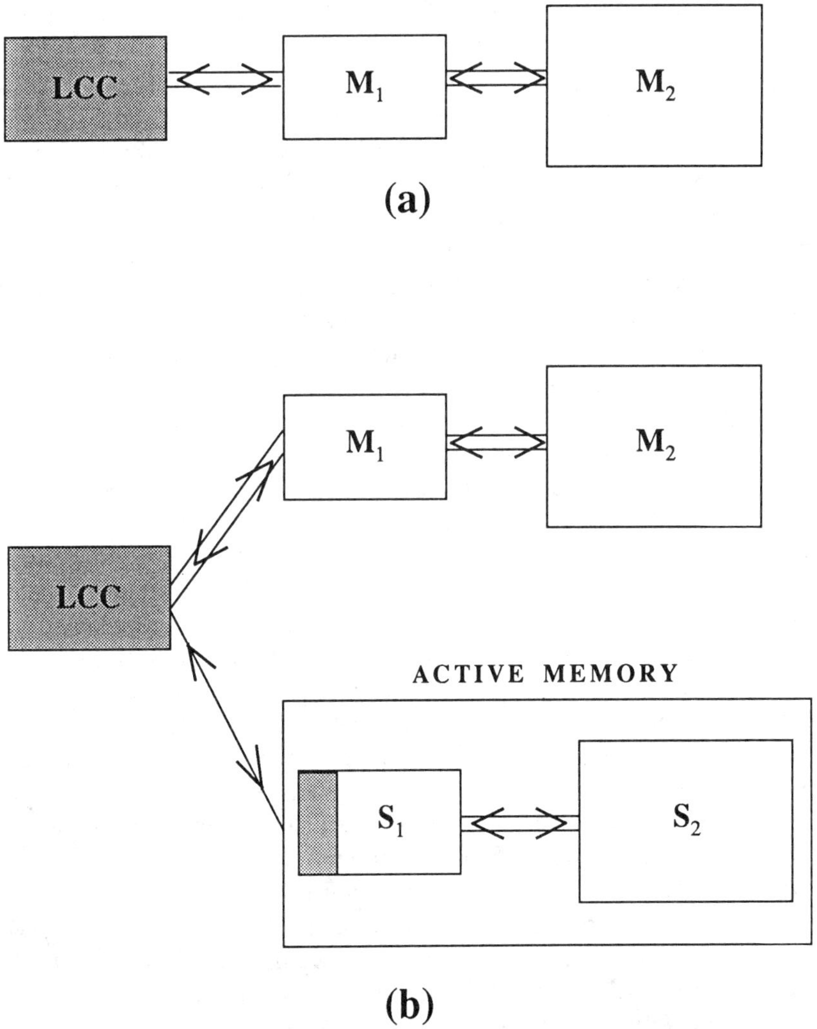

Figure 18.1 Adding active memory to a conventional computer.

i) A physical address-mapping is necessary between M1 and M2; this physical mapping does not normally reflect the logical structure of the data. Hence memory management ('paging and protection') is carried out with reference to coarse physical address boundaries.

ii) The bandwidths of both interconnecting highways has to be high, if high overall performance is to be maintained.

iii) All responsibility for the exploitation of parallelism resides within the LCC. Assuming LCC to be based on a general-purpose von Neumann computational model, responsibility for exploiting parallelism is actually moved into software (at the compiler and/or source program level) for most programming languages.

In Fig. 18.1b the system has been augmented by the addition of an autonomous unit labelled Active Memory. This may also contain a hierarchy of devices, S1 (fastest, volatile) and S2 (slowest, non-volatile), but this internal arrangement is invisible to LCC. Both S1 and S2 have limited (i.e. special-purpose) computational ability in addition to their ability to store information. Apart from explicit insert and delete commands, data is persistent within the Active Memory. This property of persistence is extended to any new data structures created as a result of operations involving existing data structures. Such action has implications for data consistency, naming conventions and version control. These are issues which are the subject of current research.

The Active Memory has a number of other unusual properties, as follows. The Active Memory is associative, i.e. content-addressable. That is to say, LCC can only refer to a data object held within the Active Memory by a unique name. The term 'name' is taken to include 'descriptor', 'interrogand', or 'pattern', so that variables and wild cards are accommodated. A consequence of this is that named objects can have varying granularity. The hidden memory management within the Active Memory is also of variable granularity, being based on logical descriptors rather than on physical addresses. The data-manipulation commands built into the Active Memory reflect the common operations on frequently-used data structures such as relations, sets and graphs. Such operations exhibit much scope for parallelism. The repertoire of commands is discussed in Section 18.3; their hardware implementation is discussed in Section 18.5. Note that the Active Memory is primarily intended for structured data arising from a finite, but useful, subset of users' abstract data type declarations. Other (possibly unstructured) data may be held as usual in M1 and M2 in Fig. 18.1b. Since the Active Memory's commands are memory-mapped, it is open to the LCC's system software to integrate (M1 + M2) and (S1 + S2) into a one-level virtual store. It is, of course, not so easy to offer persistence within the (M1 + M2) section of this integrated virtual memory – though computers such as the MONADS do this via extremely large address spaces [Rosenberg 1981].

18.3 FUNCTIONAL REQUIREMENTS

As was mentioned earlier, the structures which the active memory has to manipulate mainly consist of sets, relations and graphs. Generically, the super-type relation appears capable of describing all such structures. A list of suitable operations on these structures includes the following:

(i) relational and set primitives: insert, delete, member, select, project, intersect, difference, union, join, duplicate removal.

(ii) set aggregate primitives: cardinality, maximum, minimum, average.

(iii) recursive query primitives: transitive closure of a relation, reachable node set, nth wave of tuples, 'is there a path between two specified nodes?', return the path between two specified nodes, composition of relations.

(iv) graph aggregate primitives: shortest path, longest path, arc average, node average.

(v) special primitives: (yet to be decided, but possibly including: sort, modify, range search, fuzzy search, Euclidean distance, Hamming distance).

The third group needs more explanation. The intention is to support the evaluation of linear recursive rules. Two types of linear recursive rule are considered: single-sided (single-chain) and double-sided (n-chain). The first type are transitive closure rules. Although the second type can be evaluated by one transitive closure query plus one or more non-recursive queries, this is generally not an efficient strategy. The provision of an 'nth wave' primitive allows much better performance. This returns the nth wave of nodes starting from a specified (variable binding) node set. Successor nodes are automatically re-cycled (n-1) times to discover the end of all n-step paths from the source nodes. Another of the above primitives that needs further explanation is 'reachable node set'. This returns the set of nodes to which paths exist from a specified initial binding set. This operation applies to a base relation. The corresponding set in a virtual relation p, defined by a chaining rule such as:

```
p(x,y)  :-  a(x,v),b(v,w),c(w,y).
```

can be produced without having to materialize the whole virtual relation. The active memory implements this by chaining responder sets through the base relations a, b, c, repeatedly. Further information is contained in [Robinson 1990]. Some specimen timings are given in Section 18.5.

Lest all this appear too biased towards the deductive database paradigm, it should be noted that relational operations also seem to be at the heart of other popular AI paradigms. For example in production systems, a set of rules is applied to a set of facts by attempting to match the condition-part of a rule with fact patterns. Each of the conditions of a rule is a tuple whose terms may be values (ground term) or variables. A condition may be regarded as defining a relation, which is instantiated by a subset of zero or more facts in the factbase, a fact being a tuple of ground terms. Pattern matching can thus be defined as finding the join of the relations associated with all of the conditions of each rule. A rule is satisfied if its join is non-null.

As far as overall system requirements are concerned, we summarize here the desirable properties of the active memory which were hinted at in Section 18.2.

(a) Memory management. An active memory should provide hardware-assisted support for the 'paging' and protection of information within a hierarchy of volatile and non-volatile storage devices. These devices should be associative, i.e. content-addressable.

(b) Persistence. Through (a), the active memory should provide support for persistent objects so that any <type> system enforced by a programming language on short-term data in the active memory is also enforced on long-term data. Persistent stores require a large, uniform naming system which allows direct access to objects of various sizes, without requiring knowledge of their physical location. Any structural relationships ('cross-references') between persistent objects should be maintained.

(c) Ease of integration and extension. The procedural interface for the primitive operations given previously should be easy to integrate within the low-level software and hardware of a conventional computing system. The active memory should be modularly extendible.

(d) Speed and size. The speed of the active memory's primitive operations should at least be faster than could be achieved by hand-coded software running on a uniprocessor of compatible technology. This implies the use of parallel techniques. As far as capacity is concerned, the active memory should have a fast (semiconductor) section which is comparable in size with a normal RAM primary memory.

When sets and graphs arise indirectly, e.g. for control purposes, the quantification of size and speed is not so obvious. Examples are: lemma stores, fact dependency networks, constraint satisfaction, and truth maintenance systems. We take the latter two cases for illustration. Both constraint satisfaction (e.g. [Freuder 1978]) and truth maintenance (e.g. [De Kleer 1986]) have been used in AI applications areas such as planning and scheduling, fault diagnosis, natural language processing, scene labelling in vision, etc. Both techniques attempt to control the problem-space by using derived information. In constraint satisfaction systems, it is convenient to represent domains of values as sets; similarly, the derived values of compositions of problem-variables can be represented as sets. Algorithms then make use of operations such as intersection to work towards the final problem solution. The amount of working space required by these algorithms can be considerable. One CS system, when solving the 10-Queens problem, starts with 10 sets of ten members each and then generates fewer but larger sets until the final solution set (of 700 elements) is reached. At one intermediate stage, 5 sets each of cardinality about 7500 are generated. In Truth Maintenance systems, networks (i.e. graphs) represented as tuples are searched for matches. Such networks can become quite large: a million-node network is regarded as a minimum realistic Truth Maintenance System.

The architectural requirements (a) and (b) above depend critically on the conventions adopted for the low-level representation of information. In the next Section we describe the conventions which have been developed for a knowledge-base server known as the Intelligent File Store (IFS) [Lavington 1988]. An IFS/1 has been in use at a customer's site since December 1987. The IFS/1's storage conventions are being incorporated into a prototype active memory unit now under construction at the University of Essex.

18.4 INFORMATION REPRESENTATION AND LOW-LEVEL INTERFACE

The active memory of Fig. 18.1b must be semantics-free, in the sense of being able to support a variety of applications, programming languages and information models. As mentioned above, the active memory is associative. For convenience we refer to each entry, or line, of this memory as a tuple. The requirement to be semantics-free means that tuples may take a variety of formats. Thus the general format of a line of associative memory has two components:

<tuple descriptor> <stored information>.

The IFS/1 has been used for a variety of purposes, including the storage of sparse matrix control information. However, the IFS/1 is mainly intended to support non-numeric (i.e. symbolic) applications and for these it is convenient to describe each stored line according to the following format:

<D><L><T1><T2>...<Tm><M1><M2>...<Mn>

where:

<D> is a tuple descriptor or variant number
<L> is an optional label (e.g. godelization, etc.)
<T1><T2>... are terms in a wff
<M1><M2>... are optional modifiers for the <L> and <T> fields.

The <terms> may be lexemes (e.g. character strings), integers, labels (e.g. godel numbers), structure tokens, abstract nodes, existentially-quantified variables, etc.

The <terms> are all mapped into fixed-length internal identifiers (IDs). Thus, IDs are used to represent all primitive objects. In an earlier IFS scheme [Lavington 1988], each ID included four 'type' (or tag) bits which segmented the ID space into lexical tokens, labels, etc. The <D> field now makes this unnecessary, since the variant number may be used to define the <type> of each field, including union types. With the <D> field set to be 32 bits and each <term> being an ID of say 64 bits (configurable), an extremely large number of tuple formats of persistent primitive objects is possible.

As with the IFS/1, the active memory uses a special subsidiary associative memory called the Lexical Token Converter (LTC) as a hardware symbol table to give rapid mapping between character strings and IDs and vice versa [Wang 1989]. The LTC also enforces uniqueness of encryption for lexemes. Hardware support for <labels> is also given, in respect of enforcing uniqueness and speeding the dereference operation.

The above tuple format and ID conventions are assumed for all the hardware primitive operations described in Section 18.3. The active memory hardware primitives are presented to users via various levels of software, at the lowest level of which is an applications-independent and model-independent C procedural interface. There are procedures at this lowest level for all of the hardware actions listed in Section 18.3. For example, there are two main versions of the search (or select) command, the general forms of which are as follows:

```
p-search(patt, A)
r-search(patt, resp)
```

Both commands assume that the required C declarations have been made, and that 'patt' has been initialized to a desired interrogand pattern, including wild cards where desired. 'A' is the name by which the responder set will be known. 'resp' is an area in the user's memory to which responders may be returned. The first command, p-search, automatically inserts any responders back into the active memory, creating a persistent structure named A. There are, of course, some consequential issues concerning version-number to be resolved in practical database systems. Hardware support within the active memory for automatic versioning of structures is under consideration at the time of writing. The second command, r-search, is a variation which returns responders to the host processor into a buffer pointed to by resp. Above this lowest level, various software strategies are possible. We may, for example, wish to enrich the primitive types of the applications programming language by adding types which reflect the structure of the tuples we wish to store in the active memory.

18.5 HARDWARE REALIZATION

The underlying structure of the active memory follows that of the IFS/1 [Lavington 1988] and the IFS/1's relational algebraic processor [Lavington 1989]. Both these units employ SIMD-parallel search engines and hardware-hashed RAM to give very rapid search rates. This permits associative matching tasks to be carried out over large volumes of information in a more cost-effective manner than would be possible with CAM chips. In the active memory the storage functionality and the relational processing activity are combined within the same hardware unit. The main difference between the former IFS/1 implementation and our active memory now under construction is that the latter uses transputers in place of PAL-based finite state machines for control purposes. Using several transputers for distributed control gives greater functional flexibility, better modular extensibility, and very much shorter development times. Since the data-intensive work is still carried out by special SIMD search engines, there is little degradation of overall performance compared with the IFS/1's MSI control hardware.

Fig. 18.2 shows a section of the active memory now being built at Essex. The boxes Tbc, Tbf, Tn and Tr are TRAMS – (transputer-plus-RAM modules). The subscripts bc, bf, n and r respectively stand for: branch control, branch fan-out, node and root. The box labelled H alongside each node transputer is a memory-mapped hardware hasher. The search modules SM each consist of 1 Mbyte of 80nsec. DRAM, a 32-bit wide search engine, and a small amount of organizational logic for masking, etc. The search modules are mapped into Tn's address space for control purposes. In the prototype there are four search modules per node, giving 12 Mbytes of associative (i.e. content-addressable) memory in Fig. 18.2. Each SM pcb contains about twice the number of chips as would be the case if it was a conventional RAM board of the same capacity. Thus the cost per bit of the active memory's CAM is about twice the cost per bit of conventionally-accessed RAM. The memory per module, and the nodes in the tree, can easily be extended in future. Overflow is to disc(s), which are organised into logical hashing bins compatible with the organization of the search modules.

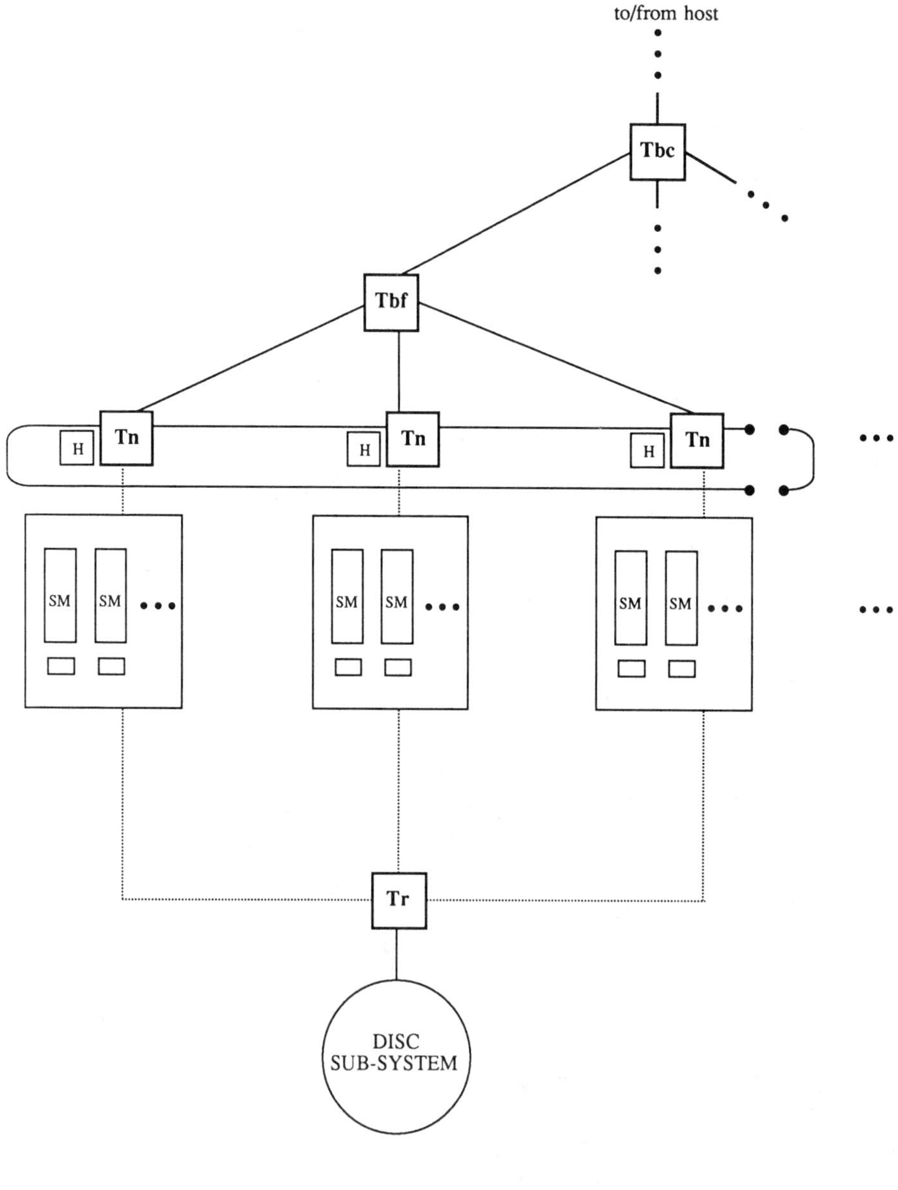

Figure 18.2 One unit of active memory, consisting of three leaves. Each leaf, or node, is under the control of a node transputer, Tn.

The associatively-accessed disc in Fig. 18.2 is naturally the non-volatile part of the active memory, for which the search modules appear as a cache. Data is moved between the disc(s) and cache in logical sets, according to a scheme known as semantic caching [Lavington 1987]. Cached sets, for example 'all people living in Ipswich', also have their set-descriptor (corresponding to <?> <lives.in> <Ipswich>) placed in the cache. As discussed in [Lavington 1987], testing cached set-descriptors is sufficient to determine whether a requested set is totally, partly, or not at all contained within the cache. It is shown that the overheads of carrying out these tests is small provided that R > > 2t, where R is the performance ratio of RAM to disc (typically > 104) and t is the number of <terms> in the interrogand which are not wild cards. Initial studies of a binary relational database gave reasonable results, indicating that an average hit-rate of 89 per cent was achieved with a cache size in the range 5 to 10 per cent of the total database size. However, we have not yet used semantic caching in earnest on very large databases. A strategy for concurrent-user control based on the same variable-granularity set-descriptors for lock specifiers has also been proposed [Lavington 1987]. A combination of pre-conflict locking and post-conflict (optimistic) locking is envisaged.

18.6 PERFORMANCE

Based on the existing IFS/1 performance [Lavington 1988, Lavington 1989] and upon Occam simulations of Fig.18. 2, we expect the active memory to yield the following approximate timings when operands are held in the RAM-based search modules. (Note that these are times measured at the nodes; they do not include any transfers to/from the host).

- Insert a tuple: 60 microseconds.
- Member operation: 40 microseconds (fixed time, independent of relation cardinality).
- Search with one wild card: 400 microseconds (independent of relation cardinality; varies with number of responders, but assumes these responders are kept within the active memory and not returned to the host).
- Join operation: join of two 1000-tuple relations in about 5 milliseconds.
- Transitive closure: up to 600 microseconds for a 1000-node graph, depending on bushyness.

The relation format for the above operations is very general, no assumptions being made about position of key fields, presence of sorted values, etc. Hand-coded software, running on a uniprocessor of compatible technology, only offers competitive speeds for very small data structures of cardinality typically less than 20.

As a practical example of the potential use of the active memory in support of management information systems, we quote the results of an evaluation carried out by the Union Bank of Switzerland [Walther 1989]. UBS used an IFS/1 to hold a relational database containing historical share-transaction information. In the first test, 100,000 5-field tuples were used to represent the following data for 87 stock titles:

> trading day, year, stock title, average price on this trading day, volume traded on this day.

In a second test, two more fields were added to each tuple to give information on the highest price and lowest price for the trading day in question.

Specimen queries such as 'return all entries for a given title over a given year' were carried out on the two sets of 100,000 tuples. When compared with two well-known relational database products running on an Apollo Workstation, the IFS/1 was observed to speed up queries by between 10 – 1000 times. The actual speed-up factor depended upon number of wild cards in the query, but was nearly independent of the position of the wild card in the interrogand. In [Walther 1989] the following additional comments are made by UBS about the IFS/1:

a) access is truly relational – the order of tuples does not matter;

b) no indices are necessary, hence inserts and updates are fast;

c) database tuning and query optimization are unnecessary;

d) the IFS low-level procedural interface is easy to use.

18.7 CONCLUSIONS

The processing of AI structures is a task ill-served by conventional architectures. An add-on unit called the active memory has been described which uses SIMD parallelism to speed up performance in a modularly-extensible, cost-effective, manner. The active memory offers a reasonably high level of functionality, well-suited to smart database and knowledge-base applications. This helps to remove some of the complexity from run-time software, by migrating tedious structure-manipulation tasks away from the CPU and into the special add-on unit. In other words, the natural data parallelism inherent in many AI structures is exploited automatically.

18.8 ACKNOWLEDGEMENTS

It is a pleasure to acknowledge the contribution of other members of the IFS team at Essex. The work described in this paper has been supported by SERC grants GR/E/05018 and GR/E/06319.

REFERENCES

De Kleer, J. (1986) 'An Assumption-Based TMS' *AI* **28** pp127–162.

Dewar, R. B. K., Schonberg, E. and Schwartz, J. T. (1983) *High-Level Programming - An Introduction to the Programming Language SETL* Courant Institute of Math Sciences, New York.

Freuder, C. (1978) 'Synthesizing Constraint Expressions' *CACM*, **21**, (11), 958–966.

Lavington, S. H. (1988) 'Technical Overview of the Intelligent File Store'. *Knowledge-Based Systems,* **1**, (3), p 166–172.

Lavington, S. H. and Davies, R. A. J. (1990) 'Active Memory for Managing Persistent Objects'. Presented at the International Workshop on Computer Architectures to Support Security and Persistence, Bremen, FRG. Proceedings to be published by Springer-Verlag.

Lavington, S. H., Robinson, J. and Mok, K. Y. (1989) 'A High Performance Relational Algebraic Processor for Large Knowledge Bases'. Presented at the International Workshop on *VLSI for Artificial Intelligence*, Oxford, July 1988. Published in: VLSI for Artificial Intelligence, eds. Delgado-Frias and Moore, Kluwer Academic Press, pp 133–143.

Lavington, S. H., Standring, M. Y., Jiang, J., Wang, C. J., and Waite,M. E., (1987) 'Hardware Memory Management for Large Knowledge Bases'. Proceedings of PARLE, the conference on Parallel Architectures and Languages Europe, Eindhoven, pp 226–241. (Published by Springer-Verlag as *Lecture Notes in Computer Science,* Nos. 258 & 259).

Robinson, J. and Lavington, S. H. (1990) 'A Transitive Closure and Magic Functions Machine' To be presented at the Second International Symposium on Databases in Parallel and Distributed Systems, Dublin.

Rosenberg, J. and Keedy, J. L. (1981) 'Software Management of a Large Virtual Memory'. *Proceedings of the 4th. Australian Computer Science Conference,* Brisbane, pp 171–183.

Walther, H. (1989) 'Performance Measurement of the Associative Memory IFS at the Artificial Intelligence Applications Institute at Edinburgh, 13 November 1989 - 24 November 1989'. UBILAB Report, Union Bank of Switzerland, Zurich.

Wang, C. J. and Lavington, S. H. (1989) 'The Lexical Token Converter – A High Performance Associative Dictionary for Large Knowledge Bases' Department of Computer Science, University of Essex, Internal Report CSM-133 (submitted to Knowledge and Data Engineering).

19 Cyclic computation of direct transitive closures in a shared-nothing architecture

J. P. Cheiney, Y. N. Huang*, C. de Maindreville***

19.1 INTRODUCTION

With the introduction of deductive capabilities in the DBMS, efficient computation of the transitive closure (TC) of a relation becomes a key issue in processing recursive queries [Biskup 89]. In the database community, algorithms based upon join loops have been largely studied [Bancilhon 86, Ioannidis 87, Lu 87, Valduriez 88a,b, Cheiney 90]. The main algorithms are Bancilhon's semi-naive algorithm and Valduriez's logarithmic algorithm. These algorithms are limited by the fact that the termination condition must be tested at each iteration in the join loop. This test is a set-oriented and expensive calculation.

Other approachs consider the computation of the TC of a matrix. Much research have been involved in this approach [Warshall 62, Warren 75, Ebert 81, Rosenthal 86, Gardarin 88]. We divide these proposals into two different categories: the algorithms sensitive to the structure of the initial relation and those unsensitive to the structure of the initial relation. The first category processes a depth first search into the graph. Ebert's algorithm [Ebert 81] is such a algorithm. The algorithms unsensitive to the structure work by numbering the nodes. All the arrangements of nodes in the graph are tested. Therefore, the existing paths can be constructed. The representative algorithms of this category are Washall's and Warren's algorithms [Warren 75].

In spite of the importance of the subject, the parallelization of transitive closure is still an open issue, parallel algorithms are very few and recent [Valduriez 88a,b, Agrawal 88, Cheiney 90].

* Ecole Nationale Supérieure des Télécommunications France.
** Institut National de la Recherche en Informatique et Automatique, France.

Some theoretical foundations for parallel algorithms reach linear complexity for the operation [Guibas 79]. However, this type of algorithm considers only the closure of graphs with fixed dimension (p nodes), assumes that the available main memory is not limited (the cost of I/O disk is omitted), supposes that the communication between sites is without delay (the cost of communication is ignored), and demands a number of processors equal to the square of the number of nodes. In the DBMS context, the number of nodes p represent the number of different values of the two attributes of the relation to be closed, these hypothesies are obviously not realistic.

We consider a multiprocessor environment where each processor has its own main memory and disk. In the remainder of the paper, we call site the triple <processor, main memory, disk>. The communication between sites is supported by messages via a bus or a network. The data is partitioned among the sites according to alphanumerical characteristics: the nodes are numbered, and the partitioning is done with the numbers. The algorithms sensitive to the structure of the graph appear less suited to the distributed context than those unsensitive to the structure. The algorithm proposed in the paper is based on the essential idea of Washall's and Warren's algorithms (i.e. it concerns all possible arrangements of the nodes on the graph). The contribution of the present paper is the ability to reorganize the scheduling of computation in order to divide the task among multiple processors.

After this introduction, we present the conventions and notations in Section 19.2, where we recall the connected research ; Section 19.3 introduces a basic theorem and the algorithm is developed in Section 19.4 ; Sections 19.3 and 19.4 constitute the heart of the paper. We give an evaluation of the algorithm in Section 19.5. Finally, we conclude the paper in Section 19.6.

19.2 CONNECTED RESEARCHS

19.2.1 Conventions and notations

We introduce some conventions and notations in this section in order to make uniform our discussion with the connected research. Note we consider a relation as a set of successor lists [Warren 75]. The reason for this is only to facilitate our discussion. Concerning implementation, an adaptation of this representation to a tuple format is very simple. We use the relation and the graph concepts without any distinction: let us consider a binary relation R(X, Y) where X and Y are defined on the same domain D. The relation R defines a graph G, where a node is an element of D and an edge (x,y) denotes a tuple (x,y) of R. The transitive closure R* of the relation R consists of the transitive closure of its corresponding graph G, i.e. a tuple (x,y) is in R* iff there exists a path from x to y in G.

For the oriented graph G, we define the elementary procedure (i,j):

Procedure (i,j)

i,j are two nodes. The notation (i,j) corresponds to the following procedure:
1) test if i is in the successor list of j ; if NO: STOP;
2) add without duplication the successor list of i to the successor list of j.
We say that the node i serves the node j.

The procedure (i,j) will be used in the remainder of the paper.

19.2.2 Warren's and Agrawal's algorithms

The proposed algorithm can be considered as a parallel version of Warren's algorithm. We present in this section Warren's algorithm using the introduced notations. Warren's algorithm is unsensitive to the structure of the graph. It works on the alphanumerical characteristics of the graph and concerns all the possible arrangements of nodes in the graph. So, the existing paths are obviously considered. In a graph representation, we use an ordering of the nodes. This ordering is fixed by the lexicographical order of the attribute values of the binary relation to be closed (these values form the numbers of nodes in the graph representation).

Warren's Theorem [Warren 75]

Let G(V) be an oriented graph. $V = \{v_1, v_2, ..., v_n\}$ *is the set of nodes of graph G.* $<$ *is a total order defined on V:* $v_1 < v_2 < ... v_n$. *Therefore, the TC of G can be computed by the following algorithm:*

```
begin
        for i=1 to n-1
                for j=i+1 to n
                        (vi,vj);
        for i=2 to n
                for j=1 to i-1
                        (vi,vj);
end;
```

This is the initial version of Warren's algorithm. Intuitively, Warren's algorithm has two steps. First, it defines a total order on the set of nodes in graph ; second, it considers the services given by each node in the order defined by the first phase.

In order to implement this algorithm in the page environment, Agrawal modified the order of the computations to minimize the disk I/O.

Agrawal's Theorem [Agrawal 87]

> *Let G(V) be an oriented graph.* $V = \{v_1, v_2, ..., v_n\}$ *is the set of nodes in graph G.* $<$ *is a total order defined on V:* $v_1 < v_2 < ... < v_n$. *Therefore, the TC of G can be obtained by series of computations* $\{(v_i, v_j) \,/\, 1 \leq i \leq n, 1 \leq j \leq n\}$ *which verify the following constraints:*
>
> 1. (v_i, v_k) *precedes* (v_j, v_k) *for all k ; for all* $i < j$;
> 2. (v_i, v_j) *precedes* (v_j, v_k) *for all j, k ; for all* $i < j$.

This implies that a node may start to serve the other nodes as soon as it is served by the inferior nodes. Agrawal's algorithm relaxes a constraint imposed by the initial version of Warren's algorithm, where a node may start to serve the others only after the inferior nodes have finished to serve all the nodes.

The idea of this algorithm is to reorganize the order of computations. The constraint is relaxed in the following way : we avoid to consider the services given by a single node, and we consider at the same time the services given by a set of nodes which can fit into a disk page. Thus the disk I/O traffic can be minimized.

Our algorithm continues in the same way as Agrawal's algorithm. In fact, it also consists in reorganizing the computations, but it exploits the possibilities of parallelization introduced by different sequences.

As we have seen, Warren's and Agrawal's algorithms define a total order on the set of nodes in graph ; each node must be served by all the other nodes in this order. This makes the nodes of the graph nonsymmetrical to each other. If the distribution of an initial relation among n sites is now realized according to alphanumerical characteristics, the pieces of data on each site are entirely symmetrical. Therefore, if we directly apply Warren's or Agrawal's algorithms in a distributed context, the parallelism can only be obtained with an increased number of transfers [Agrawal 88]. In this algorithm, as soon as there is a successor list on a particular site (served by all the inferior nodes), it is immediately broadcasted to all the sites. This implies that the number of transfers between sites is equal to the number of nodes in the graph. Note that a large part of the transfer cost is due to preprocessing and message management, in addition to data transfer. Therefore we prefer to transfer block data rather than a single successor list at a time. An improved version, presented in [Agrawal 88], allows transfers by blocks, but it implies decreasing the degree of parallelism. The contribution of the present paper is to provide an efficient, distributed solution, where the number of transfers is bound with the number of sites.

19.3 DISTRIBUTION OF DATA AND FUNDAMENTAL THEOREM

19.3.1 Distribution of data among sites

Two approaches are possible for partitioning an initial relation among p sites: distribution according to the structural characteristics of the relation; distribution according to the alphanumerical characteristics of the data (i.e. numbering of the nodes).

Structural distribution implies searching through the graph (depth first or breath first). The complexity of the partitioning algorithm is therefore the same as that of the transitive closure algorithm itself. Thus, the distribution according to the numbering of the nodes is simpler and more realistic. We choose this last approach.

The number of sites will be denoted by an integer p, and the p different sites are numbered from 0 to p–1. We use a hash function to partition the set of the successor lists of the initial relation into p disjoint subsets of successor lists. Each subset resides permanently in the allocated site. The successor list of the node i resides in the site (i mod p).

19.3.2 Fundamental theorem

We affect a different order of services to the nodes residing in the different sites, to avoid affecting the same order of services to all the nodes. The method is the following one : we first define a total order into each subset (or bucket) of nodes, this is a local ordering ; the interbucket ordering varies from one bucket to the other. For the bucket i, the inter-bucket ordering will be i+1, i+2, ..., p–1, 0,..., i. The absolute ordering between two nodes is obtained with site_number.node_local_number.

We present the theorem which formalizes this principle.

Theorem:

Let G be an oriented graph. $S = \{s_1, s_2, ..., s_n\}$, $n > 0$, is a subset of the nodes of G. q and s_{n+1} are two nodes of G. The successor lists of q and s_{n+1} include all the nodes of S reachable from q and s_{n+1} respectively via the nodes of S. Therefore, all the nodes of $S \cup \{s_{n+1}\}$ reachable from q via the nodes of $S \cup \{s_{n+1}\}$, can be obtained by the procedure (s_{n+1}, q).

Proof:
The nodes of $S \cup \{s_{n+1}\}$ reachable from q via the nodes of $S \cup \{s_{n+1}\}$ can be divided into two categories : 1) the path does not include s_{n+1} ; and 2) the path includes s_{n+1}. Due to the hypothesis of the theorem, the successor list of q includes all the nodes of the first category. For the nodes of the second category, we can assume that the paths are in the general form : $q s_{v1} s_{v2} \ldots s_{vk} s_{n+1} s_{w1} s_{w2} \ldots s_{wl}$, where k, $l \geq 0$, $k+l \leq n$, $s_{ij} \in S$. According to the hypothesis of the theorem, the successor list of q includes the node s_{vk} which is obtained via the path $q s_{v1} s_{v2} \ldots s_{vk}$; the successor list of s_{n+1} includes the node s_{wl} which is obtained via the path $s_{n+1} s_{w1} s_{w2} \ldots s_{wl}$. Thus, the procedure ($s_{n+1}$, q) obtains the node s_{wl} via the path $q s_{v1} s_{v2} \ldots s_{vk} s_{n+1} s_{w1} s_{w2} \ldots s_{wl}$.

This theorem constitutes the basis of the algorithm. We discuss two important points derived from the theorem:

1) The theorem allows to obtain all the nodes reachable from an arbitary node in an incremental way. We first define an order of services for this node. At the ith step, we consider only the services given by the first i nodes. The order of the services is private to each node : we can affect a different order of services to the different nodes.
2) In order to compute the services given to q by $S \cup \{s_{n+1}\}$, we first compute the services given to q and s_{n+1} respectively by S. But the order in which S serves q can be different from the one in which S serves s_{n+1}. Finally, the services given to q by $S \cup \{s_{n+1}\}$ can be obtained by the procedure (s_{n+1}, q).

19.4 PROPOSED ALGORITHM

A relation is distributed among p sites; a set of successor lists is stored on each site. We note n the number of nodes residing on a site. On this site, n successor lists are located.

Each site has three buffers "stable", "dynamic" and "tempo". The buffer "stable" stores the set of successor lists residing permanently on the site ; the buffer "dynamic" stores the set of successor lists circulating among the sites ; the buffer "tempo" is a working buffer. We assume that the buffer "stable" contains the set of the successor lists of the initial relation distributed on the site before starting the algorithm.

The order used in the following programs implies an order defined a priori inside each subset of the nodes. For the purpose of simplicity, we assume that the order defined in a subset is the order of the indices.

19.4.1 Basic algorithm

In this subsection, we present the algorithm. We first consider three primitives self-service, serve and finish used in the algorithm.

```
self-service(S)

    /* S is a set of successor lists, S = {s1, s2, ..., sn}, n > 0 */
    /* Each inferior node serves the superior nodes */

    begin
            for i=1 to n-1
                    for j=i+1 to n
                            (si,sj);
    end;
```

```
serve(S,T)

    /* S, T are two sets of successor lists */
    /* S = {s1, s2, ..., sn}, T = {t1, t2, ..., tn}, n > 0 */
    /* Each node of S serves each node of T. */

    begin
            for i=1 to n
                    for j=1 to n
                            (si,tj);
    end;
```

```
finish(S)

    /* S is a set of successor lists, S = {s1, s2, ..., sn}, n > 0* /
    /* Each node serves the inferior nodes  */

    begin
            for i=2 to n
                    for j=1 to i-1
                            (si,sj);
    end;
```

The following program is executed on the site s; the final results are obtained in the buffer "stable" on each site.

ALGORITHM 1:

```
begin
        self-service (stable);
        dynamic := stable;
        for i=1 to p-1
                begin
                        transfer dynamic to (s-1)mod p;
                        receive dynamic from (s+1)mod p;
                        tempo := stable;
                        serve (dynamic,stable);
                        self-service (stable);
                        if i < (p-1) then
                            begin
                                serve (tempo,dynamic);
                                self-service (dynamic);
                            end;
                end;
        finish (stable);
end;
```

On each site, we consider the services given by "stable" to "dynamic" and the services given by "dynamic" to "stable". The new contents of "stable" are obtained from the old contents of "stable" and the old contents of "dynamic"; in the same way, the new contents of "dynamic" are also obtained from the old contents of "stable" and the old contents of "dynamic". We have to use a supplementary buffer ("tempo" in the program).

In order to treat the services given between two sites, we have to consider the services given by each element individually, satisfying the constraint on the ordering of the operations. The two sets of nodes must be "self-served" before they serve the other set.

During the last iteration of the algorithm, we consider only the nodes of the buffer "dynamic" which serve those of the buffer "stable".

The Fig. 19.1 illustrates the main idea of the algorithm on p sites.

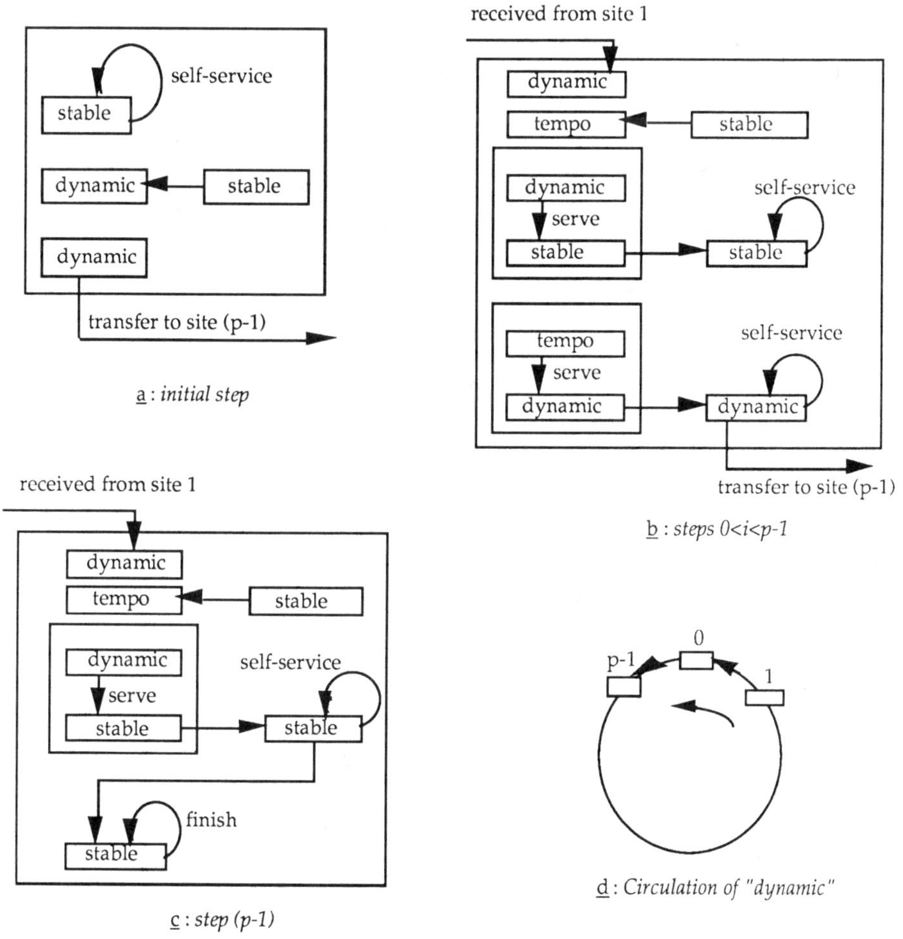

Figure 19.1 Computation on site 0.

The algorithm is cyclic. We observe the processing on site 0 (Fig. 19.1). During the initial step (Fig. 19.1.a), the nodes serve the superior nodes on each site ; site 0 then sends the result of the subset 0 to the left-hand site (Fig. 19.1.d), and it receives the result of the subset 1 from the right-hand site to fill in the buffer "dynamic". During the first step (Fig. 19.1.b, corresponding to the iterations $1 \leq i < (p-1)$ of the loop), the set of nodes coming from site 1 serves all the nodes of the set 0; at the same time, the set 0 serves all the nodes of the set 1. Then, the set 1, bringing up the services of the set 0, is sent to the left-hand site; the set 2, bringing up the services of the set 1, is received from the right-hand site. During the second step, the set 2 serves the nodes of site 0; and the set 0 serves the nodes of the set 2 also. Generally, during the ith step, the nodes of the set i, bringing up the services given by the sets 1 to i, serves the nodes of the set 0; and then, the nodes of the nodes of the set 0 serves also the nodes of the set i. Until the $(p-1)^{th}$ step, all the nodes of the set 0 have been serviced by the nodes of the set 1, set 2, ..., set (p-1) in that order. Finally, inside of the set 0, the superior nodes serve the inferior nodes. The result of the set 0 can then be obtained on the site 0 (Fig. 19.1c).

19.4.2 Improved version

The preceding subsection has presented the essential idea of the algorithm; but, we can establish some redundant computation in ALGORITHM 1: 1) self-service(stable) and self-service(dynamic) are processed at each iteration. The computations of self-service(stable) and self-service(dynamic) can be redundant from one iteration to the other; 2) the computations serve(stable, dynamic) and serve(dynamic, stable) are executed after "stable" and "dynamic" have been "self-serviced". This also implies redundant computations. In this subsection, we present an improved version avoiding these redundances.

For simplicity, we work on a matrix representation of the relation: the set of successor lists on each site corresponds to a n*(n.p) matrix where p is the number of sites and n is the number of nodes on one site.

We use a supplementary bit ".flag" associated to each element in the matrix, in order to point out if this element is produced by the procedure "self-service" or not. .flag=1: YES; .flag=0: NO. The bits .flag of all the elements are initialized to 0. We use a supplementary buffer "delta" on each site. The buffer "delta" has the same size as the other buffers.

The improved primitives are firstly presented:

```
self-service-delta (S,delta)

/* S is a matrix, S is the result of self-service(S'). */
/* the elements of S are divided into two categories: .flag=1; .flag=0. */
/* "delta" stores the services given to S'. */

    begin
        for i=1 to n-1
        for j=i+1 to n
            begin
                if S(j,i)=1
                for k=1 to n.p
                    begin
                        if ((delta(j,k)=0)and(delta(i,k)=1))
                                then delta(j,k).flag=1;
                        delta(j,k) = delta(j,k) or delta(i,k);
                    end;
                if ((S(j,i)=0) and(delta(j,i)=1))
                for k=1 to n.
                    begin
                        if ((delta(j,k)=0)and(delta(i,k)=1 or S(i,k)=1))
                                then delta(j,k).flag=1;
                        delta(j,k) = delta(j,k) or delta(i,k) or S(i,k);
                    end;
            end;
        for i=1 to n
            for j=1 to n.p
                begin
                    S(i,j) = S(i,j) or delta(i,j);
                    S(i,j).flag = S(i,j).flag and delta(i,j).flag;
                end ;
    end;
```

```
serve-delta(S,T,delta)
/* S, T are two sets of successor lists */
/* S, T reside on sites s, t respectively. */
/* Each node of S serves all the nodes of T, the result is in delta */

      begin
            for i=1 to n
                  for j = 1 to n
                        if (((T(i,s+(j-1).p)=1 and (T(i,s+(j-1).p).flag=0))
                            or (delta(i,s+(j-1).p)=1)) then
                               for k=1 to n.p
                               delta(i,k) = delta(i,k) or S(j,k);
      end;
```

The principle of the improved version is the same as in ALGORITHM 1, except that the primitives address only the delta. The following algorithm is executed on the site s.

```
ALGORITHM 2

      begin
            delta = 0;
            self-service-delta(stable,delta);
            dynamic = stable;
      for i=1 to p-1
            begin
                  transfer dynamic to (s-1)modp;
                  receive dynamic from (s+1)modp;
                  tempo = stable;
                  serve-delta(dynamic,stable,delta);
                  self-service-delta(stable,delta);
                  if (i < p-1) then
                        begin
                           serve-delta(tempo,dynamic,delta);
                           self-service-delta(dynamic,delta);
                        end;
            end;
            finish (stable);
      end;
```

19.5 EVALUATION AND COMPARISON

19.5.1 Evaluation of the algorithm

The response time is composed of the time to produce the new tuples (or paths) and the time to transfer the information between sites. The proposed algorithm consists to renumber the arrangements of the nodes of the graph. Among these arrangements, ones correspond to real paths into the graph. In a set of k nodes, the number of all arrangements is

$$A_k = A_k^1 + A_k^2 + \ldots + A_k^k$$

But,

$$A_{k+1} = A_{k+1}^1 + A_{k+1}^2 + \ldots + A_{k+1}^k + A_{k+1}^{k+1} > A_{k+1}^1 + 2A_k^1 + 2A_k^2 + \ldots + 2A_k^k > 2A_k$$

This means that the number of arrangements of nodes in a set will be at least doubled if we add a new node in this set. We assume that:

Hypothesis 1:

The probability that each of the possible arrangements corresponds to a path into the graph is the same ; the number of the arrangements of k nodes of a set is equal to 2^k

Hypothesis 2:

The time to produce a new tuple is a constant.

We use the following parameters to evaluate the response time.

n : node number on each site ;
p : site number (processor number) ;
R : number of tuples in the basic relation ;
Rnew : number of new produced tuples ;
tup : production time for a new tuple ;
msg : pre-processing time for one transfer between sites ;
t : transfer time for one tuple between the sites ;
L : length of the initial relation.

n is an equal value on each site ; this is based upon a uniform hashing assumption. Now, we give the response time of our algorithm.

Processing time:

at i^{th} step ($0 \le i < p-1$):

$$\mathrm{Trait}_i = 2.\frac{1}{p}.\frac{\sum_{k=i.n+1}^{(i+1).n} 2^k}{\sum_{k=1}^{p.n} 2^k}.R_{new}.\,tup;$$

at (p-1)th step:

$$\frac{1}{p}.\frac{\sum_{k=(p-1).n+1}^{p.n} 2^k}{\sum_{k=1}^{p.n} 2^k}.R_{new}.\,tup;$$

So, the total time for processing is:

$$\sum_{i=0}^{p-1}\mathrm{Trait}_i = \frac{1}{p}.R_{new}.\,tup + \frac{1}{2^n}.\frac{1}{p}.R_{new}.\,tup;$$

Transfer time:

We use a simple cost model considering that the transfer time is equal to the sum of a constant factor "message" and a factor proportional to the number of the tuples transfered:

$$\mathrm{TransferTime} = msg + t.\mathrm{NbTuplesTransfered}$$

at i^{th} step ($1 \le i \le p-1$):

$$\mathrm{Tran}_i = 2(msg + \frac{1}{p}R_{new}.\frac{\sum_{k=1}^{i.n} 2^k}{\sum_{k=1}^{p.n} 2^k}.t + \frac{1}{p}.R.t)$$

So, the transfer time is:

$$\sum_{i=1}^{p-1} Tran_i = 2(p-1).msg + \frac{1}{2^n}.\frac{1}{p}.R_{new}.t + 2\,R.t.$$

Finally, the response time is:

$$\frac{1}{p}.R_{new}.tup + \frac{1}{2^n}.\frac{1}{p}.R_{new}.tup + 2(p-1).msg + \frac{1}{2^n}.\frac{1}{p}.R_{new}.t + 2\,R.t\;;$$

19.5.2 Comparison

We compare here our algorithm with two other parallel TC algorithms. The first one is based on the semi-naive algorithm [Cheiney 90]. The other one is a parallel version of Warren's algorithm; it is proposed by Agrawal in [Agrawal 88]. We first recall the results of the evaluations of these algorithm, using the same parameters as in the last subsection.

Parallel semi-naive algorithm (noted dhtc)

The response time of the parallel semi-naive algorithm integrates two components : the new tuple production time and the transfer time of local results between sites [Cheiney 90].

1. New tuples production:

$$\frac{1}{p}.R_{new}.tup\;;$$

2. Transfer time between sites

$$(p-1).L.msg + \frac{1}{p}.R_{new}.t\;;$$

where L is the join loop depth.

Finally the response time is :

$$\frac{1}{p}.R_{new}.tup + (p-1).L.msg + \frac{1}{p}.R_{new}.t$$

Agrawal's parallel algorithm (noted Agtc)

The response time of Agrawal's parallel algorithm has the same two components : new tuple production time and result transfer time.

1. New tuple production:

$$\frac{1}{p} . R_{new} . tup ;$$

2. Transfer time between sites:

$$\text{for the } i^{th} \text{ node: } Tran_i = msg + \frac{1}{n.p} R_{new} . \frac{\sum_{k=1}^{i} 2^k}{\sum_{k=1}^{p.n} 2^k} .t + \frac{1}{n.p} . R.t$$

so, the time transfer is

$$\sum_{i=1}^{n.p} Tran_i = n.p.msg + \frac{1}{n.p} R_{new} .t + R.t$$

finally, the response time is

$$\frac{1}{p} .R_{new} . tup + n.p.msg + \frac{1}{n.p} R_{new} .t + R.t$$

We choose the following parameters in order to illustrate the influence of the number of sites on the response time of : (i) our algorithm, called rptc (for re-ordering and parallel transitive closure), (ii) parallel semi-naif algorithm and (iii) Agrawal's parallel algorithm. The figure 2 shows the comparative results with, particularly, the behaviour of the algorithms in function of the number of processor.

R	=	100,000 ;
Rnew	=	2,000,000 ;
L	=	100 ;
tup	=	0.2 ms ;
t	=	5 μs ;
msg	=	1 ms.

And the node number in the relation is 10,000, i.e n.p = 10,000.

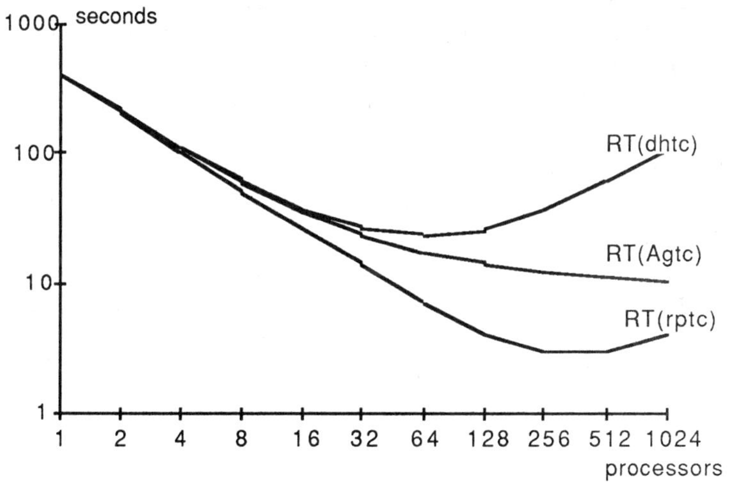

Figure 19.2 : Response time.

Table 19.1 shows the strengths and the weaknesses of the considered algorithms.

Table 19.1 : Strengths and weaknesses of algorithms.

	Proposed Algorithm	Parallel. semi naif Alg.	Agrawal's Parallel Algorithm
redundant production of new tuples	–	+	+
Transfers of intermediate results	++	–	– –
stop condition test	+++	– –	+++

A weakness of our algorithm is the production of redundant tuples. However, their number is limited. This number is the inverse of 2^n, where n is the number of nodes on one site. When the number of nodes on a site is sufficiently great, this redundance can be ignored. To transfer the intermediate results, rptc requires only O(p) transfers, while dhtc uses O(L.p) transfers and Agtc needs O(n.p) transfers: generally, n is largely greater than L. So, this is a weak point of the Agtc.

During the first i iterations of the rptc, i subsets of the successor lists pass by each site. Therefore, we obtain on each site the transitive closure of a set composed by the nodes localized on each site and the nodes having transited by the site. According to Hypothesis 1 in 19.5.1, the addition of a new node in a subgraph will double the number of possible paths (the new tuples). So, the number of new tuples produced by the first (p–2) iterations on each site is:

$$\frac{1}{p} \cdot \frac{\sum_{k=1}^{(p-1).n} 2^k}{\sum_{k=1}^{p.n} 2^k} .R_{new} = \frac{1}{2^n} \cdot \frac{1}{p} .R_{new} .$$

And the number of the new tuples produced by the last iteration on each site is:

$$\frac{1}{p} \cdot \frac{\sum_{k=(p-1).n+1}^{p.n} 2^k}{\sum_{k=1}^{p.n} 2^k} .R_{new} = (1 - \frac{1}{2^n}) \cdot \frac{1}{p} .R_{new} .$$

This means that the greatest part of the computation of TC is done during the last iteration. Therefore, the number of new tuples transferred among sites is very small: the tuples transferred in the rptc are almost the basic tuples.

Another interesting aspect of rptc is the number of connections established between sites: each site is logically linked with only two sites. In the case of dhtc and Agtc, the linkage between sites is "point to point"; each site will exchange some piece of information with all the other sites [Huang 90]. So, bus management is consequently much more complex than in our case.

The procedure which tests the termination condition is completely avoided in our algorithm and in Agtc, while it takes an important part in the response time of the dhtc. In summary, the algorithm rptc is, in the domain of the current utilization, more efficient than dhtc or Agtc.

19.6 CONCLUSION AND OPEN ISSUES

We have proposed in this paper a new parallel algorithm for computing transitive closure. This algorithm is based on a direct computation and a representation of successor lists. The termination condition test, usually very expensive, is entirely avoided. We have also shown that the speed of the production of new tuples is very high and that the volume of transfers between the sites is reduced. The evaluation of the last section shows the good behaviour of the proposed algorithm.

The detail of the implementation is not discussed in this paper; future work will investigate the matricial or successor list representation into a more general context of data and storage models.

REFERENCES

Agrawal, R. Jagadish, H.V. (1987) Direct Algorithm for Computing the Transitive Closure of Database Relations, *Proc of the 13th VLDB conf*, Brighton, England.

Agrawal, R. jagadish, H.V. (1988) Multiprocessor Transitive Closure Algorithms, *Proc. Int'l Symp. Databases in Parallel and Distributed Systems,* Austin, USA.

Bancilhon, F., Ramakrishnan, R. (1986) An Amateur's Introduction To Recursive Query Processing Strategies, *ACM SIGMOD,* Washington, USA.

Biskup, J., Stiefeling, H. Transitive Closure Algorithms for Very Large Databases, *Proceedings of WG 89,* Workshop on Graph-Theoric Concepts in Computer Science.

Cheiney, J. P., de Maindreville, C. (1989) Relational Storage and Efficient Retrieval of Rules in a Deductive DBMS, *Proc. of the 5th Int. Conf on Data Engineering,* Los Angeles, USA.

Cheiney, J. P., de Maindreville, C. (1990) A Parallel Stategy For Transitive Closure Using Double Hash-based Clustering, *Proc. of 16th Int. Conference on Very Large Data Bases,* Brisbane, Australia.

Ebert, J. (1981) A sensitive transitive closure algorithm, *Information Processing Letters* **12** (5).

Gardarin, G., Pucheral, P.(1988) A Graph Operator to Process Efficiently Linear Recursive Rules in Main Memory Oriented DBMS, *3rd Database Brazilian Symposium,* Recife-Pernambuco, Brazil.

Guibas, L. J., Kung, H. T. Thompson, C.D. (1979) Direct VLSI implementation of Combinatorial Algorithm, *Caltech Conf. VLSI,* pp509–525.

Huang, Y. N. (1990) On modelling a Type of Communication in Some Communication Intensive Applications, *Proc. of PARBASE90*, Miami, USA.

Ioannidis, Y., Ramakrishnan, R. (1988) Efficient Transitive Closure Algorithms. *Proc. of the 14th VLDB*, Los Angeles, USA.

Lu, H. (1987) New strategies for computing the transitive closure of a database relation, *Proceeding of the 13th VLDB Conf,* Brighton.

Rosenthal, A., Heiler, S., Dayal U.and Manola, F. (1986) Traversal recursion: a practical approach to supporting recursive applications *Proc. ACM-SIGMOD 1986,* Int Conf on Management of Data, Washington, USA.

Valduriez, P., Kohhafian, S. (1988) Transitive closure of Transitively Closed relations, *2nd Int. Conf on Expert Database Systems,* Tysons Lorner, Virginia, USA.

Valduriez, P., Koshafian, S (1988) Parallel Evaluation of the Transitive Closure of a Database Relation, *Int. Journal of Parallel Programming,* **17**, (1).

Warren, E. S. (1975) A Modification of Warshall's algorithm for the transitive closure of the binary relations, *Communications of the ACM,* **18**, (4), pp 218–220

WarshalL, S.(1962) A Theorem on Boolean Matrices, *Journal of ACM,* pp 11–12.

Part Seven

The EDS parallel database server

20 Information servers, present and future

G. Haworth
Marketing Manager, ICL.

20.1 THE INFORMATION SERVER

Enterprises using information technology today range over the industrial, service, government, administrative and defence sectors. They depend increasingly on their information resource to:

- reduce operational costs
- improve operational effectiveness from stock-holding to customer service
- support business development in new markets
- create lasting competitive advantage in a rapidly changing context

They often regard their information as more important than their next 'product'. They are pursuing a systems architecture which delivers highly reliable IT support for the organization and comprises:

- a framework of long-life interfaces protecting their IT investment
- a complete, coherent and robust information base
- a portfolio of applications interworking through the medium of data

Why do we accumulate large volumes of information? The target is an increasingly rich computer model of the enterprise as a whole. This model is a time machine which can be wound back to recreate history or forward to create a range of alternative futures. It can even be the means by which clients and suppliers interact most effectively with the enterprise.

For many years, the role of database management or information server has been seen as a major and increasing part of what large systems in particular do. We can recognize an information access explosion, driven by the following factors:

- growing volumes of information from increasingly many sources
- the growing interest in the value of unformatted information
- the increasing trend and ability to develop on-line systems
- the growing number of direct 'users' of information
- the increasing IT literacy, facility and sophistication of those users
- technologies to acquire, store, access, analyse and present information

Mainframes, corporate and central servers are becoming information servers. The requirement for more powerful information servers, analysed below, is the best opportunity to exploit the potential of parallelism.

20.2.1 Requirement: information resource

The word 'information' has been chosen deliberately as an umbrella for:

- formatted data: carefully manicured by DP into identifiable records
- semi-formatted text: some 80% of commonly used information representations of sound and image
- knowledge: constraints, integrity and business rules ... processes

The volume of information, judged by the sales of discs, is growing at 25–35% per annum. This is largely organic growth caused by increasing amounts of formatted data. Office systems including electronic mail and document retrieval increase the storage problem. A typed page of 4K characters can be compressed to 1 Kbyte in coded form but takes 40 Kbytes in graphic form, 400 Kbytes as image and some 20 Mb in CD quality sound.

This information needs to be stored with security levels which would be the envy of a bank. This suggests a large, central facility rather than a set of all too portable PC discs. The information needs to be retrieved in a suitably short time for online users, regardless of information volumes, transaction rates or the completeness of the data input to specify the query.

As the information base takes on a wider range of structured information objects going beyond the flat, COBOL-like record, the user will tend to identify information by content and not by some artificial identifying key. Index techniques, dependant on such keys, will become less relevant and information access will become more difficult.

20.2.2 Requirement: on-line systems

Information servers must support an increasing transaction processing load. Only on-line systems support the effectiveness needed in a budget conscious, competitive world. Fortunately, CASE tools ten times more productive than COBOL and therefore worthy of the name 'fourth generation' are available to help us build on-line systems.

The volume of online transactions is increasing by some 20–30% per annum. This growth rate is stimulated by desktop technology and by a trend to business-to-business system-sourced transactions, as in the banking and retail sectors.

Transactions are becoming more complex. The original transaction supported the fine-grain clerical task, disciplined the user into supplying numbers and codes for every entity of interest, used and supplied very little data, was entirely predictable and soon over.

Staff professionals and information workers are coming on-line in numbers. They exercise greater freedom in the use of data, ask more ambitious, higher value queries, deeper questions and have an iterative enquiry style. Decision support queries typically involve transactions more like sagas, drawing on large subsets of the warehoused data and extracting similarly large amounts to snapshot files in information centres.

Saga type transactions tend to lock up resources which they are not in fact using; they can pre-empt clerical transactions with short expected response times. Clearly, parallelism can perform decision support type queries with response times akin to classic TP.

Transactions can be characterized in terms of frequency and complexity, as judged by the load they place on the computer system. Classic TP has high rate and low complexity; the earliest knowledge based systems have high complexity and low rate. There is some evidence that the exploitation of knowledge-based techniques is being impeded by performance problems.

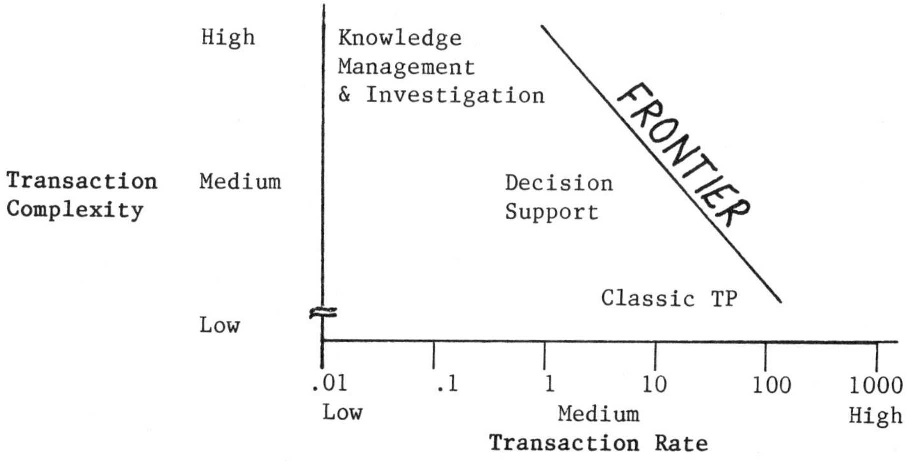

Figure 20.1 Frontier.

Complex queries over knowledge bases are to be found in:

- the IT industry: dictionary, IRDS, CASE and IPSE work
- government: the administration of rules and guide lines
- manufacturing: CAD design rules, factory floor scheduling
- distribution: storage and scheduling against penalty clauses
- utilities: scheduling and (PTTs) remote maintenance

As enterprises increase the value of their information bases by enriching both the information model and the range of queries put to the model, transactions will increase in both frequency and complexity.

Any computer system will have a throughput frontier for different kinds of transaction. Parallel information servers will advance that frontier by orders of magnitude.

20.2.3 Requirement: investment protection

Enterprises need to protect the value of their information processing systems. Their expenditure with IT suppliers represents only a small part of their investment in IT which is in turn only a fraction of this value. The full asset register includes the value of the information, the current portfolio of running applications and the skills of development staff and information workers.

Increasingly then, IT strategists are looking for a framework of long life interfaces. These allow established systems to be insulated from, and yet exploit, new technologies as they become available.

IT suppliers are similarly free to introduce new ideas in an evolutionary way behind interfaces of value to customers. Such an approach reduces or even nullifies the cost of take on for the user and was the approach adopted by ICL when CAFS was introduced.

The ANSI/ISO SQL standard is the key interface today in the database world. It is a higher level interface than the CODASYL interface, provides greater program/data independence and therefore greater protection from the effects of change. SQL is evolving and seeking to meet new requirements for user-defined abstract data types and the manipulation of knowledge.

Opinions differ as to whether SQL will evolve sufficiently or be replaced by an 'object oriented' interface between application and data. Despite SQL's admitted inelegance as a language, this author believes it will survive because of the investment already made in it.

In addition, SQL is a declarative, 'set level' language, allowing the user to say nothing about how data is to be retrieved. Notionally, a million processors could 'select' one each of a million independent records. We may therefore expect parallelism to be exploited in varying degrees in a range of SQL servers.

20.3 INFORMATION ACCESS TECHNOLOGY

Information is accessed by a combination of indexing and searching.

Indexes are subset 'projections' of the object data and can be effective in focusing our interest on just the data required. Indexing techniques are well documented and today advance only slowly. Two caveats are worth mentioning.

First, indexes cost in terms of space, initial set-up, maintenance and update. A word-level index of a body of text can occupy three or four times the volume of that text; full inversion of a database can make update prohibitively expensive. Inevitably, a balance has to be struck between the need for good read-only access to data and the need to update it quickly in TP systems.

Secondly, an index such as Cust# is obviously most effective when a query quotes a Cust# in full and requires only information for that Cust#:

```
SELECT ... WHERE Cust# = 'ABC12345'
```

Relax any of these conditions and the index becomes less effective:

```
SELECT ...    WHERE Cust# startswith 'ABC'
              WHERE Cust# contains '??C123'
              WHERE Cust# is any of {'ABC12345', ... , 'XYZ67890'}
              WHERE Customer-name = 'HAWORTH'
              WHERE Customer-name = 'H?W?RTH'
              WHERE Height is in range [5' 8", 6' 2"]
              WHERE hair-colour * 'FAIR'
              WHERE score > 3 scoring 2 for height in range, 1 for .....
```

Once an index or set of indexes have been used, the data targetted must be searched. As we can see from the above examples, this data set may not be small. In relational terms, we need to perform the operations of 'select' and 'project' on the data, choosing records which meet the criteria and passing back only those items of interest from the record.

Searching is slow and high volume TP systems seek to avoid it by offering a set of predictable transactions demanding DP-imposed record-keys.

Nevertheless, it is necessary to search information as we have seen in the emerging world of decision support, strategic planning, structured information objects and knowledge manipulation.

ICL recognized the opportunity of the 'knowledge spectrum', namely to convert raw data into information and then into high grade knowledge.

Its response to this and to the underlying search problems was to introduce the CAFS retrieval engine. We examine the CAFS concept, architecture and its subsequent use as a case study in the exploitation of parallelism.

20.4.1 The CAFS retrieval engine

The concept of CAFS is simple. Searching information is slow and moving it from disc to memory to processor is expensive. It would be better to filter the data 'at source' by the disc and at the disc's delivery rate.

ICL chose to introduce CAFS in an evolutionary way, behind interfaces used by its customers and with little or no change to existing hardware, software, applications or data.

CAFS is now a standard ICL product, a co-processor within the Series 39 architecture. CAFS engines sit in the disc channel and filter the data when given the parameters for the 'select' and 'project' operators.

CAFS exploits parallelism in three ways.

1. Multiple CAFS engines work in parallel with Series 39 processors
2. A job may drive multiple CAFS engines simultaneously
3. CAFS is a four-stage pipeline around a battery of 16 processors

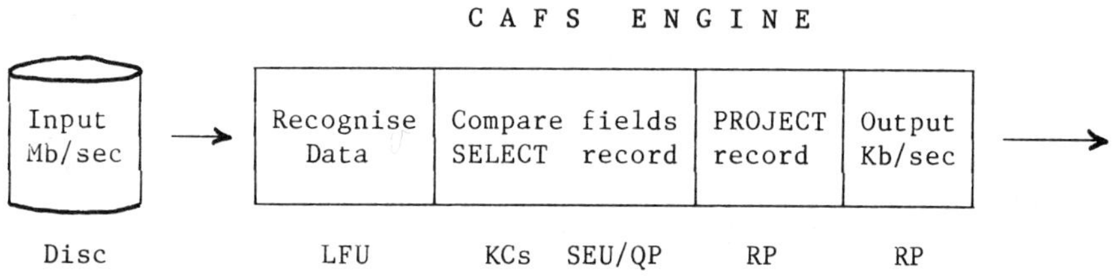

Figure 20.2 CAFS engine.

The CAFS engine architecture is as follows:

STAGE 1. The 'front office' of the CAFS engine is the Logical Format Unit (LFU). This recognizes aspects of the incoming data such as start and end of block, record and field. It triggers the rest of the engine to handle the data-stream at appropriate moments.

STAGE 2. CAFS implements the selection criterion to pick out records of interest. A free combination of boolean and 'quorum' logic may be used, involving up to 15 atomic conditions and possibly partial or uncertain information:

age < 30, name startswith 'BRE??NE', type ≠ 99

CAFS will also count the success-rate of each atomic criterion and return these scores at the end of the search. This is useful for statistics applications and also helps the user to broaden out, focus or change his query after looking at the response.

Typical selection criteria might be:

Select on score of 3+: score designer = 3, coder = 2, tester = 1

20 < age < 30 & 15000 < salary < 30000

A small army of 16 'key channel' processors (KCs) mask fields as required, apply the atomic conditions and combine their results either to select or to deselect the record in the selection evaluation unit (SEU).

CAFS is able to select information about entities 'like' or 'near' an ideal. We cannot insist on the perfect job-applicant, house or holiday; where many features are involved, it is better to net the best candidates rather than insist on the perfect candidate. The quorum processor (QP) scores a record against a stated threshold value.

STAGE 3. The CAFS Retrieval Processor (RP) performs the PROJECT function, reducing the amount of information output to the interesting fields in selected records. Perhaps it is only the primary key or some 50 bytes of a 1000 byte record which are required.

STAGE 4. The Retrieval Processor also outputs data to the host computer. Normally CAFS outputs a few Kbytes/sec for an input of 3Mbytes/sec and the output process does not cause CAFS to pause on the input process.

See [1] for a more detailed exposition of the CAFS engine's anatomy. That paper also introduces a series of papers in a volume dedicated to the many aspects of the CAFS system.

At the logical level, we have distinguished four processes being executed in parallel within CAFS; at the next more physical level, the engineering employs 36 individual processing elements.

20.4.2 CAFS performance

CAFS filters information at up to 3Mb/sec or, more meaningfully, at some 1200 pages of text per second. CAFS improves information searching by orders of magnitude because:

1. the searching function has been moved in the system architecture
2. a different mix of technologies is being applied to the job

3. parallelism is used outside and inside the CAFS engine

CAFS performance can be compared with non-CAFS performance on the same ICL Series 39. A typical example is:

LIST ... WHERE Wks Status = "1", "2", "3" AND WKS OWNER ≠ "B"

	Non-CAFS	CAFS	Ratio	Difference
Response Time	186.4 mins	4.4 mins	42:1	2 hrs22 mins
OCP Usage	1258 secs	3.3 secs	378:1	20m54.7 secs
OCP Utilization	11.2 %	1.2 %	9:1	10 %
Millions of PLI	4025	10.5	383:1	4015.5

Absolute differences are more significant than ratios. In this case, CAFS delivered the answer over two hours earlier and liberated almost two and half hours of machine time for other purposes.

Back in 1984, identical queries were run on 2966/CAFS and IBM 3081-G under independently audited conditions. The 3081-G system was rated at 9 times the 2966's power and 7 times the price. The CAFS system returned answers 4-5 times as quickly and at one sixteenth of the estimated cost.

The performance gain from CAFS depends on the type of data searched, the complexity of the query and the sparseness of the input data presented as matching criteria. Complex queries based on multiple weak criteria take the same time as simple atomic queries on CAFS but far longer when executed conventionally in software.

The CEGB (as was) cited the case of searching for two-part identifiers amongst a file of 300,000 part-identifier/description records; only a few words of product description were available. Response time was critical; the auditors were expected at the door. This query was reckoned to cost some £10,000 on a large IBM-compatible mainframe but ran in some 15 seconds at nominal cost on CAFS.

20.4.3 Interfaces to CAFS

Different users require access to information via different interfaces. CAFS can be used:

- by unchanged software (where you have lost the source!)
- by programs written in COBOL, FORTRAN, PASCAL, ...
- in reporting and statistical analysis
- by casual users of online enquiry systems
- by ICL QuickBuild TP systems using standard forms or videotex
- by INGRES and the SQL interface

- via bibliographic or office document text systems
- in investigative applications with tailored interfaces

Most DP departments will ruefully admit to having one or more programs which scan files and are *very* important, where the programmer has left and where the source code and documentation have disappeared. By telling the underlying record manager about the selection criteria, even these programs can be speeded up.

ICL provides DCI, a procedure/parameter interface to CAFS which is usable from all programming languages and application packages such as SPSS. COBOL programmers were further favoured by a relational extension of the COBOL language which used CAFS.

Users of the CASE toolset QuickBuild now use CAFS to 'head off' database searches previously specified in their application programs. The underlying DBMS, IDMS, uses DCI and CAFS rather than its own software. Several on-line systems now do not depend as much as they used to on the driver not spilling coffee on the delivery note.

The text systems ICLFILE and STATUS both use CAFS to access information which has recently arrived and not yet gone through the considerable process of being fully indexed.

As detailed below, investigators in the intelligence community depend on CAFS' ability to work with multiple weak criteria and match similar entities, for example people. In contrast to DP departments who work with a data model of a known world, these investigators are trying to discover patterns in an unknown world by browsing through semi-structured data.

20.4.4 CAFS in practice

The CAFS engine has been embedded in the Series 39 mainframe architecture and the interfaces have been made available. What benefits have customers achieved in practice?

With over 4000 CAFS engines in regular use, it is impossible to list here the many customers who have put on record the benefits they have achieved.

Southern Water [2] were amongst the first organizations to put end-users on-line to their data on a large scale. They found that 80% of CAFS traffic was 'new work' and that on-line activity did not run out of control. Users gained confidence quickly and, through experience, a new awareness of the status and potential of their data. Southern Water deservedly won the Office Automation award in 1985 for the 'best information storage and retrieval system.'

Thyssen France [3], a major specialist steel distributor, made the transition to CAFS in 1985. They were able to throw away over one hundred one-off COBOL programs. The DP manager, M Ardon said, "The COBOL program would always take a day to write and an hour to run; now the query takes three minutes to enter, six minutes to run. Speed of response has given our sales staff the edge."

ICL Manufacturing is a typical high technology operation with a long 16 hours batch reporting suite run at capacity overnight. This load was reduced to just 11 hours at a stroke when some of the reports were diverted to CAFS. The machine was switched to high value analytical work which was waiting in the wings.

In Berkshire, the public use CAFS via a videotex system [4] to identify library books of interest. Users enter one or two words, or word-stems, which are then matched against the county's 300,000 titles in some three seconds. No need for subject classification, multiple menus or microfiche. The same idea is being used to relate users to clubs of interest, events coming up and generally the range of information topics in the system.

CAFS is invaluable for the investigative systems needed by intelligence departments, defence organizations and police. These often use INDEPOL, 'the system that's wanted for questioning'. The Civil Aviation Authority monitors air safety [5] while the RAF [6] analyses the maintenance profile of its aircraft. Forensic accountants check out the legality of applications for shares in 'privatized' UK companies, foiling a £6M raid on the last (water) occasion. The Royal Hong Kong Police combat the organized crime of the Triads, using CAFS in their Criminal Intelligence, Narcotics and Commercial Crime Bureaux.

The largest civil computer system in Europe is the UK Inland Revenue's COP/CODA system within which is a National Tracing System. This holds only the information needed to link a correspondent with the correct tax office, namely name, address, National Insurance 'NI' number and tax office. The Inland Revenue often receive mail without the NI reference and sometimes with only a few characters of the handwriting decipherable.

At peak times, 20 transactions/sec access a duplexed 12Gbyte file, some 50 million name/address pairs. Two-thirds of the transactions require a CAFS scan which delivers a response in 2-3 seconds. The system uses a mix of course-grain indexing and parallel searching on 26 CAFS engines.

20.5.1 The database machine opportunity

The CAFS product demonstrates that it is possible to move functionality within an established architecture, introduce a different technology mix and exploit parallelism to achieve radically new levels of performance. CAFS also demonstrates the benefit of achieving this transparently behind existing interfaces.

The computer industry is now moving to achieve the same effect with 'database machines' behind the established interface SQL. Technology continues to move rapidly and database management is evolving to take on ideas of object orientation and knowledge manipulation. We look at these trends briefly here.

The most rapid change is in microprocessors. RISC architectures are now giving a line of processors increasing in power at 50% per annum. In RISC Mips, today's 25Mips chips will be succeeded by 40, 60 and 90Mip chips. The 100Mip chip is expected in volume in 1995. The challenge of computer system architects is to translate this increase in processor power into a similar increase in systems throughput.

Buses as a central shared resource have become a bottleneck in shared memory multiprocessor systems. VMEbus delivers 20Mbytes/sec; the Futurebus standard will deliver 110 and 180Mbytes/sec. Given the micro processor power curve above, these higher bandwidths will only postpone the processor-memory queuing problem for a short time.

Storage technology is diversifying but changing more slowly. Massive semiconductor memory and optical discs are significant new physical layers in the storage hierarchy.

Disc performance is increasing at only 10% pa, capacity at 25% pa; costs are dropping at only 20% pa. In comparison, DRAM chips increase in capacity by a factor of 4 every 4 years. The commodity chip today is 4Mbits and will be 16Mbits in 1994 and 64Mbits in 1998. DRAM cost/byte is dropping at 60% per annum.

Semiconductor memory used to be 100 times the cost/byte of disc; by 1995, the ratio will have reduced to 20. If we wish to build a high volume TP system at minimum cost today, the easiest way is often to use large amounts of RAM.

Databases are going to become richer, more accurate and more manageable models of the real world. Ideas from the language, database, artificial intelligence and information retrieval communities are now converging. Object-oriented databases are now being developed to support object oriented languages which originated with SIMULA in the late 1960s.

Abstract data types with associated 'methods' are being defined by users to model the real-world entities of interest to them. The ADT 'methods' reflect the protocols, processes or enterprise rules used to manage the enterprise's interest in those entities. 'Data' and 'process' are becoming more closely associated at define-time and run-time.

Representations of knowledge can be incorporated into databases. AI techniques then have to be incorporated into the DBMS to manage recursion, deduction, inference and logic programming. Current RDBMSs use rules and cost models to manage optimization and integrity. The opportunity therefore exists to handle these parts of the RDBMS and increase their intelligence using declarative languages.

The software industry has in the past tended to identify the most common functions in customers' application programs and embed that functionality in the software it provides. Database management systems are taking over more responsibility for the data, delivering information more intelligently and implementing, on the 'data' side of the fence, the enterprise rules associated with ADTs.

20.5.2 The EDS project

ICL is now working with Bull and Siemens to develop the information servers of the future by exploiting new technologies as available.

These servers will meet requirements, as detailed above, to:

- manage increasing volumes and varieties of information and queries
- provide a basis for more productive and reliable system development
- provide more powerful and reliable hardware platforms

The objective of the joint Esprit II European Declarative System project is to develop a smoothly scalable, highly parallel computer system, EDS. EDS will in the main be an SQL server and an information server. It will support the many data-intensive applications which the companies foresee; it will also support application-intensive and logic-intensive systems.

EDS supports the declarative languages SQL, Lisp and PROLOG, key languages for future database management systems and applications. The SQL interface goes beyond SQL2 to include object-management and deductive programming. The parallelism of EDS is transparently exploited behind these three interfaces.

An EDS system consists of from 8 to 256 Processing Elements, PEs, each one a powerful microprocessor with 2Gbytes of non-volatile DRAM. Each PE supports a Unix/Chorus environment and will run C/C+ + programs including existing relational database software.

The architecture of EDS has been designed to be in balance as the system is scaled up and despite new rounds of chip technology. A share-nothing rather than a share-everything design has been chosen because large systems are becoming more and more data intensive. Computer architecture should therefore avoid shipping data en masse. Share-everything system performance is strictly limited by:

- memory requests queueing for fixed, finite bus capacity
- the locality pattern of references of programs to cache content
- processor interference caused by synchronizing cache content

- the uneven loading of work on different processors

The shared bus introduces a factor Q ($Q < 1$) into share-everything performance based on the throughput of a standard queue. Together with the cache-coherency problem, the performance of N processors on a bus is:

$QN [1 - (N-1)p/k]$ times the performance of one processor

assuming 1 in k cycles cache accesses change the content of the cache, and where p = probability of processor 1 stealing a cache cycle from processor 2 on changing the content of cache 1.

This performance curve is a quadratic, nose up, with a defined maximum power close to Qk/4p for a maximum N of k/2p processors. For example, take k = 10, p = 1/4; maximum N = 20 processors. References out of cache could saturate the bus capacity well before 20 processors were active.

Systems using EDS will feature terabytes of data, megabytes of program and task specifications measured in hundreds of bytes. It is clearly easier to move the task to the data than the data to the task. EDS, like CAFS, implements the ideas of function-shipping and parallelism but in a different way. It uses fast inter-processor communication for transmitting light weight task specifications, processes and task syndication.

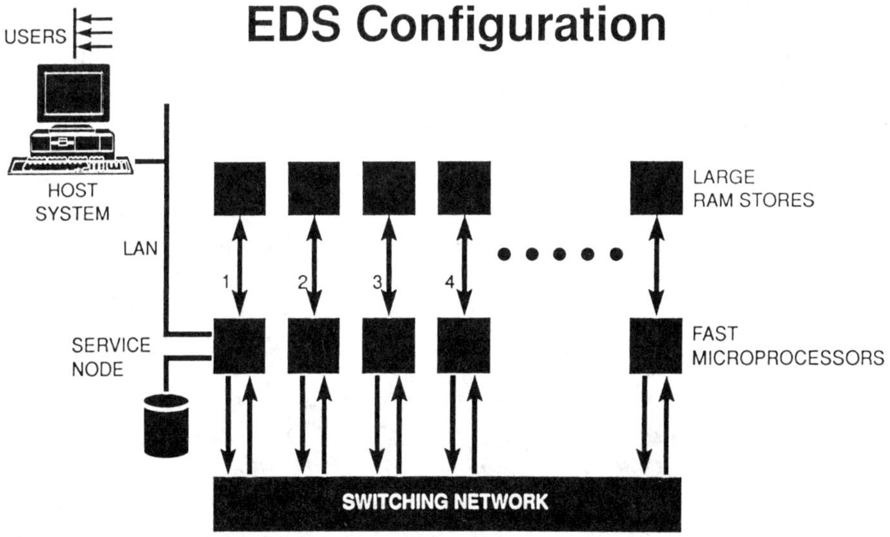

Figure 20.3 EDS configuration.

EDS' performance will be competitive with multiprocessors and scale linearly with size to produce order of magnitude advances. Performance is being measured against benchmarks profiled to reflect real workloads. A 256-element EDS machine is targetted at 12,000 TPCA (ET1) transactions second. Note that this a more demanding system test than the database test TPCB (TP1). The same machine will perform in LISP some 140 Boyer runs/second or for PROLOG, 32Mlips, logical inferences per second.

The EDS project is developing RDBMS software which will exploit parallelism to the full in the optimizer and in the operations. It is also porting existing applications to the EDS machine. These will prove that the component technologies work together. They will also demonstrate the potential benefits of EDS to leading edge customers who are now identifying their current needs and future aspirations to the project.

REFERENCES

Haworth, G. McC. (1985) 'The CAFS System today and tomorrow', *ICL Technical Journal,* **4** (4), November '85, pp365–392

Corbin, C. E. H. (1985) 'Creating an end-user CAFS service', *ICL Technical Journal,* **4** (4), November '85, pp441–454

'ICL at Work' Case Study, 'Thyssen Special Steels - Querymaster gives a cutting edge'.

'ICL at Work' Case Study, 'Berkshire County Council - showing what community spirit can do'.

'ICL at Work' Case Study, 'Civil Aviation Authority - vast improvements in Safety Monitoring with INDEPOL'.

'ICL at Work' Case Study, 'Royal Air Force - Improved Fleet Management with Illustrator'.

21 Object management in parallel database servers[1]

O. Gruber, P. Valduriez
INRIA-Rocquencourt

21.1 INTRODUCTION

Complex data-intensive applications typically access large collections of shared persistent data and therefore require a combination of database management functions and general-purpose programming. The current database solution [Vald89] is to embed a database query language (e.g., SQL) within a programming language (e.g., C). The query language provides efficient access to shared persistent data but has limited data modelling and manipulation capabilities. The programming language supplements the query language with rich data types and operations to manipulate transient objects in main memory. The embedded query language solution has two serious problems. First, dealing with two separate and incompatible languages introduces a great deal of complexity for the programmer. Second, conversion and copying of persistent (disk-resident) objects into transient (memory-resident) objects using a two-level store incurs an important performance overhead.

In order to achieve high performance for data-intensive applications, we see two important and complementary solutions: uniform object management and parallel data management. Uniform object management [Cope90] provides a uniform treatment of objects, regardless of whether they are transient vs. persistent, local vs. distant, or memory-resident vs. disk-resident. This can be achieved efficiently using a distributed single-level store where all objects are represented in a virtual address space. Uniform object management is the basis for supporting efficiently complex objects, including object identity and object sharing (the ability of an object to be referenced by multiple parents) [Khos87], as needed in object-oriented database systems [Banc88], persistent programming languages [Atki87] or post-relational database systems [Gard90].

---

1 This work has been partially funded by ESPRIT project EP2025 (EDS)

Parallel data management [Ozsu90] exploits parallelism available in data-intensive applications in order to improve performance using the recent multiprocessor computers. MIMD parallelism is best exploited by declustering [Livn87] (horizontally fragmenting) large collections of data across multiple nodes using a function applied to some attribute(s) so that inter- or intra-transaction parallelism can be achieved. Parallel data processing can improve both system's throughput and individual transaction response times. Most of the work in this area has focused on relational data management, e.g., Teradata's DBC [Nech85], Gamma [DeWi86] and Tandem's NonStopSQL [Tand87]. Bubba [Bora90] is a notable exception for it supports a more general object model [Danf89] albeit somewhat limited. In general, the multiprocessor architectural model is also fixed (more likely message-passing rather than shared-memory).

In this paper, we study uniform object management in the context of parallel and distributed computers. We describe object management in terms of a physical object model, a container model. The physical object model provides all capabilities to manage complex objects independent of any conceptual data model. This objective is reminiscent of extensible object managers like Exodus [Care86] or Geode [Bell90]. It supports simple objects and values, complex objects and collections, and distributed object sharing (the ability of an object to be referenced by remote parents) through the use of system-wide object identifiers. The container model captures the declustered placement of collections, as well as the clustering of objects. It is different from the model proposed in [Khos89] in that it is of lower level and not tied to a particular data model. However, it has the same objective of capturing declustered data placement. Full support of these models is based on the use of a globally shared-virtual memory and features available in modern distributed operating systems like Mach [Acce86]. These models apply naturally to both shared-memory parallel and distributed-memory computer models.

The rest of the paper is organized as follows. Section 21.2 presents the physical object storage model. Section 21.3 deals with parallel and distributed object management. In particular, it proposes the container model which captures locality of access in order to enhance performance in a declustered environment. Finally, Section 21.4 lists the open issues and concludes.

21.2 PHYSICAL OBJECT MODEL

The physical object model is intended to support any (rich) conceptual data model that exhibits object management features, e.g., object-oriented or post-relational. Therefore, the objectives that guided the choice of such model are generality and extensibility. The model is general in that it provides all the basic constructs to structure arbitrarily complex objects efficiently. The model is extensible in that new structures can also be added to cope with application-specific requirements. Furthermore, the model naturaly supports parallel data processing.

The physical object model is intended to support multiple object data models of higher level and therefore must be simple and general. The model includes values and objects which may be either simple or complex. Values are data structures referenced by physical addresses, defined as pairs (page, offset). Value are defined as follows.

Let D be the union of all the base types (including the value-address type). Let I be the domain of object identifiers (oids).

1. A simple value is either a base type from the following set

   D = {byte, integer, float, value-address},

   a fixed-size structure

   [A1 : D ∪ I ; ...; An : D ∪ I],

   or a variable-length byte string

   [int Size; char String[Size]].

2. A complex value is a hierarchy of simple values composed using value-addresses.
3. A close value is a value which does not contain oids.
4. An open value is a value which contains oids.
5. A simple value is able to locate the references to values (value-addresses) or objects (oids) it contains.

A simple object is a pair (oid,value), the oid refers to the value and is the only way to manipulate it. Oids are value-addresses made invariant to support sharing. Oid invariance is implemented by means of forwarders. A forwarder is a marker, left in place when the object moves in memory, which allows to find the new location of the object from the old one.

A complex object is defined as a directed graph of objects whose edges represent the "refers to" relation. In other words, simple objects may be composed using oids. Nothing prevents the object graph from having cycles.

The rationale for supporting both objects and values is to enable the application (the layer above the object manager) to trade-off between the use of values and the use of objects. Objects are more space- and time-consuming because they are identified by oids.

Collections are objects which group objects or values, and are used to compose complex objects. A collection contains the oids of the objects or the addresses of the values it groups. Collections are homogenous in the sense that a collection groups either objects or values but not both. However, collections are heterogenous with respect to type to support polymorphic data models, i.e., elements of a collection may have different types. Collections that should be available are the set, the bag (set with duplicates), the array extended with the ability to grow by the end, and the sequence. A sequence is a B-tree based data structure to support long texts [Care86]. Other collections can also be added to cope with application requirements. Complex objects are illustrated in Fig. 21.1.

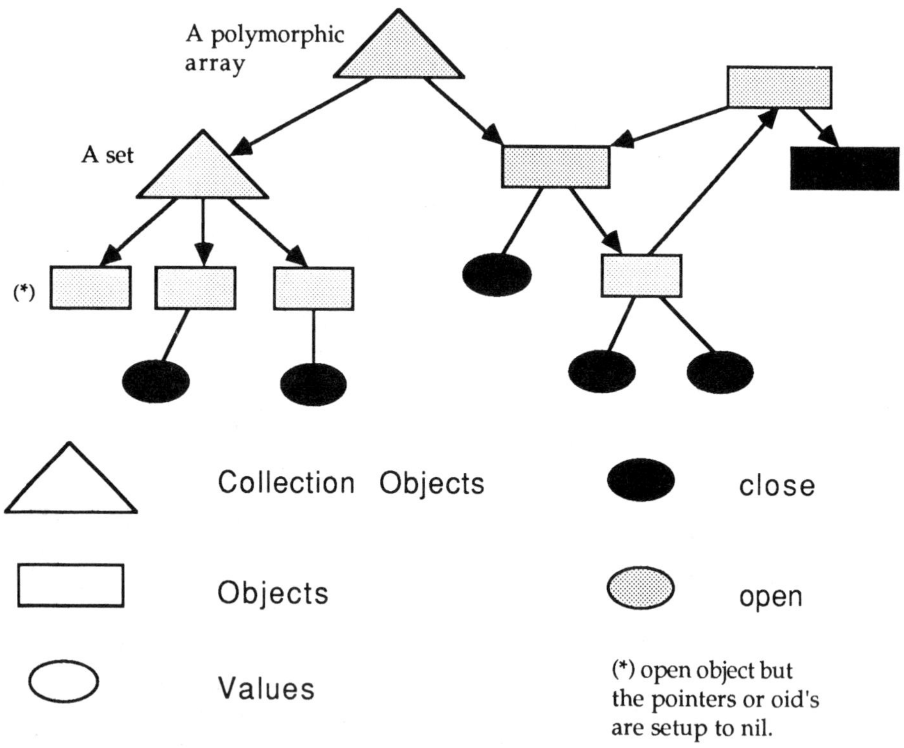

Figure 21.1 Complex objects.

We believe that future systems for data-intensive applications will fully integrate the object paradigm and will still provide set-oriented processing as relational database systems. We presented collections for structuring complex data, but they are also the support of set-oriented processing, thereby extending the notion of relation. Techniques developed to improve performance for the relational model, mainly parallelism and indexing, apply equally to collections.

To cope with increasing amounts of data, commercial database systems can exploit horizontal fragmentation to achieve adequate performance. The parallelism required for set-oriented processing based on relations is also required to process collections. Therefore, collections should also support horizontal fragmentation (declustered collections) so that parallel data access and processing can occur.

A declustered collection is a collection divided into fragments using a user-defined function called a splitter. Fragments are themselves collection objects holding only a subset of the original collection. Fragments of a collection are identified by a root index. The splitter determines the subsets of data that constitute the fragments. A good candidate for a splitter would be a hash function. The splitter may be dynamicaly changed to redistribute a collection based on new application requirements.

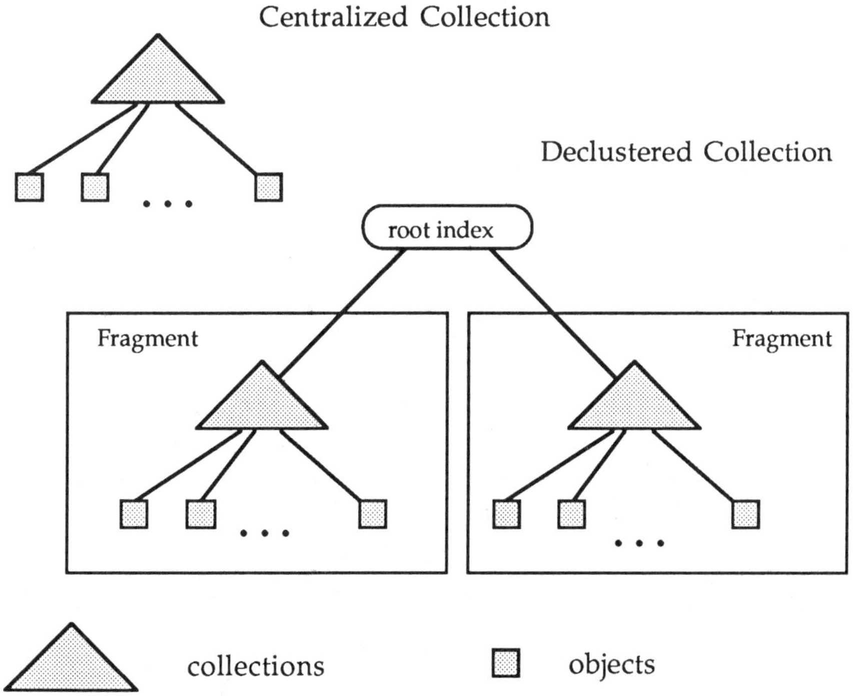

Figure 21.2 Centralized vs. declustered collections.

The speed up factor introduced by the use of indices in relational database systems also applies when indexing collections. The relations are flat structures needing primary and secondary indices. Primary indices allow to adapt the physical storage of relations for specific processing patterns whereas secondary indices allow somewhat different patterns to be also efficient. Collections are adapted data structure for certain needs and therefore already provide, by nature, the primary index optimization. However, collections also require secondary indices. One or more secondary indices may be associated with a collection. Collections may be recursively declustered and indexed since a collection fragment is a collection, i.e., fragments of a declustered collection can be indexed.

Persistent programming and database languages need to navigate through the object graph, so entry points in the graph are definable. All the objects defined as entry points are named. The names provide direct access to the named object and persistent object names are stored in a catalogue. A transient object becomes persistent by attachment to any persistent object or by naming it and storing its name in the catalogue. Consequently, all objects reachable from the catalogue are persistent. The catalogue is the unique persistent root known by the system. Persistent objects can be directly referenced (pointed to) by transient objects using their oids. The persistent object model is illustrated in Fig. 21.3.

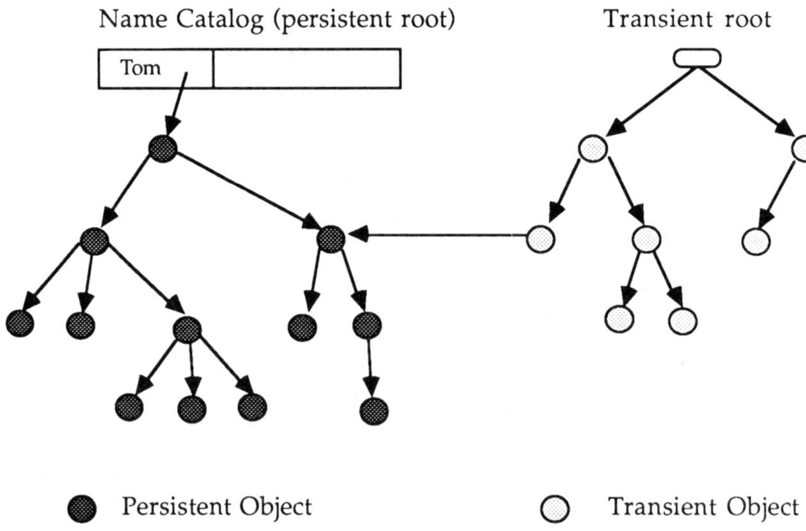

Figure 21.3 Persistent object model.

21.3 PARALLEL AND DISTRIBUTED OBJECT MANAGEMENT

In the previous section, we presented the physical object model provided to structure data and to ensure the persistency of such structures. We saw how collections support parallel set-oriented processing. This section concentrates on object management issues, how distributed uniform management is achieved and the impact of parallelism. We also present the container model, showing successively its role in distributed object management and parallelism.

21.3.1 Distributed uniform object management

Distributed uniform object management means several things. First, it makes objects to be managed in an uniform way, so object copies or translations are avoided. Second, it ensures distribution transparency for distributed application software engineering, as well as for supporting full distributed sharing of objects. We will show that this approach provides distribution transparency while the container model allows to keep the control over the locality.

Object translation or copying is one of the major hurting performance factors of traditional database systems. Multiple copies are needed between the operating system buffer and the database buffers, the back-end database buffers and the network packets to communicate with the front-end, and finally from the front-end space into the application space. Furthermore, translation is necessary to convert objects from database format into the application format, e.g., database tuples mapped into COBOL or Fortran structures.

Several research projects have investigated uniform object management. The Bubba project [Bora90] relies on a tailored operating system BOS Bubba Operating System [Clay89] on top of a share-nothing architecture. The database is divided into subparts stored on nodes; a node is a processing unit and its local memory; nodes communicate through messages. The database is managed into a single-level store per node. A single-level store names the approach which maps disk-resident data into the virtual memory of processes, so it addresses two operating system issues, mapping files in virtual memory and sharing virtual memory between processes. On each node, the local subpart of the database is mapped in the virtual space of all processes. Consequently, uniform object management is achieved at each node as shown in [Cope90]. Roughly speaking, pages of objects are moved between the disk and the cache where they are directly used by the processes, so that object extraction as well as copy or format translation are avoided. However, uniform object management is only achieved at each node, but not between nodes. Moreover, no object sharing is supported across node boundaries, and sharing is even restricted within a node.

The Ontos system [Andr89] follows the multi-client/multi-server approach. Applications running on a workstation have object faults, solved by requesting the desired objects to the servers. The servers manage C++ objects [Strou86] which are copied into the virtual address space of the applications. Ontos claims that translation is avoided. However, as far as the authors are aware, objects need to be extracted from and merged in pages and need to be copied back and forth from network packets. The Ontos architecture looks like the object server approach described in [Dewi90] about the three possible architectures for a client/server architecture. Uniform object management is partially achieved. Distribution transparency is fully achieved.

Our goal is to provide full distributed uniform object management by managing the database into a distributed single-level store. Such a store is shared by all processes around the network which access the database. Their virtual memory space is splitted in two subspaces. One is a local virtual memory for local and private data. The other, mapping the disk-resident database, is a distributed shared virtual memory [Tam90], see Fig. 21.4. This approach has several advantages.

First, large shared virtual memory is now technicaly feasible either on shared memory multi-processor or share-nothing architecture [Tam90]. The side-effect is that the shared memory paradigm is transparent to the architecture. Thus, systems developed using this paradigm can run on both architectures. In fact, the differences are concentrated within the virtual memory management which is part of the operating system.

Second, managing the database into a distributed single-level store ensures distributed uniform object management. The Bubba project shown that mapping a single-level store in a local virtual memory ensures local uniform object management[1]. In our approach, the disk-resident database is mapped into a distributed shared memory ensuring distributed uniform object management. A distributed shared memory is an extended virtual memory mechanism which is able to move pages between nodes instead of just moving them between the cache and the disk. Therefore, remote data access is provided without object extraction nor translation acheiving distributed uniform management.

---

1 Please report to the previous paragraph on Bubba or Cope 90 for more details

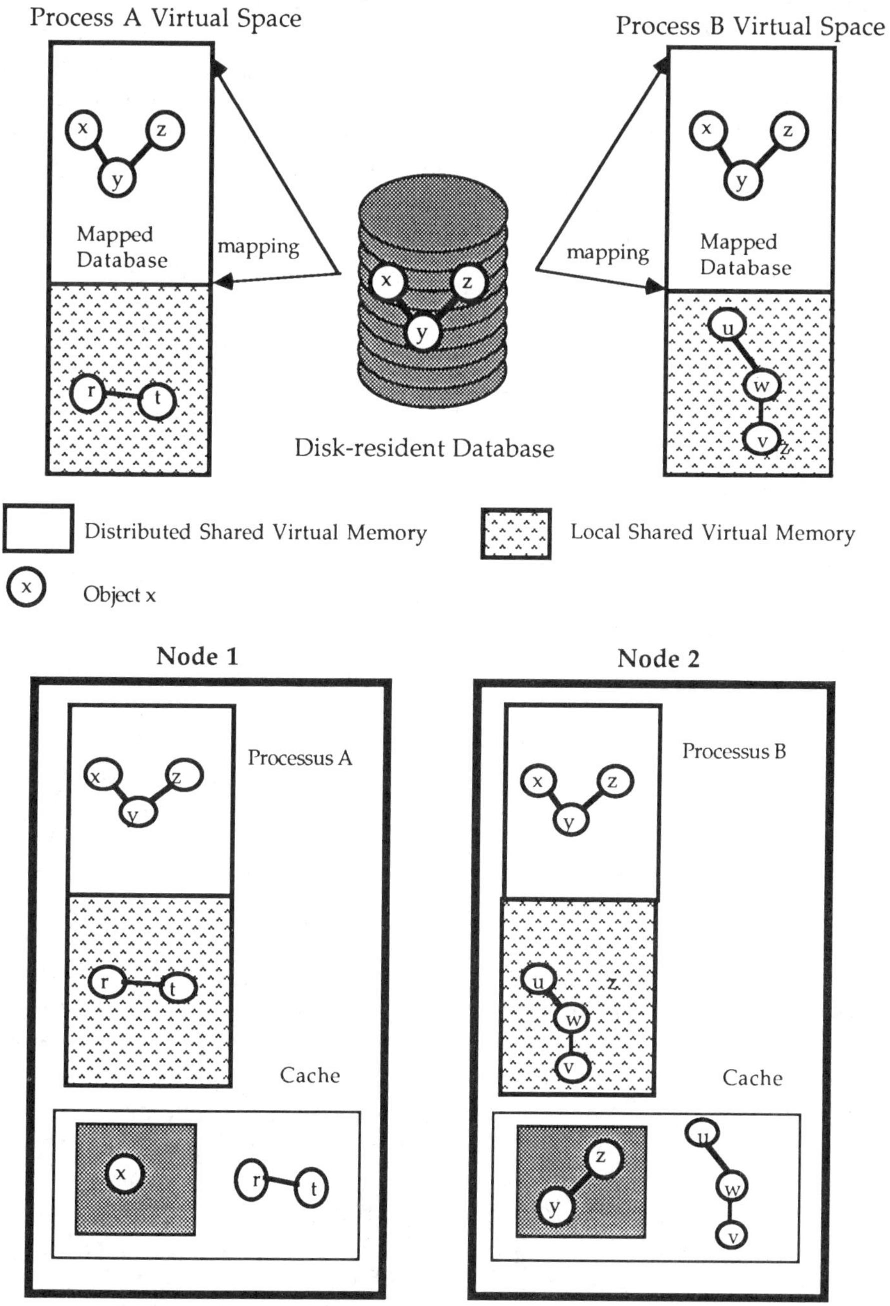

Figure 21.4 Distributed single-level store.

Third, full distributed sharing of objects is supported by construction. Distributed sharing of objects means that an object may be referenced from other objects lying at different nodes, it is often presented as the worst case of object sharing. The problem resides in remote object access and in providing identifiers which are invariant and system-wide. The problem vanishes in our approach since the object graph is built into a distributed shared memory. First, a full distribution transparency is provided, therefore remote object access is no particular case (seems to be local). Second, the virtual addresses are system-wide as previously stated, so are the oids. The invariance is still ensured by the forwarder mechanism as mentioned before.

It is important to point out the differences between our approach (we call it mapped databases) and main memory databases. Main memory databases make the assumption that all the data fit in main memory while mapped databases make the assumption that all the data fit in the virtual space. To behave efficiently, mapped databases need also the assumption that the working set of objects spreads over a set of pages smaller than the main memory size. Of course, this assumption is weak, because page faulting mechanism is taking up. However, tools are needed for clustering objects in order to verify this assumption, i.e., to exhibit access locality. This is the role of the container.

A container is intended to cluster objects together and is local to a node (see Fig. 21.5). The containers are built on top of the distributed virtual space and represent sets of pages. A container is not a segment because there is no need for the pages to be contiguous. Any page of the virtual space belongs to a unique container, hence any object belongs to a unique container. A container is bound to a single node which means that its pages are owned by that node. Therefore, objects of a container tends to be locally accessible on the owner node. If the clustering policy over container is efficient, methods running at the container node will run on local data.

Clustering includes both policies and mechanisms. Our approach is to provide the mechanisms but leave the policies to higher layers of software aware of the application knowledges. This is motivated by the lack of general clustering policy which is application-dependant. Offering mechanisms instead of fixed-policies have been shown successful in operating systems field [Sans 86, Baro 87], achieving a first step towards adaptability and extensibility.

In disk-based systems, locality is increased by clustering objects within pages, thus minimizing page faults. For the past twenty years, such clustering has been extensively used to improve buffer pool performance in systems supporting value-based data models [Chou 85]. Collections of objects or values should also be clustered when used for scan-based algorithm. A container is associated with multiple allocators of objects, each dealing with a distinct subset of the container pages. One allocator is reserved for each collection, allocating the objects of the collection. Therefore, these objects are clustered on a private set of pages. Processing the collection will exhibit full locality within that set. The caching policy for the pages of this set could be adapted to the access pattern, reusing techniques developed for relational database buffer management.

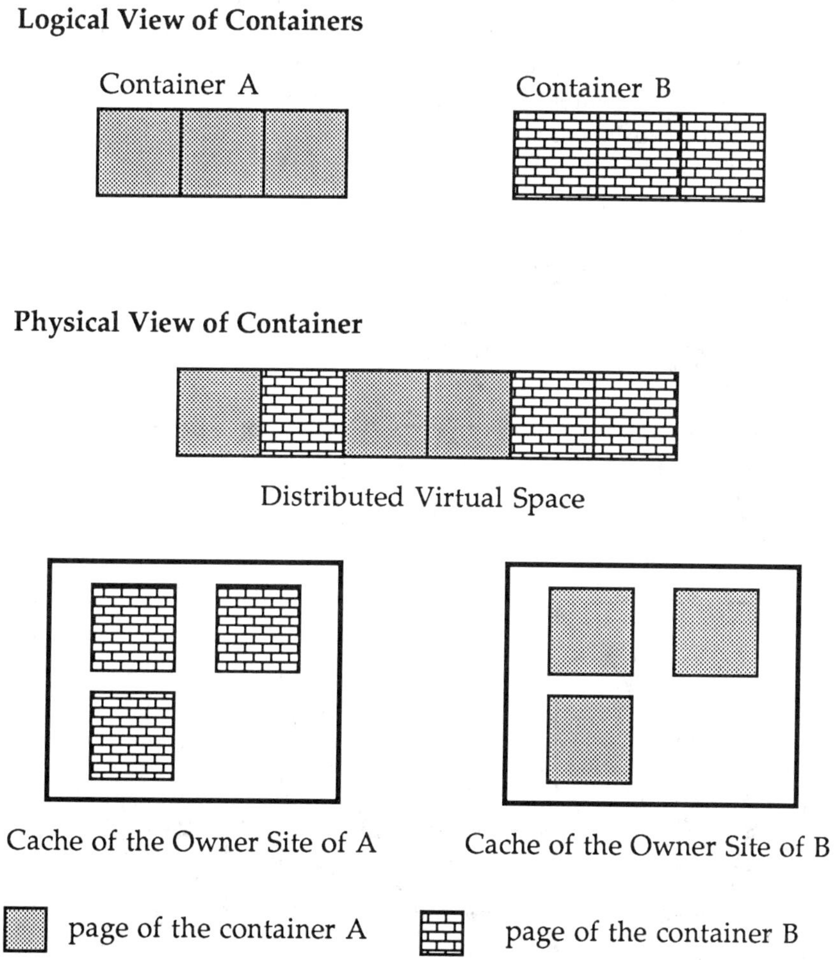

Figure 21.5 Container definition.

In object-based systems, locality is highly dependant of the applications as shown in [Benz90]. But the numerous clustering policies rely on the same simple clustering mechanism. An object can be tightly or loosely clustered with another. Tight-clustering means that both objects are in the same page. Loose-clustering means that both objects appear in the same cluster which is some entity defined as several pages.

Our cluster is defined as the subset of pages managed by an object allocator. One allocator behaves in the space of one container, so a cluster is local to a container, hence local to a node. Creating an object requires the oid of the object it will be clustered with. If loose-clustering is desired, the new object is allocated by the memory allocator that allocated the specified object. If tight-clustering is desired, the new object is placed in the page of the specified object if possible (if there is enough space), otherwise loose-clustering is ensured.

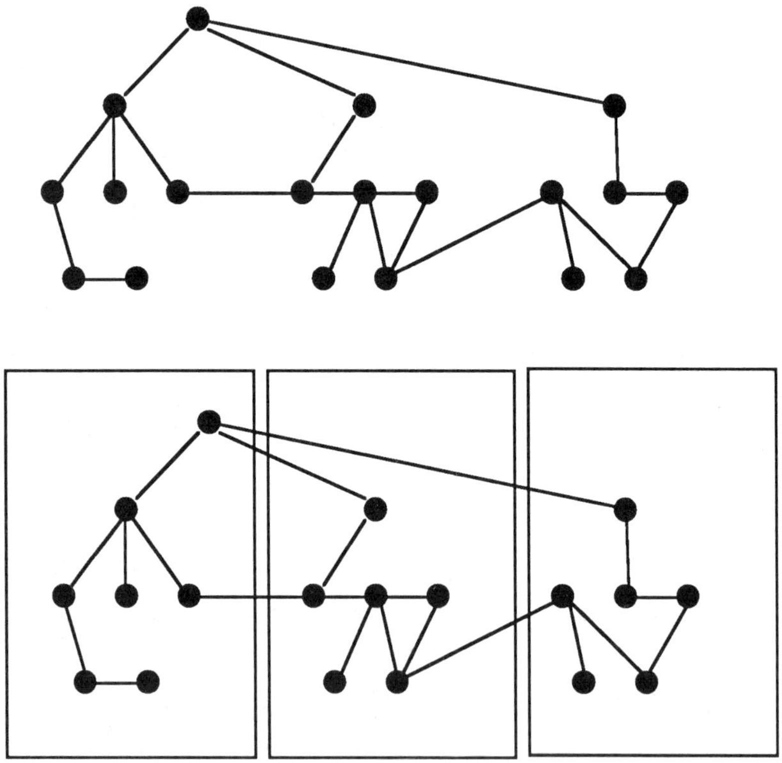

Figure 21.6 Mapping object graph onto containers.

Layers above the object manager, which are aware of application knowledges, have to define the clustering policies in order to map the object graph onto containers (see Fig. 21.6). The policy may rely on many different heuristics, for example, object taxonomy, specific application requirements, object access statistics. Hua proposes an interesting approach for automatic clustering based on the simulated annealing algorithm in [Hua90]. The method splits automatically any object graph into sub-graphs in such a way that sub-graphs contain highly connected objects but very few edges exist between sub-graphs. The method is general and does not rely on the semantics of the edges between two objects. For example, edges can be weighted to express some clustering priority between parents for shared objects.

Containers capture object clustering while keeping system-wide identification. From our past experience in the GEODE project [Bell90], clustering (object localization) should be orthogonal to object identification (object access mechanism). Indeed, if it is more or less easy to specifiy clustering when creating objects (lack of clustering semantics), it is even more difficult to be aware of object clustering when accessing objects. For instance, let us suppose that the clustering relies on the class hierarchy and that the language is polymorphic. The typing system cannot deduce anymore at compile-time where is an object. Hence, some run-time decision is necessary based on user-maintained informations, making the application more complex. Another example, let us suppose that the clustering relies on some hash function on some attribute value, how is it possible to know the bucket where is the object without having the object itself to apply the hash function?

This orthogonality from the user point of view is even more vital when the object space is distributed. If the user has to deal with two different access techniques depending on whether the object is local or not, object access becomes a dreadful burden in face of migrating objects. It is almost impossible when the object heap is shared by multiple users, each migrating the objects on its own will.

21.3.2 Parallelism

The physical object model provides means for collections to be declustered so parallel data-access and processing can occur. This section focuses on the requirements for parallelism to be efficient.

Parallelism can well improve performance provided that some conditions are satisfied, for instance, high access locality is required. The physical object model allows to decluster a collection into distinct fragments so that computation can be parallelized by replicating it over each fragment.

Each computation instance, called subcomputation, accesses objects logically clustered in a fragment. Therefore, on one hand, the objects of a fragment have to be clustered together so logical access locality becomes physical access locality. On the other hand, the subcomputations have to be moved to the fragments. In the following, we show how the container model fulfills these two requirements.

First, containers are a clustering tool which provides locality, and thus is the natural support for declustered collections. A declustered collection is mapped into several containers, i.e., a container is associated to each fragment. This mapping is supplied by the user through a mapper function which associates a fragment with a container. The set of containers that accommodates the fragments of a collection is called the home. A container may hold multiple fragments but a fragment is within a single container, ensuring locality (see Fig. 21.7).

Second, a container is bound to a unique node, its owner node. So a subcomputation is moved to the owner node of the container where the needed fragment relies.

Let us recall that the object manager supports parallelism but does not define the computations to be parallelized. The application (or parallelizing compiler), using standard operating services such as forks or semaphores, defines and controls parallelism. Supporting parallelism means the ability to structure the data so parallel data processing can occur (collections), as well as the ability to ensure correct concurrent execution. Concurrent execution can be ensured using several methods, the most commonly accepted being the transaction model. Although our transaction model has not been selected yet, we are investigating nested transactions and the impact of pessimistic and optimistic approaches over the distributed caching performance. This is the key issue for the overall performance of distributed systems.

Some management of objects is also done concurrently with the applications, for instance, garbage collection. A garbage collector first detects garbage and then collects it[1]. The detection must be serializable with the user transactions to avoid erroneous garbaging. The following scenario is an example of object loss. A transaction makes an object unaccessible by deleting its last reference. It is detected as garbage and then collected. If the transaction rolls back; then the object has been lost because it does not appear in the transaction logs. The garbage collector has to be semanticaly serializable, but it is highly unrealistic to implement it as a transaction, since it would delay the user transactions thereby degrading performance and would probably never finish, trapped in a deadlock situation. We are currently investigating a promising approach based on conservative collectors[2].

---

1 Scavenging-based collectors do both detection and collection, but the presented problem stays.

2 A conservative collector detects only a subset of the garbage to enhance concurrency with the mutators (applications), keeping objects which are uncertain garbage.

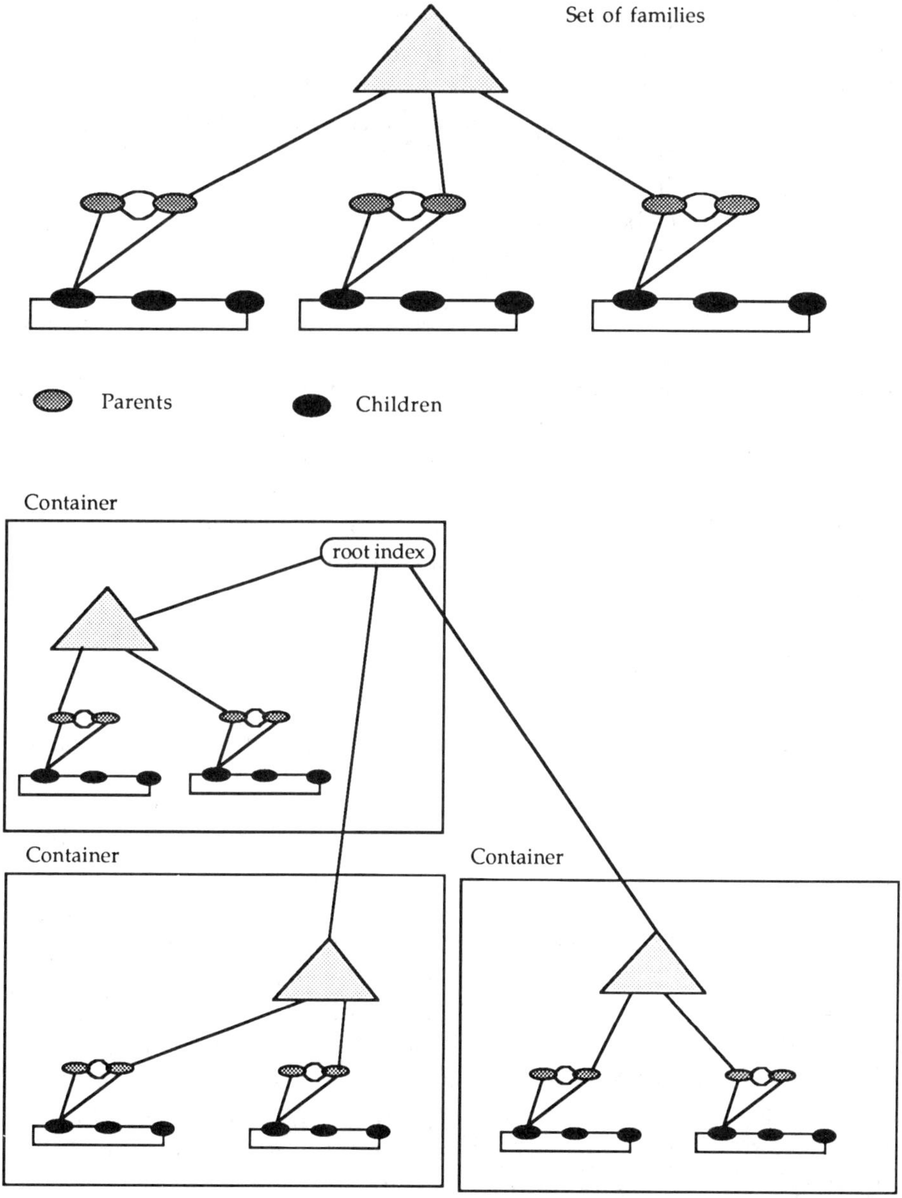

Figure 21.7 Declustering of collections onto containers.

A garbage collector is necessary for a general-purpose object manager. It is a valuable service for the applications because manual space recovery is very tough to program and error prone. Furthermore, manual garbage collection over a shared persistent object space is even impossible if object sharing between applications exists (a flavour of interoperability). Indeed, none of them could ever decide on its own whether or not an object has become unreachable. Furthermore, a distributed garbage collector is complex to design and to implement. In fact, very few distributed garbage collectors [Lisk86, Shap90] exist which have realistic assumptions. Albeit realistic, they need to be tailored for parallel data-intensive environments. We are currently tailoring the distributed collector protocol presented in [Shap90].

Declustered data placement has been fully investigated in the context of distributed and parallel relational database systems [Ozsu90]. The same techniques used to decluster collections of objects may achieve less locality. Shared objects are required to be ubiquitous if their parent collections (referencing them) are in different containers. A shared object, as any object, belongs to one container, hence only the parent collections in that container will have true local access. Other parent collections will access it through the distributed virtual memory mechanism. Albeit transparent, this access is non local.

21.4 CONCLUDING REMARKS AND OPEN ISSUES

In this paper, we have defined a basis for building a high-performance extensible object manager that can support arbitrarily complex objects with object sharing. This object manager can be extended at the lowest level to accommodate specific application requirements. It is therefore a building block for data-intensive application support-systems such as object-oriented database systems or post-relational database systems. We proposed a container model that captures both clustering and declustering of object collections within a distributed computing environment.

High-performance object management is obtained through the use of a system-wide single-level store that fully exploits virtual-memory hardware and distributed operating system capabilities. The proposed object management model can be mapped onto various physical machine architectures such as a shared-memory multiprocessor, a shared-nothing multiprocessor or even a network of workstations.

A number of important issues related to this project are being investigated. We see three major issues. First, an object-oriented PL interface to the object manager must be specified. The choice of an object-oriented language is simply motivated by our extensibility requirements.

Emphasis will be given to the type system in order to allow static type checking of programs dealing with persistent and transient objects. Safe method execution control within the object manager is also important. A related issue is the support of a global data directory that manages the ADT methods and container information. Second, a distributed virtual memory protocol must be specified with special attention to the support of dataflow execution models. A related issue is event and rendezvous support to be integrated within the operating system. Third, static and dynamic techniques for object clustering and declustering must be investigated for they will dictate the performance of the applications. A related issue is transaction management support at the lowest level of the system, e.g., concurrency control support for objects and efficient fault-tolerant techniques.

REFERENCES

Accetta, M. (1986) *et al.*, Mach: a New Kernel Foundation for UNIX Development, *Summer USENIX Conf.*

Andrews, T., Harris, C. and Sinkel, K. (1989) *The OB2 Object Database*, Ontologic Inc.

Atkinson, M. P., Buneman, O.P. (1987) Types and Persistence in Database Programming Languages, *ACM Computing Surveys,* **19**, (2).

Bancilhon, F. (1988) Object-Oriented Database Systems, *Int. Symp. on PODS,* Austin, Texas.

Baron, R. V. *et al.*, (1987) *MACH Kernel Interface Manual*, Department of Computer Science, Carnegie-Mellon University, Pittsburgh, PA 15213.

Bellosta, M. J., Bessde, A., Darrieumerlou, C., Gruber, O., Pucheral, P., Thévenin, J. M., and Steffen, H. (1990) GEODE : Concepts and Facilities, *BD3 Conf.*, Montpellier, France.

Benzaken, V. (1990) *An evaluation model for clustering strategies in the O2 object-oriented database system*, ICDT-90, Paris.

Boral, H., Alexander, W., Clay, L., Copeland, G., Danforth, S., Franklin, M., Hart, B., Smith, M., and Valduriez, P. (1990) Prototyping Bubba, a Highly Parallel Database System, *IEEE TKDE,* **2**, (1).

Carey, M. J., DeWitt, D. J., Richardson, J. E., and Shekita, E. J. (1986) Object and File Management in the EXODUS Extensible Database System, *Int. Conf. on VLDB,* Kyoto.

Clay, L., Copeland, G., and Franklin, M. (1989) Operating System Support for an Advanced Database System, *MCC Technical Report ACT-ST-140-89.*

Chou, H-T (1985) Buffer Management of Database Systems, thesis, University of Wisconsin.

Copeland, G., Franklin, M., and Weikum, G. (1990) Uniform Object Management, *Int. Conf. on EDBT,* Venice, Italy.

Danforth, S., and Valduriez, P. The Data Model of FAD, a Database Programming Language, to appear in *Information Science.*

DeWitt, D.J. *et al.*, (1986) GAMMA : a High-Performance Dataflow Database Machine, *Int. Conf. on VLDB,* Kyoto.

Gardarin, G., and Valduriez, P. (1990) ESQL : an Extended SQL with Object and Deductive Capabilities, *Int. Conf. on Database and Expert System Applications,* Vienna, Austria.

Hua, K. A., and Lee, C. *Data Clustering for Parallel Query Processing in Object-Semantic Databases,* IBM Mid Hudson Lab.

Khoshafian, S., and Valduriez, P. (1987) Persistence, Sharing and Object-Orientation : a database perspective, *Int. Workshop on DBPL*, Roscoff, France.

Khoshafian, S., and Valduriez, P. (1989) A Parallel Container Model for Data- Intensive Applications, *Int. Workshop on DBM*, Deauville, France.

Liskov, B., and Ladin, R. (1986) Highly-Available Distributed Services and Fault- Tolerant Distributed Garbage Collection, *Proceedings of the 5th ACM Symposium on Principles of Distributed Computing,* Alberta, Canada.

Livny, M., Khoshafian, S., and Boral, H. (1987) Multi-disk Management, *ACM SIGMETRICS Conf.,* Banff, Alberta.

Neches, P. M. (1985) The Anatomy of a Data Base Computer, *Digest of Papers* COMPCON, San Francisco.

Ozsu, T., and Valduriez, P. (1990) *Principles of Distributed Database Systems*, Prentice Hall.

Sansom, R. D., Julin, D. P. and Rashid, R. F. (1986) Extending a Capability Based System into a Network Environment, *Technical Report CMU-CS-86-115.*

Shapiro, M. (1986) Structure and Encapsulation in Distributed Systems : the Proxy Principle, *Int. Conf. on DCS,* Cambridge, Massachussetts.

Shapiro, M., Gruber, O., and Plainfoss, D. (1990) A garbage detection protocol for a realistic distributed object-support system, *INRIA Research Report 1320.*

Stroustrup, B. (1986) *The C++ Programming Language,* Addison-Wesley.

Tam, M., Smith, J. M., and Farber, D. J. (1990) *A Survey of Distributed Shared Memory Systems*, Distributed Systems Labatory, Dept. CIS, University of Pennsylvania, Philadelphia, PA 19104-6389.

The Tandem Database Group, (1987) Non Stop, a Distributed High-Performance High-Availability Implementation of SQL, *Int. Workshop on High Performance Transaction Systems,* Asilomar, California.

Valduriez, P., Khoshafian, S. and Copeland, G. (1986) Implementation Techniques of Complex Objects, *Int. Conf. on VLDB*, Kyoto, August.

Valduriez, P., and Gardarin, G. (1989) *Analysis and Comparison of Relational Database Systems*, Addison Wesley.

22 Capturing parallel data processing strategies within a compiled language[1]

C. Chachaty, P. Borla-Salamet, B. Bergsten
BULL Corporate Research Center

22.1 INTRODUCTION

Combining data management and parallel processing is a promising solution to efficient and fault-tolerant data processing. In order to gain efficiency, parallel algorithms have been proposed to execute relational database operations [Bitton 83, Valduriez 84]. However, in order to generate these algorithms at query compile time, a parallel language is required. This is similar to the objective of parallelizing compilers for supercomputers [Wolfe 89].

We have designed the Parallel LERA language in this context. This database language represents the logical interface between the compiler of an extended query languege called ESQL [Gardarin 90] and the parallel execution sub-system. It results from a compilation phase which uses optimization and parallelization techniques [Valduriez 89] in order to obtain maximal efficiency when executing the execution plan generated by the compiler. This approach is similar to the one adopted in the Bubba project [Boral 90] as they also chose to compile queries expressed in FAD, a database programming language, into PFAD [Hart 88].

The main design feature of Parallel LERA is to support the description of the parallel execution of a query in a shared-nothing multiprocessor environment. A Parallel LERA program is formed of components explicitly connected by data communication operations. Extended relational operations, data communication operations, and control operations can be captured into a Parallel LERA program. Data operations (relational and data comunication) implement the parallel execution methods chosen by the optimizer for the relational operations which compose the query graph. The control operations implement the control strategies chosen by the parallelizer for the management of the parallel execution of each component of the query.

1 This work has been funded by the EDS Esprit project.

The introduction of control operations provides a complete separation of data and control processing. This allows a desired execution plan to be obtained by just combining the relevant control operations with a given set of standard data operations. This approach for control goes much further in compilation than in Bubba where control strategies are part of the communication sub-system; the use of one control strategy is associated to the use of corresponding communication primitives in the PFAD program. Furthermore, our approach gives more flexibility and more optimization opportunities in the control.

The language is based on an extensible set of operations and on constructs which group these operations. The first design of the language aims to validate the approach previously described for the language. Therefore, this first definition of the language that we present in this paper does not integrate the extended aspects of ESQL.

This work is part of the EDS Esprit project which aims at building a high-performance database server on a shared-nothing computer [Andres 90].

The remainder of the paper is organized as follows: Section 22.2 presents the database server architecture, Section 22.3 describes the different parallel execution mechanisms currently supported in Parallel LERA; Section 22.4 describes the different operation types and the constructs of the language and illustrates it with examples. Finally, some implementation issues are handled in Section 22.5.

22.2 THE EDS DATABASE SERVER

22.2.1 The machine architecture

The machine architecture for the database server consists of a set of processing elements, each one associated to a local memory, and connected to a communication network that they use to exchange messages. No shared memory is available, all the synchronizations and the communications between the nodes must circulate by the network.

The distributed memory architecture (multicomputer) has been validated by various Database systems. Teradata DBC/1012 [Neches 85], GAMMA [Dewitt 86], MBDS [Demurjian 86], Tandem NonStop SQL [Tandem 87] and Bubba [Wilkinson 87] are some examples of these systems. The flexibility and efficiency of the distributed memory architecture for the database machines motivate this choice. Flexibility is due to the system uniformity, as it is possible to increase the number of nodes of the machine without modifying the architecture of the system. Efficiency results from exploiting parallelism by placing the data on the different nodes of the machine.

22.2.2 The database server functional architecture

The system is divided into two major sub-systems: the compilation sub-system (Request Manager or RM), and the execution sub-system (Data Manager or DM). The role of the RM is basically to optimize and parallelize the database queries; it generates parallel execution plans which are directly executable by the DM. These execution plans are stored in a catalogue.

Before describing both of the components of the server, the data placement model is presented. This model is used in the compilation phase in order to optimize and parallelize the queries independently of the physical location of data. This placement is close to the one chosen in Bubba [Copeland 88].

To take advantage from the parallel execution opportunities, each relation is horizontally fragmented on a set of nodes of the machine. The number of nodes is determined by different criteria such as the size and the heat of the relation. In order to let the system free to decide reorganization of data depending on some events (e.g. replacing a failing node which stores a part of the relation by another one, extending relation on a larger number of nodes, ...), compilation must be independent of the physical localization of data. The notion of "home" is introduced to realize such independence. For the compiler, a home is a logical set of nodes storing a relation of the database. Some information is available about the home: approximate number of nodes, relations stored into the home and their distribution information (attribute for example) if any. Each relational operation is then associated to a home on which it will execute. The identification of the home is made by a reference to one of the database relations stored in this home: home(R) is the set of nodes storing relation R. At run-time, the link is made between the logical home and its corresponding physical nodes. The operation is executed on these nodes as soon as it is activated by message reception.

The request manager

The RM compiles ESQL queries into a code-generated version of Parallel LERA. This compilation is achieved by different phases which are respectively the analysis, optimization, parallelization and code generation. The results of the various transformations done by these compilation steps are all expressed into variations of the same intermediate language. This intermediate language called LERA (Language for Extended Relational Algebra) [Kellett 89] is based upon relational algebra, with extensions for recursion and ADT support. Fig. 22.1 illustrates the functional architecture of the RM and indicates the exchanged intermediate languages.

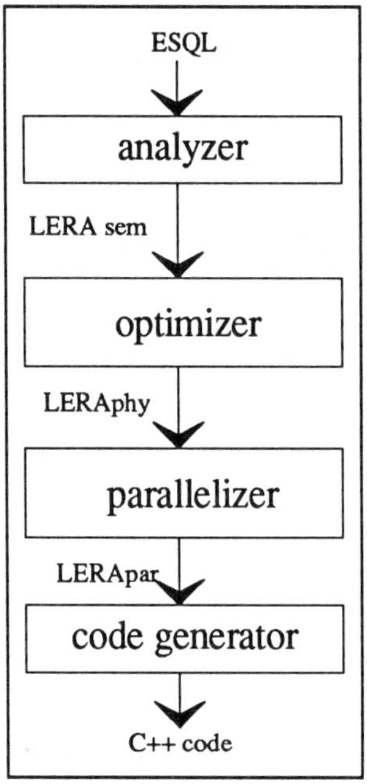

Figure 22.1 Functional architecture of the request manager.

The analysis of the ESQL query generates a LERA program which is then optimized. The result of the optimization is an execution plan for the query which minimizes a cost function expressed in terms of the parallel execution environment characteristics. This execution plan, described in LERAphy, consists of simple operations for which both operation localization and the global and local algorithms used are expressed by annotations. The parallelization step then compiles this execution plan in order to generate a parallel execution plan where data communications, and control processing needed for the schedule of the program, are explicited. This parallel execution plan is expressed in Parallel LERA. A code generation phase transforms the Parallel LERA program into C++ code which is compiled by a standard C++ compiler. The resulting object modules are either stored in a catalogue for further execution or directly executed by the Data Manager.

The data manager

When an execution is desired, the compiled code is loaded into the relevant nodes, linked to a run-time library and activated. The only part of the DM which is actually significant to Parallel LERA definition is the execution model. Its characteristics are:

- Communications between execution entities are done only by message passing
- Preloaded code is activated on message reception
- Code is activated as many times as messages addressed to this code are received

22.3 EXECUTION MECHANISMS

The parallel execution of a program needs specific control mechanisms which guarantee a valid execution. In particular, synchronization mechanisms are needed to respect the sequencing of the program operations. These mechanisms can be implemented by the run-time system and activated at query execution time, or integrated within the compiled query. For efficiency and optimization reasons, we have chosen the latter solution which avoids the use of run-time synchronization mechanisms and allows a better adaptability of the control mechanisms to each query.

In the following, after describing the parallel execution of an operation, we present the different types of sequencing between operations. Then, control mechanisms which ensure this sequencing at the execution of the query are described.

22.3.1 Parallel execution of an operation

To exploit relation distribution, each operation which uses a relation is decomposed into several sub-operations. Each sub-operation, identical to the others, executes on one node of the home of one or several relations, on the part of the data of the relation(s) local to this node. The sub-operation is derived from the initial operation by decomposing the global algorithm which implements the operation. This decomposition is specific to each algorithm. In this way, a selection operation which selects a set of tuples verifying a criterion from a given relation, is decomposed into n sub-operations by simply cutting the initial relation into n buckets, each sub-operation working on one bucket. As a relation is generally distributed on n nodes of a home, all these sub-operations can be run in parallel, each of them on one node. The same basic principle of data partitioning holds for the join operation, with some additional constraints.

Indeed, the parallelization of the join operation may include a preliminary data distribution phase. The distribution strategy is part of the global algorithm chosen by the optimizer. The parallelization deduces from this algorithm the needed data distribution. For example, to execute a hash-based join operation, if the two involved relations are not already distributed on the join attribute, the relations must first be hashed on the join attribute; the parallel execution of n local sub-joins, each on one pair of buckets, can then take place.

In the following sections, when describing the sequencing of operations, the word operation refers to the set of sub-operations which constitute the operation, each sub-operation being local to one node and executing on a subset of data.

22.3.2 Sequencing of operations

The programs that we take into account are extended relational queries. A query is represented by a directed acyclic graph (DAG) where the nodes are the operations; an arc represents an intermediate result produced by the source operation and consumed by the destination operation. Establishing the sequencing of the different operations of the graph is done by exploiting all the possibilities of parallel execution, without changing the decisions taken in the optimization step. This sequencing is used to introduce into the program all the control mechanisms necessary for the parallel execution of the request. There exist three sequencing types. They are described in the following.

Pipeline

Relational operations execute on a set of data. Making this execution operate on a single datum gives the opportunity to use pipelining, which is a special type of parallelism. Pipelining provides a finer execution grain, where small sets of data are exchanged between communicating operations. Therefore, an operation can begin executing as soon as one of the tuples that it consumes is produced. The producing and consuming operations execute therefore in parallel.

The pipelined execution avoids the storing of intermediate results as the tuples are consumed as soon as they are produced. Therefore, each time two operations exchange intermediate results, the pipelined execution will be privileged because of the parallelism that it generates and the small storage cost.

However, set-oriented semantics of relational operations is not always equivalent to the tuple-at-a-time semantics; an example of non-equivalence is the 'difference' operation. To execute these operations, we introduce another sequencing type, described in the following, which implies a set-oriented execution of these operations.

Sequential
Sequential execution of operations is the type of execution commonly used in relational database systems. It implies complete production of intermediate results by the producing operation before they can be used by the following operation. As pointed out in the previous section, it is better to avoid this type of sequencing in a parallel system because it involves storage costs and reduces parallelism opportunities. However, it appears that, sequencing two operations may be required for a correct execution of the query or for optimization reasons. A first case is the difference operation between relation A and relation B: relation B must be completely produced before the difference is executed. So the operation producing relation B must be executed in sequence with the difference operation. A second case is a join operation which operates on two intermediate results. It can be proved that, if the two input relations are pipelined from previous operations, the two streams of tuples must be locally stored to make sure that each tuple from the first input relation meets each tuple from the second relation. The optimizer may then choose another execution strategy than pipelining. This other strategy materializes (produces in a set-oriented way) one of the two input streams, in order to consume the other input in pipeline without storing it. This solution implies a sequential execution between the operation which produces the materialized relation and the join operation.

Parallel
The parallel sequencing of two operations is used when there is no dependence of one of the operations on the other, e.g. when the two operations can execute in parallel without synchronization. They can then be activated and executed independently.

In the example illustrating the control strategies and Parallel LERA in Section 22.4.4, the sequencing types described previously will be referenced to by the keywords PIPE, SEQ or PAR respectively. These keywords correspond to the constructors of an intermediate language called Abstract Parallel LERA.

22.3.3 Parallel execution control

Problem
The compilation approach chosen leads to make explicit all the execution mechanisms into the program. We indicated previously how each relational

operation is split into localized sub-operations, leaving no more global existence for the operation. All these sub-operations need being synchronized and controlled. The control mechanisms needed for a correct execution of the program are compiled and added to the program in an explicit way. These control mechanisms interact with the operations to guarantee a global execution which corresponds to the execution plan generated by the optimizer.

Each type of sequencing described before needs a different control mechanism. In particular, to guarantee a sequential execution (cf. 22.3.2) between two operations, we need to guarantee that the second operation is only activated when the first one is terminated. This implies the ability to detect the end of the execution of an operation or of a group of operations. Knowing that an operation op1 is distributed into a number of sub-operations, each localized on one node, we need to detect the local termination of each sub-operation and the global termination of op1.

If op1 is pipelined (cf. 22.3.2) with a previous operation op_0, the triggering of op1 is related to the presence of relevant data, these data being sent by op_0 . The execution is then driven by the data and operation op1 is activated on each data arrival. op1 is unable to know at a given moment if other data messages will arrive as the production of these data depends on operation op_0; so, op1 is unable to decide if its proper execution is finished or not. This implies the ability to notify explicitly the end of the data stream (EOS) to each sub-operation; this signal allows the local end detection.

In the following we present the control mechanisms which guarantee the synchronization and the end detection of operations. These mechanisms imply the introduction of specific control operations and messages. Our approach is to separate them from the data operations and messages. This choice is justified by several reasons. First, it allows to combine the same data operations (join, select, etc.) with different control structures which give different possible sequencing. Second, it allows optimization of control mechanisms by taking into account the properties of each query.

Termination detection

To detect the global termination of a distributed operation, it is necessary to detect the local termination of each of its sub-operations. The local ends are propagated to a control operation which centralizes the end signals, detects the global termination and propagates it to the rest of the program.

This termination detection is initialized at the beginning of the program by propagating an end of stream message (EOS) just after triggering the first operation(s) of the program. This message is used to build further EOS messages when the operations which generate data are terminated, and consequently are not able to produce more data on the stream. The EOS is then propagated through the graph of control operations. It is used to synchronize the operations and to detect the end of the program when reaching the last node of the graph.

Synchronization

The synchronization of two operations involves triggering the second operation when the first one is terminated. So, a control operation will trigger the execution of the second operation when it receives the end signal of the first operation. Then, the control operation triggers all the localized sub-operations corresponding to the global operation to be executed.

If n operations are executed in parallel, we might need to synchronize all these operations with another OP operation. Then we need to wait for n global termination messages before triggering operation OP.

Fig. 22.2 describes the termination detection and synchronization mechanisms for a sequential execution of OP_i and OP_{i+1}. Q is a materialized relation produced by OP_i and consumed by OP_{i+1}.

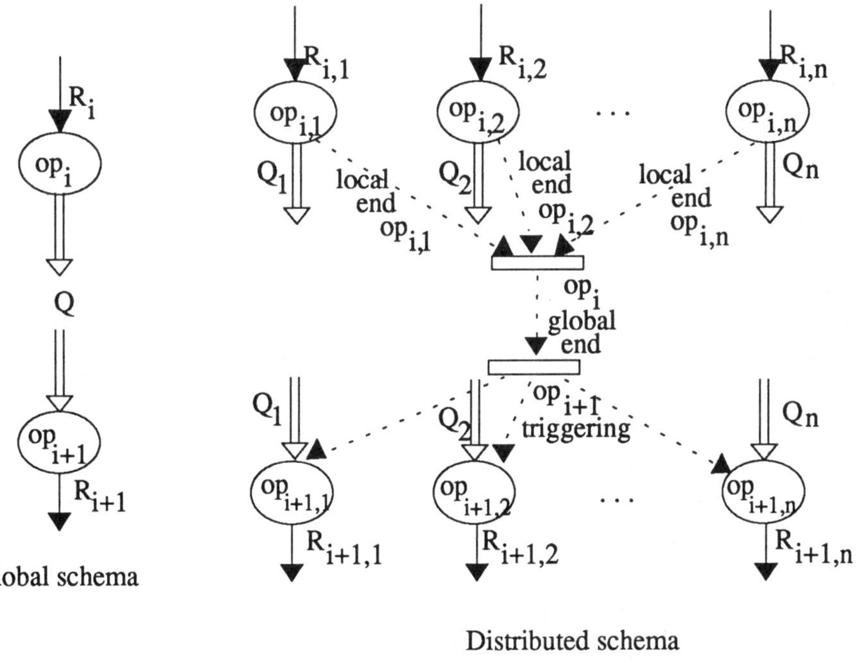

Figure 22.2 Synchronization of two operations.

22.4 PARALLEL LERA

Parallel LERA is designed to describe the parallel execution of a query. It handles localized operations and makes their interaction explicit. It supports also all types of sequencing and control mechanisms described before.

In the following, we first present different Parallel LERA operation types and then show how to group operations by using special constructs. Finally, we present the control primitives of Parallel LERA whose functionalities have been globally described previously. Parallel LERA syntax is illustrated with some examples.

22.4.1 Different operation types in Parallel LERA

Relational operations

In Parallel LERA, a relational operation represents a set of localized identical sub-operations executing on a home. An operation has one or more input relations; one of these inputs may be pipelined, the others being present in the home in a materialized form.

Example of a relational operation (a join operation):

```
I = {home(R)} join {nestedloop} ( (R, S), R.1 = S.2 )
```

The annotations indicated within {} (e.g., {home(R)}), express optimization choices for the operation. In the example above, the {home(R)} annotation indicates the set of nodes where the join operation will be executed (localization) and {nestedloop} is the local algorithm used to execute each localized sub-join operation. I identifies the result of the join operation.

Communication operations

The result of a relational operation is considered as a stream of data. The communication operations put this dataflow in the form needed by the next operation which will consume the intermediate result. The communication operations are distributed into sub-operations just as the relational operations. There is three communication operations: send, local_send and store. The send operation pipelines the data to the next operation by distributing it on the nodes of the home of the receiving operation. The distribution parameters appear in the send operation. This send operation is distributed on the same home as the operation producing the data stream which needs to be transmitted to another operation via the network. Indeed, each sub-operation of the relational operation is associated to a sub-operation of the send for the transmission of its produced data. The local_send operation is used to transmit data locally on one node in pipeline between relational operations. It is used to make communications between co-located operations asynchronous. The store operation receives a stream of data pipelined from a local or remote operation, and materializes it.

The following is an example of a communication operation (send) which transmits the result I1 of a preceding operation to the nodes of home(S), by hash on the second attribute of I1. The send operation is distributed on {home(R)}, as the operation which produces I1.

```
I1 = {home(R)} ...
I2 = {home(R)} send ( I1, home(S), hash on I1.2)
```

Control operations

Control operations which are in charge of the termination detection and of the synchronization of the program operations will be presented in details in Section 22.4.3.

In the following, "data operations" designate indifferently relational operations or communication operations.

22.4.2 Parallel LERA constructs

Parallel LERA provides two constructs, the local-op (localized operation) construct and the assoc (association) construct. These constructs are used to group Parallel LERA operations. Their semantics are described in the following sections and an example is given to illustrate the two concepts.

The local-op construct

The local-op construct isolates one execution entity into the program. It groups data operations which communicate locally on each node of a given home, e.g. exchange intermediate data in a local pipeline mode which we call internal local pipeline. The data operations which are part of the local-op represent a sub-graph which has a single root (either a dataflow or a triggering message), and one or more leaves (data communication operations: send, local_send or store). For each message received, all the data operations in the local-op are executed synchronously. A local-op is the basic unit for synchronization.

The assoc construct

An association isolates into the graph of the parallel execution plan, a component which is a sub-graph of data and control operations, located on one home. This component is composed of local-ops and associated control operations which communicate locally on each node of the home. Each element of an association is distributed on all the nodes of the home where the association is located. Two local-ops located in the same association exchange data in one of two modes: the first mode is a local pipeline called external local pipeline, and the second mode is through a stored intermediate relation. Local-ops exchange data in external local pipeline by using the local_send communication operation and so, execute asynchronously. Localized control operations interact with the local-op units and participate to the synchronization of the program.

The following is an example of two local-ops located in the same association and exchanging I3 in the external local pipeline mode. The last operation of the second local-op is a send which transmits the I5 dataflow to other nodes.

```
...
{home(R)}
Assoc
Local-op (T)
                I2 = select(R, R.1 = 10, R.2)
        I3 = local_send(I2)
End local-op;
Local-op (I2)
        I4 = difference(I3, S)
        I5 = send(I4, home(T), hash on I4.2)
        End local-op
... control operations associated to the Local-ops ... End assoc
...
```

22.4.3 Control operations of Parallel LERA

The control operations of Parallel LERA are added to the graph of the relational query. The control flow propagates in parallel to the dataflow propagation. It acts on the data operations when data pipelining is not used, i.e. when explicit triggering is necessary.

In the following sections, we present the semantics of the control operations and illustrate them with examples. We first describe the termination detection operations and then the synchronization operations.

Termination detection of an operation

Two control operations are needed to detect the termination of a distributed data operation OP: the first operation is distributed on the home of OP and is called LWP (Local Wait then Propagate). It detects the local end of each sub-operation of OP. The second operation is centralized and called GWP (Global Wait then Propagate). It detects the global termination of OP.

Local termination: the LWP

The LWP (Local Wait then Propagate) operation is distributed on the same nodes as the distributed data operation OP that it controls. Each sub-operation LWPi of the LWP is associated to a sub-operation OPi of OP executing on one node. The LWPi is activated when it receives a message (EOS for End Of Stream) indicating that no more data will be sent to OP. Then the LWPi waits for OPi to be entirely executed on all received data, before propagating a local termination message (SEOS for Single End Of Stream).

In fact, as the basic unit for synchronization is a local-op, an LWP operation is associated to a local-op rather than to a simple data operation. One parameter of the LWP refers to an output result of the local-op, therefore identifying the related local-op and also the data stream for which the LWP propagates the SEOS. If several output results are produced by the local-op, an LWP operation will be associated to each of these results. In the following, we recall the example previously used to illustrate the constructs of Parallel LERA, and add the LWPs which are necessary to detect the local termination of the local-ops and propagate the SEOS messages.

```
...
{home(R)}
Assoc
Local-op (T)
                I2 = select(R, R.1 = 10, R.2)
        I3 = local_send(I2)
End local-op;

C2 = LWP (C1, I3)       C1 is the EOS propagated to the LWP

Local-op (I3)
        I4 = difference(I3, S)
                I5 = send(I4, home(T), hash on I4.2)
End local-op

C3 = LWP (C2, I5)

End assoc
...
```

Global termination: the GWP

The GWP (Global Wait then Propagate) operation is a centralized operation associated to a distributed data operation OP. It executes on one node and receives the local termination messages (SEOS) propagated by the localized LWPi each associated to an OPi. Once the GWP has received all the SEOS, it propagates a message indicating the global termination (EOS) of OP. The number of SEOS that the GWP waits for is equal to the number of nodes in the home of OP.

In Figure 22.3, we present an example where the LWP and the GWP operations are used in association with a local-op. The local-op is composed of a join operation locally pipelined with a send operation. The example is illustrated by the Parallel LERA operations graph, and also by the corresponding program. The annotation {one-node-home} indicates the localization of the GWP operation: as the operation is centralized, any node of the system, chosen at run-time, can execute it.

```
{one-node-home}
Assoc
C1 = GWP(...)
End_assoc

{home(R)}
Assoc
        Local-op (I1)
        I2 = join {nestedloop}((R,I1),R.1 = I1.2)
        I3 = send (I2,home(S), broadcast)

        End_Local-op
        C2 = LWP(C1,I3)
End_assoc

{one-node-home}
Assoc
C3 = GWP(C2)
End_assoc
```

Synchronization and explicit triggering: the TP operation

The TP (Trigger and Propagate) control operation is introduced to make the synchronization and the explicit triggering of operations. The exact functionality of this operation is described below.

Suppose that we want to execute two operations OP_1 and OP_2 in a sequential way. The global termination detection of OP1 is done by its associated GWP operation which generates an EOS and sends it to the TP operation. The TP operation, activated by the EOS reception, triggers operation OP2. In this way, we guarantee that OP2 is not activated until the execution of OP1 is completed. OP2 needs explicit triggering because it does not receive any dataflow. The TP operation then propagates to the LWP operation associated to OP2 an end of stream message which will initialize the termination detection of OP2.

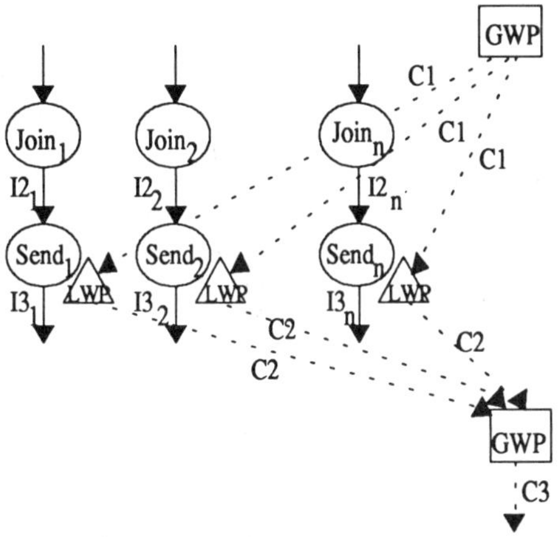


```
{one-node-home}
Assoc
   C1 = GWP(...)
End_assoc

{home(R)}
Assoc
   Local-op (I1)
      I2 = join {nestedloop}
                ((R,I1),R.1=I1.2)
      I3 = send (I2,home(S),
                 broadcast)
   End_Local-op
   C2 = LWP(C1,I3)
End_assoc

{one-node-home}
Assoc
   C3 = GWP(C2)
End_assoc
```

Figure 22.3 Example of termination detection with LWP and GWP operations.

The set-oriented synchronization between OP1 and OP2 made by the TP operation described in the previous section can be extended to support a synchronization between a group of m operations with another group of n operations. The TP operation then waits for m EOS messages, before sending n (trigger + EOS) to the second group of operations. Figure 22.4 is an illustration of the TP with m=2 and n=1. It shows how the TP operation explicitly triggers an operation and propagates the end message when the preceding operations terminate.

```
one-node-home}
Assoc
        C1 = GWP(...)
        C2 = GWP(...)
        (T1,C3) = TP(C1,C2)
End_assoc

{home(R)}
Assoc
        Local-op (T1)
        I2 = diff {nestedloop} (R,S)
        I3 = send (I2, home(Q), hash on I1.1)
        End_Local-op
                C4 = LWP(C3, I3)
End_assoc
```

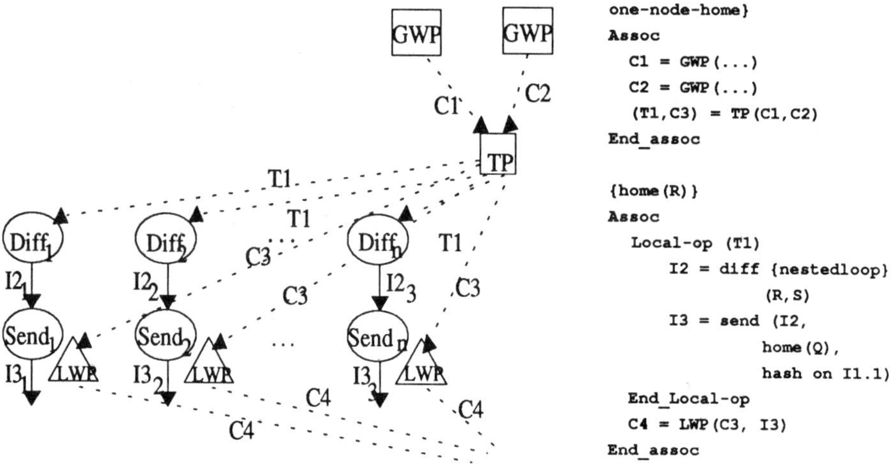

Figure 22.4 An explicit triggering with the TP operation.

22.4.4 Example

Let us consider a database composed of the following

CAR (car_id, brand, type),
CAR is randomly distributed on the nodes of the home
BUY (person_id, car_id, date)
BUY is distributed by hash on car_id attribute
CONTROL (car_id, organization_id, date)
C (for CONTROL) is distributed by hash on organization_id attribute

and the SQL query is to find Renault cars which have been bought and not controlled since the first of January 1986:

```
SELECT BUY.car_id FROM BUY, CAR
WHERE BUY.date > '010186' and BUY.car_id = CAR.car_id
and CAR.brand = 'Renault'
and CAR.car_id not in SELECT C.car_id FROM CONTROL C
                      WHERE C.date > '010186'
```

A possible execution plan generated by the optimizer is:

```
I1   = select {home(C), select} (C, C.date  '010186', (C.car_id))
I2   = select {home(CAR), select}
           (CAR, CAR.brand = Renault, (CAR.car_id))
I3   = difference {home(BUY), hashdiff} (I2 {pipe}, I1 {materialized})
I4   = select {home(BUY), select}
       (BUY, BUY.date  '010186', (BUY.car_id))
I5   = join {home(BUY), assocjoin} (I4 {materialized}, I3 {pipe},
         I4.car_id = I3.car_id, (I4.car_id))
```

Given the localization of the operations, the global execution algorithms for the operation and the indications for the input relations specified in the annotations, some communication operations must be added to the program. After these operations are introduced, the schedule of the program is established. The control operations corresponding to this schedule are integrated within the program. The Parallel LERA program corresponding to the request is represented by a graph in Fig. 22.5. The grey boxes on the figure represent the local-op constructs and the dotted boxes represent the assoc constructs.

Then, we give the Abstract Parallel LERA program which makes the schedule of the program explicit.

```
SEQ    after executing the two selections in parallel,
PAR    and materializing the two results on home(BUY), ...
       PIPE
              I1 = select {home(C)} (C, C.date  '010186', (C.car_id))
              J1 = send {home(C)} (I1, hash on car_id, home(BUY))
              J2 = store {home(BUY)} (J1)
       ENDPIPE
       PIPE
              I4 = select {home(BUY)}
                        (BUY, BUY.date > '010186', (BUY.car_id))
              J3 = store {home(BUY)} (I4)
       ENDPIPE
ENDPAR
PIPE   ... the execution of the selection on CAR is pipelined ...
       I2 = select {home(CAR)} (CAR, CAR.brand = Renault, (CAR.car_id))
```

```
J4 = send {home(CAR)} (I2, hash on car_id, home(BUY))
```

...on the difference and the join

```
I3 = difference {home(BUY)} (J4, J2)
I5 = join {home(BUY)}
            (J3, I3, J3.car_id = I3.car_id, (J3.car_id))
ENDPIPE
ENDSEQ
```

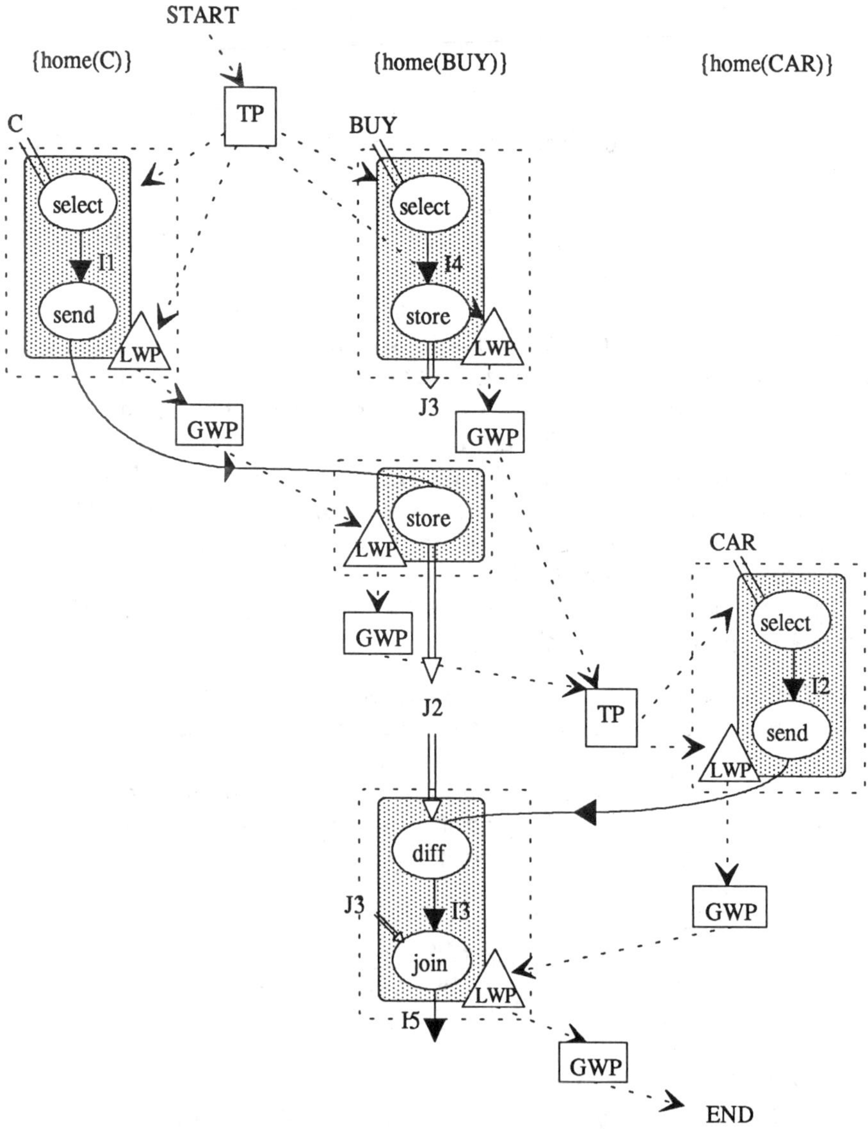

Figure 22.5 An example of a Parallel LERA graph.

22.5 IMPLEMENTATION ISSUES

The description of Parallel LERA semantics is independent from the implementation of the run time system. This feature, which was a main goal for the language definition, was made possible by two choices:

- First, the language is based on an extensible set of operations. All these operations are designed with respect to the same operational principles which are the properties of the execution model. Any run time system which respects these properties is a possible candidate to the execution of Parallel LERA programs.
- Second, a code generation phase converts a Parallel LERA program into compiled object modules. This code generation phase makes the mapping between the concepts of Parallel LERA and the run time system on which the program will be executed.

This design gave us the possibility to implement Parallel LERA on several different run time systems by the mean of one code generator for each system. One implementation was done on Flagship, a shared-nothing multiprocessor, developed by ICL. Another prototype was developed on a uniprocessor Unix system. This last implementation emulates parallelism by creating processes for the associations in Parallel LERA, and co-routines for local-ops inside each association. We are currently extending these results to a shared-memory multiprocessor (Multimax ENCORE with 10 processors running the Mach operating system).

A prototype of the compiler which compiles ESQL queries into Parallel LERA programs has been developed. This compiler is shared among the different data server prototypes previously cited. It is composed of several modules integrated within a single compilation process.

22.6 CONCLUSION

We designed a language which expresses the parallel execution of a relational query and its associated control. Extensibility and expression power are its most important features. It is extensible because it relies upon a library of operations which can evolve and integrate new operations used to implement new execution strategies. It is powerful because it enables a program to control its proper execution with the best adapted control strategies.

Three execution modes between relational operations are currently handled: parallel, pipeline and sequential. Base relations are generally distributed across a given number of nodes of the system in order to induce intra-operation parallelism. Thus, Parallel LERA operations are generally executed where the data reside and communicate by message passing. Optimization mechanisms used to reduce data and control communication volume has been described.

The implementation of Parallel LERA among several run time system prototypes have been addressed. This insists that the semantics of the language does not depend on a particular run time system implementation, but on the execution model properties. This made the prototyping possible on shared-nothing architecture as well as on a shared-memory architecture.

Studies on implementation of deduction show that the addition of special operations to handle recursion, without change to the constructs and other concepts of Parallel LERA, is enough to integrate deduction. We expect that handling objects will be integrated in a similar way.

22.7 ACKNOWLEDGEMENTS

Many people aside from the authors have contributed to the design of the language described in this paper, including Steve Kellet, Benont Dageville and Patrick Casadessus. Benont Dageville and Patrick Casadessus also prototyped parts of the compiler and participated with Didier Terral to the design and implementation of the executor, therefore validating the design of the language. We benefited from the helpful comments of Patrick Valduriez who reviewed the first version of the paper.

REFERENCES

Andres, F. et al. (1990) EDS - Collaborating For a High Performance Parallel Relational Database, *Esprit Conference,* Brussels.

Bitton, D., Boral, H., DeWitt, D. J., and Wilkinson, W. K. (1983) Parallel Algorithms for the Execution of Relational Database Operations, *ACM Transactions on Database Systems,* September 1983.

Boral, H. et al. (1990) Prototyping Bubba, A Highly Parallel Database System, *IEEE Transactions on Knowledge and Data Engineering,* **2**, (1), March 1990.

Copeland, G., Alexander, W., Boughter, E., and Keller, T. (1988) Data Placement in Bubba *Proc. ACM SIGMOD Conference on Management of Data,* May 1988.

Demurjian, S., Hsiao, D., Menon, J. (1986) A Multi-Backend Database System for Performance Gains, Capacity Growth and Hardware Upgrade, *International Conference on Data Engineering*, Los Angeles.

Dewitt, D. J., Gerber, R. H., Graefe, G. M., Heytens, L., Kumar, K. B., and Muralikrishna, M. (1986) GAMMA A High Performance Dataflow Database Machine, *Very Large DataBases*, Kyoto.

Gardarin, G., and Valduriez, P. (1990) ESQL2 : An Extended SQL with Object and Deductive Capabilities, *Databases and EXpert systems Applications,* Vienna, August 1990.

Hart, B., Danforth, S., and Valduriez, P. (1988) Parallelizing a Database Programming Language, *International Symposium on Databases in Parallel and Distributed Systems*, Austin.

Neches, P. M. (1985) *The Anatomy of a Database Computer System,* COMPCON, San Francisco.

Tandem Database Group Non Stop SQL, a Distributed High-Performance, High Availability Implementation of SQL *International Workshop on High Performance Transactions Systems,* Asilomar 87

Valduriez, P., and Gardarin, G. (1986) Join and Semi-join Algorithms for a Multiprocessor Database Machine *ACM TODS,* **9**, (1), March 1986.

Valduriez, P., and Danforth S. (1989) Query Optimization in Database Programming Language *International Conference on Deductive and Object Oriented Databases,* Kyoto, December 1989.

Wilkinson, K., and Boral, H. (1987) KEV The Operating System Kernel of BUBBA, *International Workshop on Database Machine,* Karuizawa.

Wolfe, M. (1989) *Optimizing Supercompilers for Supercomputers*, MIT Press.

23 Performance evaluation of an OLTP application on the EDS database server using a behavioural simulation model

K-F Wong and M. Paci
European Computer-Industry Research Centre (ECRC) GmbH

23.1 INTRODUCTION

The European Declarative System (EDS) is a 4 year project, the first 3 years of which are funded under the ESPRIT II (European Strategic Programme for Research and Development in Information Technology) initiative [Anc90]. The project involves a total of 650 persons/year and started at the beginning of 1989. Its aim is to design and implement a complete hardware and software platform which will be used to develop advanced information systems for business professionals. BULL (France), ICL (UK), SIEMENS (West Germany) and ECRC (Europe) are the main partners of the project.

A major goal of the EDS project is the production of a high performance, highly parallel database server [WaToWa 90]. The EDS database server is being built upon a shared-nothing multiprocessor architecture. Using the state-of-the-art parallel database and non-volatile main memory technologies, it provides high performance, reliability and availability. It is designed to handle a continuum of database applications, ranging from simple on-line transactions to large complex decision support queries. Design and development of the EDS database server involve immense efforts and time and require close collaborations of many engineers and researchers from numerous organisations [And 90]. As an intermediate product, an EDS prototype system will be developed by 1992. In order to evaluate the performance of the server prior to the availability of a prototype system, a high level behavioural simulation model of the server is being implemented. In addition, the simulation will serve the following roles:

- To evaluate the server's performance in running different applications. In particular, parallel processing of complex decision support queries will be extensively studied.
- To study the effectiveness of the EDS database interface to other parallel programming languages; especially the ElipSys (ECRC Logic Inference System) [Won 90] database connection.
- To identify system bottlenecks and hot-spots by studying the run time profiles of typical database applications.
- To investigate the performance of the system under different parallel algorithms and techniques.
- To serve as a design tool for engineers in configuring EDS systems under different application requirements.

High-level simulation at the behavioural level is effective for simulating large multiprocessor systems. For large multiprocessor systems, such as EDS which can be configured with up to 256 processors, it is expensive to simulate each processor at gate, register or instruction level. The time required to evaluate a real-sized application running on one of these levels can be intolerablely long even with a moderate number of processors. To make the simulation practical, behavioural level simulation is commonly used. Simulation in such high level can greatly improve simulation time and makes modeling of large and complex systems affordable.

A two-layer simulation approach is adopted by the EDS model. At the configuration layer, the shared-nothing architecture consisting of multiple processor elements interconnected by a message-passing network is simulated. At the execution layer, the behaviour of the parallel database server is modelled. This involves the tracing of the critical paths of all database operations during a query evaluation. A drawback of many existing simulation systems for database servers is that they cannot handle multiple queries. This is not a limitation in the EDS model because of the flexibility offered by the two-level simulation strategy. Multiple queries can be evaluated at different processing modules concurrently.

Conceptually, the EDS simulation model can be viewed as a parallel queuing network with multiple queuing stations (i.e. the processing element modules). Stations can send jobs to each other in the form of messages via a central routing agent (i.e. the network). Different, however, from classical queuing networks approaches, the EDS model adopts a simulation rather than an analytical strategy [GePu 87]. An analytical strategy would be extremely complex to implement and require many prior assumptions which would limit the accuracy of the results.

This paper describes the design, implementation and an application of the simulation model. The rest of the paper is organized as follows: in section 23.2 the hardware and software architectures of the EDS system are briefly described. Section 23.3 describes the design and implementation of the EDS behavioural simulation model. A typical On-Line Transaction Processing (OLTP), namely debit/credit, application was evaluated using the EDS simulation model. The OLTP simulation is explained and the results are analysed in section 23.4. Finally, in section 23.5, the conclusion is given.

23.2 THE EDS SYSTEM

Hardware: The EDS parallel machine [WaToWa 90]. consists of a message passing network which provides a number of identical connection ports that can support up to 256 functional elements (Fig. 23.1). A functional element may be one of:

(1) Processing Element - It is responsible for query and program execution.

(2) Diagnostic Element - It supports system diagnostics and provides early I/O and Host connection support.

(3) I/O Element - It provides the magnetic discs as back-up and mass storage.

(4) HOST Element - It provides the interface to a number of host machines.

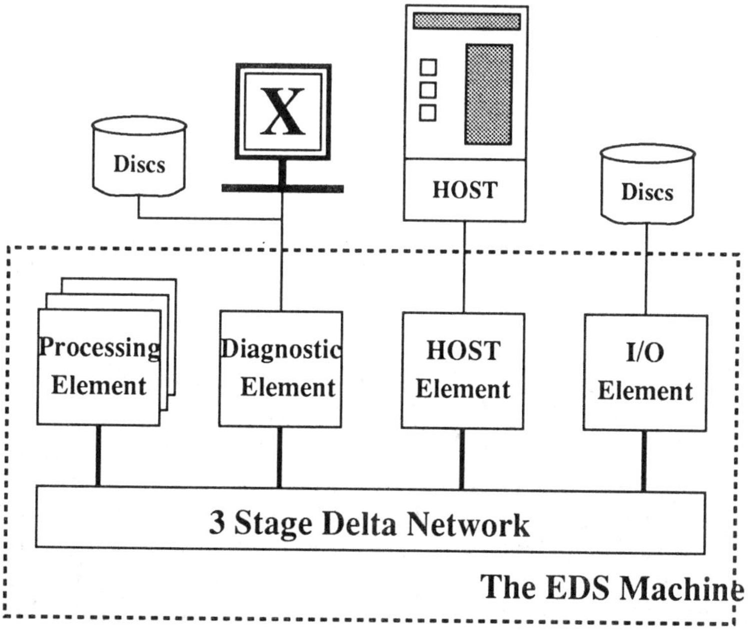

Figure 23.1 The hardware architecture of the EDS system.

The processing element which is the execution engine of the EDS machine comprises of 4 components: a Store Unit, a Processing Unit, a System Support Unit and a Network Interface Unit. The Store Unit consists of 64 Mbyte of non-volatile RAM (extendible to 2G). The Processing Unit is based on a SPARC processor. To achieve maximum flexibility the design of the PE is centered around the M-bus (a *de facto* standard defined by SUN for SPARC processors). This makes it easy to replace existing SPARC processors with similar but more powerful processors in the future; and thus ensures that the design will keep up with technological evolution. The core of the System Support Unit is a low-cost SPARC processor. It runs in parallel with the Processing Unit. Its main role is to reduce the load of the Processing Unit by performing low-level tasks such as message passing control. The Network Interface Unit provides a 20MB/s dual (Tx and Rx) communication channel between the PEs and the network.

The interconnection network is a 3 stage, byte-wide delta-network. The basic building blocks are 8x8 crossbar switches. The mode of operation is based on a combination of both packet-and circuit-switching. The switches store packets in internal buffers, as in packet-switched networks. However, if the required output link is available, the switch does not wait until a packet has been received completely before starting to transmit the packet to the next stage. By doing so, the network behaves as a circuit-switched network and provides a very short latency.

The EDS system is a main memory system. Secondary disc memory is not used for storage (except for backup, optional). Data can be distributed and stored in non-volatile RAMs on one or more PEs. The storage size of the EDS machine is scalable. A maximum of 256 PEs can be incorporated in the machine. Since each PE contains 64M to 2G bytes of memory, the EDS system is able to handle up to 0.5 terabytes of data.

Software: The EDS software architecture is designed for three non-numeric applications in parallel : database, Lisp and logic programming, namely ElipSys [Won 90]. A key feature is that these three paradigms are able to interwork on the EDS machine. Moreover, a Unix subsystem is supported. The parallel languages, database and Unix subsystems (Fig. 23.2): are being implemented on top of the EDS kernel, known as the EDS Machine Executive (EMEX). EMEX is responsible for overall resource management of the EDS system. It supports (1) a light-weight process model which implements the concepts of threads, teams and tasks; (2) message passing inter/intra process communications coupled with efficient buffer management; and (3) a memory model which employs a virtual address scheme that can spread across an arbitrary number of PEs. These facilities are essential for large scale parallelism. The language subsystems can invoke EMEX facilities by using the Process Control

Language (PCL). PCL has similar design objectives to other distributed operating systems (e.g. Mach and Chorus); this implies that porting existing applications written for such systems to the EDS machine will be possible. Conceptually, PCL may be regarded as a software bus which allows the different subsystems to coexist in the EDS machines. At the lowest level, EMEX accesses the underlying parallel hardware via the Primitive Machine Interface (PMI).

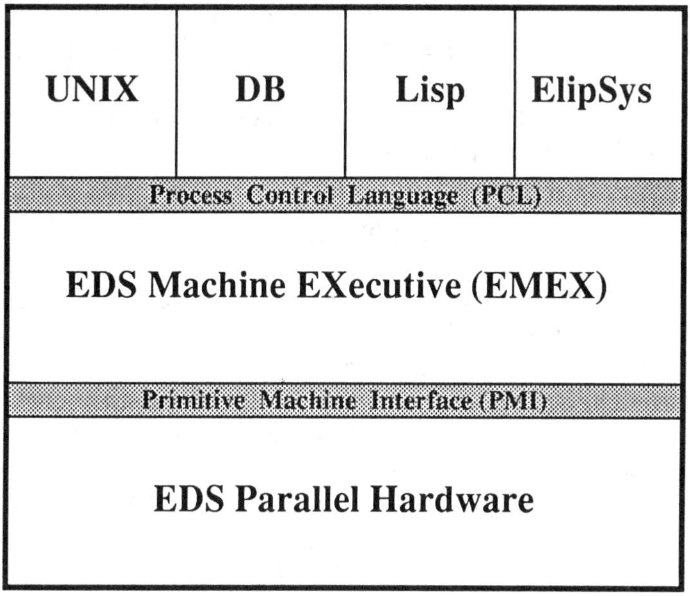

Figure 23.2 The software architecture of the EDS system.

One major drawback of Lisp and logic programming languages which has been hindering their widespread acceptance is their inability to handle large data sets. In the EDS system, this is overcome by interworking between the Lisp and Prolog subsystems and the database subsystem. Effectively, the database subsystem will play a double-role : (1) a standalone database server; and (2) an extensional database to the Lisp/Prolog subsystems. Therefore, it is one of the core elements of the whole EDS design and its efficiency can influence the performance of the overall system. A shared-nothing architecture, like the EDS machine, has been proved suitable for parallel database applications (e.g. Bubba [Bor 90]); it can provide a scalable and reliable platform which is essential for large databases that may increase in size.

The EDS database subsystem supports an Extended SQL (ESQL) interface and consists of 2 main components the Request Manager and the Data Manager [WaTo 90]. The former is responsible for compiling a ESQL query to an optimized intermediate program which is directly executed by the Data Manager. Physically, the Request Manager and the Data Manager are PCL tasks. The ESQL query, the compiled intermediate program and the query results are passed between tasks using the PCL message passing facility. Database queries are optimized to operate on data distributed across the non-volatile main memory provided on each processing element. A dedicated modular software system, namely the Object Manager, operating on each processing element is responsible for providing data consistency and operation atomicity. The performance target of the EDS server running on a system with 256 processing elements is 12000 tps at 30% utilization for OLTP applications.

23.3 THE EDS SIMULATION MODEL

For performance evaluation of the EDS database server for various applications, a high level simulation model is developed. The implementation of the simulation model is divided into 2 layers: the configuration layer simulates the shared-nothing architecture of the underlying EDS machine; and at the execution layers the behavioural simulation of the parallel database server is performed.

At the configuration layer, the EDS simulation model resembles the architecture of the EDS machine which consists of up to 256 processing elements interconnected by a 3-stage delta network. (Notice that the roles of the other functional elements – i.e. I/O, HOST and Diagnostic elements – are subsumed by the processing element in the simulation model.) Each processing element and the network are represented as independent VHDL entities in the simulation model. Processing element entities (PEs[1]) communicate with each other by a message passing mechanism. The same mechanism is used for the interface of a PE to the external environment. A message comprises seven fields, viz:

---

1 Throughout this document the abbreviation PE stands for a VHDL module representing an EDS processing element.

PIDSender	PIDReceiver	MessageType	Content0	Content1	Content2	Content3

PIDSender	identification (ID) of the message sending PE
PIDReceiver	identification (ID) of the message receiving PE
MessageType	message type (e.g. BEGIN_TRANSACTION)
Content0	content of the message (1 byte)
Content1	content of the message (1 byte)
Content2	content of the message (1 byte)
Content3	content of the message (1 byte)

Each PE is assigned with an unique identification (ID) number. An ID number represents the address of a PE on the EDS machine. When a message is sent, the IDs of the sender and the receiver PEs must be included in the header of the message. The MessageType field contains the instruction (or command) which the sender issues to the receiver. Instructions are intermediate operations corresponding to fragments of a database query. Some instructions require arguments (e.g. A and B in A JOIN B). Arguments are packaged in the subsequent content fields. The order in which arguments are contained in the content fields is pre-defined and remains fixed throughout a transaction.

The message format of the simulation model is slightly different from the same on the physical EDS machine. For example, the size of the message content of the former is generally smaller than a physical message; and also, at the programmer level, a physical message can be any size. The reduced size and the fixed format of the simulating message make storing and decoding of the message more efficient. The message format is adequate for the purpose of performance evaluation. This is because the crucial information describing the database operation to be performed by the receiving PE is clearly stated in the MessageType field.

Upon receiving a message on a PE, the simulation model works out the worst-case execution time for the operation specified in the MessageType and adds the time to the overall execution time of the corresponding transaction. The ultimate execution time of the transaction is stored in an external file for post-analysis.

In addition to calculating the execution time the execution path of a query – i.e. the PEs participated in the execution, the messages they send and receive and the chronological sequence in which the messages are handled – is traced and can be displayed graphically in waveform diagrams.

This facility is very useful and allows one to inspect the simulation results visually in between successive simulation runs.

The simulation model is implemented using a high level simulation description language, namely VHDL. Although, VHDL is originally designed for specification and design of digital hardware systems [LiScUs 90], the different levels of design abstraction which the language supported – from gate-level to architectural level – makes it also applicable to designs in other domains. VHDL preserves many useful features (e.g. strong typing, modularity, etc.) of conventional programming languages (e.g. Pascal); and in addition, the notions of time, events, signals and concurrent process are introduced to the semantics of the language. Combination of such features facilitates mixed-level system designs which is useful for modelling the EDS database server.

The growing popularity of VHDL[2] brings about numerous VHDL tools and environments from many commercial vendors. For that reason, there was little problem in finding a simulation system for developing the EDS simulation model. The VantageSpreadsheet(TM) was selected because the system offers an incremental change update capability, different formats for displaying results, and an easy-to-use graphical interface. A modular design approach is employed in the development of the EDS simulation model. Modularity, coupled with the VANTAGE incremental change facility, simplifies the procedure of adding/reducing processing element modules to/from an existing simulation run.

23.3.1 The network module

The behaviour of the network

The network[3] interconnects all PEs and provides common communication channels for data exchange between all distributed processing elements. At the programming level, data exchange between PEs is either implicit – through page copying initiated by remote access to non-local shared virtual memory – or explicitly by send/receive kernel calls.

Each processing element (PE) is connected to the network through an I/O port. A port consists of two channels – one for input and one for output, and together they provide duplex communication. The network detects all messages sent to its input channels and routes them to the appropriate receiver PEs specified in the PIDReceiver field of the messages.

---

2 VHDL is an industrial IEEE standard [IEE 88] fully supported by the US government.

3 Unless it is mentioned explicitly, the term network refers tothe network module under simulation and not the physical EDS delta network.

The minimum delay of a message through the network is equal to the latency of the network. This is independent of the positions of the sender and the receiver. Currently, the calculated nominal latency, 8.1 usec, is adopted. The time spent by a message travelling through the network depends heavily on the network traffic. For conflict-free routing, the minimum delay is introduced to the evaluation. On the other hand, when the network detects that several messages are sent to the same PE, it puts the messages into the queue associated with that PE and later dispatches them in the order they are received. Whenever a message on the top of the queue is dispatched, a delay equals to the network latency is incurred. For instance, if a message is queued in the 4th position, it will wait for 4 latency delays before it is sent. Fig. 23.3 shows the behaviour of the network module handling multiple messages.

Another role of the network is to detect erroneous messages which are sent to disconnected ports. Such messages are returned to the sender with their MessageType field changed to indicate that a network error has been encountered.

Implementation

The VHDL module of a reduced network connected to 4 PEs is shown in Fig. 23.4. In the diagram boxes with thick lines represent VHDL module, boxes with thin lines are VHDL processes and arrows represent message flows. There are 2 classes of VHDL processes in the network module: central (process -1) and PE related (process x.1 and x.2, where x is the ID of the associated PE). At initialization, the central process, Distribute Messages, first set up the configuration of the network. Information regarding to which PEs are connected are read from an external text file and stored internally in a mapping table. In VHDL, each process is sensitive to a number of signals. A change in state of a signal may activate certain processes. For the implementation of the network, this feature is very useful: instead of frequently loops and polls for new incoming messages at each PE port, a process is dedicated to the input port of a PE and it triggers at every new message arrivals. During normal operation, This input process, the CheckInputMessage process (x.1), also checks the destination of a message and returns it to the sender when it is directed to an disconnected port. Valid messages are directed to the central process, process -1. The DistributeMessages (-1) process which detects contention and distributes messages to the appropriate output processes, process x.2 QueueSendMessages. Internally, the QueueSendMessages process contains a message queue which acts as a temporary resort for holding conflicting messages (see previous paragraph).

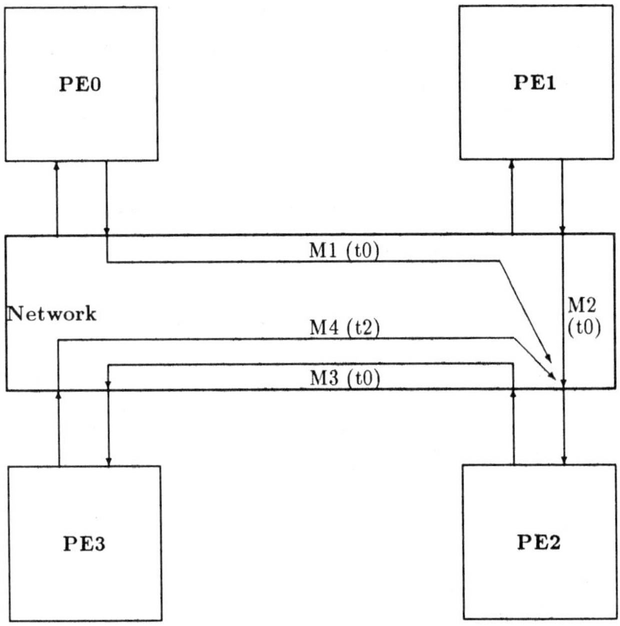

Order in which messages are sent (Tx) and received (Rx) by the Network :

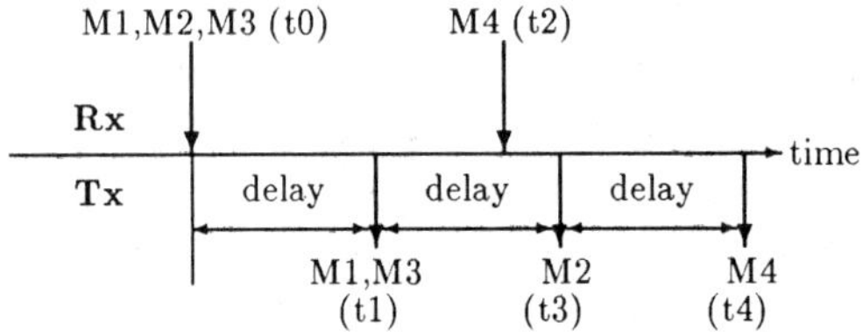

Description: *Messages M1, M2 and M3 arrive simultaneously at the network in time t0. As M3 is the only message going to PE3, PE3 receives it at t1, after one time delay (equals to the network latency, 8.1 us). On the other hand, M1 and M2 compete for the same PE. In that case, the network forwards one of the two (namely M1) to its destination after a time delay at t1 and put the other to the end of an internal output queue associated with PE2. As soon as M1 is sent (t1), the next element in the queue, M2, is dispatched and sent after another time delay (at time t3). Therefore, M2 is received by PE2 two delay times later. During the two sending events, if a new incoming message, e.g. M4 arriving at t2, attempts to reach PE2 before the output queue is empty (at time t2), the message will be added to the end of the queue and be sent after M2 at t4.*

Figure 23.3 Behaviour of the network in handling multiple messages.

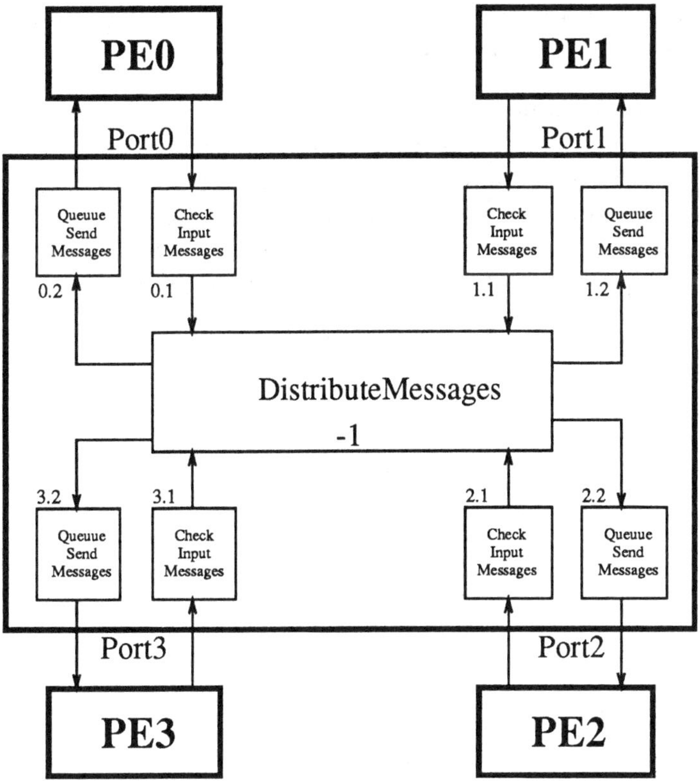

Fig. 23.4 The implementation model of the network connected with 4 PEs.

The network module is implemented in a flexible way and can accommodate future architectural changes. It is scalable and can connect to an arbitrary number of PEs. At present, a network of 256 PEs is being used. Also, the transmission delay time (currently 8.1 us) exists as a GENERIC parameter (VHDL term, see [LiScUs 90]) and can be modified easily in order to account for different load conditions.

23.3.2 The processing element module (PE)

Each processing element is simulated by a separate VHDL module. The PE module is developed in parallel with the network. A top-down design approach is practiced: the functional requirements of a PE are first identified using structured analysis (SA) [De 85] prior to implementation.

The concepts of data flow and data transformation in structured analysis bear close resemblance to signals and processes in VHDL. In general, application of CASE techniques to VHDL simulations can reduce design time and simplify implementation [KiLeSi 90].

Design of a PE module

Context Diagram (-1): The top level context diagram of a PE module is illustrated in Fig. 23.5. The diagram shows the interaction of the PE module with the external stimuli. A PE accepts a Query from a HOST, processes it and returns a Reply to the HOST. During the course of processing, it may need to send or receive RemoteRequests to/from other PEs.

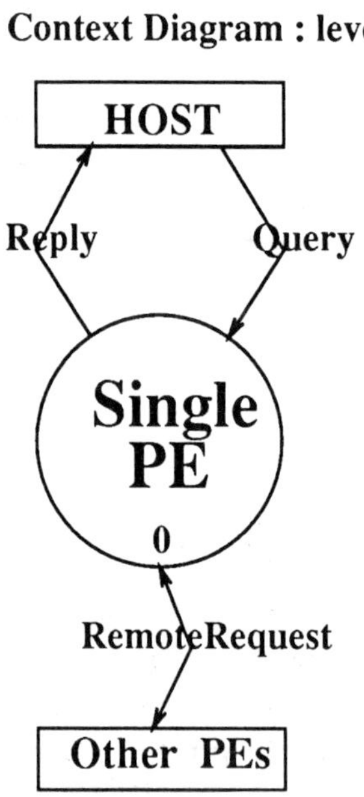

Figure 23.5 Structured analysis of a PE: context diagram.

Level 0: A PE module internally consists of four activities (in structured analysis, activities are referred to as data transformations [De 85]), see Fig. 23.6:

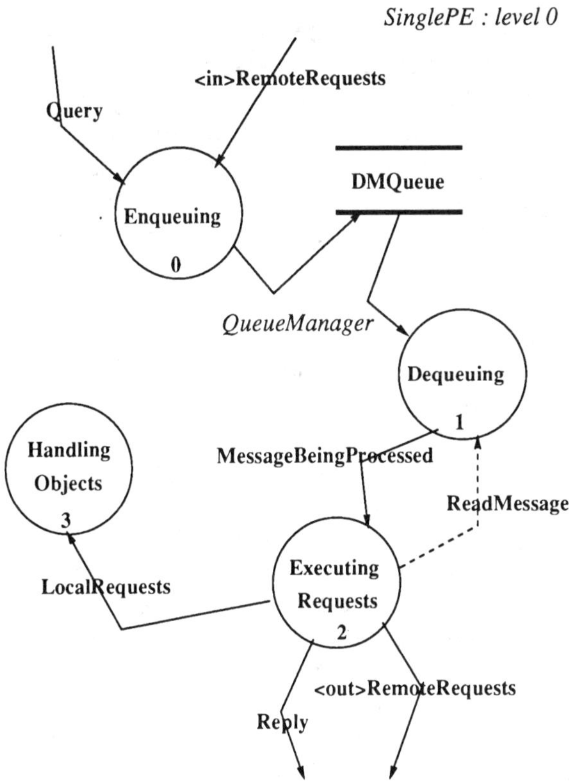

Figure 23.6 Structured analysis of a PE: Level 0 diagram.

(1) Enqueuing: The Enqueuing activity receives an incoming message to the PE, either from the Query or the <in> RemoteRequests input and places it to the next free location of the DMQueue. DMQueue is a common data store shared between the En- and De-queuing activities.

(2) Dequeuing: When the ReadMessage control signal is asserted, the Dequeuing activity dispatches the first message, namely MessageBeingProcessed, from the top of the DMQueue and sends it to the ExecutingRequests activity.

(3) ExecutingRequests: The ExecutingRequests activity receives the MessageBeingProcessed from the Dequeuing activity. According to the instruction specified in the MessageType field, it calculates the corresponding execution time, adds it to the overall transaction time and passes further <out> RemoteRequests to other PEs or Reply to

the HOST. After finishing an instruction, it asserts the ReadMessage control signal asking the Dequeuing activity for a new message.

(4) HandlingObjects: During the course of execution, the Executing Requests activity frequently sends LocalRequests to the Handling Objects activity. LocalRequests are database operations such as update, select, write, read, start transaction, end transaction, etc. These operations are performed by a local Object Manager on the physical EDS database server. The HandlingObjects activity is responsible for calculating the execution time of the operation specified in the LocalRequests.

Implementation

The schematic view of a PE module is shown in Fig. 23.7a. An external message is sent to or received from a PE via a pair of external communication ports (ExtIn and ExtOut respectively). Similarly, a PE can send or receive messages to/from the network via the NetIn and NetOut communication ports. Internally, a PE module is made up of 2 VHDL entities: the ObjectManager and the DataManager. Fig. 23.7b shows the structured design (SD) of the module based on the preceding analysis. The ObjectManager implements the HandlingObjects activity; and the other 3 activities are implemented in the DataManager. Such a modular arrangement makes the simulation more flexible: for example, different concurrency control strategies, access methods and reliability algorithms which can be augmented to the simulation model by simply modifying the ObjectManager entity.

The DataManager entity is composed of two VHDL processes, namely QueueManager and ReadQueue. The former consists of 2 sub-processes which simulate the behaviour of the Enqueuing and Dequeuing activities and their shared data store, DMQueue. Since VHDL does not support global variables, the two activities must be grouped in the same process in order to enable them to share the DMQueue. The DMQueue is a circular buffer with separate read and write pointers. If the two pointers are equal when a new message arrives, a fatal error is reported and the simulation is aborted. On the other hand, if the same occurs during a read operation, ReadQueue will be blocked and await a new message to arrive.

ReadQueue implements the ExecutingRequests activity. The action taken by the ReadQueue process is application dependent. At the implementation level, the program body of ReadQueue comprises of different sets of CASE statements. Each set accounts for all possible database instructions which can appear in the messages of a specific application, e.g. the debit/credit benchmark described in section 23.4. CASE statements are similar. Each of them sends a message to either ExtOut or

NetOut after waiting for a time which is equal to the execution time of the database operation specified in the message. A full list of the performance figures which the execution times are based on are given in appendix A.

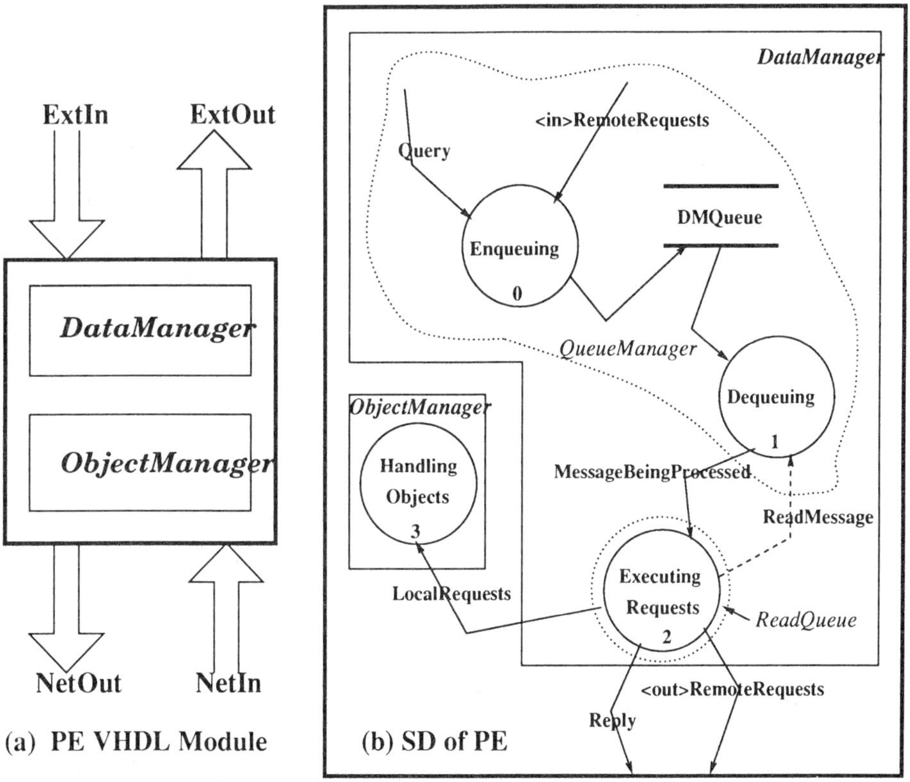

Figure 23.7 The VHDL module and the structured design (SD) diagram of a single PE.

23.4 SIMULATING THE DEBIT/CREDIT APPLICATION

23.4.1 Background

As the first study, the behavioral simulation model is used to evaluate the performance of a the EDS database server for running a typical OLTP application, namely the debit/credit benchmark. The debit/credit benchmark is a standard test suite specially designed for measuring transaction processing power of database systems [Ano 85,Tra 89]. It is also a popular yardstick for performance comparison between different database systems.

The debit/credit benchmark is concerned with an activity in a central banking database system. The bank has a number of branches and each branch has a number of tellers and customer accounts associated with it. The database system maintains the cash balance between the accounts, the tellers and the branches. A debit/credit transaction represents a customer depositing and withdrawing money from an account. This is entered at a branch by a teller. The required information describing the transaction is sent as a message (physically 100 bytes) to the database server. This information contains:

- AccountID - the customer's account number.
- TellerID - the identifier of the teller through which the transaction is made.
- BranchID - the identifier of the branch at which the transaction is made.
- Delta - the change to be made to the account.

The transaction is received by the server and according to the amount specified in Delta, it debits or credits the customer's Account and updates the balances of the appropriate Teller and Branch. It also records every transaction in a history file.

23.4.2 Execution of a debit/credit query on the EDS system

On the EDS system, the account, teller, branch and history data will be stored as tuples in four separate tables. The tuples will have the following format:

Account Tuple:

AccountID	an unique primary key of the Account relation
BranchID	a foreign key identifying the account owning branch
Account Balance	data content

Teller Tuple:

TellerID	an unique primary key of the Teller relation
BranchID	a foreign key identifying the account owning branch
Teller Balance	data content

Branch tuple:

BranchID	an unique primary key of the Teller relation
Branch Balance	data content

History tuple:

AccountID	account updated by a transaction
TellerID	teller through which the transaction is made
BranchID	branch to which the teller belongs
Delta	debit or credit amount specified in the transaction
TimeStamp	Date and time when the transaction takes place

These relations will be partitioned horizontally across the EDS machine. The processing element on which a tuple resides is commonly referred to as the "home" of the tuple. Apart from the history relation, partitioning will be centered on the branch relation, i.e. account and teller relations belonging to a branch will be stored on the same PE. The history relation will be partitioned across all PEs. After the account, branch and teller relations have been updated, a new tuple must be inserted to the history relation of the account owning PE.

A debit/credit query is executed on the EDS system as follows: when a debit/credit database session is started, a Transaction Controller (TC) task will be created. In the EDS database server, the TC is a Data Manager task [And 90] dedicated to coordinating the execution the database query. The TC will be responsible for the coordination of the execution of all queries of that session; e.g. it will control the two-phase commit protocol. A user query issued from a host machine will be received by a HOST element as a message. The message will contain the basic query information i.e. AccountID, BranchID, TellerID and Delta and will be sent directly to the TC. The TC will apply a hashing function to the AccountID to locate the "home" of the account tuple – the account owning PE. On the account owning PE, the server (server1, say) will update the account tuple. Typically, 85 transactions out of 100 are issued at the local branch [Tra 89]. For those cases, the account owning "home" will also be the branch owning "home" and server1 will also update the other 3 relations. Upon completion, server1 will notify the TC and the latter will initiate a two-phase commit cycle. For the remaining 15%, the branch owning PE will exist remotely. Server1 will then locate the branch owning "home" by applying a hashing function on the BranchID and send a "update branch" command message to it. The server on the remote PE (server2, say) will update the teller and branch tuples and notify server1 as soon as the updates are complete. When the teller/branch updates are finished, server1 will insert a new tuple to the history relation recording the event and then inform the TC to start the two-phase commit operation at the end of the insertion. When the transaction is successfully committed, the TC sends a result message (physically 200 bytes) to the host via the HOST element; otherwise, the transaction is aborted and an error message is sent to the host instead.

23.4.3 The Algorithm

Structured Analysis (SA) techniques [De 85] are used to understand the behaviour of the debit/credit application. The Data Flow Diagram (DFD) describing the structured analysis is shown in Fig. 23.8. The functionality of each bubble, i.e. activity, is described in this section using a pseudo specification language. The description is easy to understand because the only control structure of the pseudo language is IF-THEN-ELSE. Database operations are initiated by message passing between activities. Messages are shown as dataflows in the DFD. The number (embraced in []) associated with a message indicates the order of its appearance during the query execution. In order to understand the analysis, one must start from the first message (i.e. [1] QUERY_DEBIT_CREDIT) and follow through the sequence of operation.

ProcessingQuery (Activity 1)
COMMENT: This happens on the HOST element PE which accepts user queries.

IF ([1]QUERY_DEBIT_CREDIT) THEN

(1) Get the query message from the HOST. This involves an interrupt and acquisition of a buffer for holding the query message.
(2) Form a short message with TYPE = [2]START_DEBIT_CREDIT and send it to the Transaction Controller (TC).
(3) Service another request pending at the input queue.

ENDIF ;

IF ([13]RESULT_DEBIT_CREDIT) THEN

(1) Return a [14]REPLY_DEBIT_CREDIT (256 bytes) message to the HOST and from the HOST to the terminal.
(2) Service another request pending at the input queue.

ENDIF;

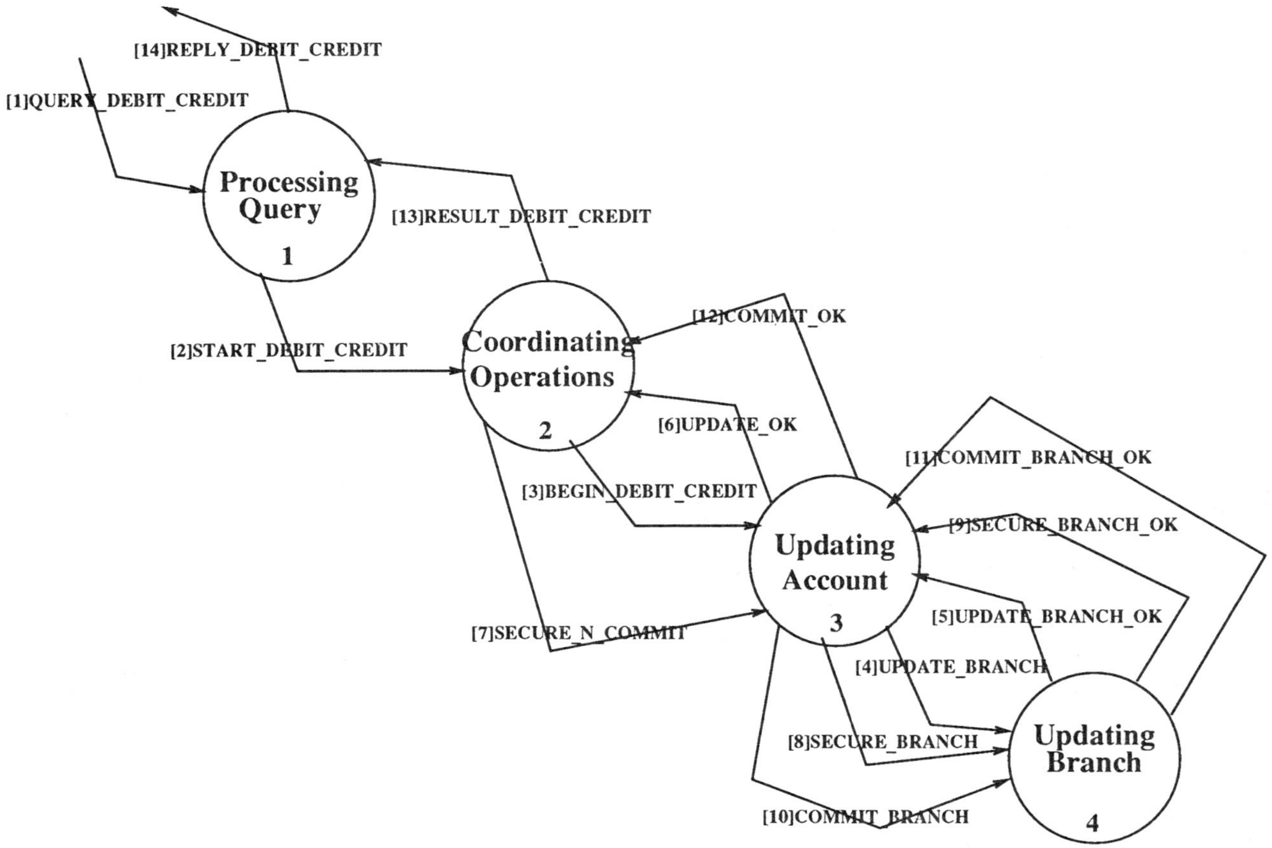

Figure 23.8 Structured analysis of the debit/credit application on the EDS simulation model.

CoordinatingOperations (Activity 2)

COMMENT : This happens on the Transaction Controller (e.g. PE1).

IF ([2]START_DEBIT_CREDIT) THEN

(1) Create a new execution thread.
(2) Start a transaction (START_TRANSACTION system call).
(3) Locate the account owning PE by hashing the AccountID.
(4) Form a [3]BEGIN_DEBIT_CREDIT message and send it to the account owning PE.
(5) Go to sleep and schedule another execution thread.

ENDIF ;

IF ([6]UPDATE_OK) THEN

(1) Send a [7]SECURE_N_COMMIT message to the account owning PE.
(2) Go to sleep and schedule another execution thread.

ENDIF ;

IF ([12]COMMIT_OK) THEN

(1) Terminate the transaction (END_TRANSACTION system trap).
(2) Return a [13]RESULT_DEBIT_CREDIT (256 bytes) message to the HOST Element.
(3) Kill the current execution thread.

ENDIF ;

UpdatingAccount (Activity 3)

COMMENT : This happens on the account owning PE.

IF ([3]BEGIN_DEBIT_CREDIT) THEN

(1) Create a new execution thread.
(2) Lookup, select, lock and update the account record (UPDATE_ACCOUNT system trap).
(3) Locate the branch owning PE by hashing the BranchID.
(4b) IF the branch owning PE is foreign THEN
(4.1)Send a [4]UPDATE_BRANCH message to the branch owning PE.
(4.2)Go to sleep and schedule another execution thread.
(4el) ELSEIF the Branch relation is stored locally THEN
(4.3)Lookup, select, lock and update the branch and teller records.
(4.4)Insert a new history record to the history relation.
(4.5)Send a [6]UPDATE_OK message to the Transaction Controller.
(4.6)Go to sleep and schedule another execution thread.
(4e) ENDIF ;

ENDIF ;

COMMENT : The Branch owning PE has finished updating.
IF ([5]UPDATE_BRANCH_OK) THEN

(1) Insert a history record to the history relation.
(2) Send [6]UPDATE_OK message to the Transaction Controller.
(3) Go to sleep and schedule another execution thread.

ENDIF ;

COMMENT : Whether a transaction is foreign or local was initially determined by the BEGIN_DEBIT_CREDIT operation at the account owning PE.

IF ([7]SECURE_N_COMMIT) THEN

(1b)
(1.1)Send a [8]SECURE_BRANCH message to the branch owning PE.
(1.2)Secure the updated account and the new history records.
(1.3)Go to sleep and schedule another execution thread.
(1el)ELSEIF the branch and teller relations are stored locally THEN
(1.4)Secure the branch, teller, account and history records.
(1.5)Commit and unlock the relations.
(1.7)Send a [12]COMMIT_OK message to the Transaction Controller.
(1.8)Kill the current execution thread.
(1e) ENDIF
ENDIF ;

IF ([9]SECURE_BRANCH_OK) THEN
COMMENT : The branch and teller relations must be foreign in here.

(1) Send a [10]COMMIT_BRANCH message to the branch owning PE. (Commit the branch owning PE first before committing itself).
(2) Go to sleep and schedule another execution thread.

ENDIF ;

IF ([11]COMMIT_BRANCH_OK) THEN
COMMENT : The branch and teller relations must be foreign in here.

(1) Commit and unlock the account relation.
(2) Send a [12]COMMIT_OK message to the Transaction Controller.
(3) Kill the current execution thread.

ENDIF ;

UpdatingBranch (Activity 4)
COMMENT : This happens on the Branch Owning PE.

IF ([4]UPDATE_BRANCH) THEN
(1) Create a new execution thread.
(2) Lookup, select, lock and update the branch and teller records.
(3) Send a [5]UPDATE_BRANCH_OK message to the account owning PE.
(4) Go to sleep and schedule another execution thread.
ENDIF ;

IF ([8]SECURE_BRANCH) THEN
(1) Secure the branch and teller records.
(2) Send a [9]SECURE_BRANCH_OK message to the account owning PE.
(3) Go to sleep and schedule another execution thread.
ENDIF ;

IF ([10]COMMIT_BRANCH) THEN
(1) Unlock and commit the branch and teller updates.
(2) Send a [11]COMMIT_BRANCH_OK message to the account owning PE.
(3) Kill the current execution thread.
ENDIF ;

23.4.4 Implementation

The preceding algorithm is implemented using the high level EDS simulation model. The following assumptions were made:

- A HOST element is simulated by a special-purpose PE. This PE does not involve in the database execution of the query. It is solely dedicated to EDS–HOST communication.
- All transactions are successful. Therefore transaction aborts never take place.
- All queries have been pre-compiled and the HOST element can communicate with the Transaction Controller directly.
- PEs are paired. One acts as the main processing element and the other provides the duplex facility. All accesses to the database store are replicated. Duplex facility runs in parallel with the main database operations.
- Group commit is assumed and the log buffer is infinitely large. Therefore, flushing of the buffer takes place only occasionally and does not affect the normal database operations.

At the VHDL programming level, the implementation is simply a set of CASE statements within the ReadQueue process of the DataManager entity (see section 23.3.2). CASE statements are similar. Each of them WAIT (or suspend) for a time equals to the elapsed time of the database operation specified in the message which the DataManager is dealing with; then send a message to either ExtOut or NetOut. Currently, the performance figures being used are mainly extracted from 3 sources:

(1) Worst case timing of the EDS kernel.

(2) The EDS message passing overheads.

(3) Performance estimates of the EDS database operations.

The performance figures are listed in appendix A. Altogether 14 message types (or database operations) corresponding to the dataflows in Fig. 23.8 are supported; they are (in their order of appearance):

[1] QUERY_DEBIT_CREDIT
[2] START_DEBIT_CREDIT
[3] BEGIN_DEBIT_CREDIT
[4] UPDATE_BRANCH
[5] UPDATE_BRANCH_OK
[6] UPDATE_OK
[7] SECURE_N_COMMIT
[8] SECURE_BRANCH
[9] SECURE_BRANCH_OK
[10] COMMIT_BRANCH
[11] COMMIT_BRANCH_OK
[12] COMMIT_OK
[13] RESULT_DEBIT_CREDIT
[14) REPLY_DEBIT_CREDIT

The actions taken by the EDS database server depends on the type of the incoming message. In the simulation model, only the execution times of the actions are used. The summation of the execution times of the corresponding actions gives the total WAIT time of each CASE statement.

23.4.5 The test suite

Four simulation tests with varying combinations of query and input multiplicity were performed. Query multiplicity is determined by the number of queries input to a PE and the number of PE receiving the queries defines the input multiplicity. Both of them may either be single or multiple. The tests are:

(1) Single Query Single Input (SQSI).
(2) Single Query Multiple Inputs (SQMI).
(3) Multiple Queries Single Input (MQSI).
(4) Multiple Queries Multiple Inputs (MQMI).

For the first 3 tests, a network of 256 PEs were used in the simulation and each PE was implemented with a 256 entry DMQueue. Due to memory restriction, test 4 was performed using a reduced EDS architecture with 64 PEs instead. The results, however, would have been similar with 256 PEs. This was proven by re-running the first 3 tests with a 64 PE system.

Either 3 or 4 PEs were involved in a debit/credit transaction. One PE was chosen as the HOST element; a second PE was chosen to be the Transaction Controller and a third acted as the account owning PE (server1). For local queries, all relations – account, history, branch and teller – were stored on the same PE; therefore, the account owning PE was also the branch owning PE. On the other hand, in the case of remote queries where branch/teller and account/history relation pairs were kept in different PEs, a fourth PE was introduced as the branch owning PE (server2). The role of PE were designated arbitrarily at the beginning of a query.

The metrics of the tests were system throughput – the rate at which queries are processed, and response time – the difference between the arrival time and the reply time of a query at the HOST element. There are two main objectives for the tests: first, to identify the general effects (both positive and negative) of multiprocessing for simple OLTP application; and second, to evaluate the performance of the EDS database server for debit/credit transactions.

Negative effects of multiprocessing

(I) Test 1: The contention-free situation (SQSI):
A single local query was input to the simulation model via PE0 (i.e. the PE whose ID is 0). PE0 acted as the HOST element. The times which the query message and the reply message appeared at PE0 were measured. Their difference gave the response time of the query, RT_{SS}^{l}. The same procedure was repeated for a single remote query and the query response time RT_{SS}^{r} was recorded.

Under the specification of the debit/credit benchmark, local and remote queries typically have an 85%:15% ratio. Based on this, the nominal response time of the debit/credit tran-saction RT_{SS} was calculated, viz:

$$\begin{aligned} RT_{SS} &= 0.85 \text{ x } RT_{SS}^{l} + 0.15 \text{ x } RT_{SS}^{r} \\ &= 0.85 \text{ x } 4.288 + 0.15 \text{ x } 4.847 \\ &= 4.372 \text{ msec} \end{aligned}$$

This is, in fact, only a theoretical value because there was only one query running in the system. Since there was no resource contention, the query utilized the machine fully. However this situation never happens in practice for queries may arrive at more than one PE and also continuously in streams. Multiple queries and inputs inevitably cause adverse effects.

(II) Test 2: effect of parallelism (SQMI):
To study the effect of parallelism, the full network of 256 PEs were used. Single queries were input to all the PEs in parallel simultaneously. One out of every seven queries were made to be remote. Designation of the roles of the PEs were as follows: PE_x, PE_{x+1}, PE_{x+2} and PE_{x+3} were chosen to be the HOST element, the Transaction Controller (TC), the account owning PE (server1) and the branch owning PE (server2, for remote queries only), respectively, where x ranges from 0 to 255; and $x+1$, $x+2$ and $x+3$ wrapped around when they exceeded 255. This arrangement gave an even role distribution so each PE served all the four roles.

The response times of the queries were averaged, RT_{sm} and is equal to 5.168 msec. The increased response time ($RT_{sm} - RT_{ss} = 0.79$), is due to the queries competing for CPU resources i.e. the PEs. It accounts for 15% of the overall execution time.

It is interesting to note the ratio between RT_{sm} and RT_{ss} (5.168/4.378 = 1.18) which shows the degree of parallelism for running a single query on the EDS machine. This value is comparable to the same derived for a similar distributed memory machine, the Flagship machine [WaToWa 90], developed in ICL. The Flagship machine exhibits a degree of parallelism of 1.15.

(III) Test 3: effect of streaming (MQSI):
In practice, query input on each PE arrives continuously in streams for OLTP applications. The streaming effect on a single PE is investigated in this test. The full EDS configuration with 256 PEs was simulated. Multiple queries were streamed into PE0 (the HOST element). The roles of the Transaction Controller (TC), the account owning PE and the branch owning PE were dedicated to PE_x, PE_{x+1} and PE_{x+2} in a round robin fashion, like the SQMI test. The query input to a PE was purely random and assumed Poisson arrival with an exponential distribution[4]. Each query stream consists of 256 queries or more separated by a randomly generated interarrival time.

---

4 A process is Poisson if the the times between successive arrivals i.e. the first-order interarrival times, are identically distributed, exponential random variables [Dei84,pp388–392].

Result of the MQSI Test (Test3)										
$\bar{\tau}$ (msec)	1.5	2.0	3.0	4.0	5.0	6.0	7.0	8.0	9.0	10.0
RT_{ms} (msec)	> 1200	30.70	7.74	6.58	6.03	5.73	5.26	5.14	5.05	4.96

Table 23.1: Results of the MQSI test.

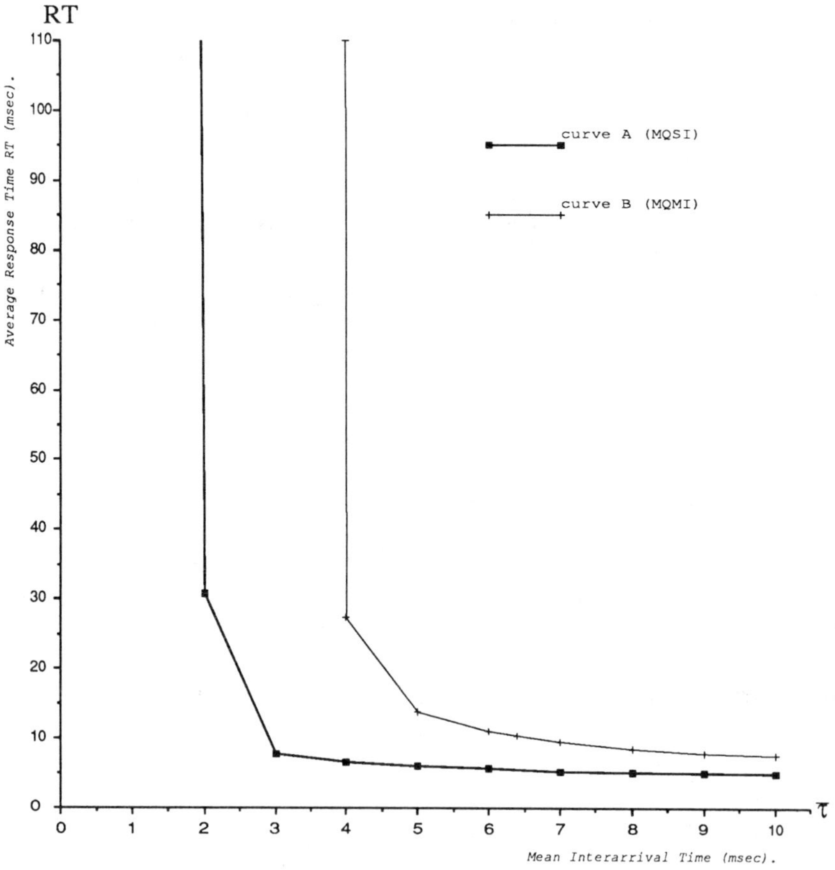

Figure 23.9 Average query response times RT_{ms} under variable interarrival times τ for the MQSI and MQMI tests.

The mean interarrival time τ and hence λ was varied from 10 to 1 msec and the average query response times were measured. The result of the test is tabulated in Table 1 and plotted on curve A in Fig. 23.9. The response times RT_{ms} were measured at steady state when RT_{ms} saturated. For some measurements, the size of the DMQueue was increased in order to achieve steady state.

Intuitively one would expect that as long as the interarrival time between queries is greater than 4.378 msec ($>RT_{ss}$), the EDS database server would give a constant response time. This is true if and only if the queries arrive at fixed regular intervals greater than 4.387 msec. Nevertheless, in reality query arrival is completely random. One only knows the mean interarrival time τ. Under the characteristics of the Poisson arrival, the probability of two successive queries arriving at less than 4.378 msec tends to 0 as τ tends to infinity. In general, given a finite τ, >4.378 msec, there are always some interarrival times less than 4.378 msec thus causes resource contention. The rate of contention increases as τ decreases. That explains the increase in response times RT_{ms} of curve A. Notice that RT_{ms} increases steadily as τ decreases from 10 down to approximately 2 msec; and after that RT_{ms} increases steeply. This is because below $\tau = 2$ msec, the rate of input is faster than the rate of processing; so unless one had a sufficiently large input queue, the system would be unable to cope with the query input rate. The large queue would function as a temporary buffer for holding all waiting queries. However, as the number of waiting queries accumulates in the queue, the average query response time escalates. For this reason, the system in fact can never reach steady state. This explains the steep gradient beyond $\tau = 2$ msec.

(IV) Test 4: combined effect (MQMI):

A similar test as (III) was performed; but this time streams of queries are input simultaneously to all connected PEs in parallel. The size of the simulation model was reduced to 64 because of memory limitation. Steady state response times were recorded with varied interarrival times. The result is tabulated in Table 2 and plotted on curve B in Fig. 23.9. Comparing curve A with curve B, both are similar and the latter increases monotonically until $\tau = 4$ where the system begins to fail to saturate. The rate of increase in response time is much faster in curve B. This is because at each PE there are more than one input streams. In addition to the query stream at the external input port, query fragments from several other PEs are arriving at the network input port. Both ports share a common input queue. Therefore, the rate at which messages accumulate in the queue is much quicker and the skewing between fragments of a query also increases much faster than the same of the MQSI case. The nominal interarrival time for parallel input which was obtained in the SQMI test is 5.168 msec. Similar to the MQSI case, this nominal value could only be reached if τ tends to infinity because of the randomness of the query input.

Result of the MQMI Test									
$\bar{\tau}$ (msec)	3.0	4.0	5.0	6.0	6.4	7.0	8.0	9.0	10.0
RT_{mm} (msec)	> 507.07	27.27	13.79	11.03	10.40	9.52	8.49	7.84	7.55

Table 23.2: Result of the MQMI test.

It is important to know that the MQMI test closely simulates the behaviour of the EDS database server at normal operation. Therefore, its result reflects the performance of the actual EDS system.

Positive effects of multiprocessing

The Effect of Pipelining: When τ goes below the nominal interarrival time, 5.168 msec for the MQMI test and 4.378 msec for the MQSI test, one would intuitively expect that the system could no longer cope with the input rate. As shown by the curves in Fig. 23.9, this is not so. The limitation is relaxed due to the pipelining technique of the EDS database server. The execution of a debit/credit query is performed by 3 or 4 PEs in series depending on whether a query is local or remote. Each of the PEs executes a fragment of a query in series. As soon as a query fragment is completed on a PE, it will notify the next PE by message passing. Before the notification takes place, the next PE does not stay still, it may be executing fragments of another query. The processing rate of a query stream is determined by the number of PEs involved in the pipeline and the execution time of the most time-consuming fragment – the bottleneck of the pipeline. This is application dependent and for the debit/credit transaction, it is approximately 4 and 2 msec for multiple and single inputs.

The effect of multiple inputs in parallel:

One of the advantages of the EDS shared-nothing architecture is the increase of system throughput using parallel input streams. Parallel input streams allow multiple transactions to be initiated simultaneously (i.e. frequently referred to as intertransactional parallelism). The advantage is revealed by plotting the MQMI response time RT_{mm} with the total system throughput ($\lambda = 256/\tau$), see Fig. 23.9). The target throughput of the EDS server for the debit/credit benchmark is 12000 tps at 30% utilization. Referring to Fig. 23.10, this can handle by the server comfortably. At 12000 tps, the corresponding response time is 10.4 msec. Furthermore, the EDS server can sustain a maximum throughput of 64000 tps which is 19200 tps at 30% utilisation with a tolerable response time of 27.27 msec.

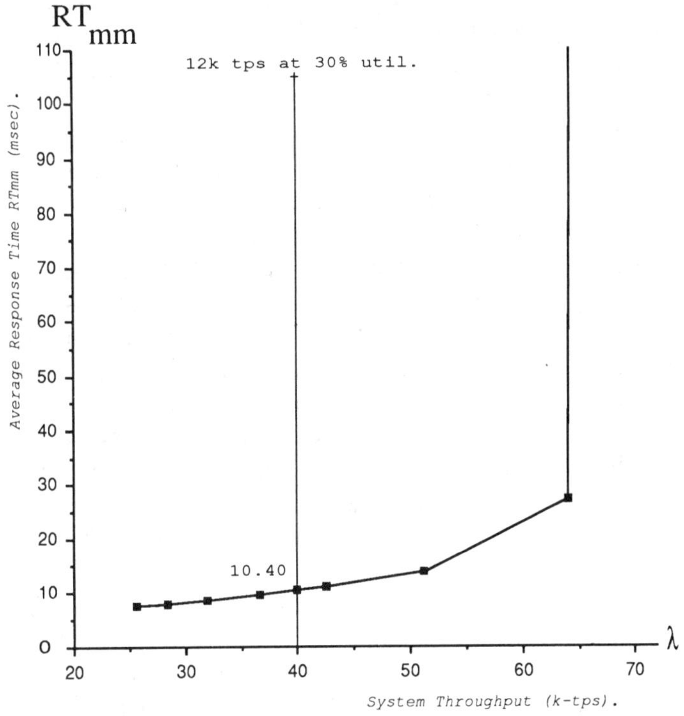

Figure 23.10: Average query response times of the MQMI test RT_{mm} under variable transaction rate.

23.5 CONCLUSION

A behaviour simulation model is developed for investigating the performance of the parallel EDS database server running on the shared-nothing EDS machine. It simulates the EDS system in 2 layer: the configuration layer models the shared-nothing architecture and the execution layer simulates the parallel database server The simulation model is implemented using VHDL – a standard simulation language which supports modular and mixed level simulation. A typical on-line transaction processing (OLTP) application, namely debit/credit, is extensively studied using the simulation model. One important conclusion of the simulation is: the EDS system can comfortably fulfil the EDS target throughput of 12000 tps at 30% utilization; in fact, its maximum throughput at 30% utilization is 19200 tps.

A novel evaluation strategy was devised for the debit/credit simulation. This includes a suite of four tests with different combinations of query and input multiplicity, namely SQSI, SQMI, MQSI and MQMI. The quantitative results are EDS specific and are presented in section 23.4.5. Moreover, the tests were used to study the effects of multiprocessing for OLTP applications in general. It is shown that:

A single query fed to a single input (SQSI) is an ideal contention-free situation which can never happen in practice. By introducing multiple inputs, the query response time inevitably increases because of resource contention; in the single query case (SQMI), this increase accounted for 15% of the execution time. A stream of multiple queries to the system (MQSI) introduces even more contention and hence longer response times. At a constant mean interarrival time, response time increases monotonically and saturates at a steady state. Furthermore, response times gradually increase with decreasing mean interarrival time τ and up to a certain point, the system fails. When that happens a steady state can never be reached and the response time increases continuously until the input queue overflows.

Multiprocessing for OLTP applications on a shared-nothing architecture cannot improve response time; so what is it good for? The advantage of multiprocessing for OLTP application (on a shared-nothing architect) lies in increased transaction throughput. This is brought about by multiple parallel query inputs and the pipelining technique of the database server. The former offers inter-query parallelism and the latter introduces a restrictive form of intra-query parallelism. Interarrival time limits are relaxed due to the latter and because of this the throughput is increased indirectly. The restriction in intra-query parallelism is due to the temporal dependency of the program fragments within an OLTP query.

In order to further improve the performance, one must minimize resource contention. This will avoid skewing and thus reduce the discrepancy between the actual and nominal response times. To do so, one must widely decluster the database tuples – i.e. to store them on as many processing elements as possible. This will reduce the probability of any two queries accessing the same data store. Therefore, a high degree of data declustering in general favours OLTP application on a shared-nothing database server.

The major activity in the future is to use the simulation model to study the behaviour of other applications. Complex queries, especially decision support systems based on ElipSys [Won 90], will be ones of the immediate targets. The simulation model as it stands is sufficient for simple OLTP applications. For evaluation of complex queries, a direct query interface and an architecture configuration utility will be required. Ideally, the query interface should accept ESQL directly; but the implementation of such an interface would require too much efforts. A more practical choice is to simulate queries expressed in the intermediate program format (see section 23.2). The architecture configuration utility will allow users to specify the internal configuration of the EDS machine and some rudimentary system specifications (e.g. selectivity of a database). This will make the simulation model more flexible.

LIST OF SYMBOLS AND ABBREVIATIONS

λ	mean query interarrival rate
τ_i	ith interarrival time in a query stream
τ	mean query interarrival time
DFD	Data Flow Diagram in Structured Analysis
DMQueue	Data Manager Message Queue
EMEX	EDS Machine Executive
ESQL	Extended Structured Query Language
MQMI	Multiple Queries Multiple Inputs
MQSI	Multiple Queries Single Input
OLTP	On-Line Transaction Processing
PCL	Process Control Language
PE	Process Element (in the paper, it always refers to the VHDL entity)
PE_x	PE with identity equals to x
PMI	Primitive Machine Interface
RT_{mm}	average response time in the MQMI test
RT_{ms}	average response time in the MQSI test
RT_{mm}	average response time in the SQMI test
RT_{sm}	average response time in the SQSI test
RT_{ss}^{l}	response time of local query in SQSI test
RT_{ss}^{r}	response time of remote query in SQSI test
SA	Structured Analysis
SD	Structured Design
SQL	Structured Query Language
SQMI	Single Query Multiple Inputs
SQSI	Single Query Single Input
TC	Transaction Controller task
tps	transactions per second

ACKNOWLEDGEMENTS

The work described in this paper is partially funded by the Commission of the European Community (CEC) under the prject EP2025. The authors would like to thank all members of the Distributed and Parallel System (DPS) group at ECRC for their useful discussion. Special thanks are due to Dr. M. J. Reeve who is very supportive and encouraging for the Performance and Modelling work.

APPENDIX A: PERFORMANCE FIGURES

The performance figures which the simulation model uses to evaluate the execution time of a database query is listed in this appendix. These figures are mainly extracted from 3 sources:

(a) Worst case timing of the EDS kernel.

(b) Message passing overheads.

(c) Performance estimates of database operations.

A.1 The list:

COMMENT : Ethernet connection with an average bandwidth of 600K bytes/sec.
CONSTANT EDS_HOST_BANDWIDTH : time := 1.7 us

COMMENT : Nominal network latency.
CONSTANT NETWORK_LATENCY : time := 8.1 us

COMMENT : Link Level message passing timing :
This time includes GetRxBuf + RxMess + Assemble Ack + Send Ack.
CONSTANT LINK_RECEIVE_SHORT_MESSAGE : time := 7.6 us

COMMENT : Worst case Timing of user level kernel calls.
CONSTANT PCL_THREAD_CREATE : time := 25 us
CONSTANT PCL_THREAD_DESTROY : time := 15 us
CONSTANT PCL_THREAD_RESCHEDULE : time := 32 us
CONSTANT PCL_TEAM_CREATE : time := 300 us
CONSTANT PCL_TEAM_DESTROY : time := 200 us
CONSTANT PCL_TASK_CREATE_LOCAL : time := 100 us
CONSTANT PCL_TASK_DESTROY_LOCAL : time := 50 us
CONSTANT PCL_TASK_CREATE_REMOTE : time := 250 us
CONSTANT PCL_TASK_DESTROY_REMOTE : time := 200 us

CONSTANT PCL_PORT_CREATE : time := 20 us
CONSTANT PCL_PORT_CONNECT_LOCAL : time := 30 us
CONSTANT PCL_PORT_DESTROY_LOCAL : time := 15 us
CONSTANT PCL_PORT_CONNECT_REMOTE : time := 135 us
CONSTANT PCL_PORT_DESTROY_REMOTE : time := 120 us
CONSTANT PCL_MESSAGE_LOCAL_SHORT_SBUF : time:= 5 us
CONSTANT PCL_MESSAGE_LOCAL_LONG_SBUF : time := 5 us
CONSTANT PCL_MESSAGE_LOCAL_SHORT_DBUF:time:=10us
CONSTANT PCL_MESSAGE_LOCAL_LONG_DBUF : time :=12us
CONSTANT PCL_MESSAGE_REMOTE_SHORT : time := 65 us
CONSTANT PCL_MESSAGE_REMOTE_LONG : time := 75 us

COMMENT : Low level System calls
CONSTANT SYSTEM_CALL : time := 5 us
CONSTANT RETURN_FROM_CALL : time := 2 us
CONSTANT EXCEPTION : time := 19 us
CONSTANT GET_SHORT_BUFFER : time := 30 us
CONSTANT GET_LONG_BUFFER : time := 50 us
CONSTANT PROCESS_INTERRUPT : time := 5 us

COMMENT : Assume message passing time is split equally between Rx and Tx.
CONSTANT RECEIVE_REMOTE_SHORT : time := 33 us
CONSTANT RECEIVE_REMOTE_LONG : time := 38 us
CONSTANT SEND_REMOTE_SHORT : time := 33 us
CONSTANT SEND_REMOTE_LONG : time := 38 us

COMMENT : Execution time for the DB operations.
CONSTANT START_TRANS : time := 180
CONSTANT INDEX_RECORD : time := 36
CONSTANT LOOKUP_RECORD : time := 36
CONSTANT UPDATE_RECORD : time := 72
CONSTANT SELECT_RECORD : time := 306
CONSTANT SECURE_RECORD : time := 72
CONSTANT INSERT_RECORD : time := 36
CONSTANT RELEASE_LOCK : time := 36
CONSTANT COMMIT_UPDATE : time := 36
CONSTANT END_TRANS : time := 36

REFERENCES

Anceau, F. *et. al.* (1990) The European Declarative System. In *1990 ESPRIT Conference,* Brussels, Belgium, 12–15.

Andres, F. *et al.* EDS- Collaborating for a High Performance Parallel Relational Database. In *1990 ESPRIT Conference*, Brussels, Belgium, 12-15, November 1990.

Anon *et. al.* A Measure of Transaction Processing Power. *Datamation*, **31** (7):335–339, April 1985.

Boral H. *et. al.* Prototyping Bubba, A Highly Parallel System. *IEEE Trans. on Knowledge and Data Engineering,* pages 4–24, March 1990.

De Marco, T. *Structured Analysis and System Specification.* Yourdon Press, New York, 1985.

Deitel, M. T.. *An Introduction to Operating Systems.* Addison Wesley, 1984.

Gelenbe, G. and Pujolle, G. *Introduction to Queuing Networks.* John Wiley and Sons, 1987.

IEEE. *IEEE Standard VHDL Language Reference Manual.* IEEE, New York, 1988. IEEE Std 1076-1987.

Kivela, J. E., Leppanen, T. and Sipola, M. VHDL Supported by Graphical CASE-tools for High Level System Design and Implementation. In *1st European Conference on VHDL Methods,* Marseille, France, 4–7 September 1990.

Lipsett, R., Scaefer, C. and Ussery, C. *VHDL: Hardware Description and Design.* Kluwer, 1990.

Transaction Processing Performance Council (TPC). *TPC Benchmark A Standard Specification.* ITOM International Corp., L.A., U.S.A., November 1989.

Watson I. *et. al.* Flagship: A Parallel Architecture for Declarative Programming. In *15th International Symposium on Computer Architecture,* Hawaii, May 1988.

Wong, K.F. *et. al.* The European Declarative (EDS) as a Platform for Parallel Logic Programming. In *2nd IEEE Symposium on Distributed and Parallel Processing,* Dallas, Texas, U.S.A., 9–11 December 1990.

Watson, P. and Townsend, P. The EDS Parallel Relational Database System. In *PRISMA Workshop,* the Netherlands, 24–26, September 1990.

Ward, M., Townsend, P. and Watzlawik, G. EDS Hardware Architecture. In *CONPAR 90 - VAPP IV,* Zurich, Switzerland, 10–13 September 1990.